Parliamentary History

Parliamentary History

A Yearbook

Volume 1
1982

ALAN SUTTON

Alan Sutton Publishing Limited
17a Brunswick Road
Gloucester

First published 1982

British Library Cataloguing in Publication Data

Parliamentary history. — Vol.1—
    1. **Great Britain.** *Parliament* — **History** —
    Periodicals
    328.41'005   **JN500**

ISBN 0-86299-013-0
ISBN 0-86299-014-9 Pbk

ISSN 0264-2824

Typesetting and origination by
Alan Sutton Publishing Limited.
Photoset Bembo 10/11.
Printed in Great Britain by
Redwood Burn Limited
Trowbridge, Wiltshire

PARLIAMENTARY HISTORY

A Yearbook

Published by Alan Sutton Publishing Limited for The Parliamentary History Yearbook Trust.

Grateful thanks are due to the British Academy and the Twenty-Seven Foundation for their generous grants towards the publication of this volume.

Cover illustration: The Parliament House (House of Commons), Westminster Hall and the Abbey by Wenzel Hollar (1647). Reproduced from a photograph supplied by the Courtauld Institute of Art, University of London.

All contributions (which must not be longer than 10,000 words) should be typed on A4 paper (double spacing throughout), with footnotes typed separately. 'Notes for Authors' are available on request.

Articles, notes and documents and other material submitted for publication should be sent to the Editor, Eveline Cruickshanks, at the Institute of Historical Research, Annexe, 34 Tavistock Square, London WC1H 9EZ; or, in the USA and Canada, to Richard Davis (Chairman of the American Associate Committee) at the Department of History, Washington University, St Louis, Missouri 63130; books for review and completed reviews to the Reviews Editor, David Hayton, also at 34 Tavistock Square, London WC1H 9EZ.

EDITOR'S PREFACE

Parliamentary History: A Yearbook is being launched in response to growing interest and current controversies in parliamentary history on both sides of the Atlantic. As well as articles, shorter notes and documents, considerable space will be given over to reviews of books, with lengthy review articles on books or topics of major importance. Reports on conferences will also be included and there will be a regular bibliography of relevant work on parliamentary history.

The *Yearbook* will cover the history of parliamentary institutions in the British Isles (including the Scottish and Irish Parliaments) from the Middle Ages to the twentieth century, their origins, development and historical importance. The aim is to provide an open platform for current research into parliamentary history, and several articles representing the great contribution made by American scholars to British parliamentary history are contained in the first issue. Contributions on any aspect of parliamentary history will be welcome, institutional and political, including the history of legislation and procedure, parliamentary management and political 'structure', elections and the electorate, as well as the architecture and representative art of the various Parliaments.

The Editor and Editorial Committee would like to thank the Institute of Historical Research, University of London, and the History of Parliament Trust for their generosity in giving *Parliamentary History* house-room, although we have no official connexion with either institution and they are in no way responsible for the views expressed in or the editorial approach of this publication. We are very grateful to members of our Editorial Advisory Board and to a number of other distinguished parliamentary historians for their assistance and advice, which have helped us overcome the problems of embarking on such a venture at this particular time.

Eveline Cruickshanks

CONTENTS

LORDS AND COMMONS: RELATIONS BETWEEN THE TWO HOUSES OF PARLIAMENT, 1509–1558*

HELEN MILLER

University College of North Wales, Bangor

The difference in size between the two Houses of Parliament became more marked in the early sixteenth century. The membership of the House of Commons was increased from 296 to 400 between the accession of Henry VIII and the death of Mary. The House of Lords also started to expand but was then suddenly cut back. For the Parliament of 1510 individual writs of summons were sent to 21 bishops, 27 abbots and priors, and 36 lay peers. Henry Stafford was created Earl of Wiltshire during the session, bringing the membership of the House of Lords in Henry VIII's first Parliament to 85. When the writs went out for his fifth Parliament in 1529, 48 lords spiritual were again summoned to attend, this time with 44 lay peers, augmented within a few weeks of the opening ceremonies to 51. The dissolution of the monasteries ensured from 1540 the permanent predominance of the laity in a smaller House of Lords; its total membership thereafter was usually between 70 and 80.[1]

The natural wastage of the lay nobility through the failure of male heirs, reinforced during this period by a series of attainders, would have seriously reduced the number of lords temporal had it not been for the creation of new peers. From 1529 the replenishment of the peerage was especially significant for relations between the two Houses of Parliament since it introduced into the House of Lords a number of men with experience of the House of Commons. The incomplete record of the names of Members of the earlier Tudor Parliaments perhaps makes this

* I am grateful to the Trustees of the History of Parliament and in particular to the editor of the early Tudor section, the late Professor S.T. Bindoff, for permission to publish this article, which is based upon the constituency accounts and biographies prepared for *The History of Parliament: The House of Commons 1509–1588* (3 vols., 1982). Further references for statements in the article will be found in the published volumes.

progression from one House to the other appear more of a novelty than it was: Thomas Howard, second Duke of Norfolk (M.P. for Norfolk in 1478), Henry, Lord Marny (M.P. for Essex in 1491) and Nicholas, Lord Vaux (M.P. for an unknown constituency in 1515) may not have been the only members of Henry VIII's House of Lords before 1529 to have sat in the House of Commons.[2] Nevertheless, the decision to summon to the House of Lords four Members of the Reformation Parliament within weeks of their election to the Commons was unprecedented. Both knights of the shire for Lincolnshire, John Hussey and Gilbert Tailboys, took their seats in the Lords on 1 December 1529, with Andrew Windsor, who had been returned by Buckinghamshire; the next day they were joined by Thomas Wentworth, one of the knights for Suffolk. Hussey certainly and Windsor in all probability had been M.P.s before 1529 and could bring to the upper House not only years of service as officers of the royal household but practical knowledge of the working of the House of Commons; Tailboys and Wentworth, also, may have been elected to the Parliament of 1523, for which the official returns are missing. From 1529 the majority of peers created by Henry VIII were men who had previously been M.P.s — all but two in this category had indeed been Members of the Reformation Parliament. Besides those already mentioned they were Thomas Cromwell (created a baron in 1536), William FitzWilliam (Earl of Southampton 1537), Thomas Audley (baron 1538), William Paulet and John Russell (barons 1539), Gregory Cromwell (M.P. 1539, baron under a new creation in 1540), John Dudley (Viscount Lisle 1542), William Parr (Lord Parr of Horton 1543), Thomas Wriothesley (M.P. 1539, baron in 1544) and Thomas Wharton (baron 1544).[3] After the death of Henry VIII the pattern is still more striking. During the reign of Edward VI seven new peers were created, of whom six had sat in the House of Commons: Richard Rich (whose parliamentary experience went back to 1529), Thomas Seymour, William Willoughby, William Paget, Thomas Darcy and William Herbert. The youthful Edmund Sheffield, ennobled in 1547, was the only new baron never to have been a Member of Parliament. Mary created six new peers, of whom five had been in the Commons: John Brydges (another veteran of 1529), Edward North, John Williams, Anthony Browne and Edward Hastings. The one exception was William Howard, created Lord Howard of Effingham in 1554. An analysis of the lay members of the Tudor Privy Council has shown that from the 1530s election to Parliament was a useful first step towards selection for Council membership.[4] The same appears to have been true for entry into the House of Lords.

In neither case is it argued that membership of the Commons was necessarily the reason for the further advancement, although Cromwell certainly sought election to Parliament as a means to further his career. Most of the newly created noblemen had entered Parliament as knights of the shire. (For some, though, their county seats may be merely their first recorded constituency, the evidence for an earlier election to a borough seat having been lost.)[5] Seven new peers first sat in the House of

Commons as representatives of boroughs. Thomas Cromwell's constituency in 1523 is not known, although it would have been a borough; in 1529 he was returned for Taunton, one of the boroughs of the bishopric of Winchester, through the patronage of the steward of the diocese, Sir William Paulet. Audley in 1523 and Rich in 1529 were elected by Colchester, Audley after the town had received a letter from Henry VIII, Rich at the request of the Earl of Oxford, whose residence at Wivenhoe was four miles from the borough. Thomas Wharton was returned in 1529 for Appleby, where he must have had the backing of Henry Clifford, first Earl of Cumberland. The three others were from families able to secure their own election. William Herbert is first known to have been elected in 1542, for Wilton; he had obtained a lease of Wilton Abbey two years earlier. Anthony Browne was elected in 1545 by Guildford, where his father was a property owner and royal official, and Edward Hastings, also in 1545, by Leicester, no doubt with the aid of his brother, the second Earl of Huntingdon. All seven had, it seems, graduated to county seats before they left the Commons for the House of Lords.[6]

The growing significance of the House of Commons in the experience of the House of Lords is confirmed by the number of heirs to peerages seeking election to it.[7] The majority were heirs to titles of Tudor creation: Gregory Cromwell, Thomas Wharton, Francis Russell, Thomas Wentworth, Thomas Windsor, John Mordaunt, Roger North, Henry Paget and William Stanley (heir to Lord Monteagle). All expected to inherit baronies at the time of their election and the promotion of John, Lord Russell to an earldom in January 1550 raised the question of the eligibility of Francis Russell to continue to sit in the lower House — although there is no sign of any concern for the status of Gregory Cromwell in 1540, when his father became Earl of Essex. The House of Commons on 21 January 1550 ordered that Russell 'shall abide in this house in the state he was before', and he remained as M.P. until the Parliament was dissolved in 1552. But when a new Parliament was called to meet in March 1553, he was sent a writ of summons to attend in the Lords in his father's barony, *vita patris*. This was a not unusual procedure for heirs to the higher titles of nobility and writs also went out early in 1553 to the sons of John Dudley, Duke of Northumberland, and Francis Talbot, Earl of Shrewsbury. (The proper treatment of the heirs to great titles was discussed by Northumberland in a letter to William Cecil before the opening of this Parliament.[8]) Yet Thomas Radcliffe, styled Lord FitzWalter, was not summoned in the barony of his father; he sat in the Parliament of March 1553 as M.P. for Norfolk. After the accession of Mary, however, he was summoned to attend in the House of Lords, as Lord FitzWalter, in each Parliament until he succeeded to the earldom of Sussex in 1557. Francis, Lord Russell, on the other hand — although a writ *v.p.* had in Henry VIII's reign always set the precedent for subsequent Parliaments — was never summoned by Mary until he became second Earl of Bedford in 1555; having once taken his seat in the House of Lords it is doubtful whether he could have gone back to the House of Commons and he appears therefore to have been in effect disbarred from Parliament in the first two years of Mary's reign. Apart from Radcliffe, heir to an old barony as well as to a new earldom, the heirs to pre-Tudor peerages elected to the House of Commons were all sons of barons: John Neville, William Stourton, Henry Parker, William Brooke and Thomas Dacre. One other might fairly be counted with them. Henry Stafford, M.P. for Shropshire in 1555, was son and heir of Henry, Lord Stafford under a new creation by the Act of Parliament of 1547 which ended the corruption of blood resulting from his father's attainder in 1521; but the barony had been an ancient one and by resolution of the House of Lords in February 1558 the family was restored to its old precedence.

Lord Stafford's restoration to his title in 1547 had presumably been helped by the presence in the House of Commons of his bastard brother, also Henry Stafford, as M.P. for Stafford: the castle and manor of Stafford had been restored to the family in 1531. Two other manorial parliamentary boroughs forfeited by Edward Stafford, Duke of Buckingham, were never recovered by the Staffords: Great Bedwyn and Bletchingley. A number of other parliamentary boroughs were still in the possession of the families which had owned them in the fifteenth century: Arundel was held by the FitzAlan Earls of Arundel and Bramber, Horsham, Lewes and New Shoreham by the Howard Dukes of Norfolk; until the destruction of their families the Courtenay Earls of Devon owned Plympton Erle and Margaret Pole, Countess of Salisbury, the borough of Wilton. Other noble families of pre-Tudor creation owned boroughs which began to return Members to Parliament between 1509 and 1558: William, eleventh Lord Willoughby owned Orford, enfranchised by 1523, the Stanley Earls of Derby the boroughs of Thirsk and Brackley, whose first known Members sat in the Parliament of 1547, and the Dacres of Gilsland the barony of Morpeth, of which the borough was enfranchised for Mary's first Parliament. Thomas Howard, Duke of Norfolk acquired the manor and castle of Castle Rising in 1544 by an exchange with Henry VIII; as we shall see, Castle Rising first returned Members to Mary's last Parliament. New peers, too, had or acquired parliamentary boroughs. The ancestors of Walter Hungerford, made a baron in 1536, owned Heytesbury and Cricklade and the greater part of Chippenham in the fifteenth century.[9] On Hungerford's attainder in 1540 they escheated to the Crown. William Willoughby, created Lord Willoughby of Parham in 1547, inherited Orford from his uncle, who died in 1526 leaving only a daughter. William FitzWilliam, later to become Earl of Southampton, bought the manor of Midhurst; after his death the estate passed to his half-brother and then to the latter's son, Anthony Browne, who was ennobled as Viscount Montagu. John Russell, created a baron in 1539, in the same year received a large grant of lands which included the borough of Tavistock. William Herbert was granted the borough of Wilton after the attainder of the Countess of Salisbury and the borough of Shaftesbury in April 1553, by which time he had been created Earl of Pembroke. In

1547 John Dudley, Earl of Warwick asked for and obtained the lordship, manor, town and castle of Warwick. In the same year Thomas, Lord Seymour of Sudeley was granted the four parliamentary boroughs in Sussex forfeited by the Duke of Norfolk and the reversion to the borough of Cricklade and the castle, lordship and manor of Devizes which formed part of the jointure of his wife, Catherine Parr. Edward Seymour, Earl of Hertford was granted the reversion to the manor of Great Bedwyn in 1544 and in 1547, as Duke of Somerset, the borough of Plympton Erle, the lordship of Canford — including the borough of Poole which from 1536 to 1538 had also belonged to the Courtenays — and the lordship, manor and town of Ludgershall, with the reversion to the boroughs of Marlborough and Wootton Bassett after the death of Catherine Parr; in 1548 he was given the lordship and manor of Reading by the King and acquired the borough of Wells from the Bishop of Bath and Wells.[10]

The constituency surveys in *The History of Parliament: The House of Commons 1509–1558* show the use made of their opportunities as borough-owners by members of the House of Lords. The many missing names of the Members for the early Parliaments of Henry VIII's reign make it unsafe to generalize about patronage in the years up to 1529, but from that date it is clear that all the noble owners of parliamentary boroughs or manorial boroughs — with the possible exception of Lord Hungerford — nominated Members for them, at least from time to time.[11] The new owners were among the most active patrons. There is indeed some possibility that Thomas, Lord Seymour had been especially concerned to obtain Norfolk's parliamentary boroughs in his grant of August 1547: at all events, he speedily made use of them since his influence is clear in all four boroughs in the elections of that autumn. He seems also to have taken advantage of another property in the same grant — the seven hundreds of Cirencester, of which he was already bailiff — to engineer its return of two Seymour connexions to the Parliament of 1547, in spite of the fact that the only previous election in Cirencester had been in 1337; the borough did not return M.P.s again until 1571.

The lords spiritual, by contrast, made little of their possession of parliamentary boroughs. The abbots in the House of Lords apparently made no attempt to nominate any Members of the House of Commons, although the Abbots of Tavistock, Malmesbury and Reading were all lords of the boroughs in which their abbeys were situated, and the Abbot of Reading also owned the borough of Leominster. Most bishops' sees were in cities that returned Members to Parliament but only Salisbury and Wells belonged to their bishops and in neither were episcopal nominees returned as M.P.s. The Bishop of Salisbury also owned the manor of Milford, which included (or was adjacent to) the borough of Old Sarum, but he made no electoral use of it and in 1549 leased the manor to Sir William Herbert, whose influence at once began to be seen in the borough's returns. The Bishop of Norwich owned Bishop's Lynn (later King's Lynn) until 1524 and the Archbishop of Canterbury the manors of Saltwood and Aldington — with the right to appoint the bailiffs of Hythe and Romney — until they were exchanged with the Crown in 1540, but there is no evidence that either acted as parliamentary patron. In the first Parliament of Edward VI's reign or late in the reign of Henry VIII two episcopal boroughs began to return M.P.s: Lichfield, where the Bishop of Coventry and Lichfield in 1548 made over his rights to the newly incorporated town, and Peterborough, where the Bishop or the Dean and Chapter occasionally nominated the Members, but where the dominant electoral influence was that of John, Lord Russell, later first Earl of Bedford, the high steward of the city. The Archbishop of York nominated the two M.P.s for Ripon in 1558 after the return to him of the borough which had been exchanged with the Crown in 1545 and enfranchised for the first Parliament of Mary's reign. But only the Bishop of Winchester was a patron on any scale, with three parliamentary boroughs owned and utilized by his see: Taunton, Downton and Hindon.

The possession of a parliamentary borough or manor gave the most direct control over elections to a member of the House of Lords interested in exercising it. Even to a Bishop of Winchester or to a great lay peer it became at election time the centre-piece in a mosaic of power and influence. The biographies in the *History of Parliament* volumes of seven of the leading noblemen who had been Members of the lower House — as Thomas Cromwell, Thomas Seymour, John Dudley, William Paget, William Herbert, John and Francis Russell — show where and how they secured the election of their nominees. But other noblemen who had never been M.P.s were also parliamentary patrons of some significance. A brief reference to the patronage exercised by seven of them, too, and by Stephen Gardiner may help to provide a more balanced view of the electoral role of members of the House of Lords.

The most active peers were all members of the high nobility. Influence over elections followed from their ownership of lands and offices, and might be used simply as an expression of social dominance. The Cliffords owned the barony of Westmorland; the head of the family was the hereditary sheriff of the county and the knights of the shire were elected at Appleby Castle, of which he was constable. In both shire and borough elections — held on the same day — members of the family, servants and clients were returned to Parliament throughout this period. William, Lord Parr, the future Earl of Essex and Marquess of Northampton, who owned the barony of Kendal in south Westmorland, and Thomas, Lord Wharton exercised no more than intermittent patronage in the county. This was in spite of the fact that Henry, Lord Clifford, created Earl of Cumberland and made Lord Warden of the West March in 1525, had lost effective political authority by the late 1530s to Wharton — M.P. for Appleby in 1529 — when Henry VIII transferred the substance of power to him as deputy warden.[12] The second Earl of Cumberland, who succeeded his father in 1542, was never a figure of more than local significance. His lack of interest in national politics is shown by his infrequent attendance in the House of Lords.[13] But this very reluctance to go to London — family tradition had it (with some exaggeration) that he visited the capital only three times between 1547 and his death in 1570[14] — provided a motive for ensuring the presence in the House of Commons of men whom he could trust. On 7 January 1549 Thomas Jolye, M.P. for Appleby and the earl's servant, wrote to Cumberland to report the action he had taken to stop the passage of a bill — inspired he was sure by Lord Wharton — designed to deprive the Cliffords of their hereditary shrievalty.[15] The Bill 'for sheriffs of England to be but one year' progressed no further in the House of Commons.[16]

Cumberland also succeeded his father as steward of the Duchy of Lancaster's honour of Knaresborough and exercised electoral influence there after four of its boroughs were enfranchised in Mary's reign: Boroughbridge, Knaresborough and Ripon in 1553 and Aldborough in 1558 (by which time Ripon had been returned to the Archbishop of York). Here he probably saw himself primarily as an agent of the Crown, particularly in the autumn of 1554 when elections were held for the Parliament which was to end the schism with Rome. At that time Cumberland insisted in a letter to John Holmes, for whom, as he said, he had 'devised a place' at either Boroughbridge or Knaresborough, that he expected him to support the royal policy of 'godly reformation'.[17] The office of chancellor of the Duchy of Lancaster was never given to a peer — although FitzWilliam and Paget were ennobled as chancellors — and if noblemen exercised Duchy patronage it was normally through such local stewardships. In Cumberland's case, the patronage was shared with the chancellor of the Duchy and with the President of the Council of the North, Francis Talbot, fifth Earl of Shrewsbury.

Shrewsbury himself dominated the elections at Newcastle-under-Lyme, within the Duchy honour of Tutbury of which he and his father were stewards from 1509 to 1560: the chancellor of the Duchy never intervened. After he became President of the Council of the North in 1549 he was also active in two Yorkshire boroughs enfranchised in 1547, Hedon — within the honour of Holderness, in the hands of the Crown since Buckingham's attainder in 1521 — and Thirsk, where he would have had to collaborate with the Earl of Derby, the owner of the borough. In Derbyshire his influence may be seen from time to time in the elections to both county and borough seats; in Nottinghamshire, where the family had been granted many monastic lands, it is hardly visible; Shrewsbury made occasional interventions in Shropshire, in which his estates were also considerable. In no county did he have the dominance enjoyed in Lancashire by Edward Stanley, third Earl of Derby.

The Stanleys were the only noble family to hold lands on any scale in Lancashire. By virtue of his vast estates in the county Derby effectively controlled the choice of knights of the shire to the exclusion of Duchy influence, and shared with the Duchy the patronage of its Lancashire boroughs, especially Liverpool and Wigan, the two boroughs enfranchised late in the reign of Henry VIII. Further afield, at Brackley, the earl's borough, the Members were Derby's servants and friends, with one exception: the 18-year-old Henry Sidney, son of the Lord Chamberlain, was returned as the senior Member in 1547, when the borough first began to send Members to Parliament. Only in his other newly enfranchised borough of Thirsk was Derby less than a free agent.

Cumberland, Shrewsbury and Derby all benefited from the creation of new parliamentary boroughs, although only Derby was the owner of his. The FitzAlan Earls of Arundel had their one borough, but the cluster of noble and gentry families in Sussex prevented any large extension of their influence outside it. In 1539, certainly, the help of the young Henry FitzAlan, Lord Maltravers, was sought by William FitzWilliam, Earl of Southampton, busy organizing the county election on behalf of Thomas Cromwell.[18] But there is no evident link between any knight of the shire and the FitzAlan family until the Parliament of April 1554, ten years after Maltravers had become twelfth Earl of Arundel. The earl's patronage in the county was generally confined to Arundel itself, with occasional interventions at Chichester, five miles from his main residence, and at East Grinstead, a Duchy of Lancaster borough where his father had acquired Imberhorne, one of the six or seven manors of the parish.[19] East Grinstead was closed to his influence, however, in 1555, when Imberhorne was included in a land exchange with the Queen.[20] Whatever he privately thought of this deal, Arundel was a loyal supporter of Mary and took seriously his responsibilities as one of her Privy Council. He evidently saw to it that the circular letter calling for the return of local residents only to the Parliament of November 1554 was obeyed in both Arundel and Chichester, although it appears that this effectively ended his patronage at Chichester, too, at least until 1571. However, the earl's connexion with Guildford gave him some say in the election of the borough's Members. He was also a leading landowner in Shropshire and seems to have had considerable influence over the choice of the knights of that shire: the return of Sir Henry Stafford in 1555, after he had been twice defeated in the Staffordshire elections of 1553, was probably managed with Arundel's support.

One of the Queen's religious opponents was an active parliamentary patron. Henry Manners, second Earl of Rutland owned fewer lands in Nottinghamshire than the Earl of Shrewsbury when he came of age in 1547, but he was quick to establish his influence in the county. In 1547 Rutland was appointed constable of Nottingham Castle — an office held by his father at the time of his death in 1543 — and his influence over the borough's representation can be seen in all the elections from then on, with one exception: for the Parliament of March 1553 two townsmen were returned. This is surprising because Rutland was a friend and supporter of the Duke of Northumberland and was particularly active elsewhere in this election. Both knights for Nottinghamshire in March 1553 were connected with him, one of them being comptroller of his household, and both Lincoln and Grantham acceded to his request for the nomination of one of their Members.[21] Rutland was lessee of Lincoln's fee farm to the Crown, which the city was anxious to buy from him; he retained the nomination of one M.P. in subsequent Parliaments, naming his secretary, a fellow Protestant, in all Mary's Parliaments except the last, when he summarily replaced him — after his election — by a servant of the Lord Chancellor, presumably on the instruction of the Crown. Rutland's nominee at Grantham for the Parliament of March 1553 was also a strong Protestant. He was re-elected to Mary's first Parliament at a time when Rutland himself was confined to his house, and voted against a government religious bill in the Commons. Rutland, pardoned after the opening of this Parliament, showed more discretion in the choice of later Members for Grantham, although one of his possible nominees was also an opponent of the government's policy on religion.

The ability to respond to a request from court or Council for a seat in Parliament for an official candidate — however unwelcome in itself it may have been — was nevertheless one of the advantages of possessing electoral influence. Parliamentary patronage was a part of the wider patronage system, that network of favours and obligations which formed the substructure of Tudor government, linking the members of the ruling *élite* with one another and with the Crown. From time to time even a great nobleman might best serve his own interest by deferring to the wishes of others nearer to the centre of power. But the parliamentary patronage of the nobility was not often under any such constraint. The choice of servants, relatives and friends for seats in the Commons was generally, it seems, intended to please them and to give to the nobleman a spokesman or at least an informant in the lower House. Shrewsbury and Derby, Arundel and Rutland were active members of the House of Lords, but personal contact with Members of the Commons was as useful to them as to the absentee Cumberland. Most valuable of all, perhaps, was the trusted servant. A second secretary of the Earl of Rutland joined his colleague in the Parliament of 1555; Shrewsbury found seats for a number of his attendants and Arundel for members of his council and household; Derby secured the return of his receiver, his steward and the comptroller of his household, generally more than once, and of his councillor and brother-in-law six times in succession. Any nobleman probably had acquaintances in the House of Commons more influential than such men could hope to be, but when it came to furthering his concerns they at least could be relied upon; and — for all the constitutional significance of Parliament — much legislation affected the economic interests of the great landowners rather than the political life of the nation.

Only the King's chief ministers treated the selection of M.P.s as an aspect of government in the narrower sense. Their high offices gave them the opportunity to use the parliamentary patronage of others, providing an added dimension to their electoral activities. Yet for them, too, their own possessions were an invaluable base on which to build a following in the House of Commons, whether for themselves or for the Crown. In 1539 Thomas Howard, Duke of Norfolk, in the North of England surveying coastal defences, made a note for Cromwell of 'such towns as in times past I could have made burgesses of parliament of, in the shire of Sussex', naming Horsham, Shoreham, Steyning, Lewes, and Gatton 'where Sir

Roger Copley dwelleth', and adding that 'as for Reigate, I doubt whether any burgesses be there or not'. The oddities in this list suggest that Norfolk had not himself been much involved in previous elections. By Steyning he must have meant Bramber, while Reigate had not only featured, with Gatton — also in Surrey — on a list of boroughs controlled by a mid fifteenth-century Duke of Norfolk, but had actually returned one of Norfolk's servants in 1529. Nevertheless, he had at least tried to be specific about his own patronage, and Cromwell seems to have taken up the reference to Gatton, putting pressure on Sir Roger Copley to return one of his friends. By contrast, the rest of the duke's note contained no more than a general assurance that he had been attentive to electoral matters. 'In all the shires in my commission sauf Lancashire, I have put such order that such shalbe chosen as I doubt not shall serve his highness according to his pleasure, and in like wise I did in Norfolk and Suffolk before my last coming thence.'[22]

Stephen Gardiner went further than Norfolk by claiming for his nomination of M.P.s not merely precedent but some sort of constitutional right. From the Fleet prison in November 1547 he hinted darkly at the trouble that might follow the usurpation of his patronage by the government, suggesting that Protector Somerset would do well to consider 'whether mine absence from the upper house, with the absence of those I have been used to name in the nether house, will not engender more cause of objection, if opportunity serve hereafter, than my presence with such as I should appoint were there'.[23]

This was to push his case to the limit; no notice was taken of it, then or later. The membership of the first Parliament of Edward VI's reign reflected the dominance of the Protector, although, preoccupied with the Scottish campaign, he probably left much of the detailed preparation to his friends and colleagues. In the boroughs of Plympton Erle and Poole, granted to him in July 1547, three of the Members seem to have been nominees of the government rather than of Somerset himself; the fourth was his servant. But the Wiltshire boroughs granted to him at the same time — although two were his only in reversion after the death of his sister-in-law, Catherine Parr — provided seats for his eldest son, his physician and his close political associate, Sir Thomas Smith. Reading — whose lordship was not to be given to Somerset until the following year — was already open to his influence, both seats going to his supporters. His secretary was returned for Chipping Wycombe, probably with the help of the borough's high steward, and the chamberlain of his household for Scarborough. At Cirencester, the borough controlled by Thomas, Lord Seymour of Sudeley, one of the Members returned was also a servant of Protector Somerset, a choice which may have been designed to win his approval for the borough's enfranchisement.

This Parliament attainted both Seymour brothers before it finished, following the precedent of Cromwell's 'tractable' Parliament in 1540. Intervention in the elections was after all only the initial stage in the management of Parliament. Yet it was an essential preliminary, and

Norfolk and Gardiner when they returned to power with the accession of Mary reasserted control over their patronage. Gardiner, restored to the bishopric of Winchester, named household and diocesan servants to the see's boroughs in each Parliament until his death; the treasurer of the diocese was elected knight of the shire for Hampshire for every Marian Parliament. The bishop in the early part of the reign made persistent efforts to use Parliament for a political purpose, mobilizing his friends in both Houses in a campaign against the Spanish marriage and trying to promote his own legislative proposals.[24] Norfolk, with a more limited aim, was more successful. He was intent on securing the annulment of the Act of Attainder passed against him in January 1547 and his Sussex boroughs provided seats for his friends and servants in the first Marian Parliament, while the two knights of the shire were former servants of his. The dispersal of his lands by the Crown had, however, created rival claims to their possession, some of them vested in men who sat for the duke's boroughs. Either he relied too implicitly on their loyalty or he thought it better to have the whole matter settled in Parliament after both sides had stated their case. His attainder annulled, and the question of the lands referred to arbitration, the old duke was no longer concerned to be an active patron. In the next Parliament — the last of his life — he was content to respond to requests for seats in the Commons from his neighbours in the county. It was not until Mary's last Parliament that the influence of the Howards in Sussex was restored by the 19-year-old fourth Duke of Norfolk. The young duke was active in East Anglia as well. He was high steward of Great Yarmouth, which now returned his secretary as its M.P. Norfolk had also succeeded his grandfather as high steward of Cambridge. Although no previous high stewards had exercised parliamentary patronage there, he wrote to the borough for a seat for his household official, Sir Nicholas Lestrange. Cambridge refused him.[25] Thereupon Castle Rising, the duke's borough, which had never before returned anyone to Parliament, returned Lestrange and Sir John Radcliffe as its duly elected Members of Parliament. Their appearance at Westminster provoked no challenge. By this manoeuvre Castle Rising was enfranchised and the Duke of Norfolk acquired one more parliamentary borough, this time in his home county.[26]

The incident serves to highlight the key factor in the relationship between Lords and Commons in the early Tudor period: the individual, his possessions and his interests. The Journals of Parliament conceal as much as they reveal of the interaction between the two Houses. Only a series of biographical studies can illuminate the realities beneath the formal record.

Notes

[1] Figures for the Parliaments of Henry VIII's reign (except that of 1523) from writs of summons in the P.R.O. Figures for 1547–58 from M.A.R. Graves, 'The Tudor House of Lords in the Reigns of Edward VI and Mary I: A Study of Composition, Quality, and

Attendance' (Otago, New Zealand, Ph.D. thesis, 1974). Dr Graves kindly deposited a copy of his thesis with the History of Parliament Trust and gave permission for it to be used.

[2]   J.C. Wedgwood, *History of Parliament* (2 vols., 1936–8), I, p.xxxiv discovered 15 M.P.s between 1439 and 1509 who were later ennobled.

[3]   Peers created by Henry VIII, 1529–47, who had never been M.P.s: Edmund, Lord Bray, Thomas, Lord Burgh and Henry Pole, Lord Montagu (1529), John, Lord Mordaunt (1532), Edward Seymour, Viscount Beauchamp (1536), Walter, Lord Hungerford (1536), William, Lord Parr (1539), William, Lord Eure (1544) and Thomas Lord Poynings (1545).

[4]   G.R. Elton, 'Tudor Government: The Points of Contact: I. Parliament', *Transactions of the Royal Historical Society*, 5th . XXIV (1974), 199.

[5]   Windsor's constituency, if he first sat in 1510, is unknown, as is Paget's if he entered Parliament at a by-election in 1533; Buckinghamshire and Middlesex respectively are their first recorded constituencies. Russell, too, was possibly returned for a borough before his election for Buckinghamshire in 1529.

[6]   Cromwell's constituency in 1536 is not known for certain, but was probably Kent.

[7]   Wedgwood found only 10 M.P.s, 1439–1509, who succeeded to peerages: *History of Parliament*, I, p. xxxiv.

[8]   P.R.O., S.P. 10/18/8.

[9]   Wedgwood, *History of Parliament*, II, 705–6, 708.

[10]   Phyllis M. Hembry, *The Bishops of Bath and Wells 1540–1640* (1967), p. 113.

[11]   Although not all were proprietary boroughs: this subject is discussed by Norah M. Fuidge in an unpublished paper, 'The Status of the English Boroughs and their franchise'.

[12]   M.E. James, 'The First Earl of Cumberland (1493–1542) and the Decline of Northern Feudalism', *Northern History*, I (1966), 45–6.

[13]   Graves, biography of Cumberland in 'The Tudor House of Lords in the Reigns of Edward VI and Mary I'.

[14]   *Clifford Letters of the Sixteenth Century*, ed, A.G. Dickens (Surtees Soc., CLXXII, 1962), p. 149.

[15]   *Ibid.*, pp. 102–3.

[16]   Bill read once, 5 Jan. 1549: *C.J.*, I, 5.

[17]   *L.P. Hen. VIII*, XIV (1), 520.

[19]   *Ibid.*, XVI, 878 (93).

[20]   *Cal. Pat. Rolls*, 1555–7, p.2.

[21]   H.M.C., *14th Rept.*, VIII, 47; B.L., Lansdowne MS. 3, f.75, printed in H.A. Merewether and A.J. Stephens, *The History of the Boroughs and Municipal Corporations* (new edn., 3 vols., Brighton, 1972), II, 1172–3.

[22]   B.L., Cotton MS. Calig. B. VI, f.373, calendared in *L.P. Hen. VIII*, X, 816.

[23]   *The Letters of Stephen Gardiner*, ed. J.A. Muller (Cambridge, 1933), p. 424.

[24]   M.A.R. Graves, 'The House of Lords and the Politics of Opposition, April–May, 1554', *W.P. Morrell: A Tribute*, eds. G.A. Wood and P.S. O'Connor (Dunedin, 1973), pp.1–20; D.M. Loades, *The Reign of Mary Tudor* (1979), pp. 168–70.

[25]   C.H. Cooper, *Annals of Cambridge* (5 vols., Cambridge, 1842–1908), II, 140.

[26]   Norfolk nominated to both seats at Castle Rising for each Elizabethan Parliament until his trial for treason.

THE EMERGENCE OF STANDING COMMITTEES FOR PRIVILEGES AND RETURNS

MARY FREAR KEELER

The Committee for Privileges, ancestor of the powerful Committee of Privileges in later times, began in the House of Commons in the reign of Queen Elizabeth I. Although its counterpart in the upper House was not used until 1621, the Commons committee became a standing committee, drew into its responsibilities the examination of irregular election returns and other matters relating to the membership of the House, and developed into an instrument by means of which leaders in Parliament, whether of factions or of the government, might exercise influence. As the House added to the committee's functions, particularly in the next reign, its importance on matters of privilege tended to diminish, although its name preserved that sign of its origin.[1]

Although Wallace Notestein and Sir John Neale have commented on committee development in parliamentary history,[2] neither dealt very specifically with the privileges committee. It was described as he understood it by Henry Scobell in *Memorials of the Methods . . . of Parliament*[3] and by John Hatsell in *Precedents and Proceedings in the House of Commons*;[4] and brief comments on its origins have been made by later scholars such as Joseph Redlich, G.W. Prothero, Sheila Lambert and Peter Hasler;[5] but a detailed study of the committee's development throughout its formative period has not been undertaken. The present article is concerned with the origin of the committee and its functions in Elizabeth's time and with its development in the successive Parliaments of her reign.[6]

In contrast with the four other committees which, by Scobell's time, were considered 'standing committees' that were appointed early in a session, the privileges committee did not come to include all Members of the House,[7] but continued to be a select committee. If it seemed advisable to bring in other Members whose knowledge might be useful on particular occasions, the House voted to add their names to the list and at least some, but not all, of the men so added remained with the committee.[8] Non-members might attend the committee occasionally but without the vote;[9] a motion in 1624 to grant voting power to 'all that come' was denied as being contrary to precedent.[10] Because it remained a select committee[11] and came regularly to have a nucleus of men with parliamentary experience, a continuity of service developed that affected its procedure and functions. The usefulness of such a committee became evident expecially in the Parliaments of the early Stuarts.

The privileges with which the Elizabethan committees were concerned were not new. As summarized in Speaker Gargrave's speech in 1559 they were liberty of access to the sovereign, pardon for the Speaker for errors he might unwittingly make, freedom of speech for Members in debate in the House, and freedom from arrests and lawsuits for Members and their servants during a session.[12] The ones about which questions arose during Elizabeth's time were the last two of these, which involved the respective authorities of Queen and Parliament and, with regard to the last, are related to the Commons' insistence that, as part of the High Court of Parliament, it could act as a court. Authority to control its own Members, from which grew its claims regarding elections, was a more recently asserted privilege.[13] So also, though occurring less frequently than in later times, were privileges claimed in relation to the House of Lords.[14] The committee's role on matters of privilege, especially those relating to arrests and lawsuits, was chiefly in investigating facts and precedents and making recommendations. As precedents hardened into custom, however, decisions by the House without referral to the committee occurred frequently, and its role in this respect declined.

Using a committee to consider elections developed later, and separate committees performed the two functions for the House until well past the middle of Elizabeth's reign. Only in 1593 did the Commons direct a single committee to consider both privileges and election returns. Occasionally and without fanfare the Commons had used small committees to search for facts about elections or Members' qualifications in Elizabeth's earlier Parliaments, but only in the later ones did the regular naming of a committee to consider elections take hold. This procedure is concomitant with the growing self-consciousness of the Commons, a marked continuity of experienced leadership,[15] an increasing use of committees for a variety of purposes and, as Neale has observed, the assertion by this time that the House could function as a court.[16] Related to the development also was the increase in the number of Members elected as more boroughs were 'restored'. Questions arose about the right of 'new' men to take their seats and about residency qualifications and patronage.[17] Asking a committee to ascertain facts was a practical procedure.

The early cases in which the Commons used committees to consider questions of privileges and elections, as tracing through successive Elizabethan Parliaments reveals, were matters of personal concern to members; i.e. freedom from arrest or eligibility to serve as M.P.s.

Frequently the House made decisions without using a committee when Members complained about lawsuits or arrests,[18] but it sometimes named small *ad hoc* committees to ascertain facts in complicated cases or even to propose how a case might be settled. Examples are that of John Smith (1559), sued on a charge of outlawry but ultimately permitted by a close vote of 112–107 to remain as a Member;[19] the arrest of a Member's servants (1563) about which the committee arranged a temporary settlement before making its report, and the imprisonment of a Member that year, which was investigated by a different committee;[20] the Member imprisoned (1566) about whom a committee of distinguished lawyers was sent to the Lord Keeper for information and to ask for his temporary release, and another involved in a lawsuit about which a committee of five arranged for mediation between the parties.[21] In 1576, in the case of Arthur Hall's servant, Smalley, one committee investigated the facts of his arrest and afterwards the House used a different one to consider 'the manner of his delivery'. Sending its own serjeant with the 'warrant of the mace' followed the precedent of the Ferrers case of 1543, confirming the claim of power of the House alone to maintain its privileges.[22] In this session also an *ad hoc* committee examined the question of Peter Wentworth and the privilege of freedom of speech.[23] A somewhat larger committee examined the evidence regarding Arthur Hall's book in the third session (1581) before the full debate in the House and its vote to expel him and order a new election.[24]

In the next Parliament (1584–5), about midway in the session, a committee referred to specifically as the 'Committee for Privileges' was named 'to examine the state and manner of serving process upon any Members of the House from time to time', and to impart information needed by the House for making decisions.[25] A few days before, the Commons had been informed of subpoenas from Chancery and Star Chamber served upon two Members, with the arrest of one M.P. A committee sent to Chancery with a request that the customary parliamentary privilege be observed had been told by the Lord Chancellor that 'he thought this House had no such liberty of privilege for subpoenas as they pretended'.[26] Two experienced Members were thereupon named to search for precedents regarding that privilege so that they might inform the House of 'the state of the liberties and privileges'. Two days later the House established the committee of three Members for examining such cases for the remainder of the session. When a fourth Member was added on 23 February, it was described as the 'Committee for Privileges, and touching serving of process upon Members of the House and their Servants'.[27] Although no reports from the committee appear in the records of the session, it may have supplied information for the decisions made later regarding the cases of Richard Cooke M.P. and the servants of two Members.[28]

In each of the next two Parliaments similar small committees were named early in the session 'for examining and reporting cases of privilege'.[29] However, for difficult cases requiring searches for facts and precedents in both 1586–7[30] and 1589[31] the House appointed *ad hoc* committees of somewhat similar membership.

Although the committees named to consider privileges in the first three decades of Elizabeth's reign did not regularly consider problems of elections, questions had arisen about the eligibility and the increasing number of Members, and had been handled. John Smith, whose privilege had been investigated in 1559, was permitted to keep his place in spite of a charge of outlawry.[32] In 1563, a roll-call revealed the presence of a number of men whose names were not on the clerk's list of duly returned Members, chiefly ones selected by newly restored boroughs. Shortly afterwards the Speaker announced that the Lord Steward had decided they should take their places, but should bring in their letters patent showing their right to sit.[33] In this Parliament also, when Members who had been 'doubly returned' announced the place for which they wished to sit, the House followed the already established procedure of 'requiring' a new election for the vacated seat. The wording for such cases in the second session (1566) was: 'it was resolved that a new writ should go out.' A Commons order, transmitted by the Speaker to the Crown Office, was now a part of the procedure for ordering the new election,[34] but no committee work was involved here.

In 1571, however, when questions about the eligibility of new Members recurred after a roll-call on 5 April, the House recognized the burgesses for East Grinstead but appointed a committee of seven men to confer with the Attorney-General and the Solicitor regarding others from nine boroughs that had not sent burgesses to the preceding Parliament. Upon hearing the committee's report on 9 April, the House 'Ordered by Mr Attorney's assent, that the Burgesses shall remain according to the returns; for that the validity of the Charters of their Towns is elsewhere to be examined, if cause be'.[35] Evidently, the committee had not presumed or had not had time to examine the charters, but had decided the election warrants brought in by the new burgesses were sufficient proof of election. A review by a committee rather than by the Lord Steward as in 1563 represents a small move toward the claim of the Commons' authority to review and pass judgment on election returns. No committee appears to have been used, however, when the House decided on 10 May to expel Thomas Long because he had gained his election through bribery.[36] Concern about the quality of its Members, especially about inexperienced men who owed their seats to noble patrons, led the House to consider a bill requiring residency for borough Members. The bill, however, was not enacted.[37]

In Elizabeth's next Parliament, her longest (1572–83), no questions about membership seem to have occurred until the second session (1576). The House then acted without using a committee to retain Members absent on 'ambassage' or ill, as well as a peer's son who had no vote in the upper House, and Serjeant Jeffries, despite his responsibilities there as Queen's Serjeant.[38] Once more the Commons named an *ad hoc* committee to 'confer together touching the number of Knights and Burgesses',[39] but nothing came of it.

In the third session (1581), however, meeting after an interval of five years, the House again faced the question of retention of seats for various absentees, with a challenge this time to the Lord Chancellor's authority for sending writs for new elections.[40] On 19 January, even before the Speaker had been presented to the Queen, Thomas Norton of London, one of the 'radicals' of this period, asked why the new men so chosen were present and questioned the validity of writs issued without authorization from the House.[41] He had in mind, no doubt, the decisions regarding absentees in 1576. Several law officers of the Crown replied that 'it sufficeth to make suggestion in Chancery' regarding a vacancy and that to challenge the Lord Chancellor's authority was to 'scandalize' the work of his court.[42] They advised, however, that the new Members be accepted 'until the matter be further cleared upon the examination and judgment of the said House'. The clerk's notes suggest that the new men may have been received,[43] but a formal vote was probably not taken, since the Speaker-elect had not yet been presented and the House was not formerly organized.[44]

Although the question of election writs was set aside for a time, the House acted on its own authority when, on 21 January, it accepted as a Member a man who had been indicted for felony, reasoning that indictment did not mean a proved charge.[45] It voted also on 8 February that Walter Vaughan should keep his seat, in spite of an outlawry charge against him, after the matter had been investigated by the Speaker and two other Members.[46]

More than a month into the session the problem of the new Members elected on the Lord Chancellor's writs came up again when the House was called on 24 February. Now the Commons ordered that all of those returns should be examined as well as the orders and precedents of the House 'in like cases', and named a committee of 12 for the work.[47] Thomas Cromwell reported from the committee on 18 March and the House, after some debate, reversed the plan advised earlier by government spokesmen, voting to discharge without penalty the new Members not 'duly returned . . . as in lieu and place of others absent . . . and not dead', unless special order should be taken by the House to the contrary. The former incumbents still living, except two who were too ill to attend, were declared to be the legitimate Members. Among the absentees whose incumbency was recognized were some Members employed in government service. The resolution reiterated further that 'during the time of the sitting of this court' no writ for election should go out 'without the Warrant of the House first directed for the same to the Clerk of the Crown, according to ancient jurisdiction and authority of this House in that behalf accustomed and used'.[48] This decision on the Members agreed with the position taken in 1576.

In the next Parliament, which began in late November 1584, about two weeks after the opening (on 8 December), the Speaker himself (Serjeant Puckering) asked the opinion of the House about the validity of several shire elections. Following defensive comments by one Huntingdonshire

Member, the House referred investigation of the matter to a small committee of Privy Councillors and lawyers (Mr Treasurer, Mr Vice-Chamberlain, Mr Solicitor and the Recorder of London). On 12 December, the date that had been set for their meeting, the last two were directed particularly to examine the records of the Huntingdonshire election. On the day before the Christmas recess, 21 December, the Solicitor reported that, after examining various writs and returns, only the Huntingdonshire election seemed to be in question. He added that because actions of the sheriff were involved, the case was not 'in their opinions for this House to deal with' or to declare the election void; however, 'because that resteth now chiefly upon matter of Precedents to see how this House may decide this cause', he and the Recorder would make a further search for precedents with the clerk of the upper House and report 'as cause shall require'.[49] Since no later report is recorded, the case was evidently dropped. The Queen's legal officers, while nodding to the Commons' repeated claim about investigating elections, had handled their assignment effectively. Yet, although circumscribed in membership and activity, this small committee on elections represents a link between those of 1581 and 1586.[50] As to one M.P. who was doubly returned, the House used no committee before ordering that a warrant be sent to the Clerk of the Crown for a new writ for filling the vacancy.[51]

In the 1586 case of the Norfolk election, the Commons asserted more strongly their claims of authority, possibly taking advantage of the confusion during the early days of the session. The Council's mistake in ordering a second election writ, as the Lord Chancellor himself acknowledged later, inevitably stirred criticism both in Norfolk and in Parliament and, during the delays about getting the session started, the matter was talked about.[52] It is not surprising, therefore, that the Speaker's announcement on 3 November of the Queen's view that it was 'impertinent' for the House to concern itself with matters of the Lord Chancellor's office[53] led to discussion by the House and its decision on 9 November to name a committee of 15 in the interest of the 'liberties of this House in the examination and judgment of the returns' regarding the Norfolk events so that the House might determine its own course.[54] Thomas Cromwell, spokesman for the 1581 committee, now reported on 11 November the present committee's approval of the first return, adding that it might be a perilous precedent for the 'Liberty and Privilege of this House to admit or pass over any such Writ or Return in such manner as the second Writ carrieth'. Furthermore, although they had learned that the Lord Chancellor and other judges now agreed on the validity of the original return, the committee had declined to send a delegate to ask for confirmation of that view, arguing that to do so would be prejudicial to the principle that only Members of the House should decide on cases of this sort. The House promptly accepted the committee's finding. Remarks made thereafter by Treasurer Knollys and Recorder Fleetwood, in which the latter rather fulsomely restated the Commons' claims, were doubtless intended to set the matter at rest so that the main business of the session, the question of Mary Queen of Scots, might proceed.[55]

In dealing with the Norfolk case not only had the Commons reasserted the principle that the House alone should decide questions about its membership but had challenged the authority of both the Chancery and the Privy Council.[56] The committee they used on this occasion, larger than that of 1584 and including more non-official members, provided another step toward a regularly appointed committee to consider election matters.

In the next Parliament (1589), however, the Commons appears to have yielded somewhat with regard to Chancery procedures, although a committee to deal with rumoured abuses in elections was set up on 8 February, one day after the appointment of the now customary Committee for Privileges. Already the House without a committee had taken the customary action about a doubly returned Member and presumably ordered writs for replacing two Members reported as being too ill to attend.[57]

The committee, appointed upon a motion by Sir Edward Hoby, a younger Member with radical inclinations, was assigned to consider a wide range of 'abuses' regarding elections and to go over with the Clerk of the Crown his book of returns and the returns from the sheriffs.[58] Eleven or 12 Members were quickly named, including Watson, the Clerk of the Crown who was also an M.P., and another man was added after he proposed that the committee consider also the problem of poor attendance. Five more were added[59] when a review of the question of replacing ill Members was ordered on 10 February.[60]

In dealing with their assignment the 1589 committee modified the stand that had been taken in 1586. There was a different Lord Chancellor by this time, Sir Christopher Hatton, who in his previous parliamentary experience had, as a courtier, generally been a spokesman for the Crown;[61] and the post-Armada session was one of general good feeling toward the Queen.[62] The presence of the Clerk of the Crown as a committee-member also may have been a moderating influence. At any rate, Mr Treasurer Knollys reported on 11 February the committee's agreement on the following points: the House should take notice of returns 'only in such sort' as certified by the Clerk of the Crown in Chancery, 'without any intermeddling at all in any business of the Sheriffs' or other election officials; if no return at all had come in, the House should through its Speaker authorize the Crown Office to send an election writ; no ill Member should be replaced unless he had an 'irrecoverable' sickness. However, in spite of the first point, the committee had found the return for Appleby faulty and recommended a new election. This report was 'well liked' by the House, as was the committee's recommendation that absenteeism should be discouraged by fines.[63] Apparently, the committee did not consider the unusual situation of the Lincolnshire sheriff who served as a Member this year.[64]

Two weeks after the first report, Recorder Fleetwood notified the House of an irregularity regarding New Romney's election and, in spite of the ruling of 11 February, the case was referred to the same committee. Thomas Cromwell reported this time (3 March), indicating that no decision had been reached within the committee. He stated as his own view, however, and one which the House presently decided to follow, that the New Romney man should be seated, even though local officials had neglected to certify his election to the Crown Office.[65]

It seems clear that this Parliament, influenced by men like Cromwell and Fleetwood, intended to keep an eye on election matters, although it was willing to make concessions to the role of the Crown Office. It is evident also that, in naming a committee to consider cases of questionable elections, in using it repeatedly and expanding its functions, and in appointing to it men with experience on such committees as well as knowledge of privilege cases, the House was developing a useful instrument. In the next Parliament a committee on election returns was called for early, and its work was combined with that of the committee for privileges.

On the first full business day of the 1593 session, 26 February, George More, a Surrey Member, moved that a committee be appointed to consider irregularities in the Southwark election.[66] Before the nominations were made Robert Wroth moved for 'a committee for the Liberties and Privileges of the Members of the House and their Servants', and the House responded then by voting to name a single committee charged with dual functions:

> [to] examine and make report of all such Cases touching Elections and Returns . . . and also all such Cases for privilege as in any wise may occur or fall out during the same Sessions of Parliament; to the end this House upon the Reports of the same Examinations may proceed to such further course in every the same Cases [*sic*] as to this House shall be thought meet.[67]

One of Wroth's concerns, although it was not mentioned in the records until 10 March, was the Council's orders of the previous day for the imprisonment of Peter Wentworth and other Members.[68]

The committee now appointed, with an established day for meeting, was larger than its predecessors, including all of the Privy Councillors who were M.P.s and 30 others, with permission for any Members of the House to attend its meetings 'as occasion shall serve'. The roster of the committee included a number of men who had served on earlier election or privilege committees.[69] The reports made by various members of the committee related to both privileges and elections, with Serjeant Yelverton making the first report on 1 March, supplemented by several speakers, and Sir Edward Hoby reporting on 6 and 7 March.[70] The motion by Wroth on 10 March regarding imprisoned M.P.s evidently did not come from the full committee, since he was promptly rebuffed by the Privy Councillors present.[71]

Although members of the committee did not succeed in efforts in behalf of the offending M.P.s, the committee examined a few other privilege cases, especially that of Thomas Fitzherbert, whose arrest was related to election matters also. After Yelverton's report on 1 March, discussion followed in the House on several days, with Speaker Coke intervening for guidance on procedure and the decision. Seeking to maintain its position as a court and its authority to decide on the eligibility of its Members, the Commons voted on 5 April that Fitzherbert was by his election a Member, but that he could not be granted privilege especially because his arrest had occurred before his election had been certified and before the date on which parliamentary privilege began.[72]

In handling other election cases, all involving irregularities in the returns, the committee on 6 March reported its views and suggestions regarding three of them. This time the House, instead of making its own decisions, voted that the Speaker should consult the Lord Keeper's views about allowing two of the returns to stand as the committee recommended or issuing new writs in all of the cases 'at his Lordship's pleasure'. The outcome was that he disallowed only one, and decided that the other two should stand 'without taking notice of any matter of fact therein, or in the election at all'.[73]

The combined committee for returns and privileges of 1593, although more firmly established procedurally, performed its work with less boldness than had its predecessors. Although a few Members spoke out strongly,[74] the rest of the committee and also the House in making its decision yielded more readily to royal authority, whether pronounced by Privy Councillors, the Speaker, or the Lord Keeper. A partial explanation of the different mood in the Commons may be the absence of the older Members, especially Thomas Cromwell and Recorder Fleetwood, as Neale has pointed out. Certainly, too, the early removal from the scene of some of the more daring of the current Members served as a warning to others.[75] The presence of all the Privy Councillor M.P.s on the committee, and the interposition of Coke, at the same time Speaker and Solicitor-General, with his heavy emphasis on points of law, must be considered as well. Although the privileges of the Commons and their claims about determining their own membership were referred to often in debate, the will to press forward on their claims yielded to a spirit of compromise.

On these matters the Parliament of 1597 was less docile. The new Speaker was Serjeant Yelverton,[76] who had been a reporter for the 1593 committee and had shown his interest in privileges and election matters. Also, although various older spokesmen for the Commons' claims on those areas were absent, newer men were emerging to argue the case. It was Speaker Yelverton who, on the first day of regular business (5 November), put 'the House in remembrance of a committee' to deal with any causes 'touching privileges and returns' during the session and to make reports 'as occasion shall serve'.[77] Those appointed to the single committee included all the Privy Councillor M.P.s and 35 others. In addition to such legal officers as the Recorder of London, the attorneys of the Duchy of Lancaster and the Court of Wards, the Solicitor-General, the Master of Requests, and Serjeant Hele (of Exeter), many were veterans of this and other kinds of committees, obviously experienced Parliament-men.[78] Another Member was added later when he raised a question touching his privilege.[79] The chairmanship again was indefinite, the various reporters being John Brograve, attorney for the Duchy, George More, and Sir Edward Hoby.[80]

One privilege case about a Chancery subpoena served upon Thomas Knyvet demonstrates this Parliament's efforts to be less dependent upon the Lord Keeper. Brograve reported on 8 November that the committee had found in favour of the Member's privilege and recommended sending two Members to confer with the Lord Keeper about it. The House responded by approving the plan and 'requiring' that official to revoke the subpoena. It is scarcely surprising that Hoby brought back the word that the Lord Keeper, questioning the word *require*, had been unwilling to give an immediate answer.[81] The decision of the House to send committee-members rather than the Speaker to confer with the Lord Keeper is markedly different from the procedure insisted upon by the Speaker, Coke, in 1593. As to the election case on which Brograve reported also, the House voted to accept the committee's recommendation about the returns in question. Although the Crown Office had reached the same decision earlier, the Commons used its committee to make its own study before deciding which return was valid.[82]

Although three more privilege cases involving subpoenas were handled by the House on 28 March without reference to the committee,[83] the Commons continued to use the committee on election matters. When George More reported on 12 November the committee's view that Ludlow's election return was irregular, the House considered fining one of the local officials but, unable to decide which one to blame, referred the matter back to the committee, with instructions to seek the opinion of judges if they could not decide on the matter themselves.[84] In early December, with Sir Edward Hoby apparently taking the lead, the committee was conducting a search of Members missing from the book of the Clerk of the Crown, and the House ordered its clerk to search for precedents so that the House could decide on the cases Hoby had reported. Although a date was set for the review by the House,[85] no further action appears in the records. Evidently Hoby, who had emerged as a leader in the committee, was unable to push the House into action.

In Elizabeth's last Parliament (1601) a 'Committee for Returns and Privileges' was appointed early for examining problems in those areas on which the House would have to decide. The committee list, which included all the Privy Councillor M.P.s and 30 others, many of whom were familiar with the committee's work, was given to Sir Edward Hoby.[86] Although several reports were made by Hoby, other spokesmen for the committee were Serjeant Harris, Sir Francis Hastings, the Solicitor and Sir Robert Cecil. A record of one of its meetings has been preserved in one of the private diaries of this session.[87]

Again the committee was used for investigating problems and recommending action to the House, although less often on privileges than on questions of eligibility of Members or irregularities in elections or returns. Decisions about alleged violations of privileges were often dealt with immediately by the House, the committee being used only in the more unusual cases.[88]

An election case from Rutland raised the question of whether a sheriff might serve as a knight of the shire. Members of the committee, when their report was debated on 4 November, differed in their views, with Sir Edward Hoby arguing from precedents of 1589 and 1593 that an official might return himself,[89] but lawyers arguing that the wording of the election writ forbade such action by a sheriff. When the House voted that the sheriff's election should be voided, Hoby reminded the Speaker that he must send the warrant for the new election writ.[90]

Another election case involving precedent was that of Denbighshire, whose sheriff had sent in no return. When on 5 November Secretary Cecil, speaking for the committee, asked the opinion of the House on the case and ventured to propose that the Speaker 'attend' the Lord Keeper regarding it, Hoby and others quickly objected, insisting that the Speaker's warrant to the Clerk of the Crown was the correct procedure for securing a new election writ. Cecil promptly acknowledged his verbal slip and the Speaker confirmed the writ procedure. That afternoon the committee reviewed precedents from 1581 and 1584 that upheld their point.[91] When the House learned on 13 November that Lord Keeper Egerton had declined to issue the new writ because he believed the Speaker's warrant should have come to him directly, Hoby argued strongly against that view. Other committee-members, however, urged some concession to the Lord Keeper,[92] and Cecil then proposed that a delegation of four knights from the House should confer with the Lord Keeper about his delay and that another six Members should conduct a further search for precedents, to discover 'whether the privileges in former ages have danced a Pavin to and fro and according to the time have been altered'. The groups he proposed were appointed,[93] and made their reports the next day.

There was further debate on 14 November when the reports came in. As to precedents, Hastings and Hoby reported examples, back to the time of Lord Keeper Bacon, of writs about elections going directly to the Clerk of the Crown,[94] but More cited instances in 1593 when warrants had gone to the Lord Keeper.[95] Secretary Herbert reported the Lord Keeper's hope that, rather than having further 'improvident' precedents, contrary to 'the most ancient ways', the House would now settle its resolution so that there 'might be a sufficient Warrant unto him to put in Execution our Commands'. The debate ended with a vote whereby the procedure of sending the warrants to the Clerk of the Crown was approved 'by a little'.[96] When he was informed of this action Lord Keeper Egerton, 'after a small pause', declined further contention because of the pressure of business, and agreed to perform the desire of the House. Egerton's position at this time, however, foreshadowed the further conflict that came in the next reign.[97]

From this review of the development of the committee, it is clear that, by the end of the reign of Elizabeth I, the House of Commons had found within its committee structure a means by which it might assist its Members with regard to their privileges and even influence its own composition through examination of election cases and returns. With the possible exception of the Norfolk case in 1586, however, the Commons seems to have been swayed during this period more by its interest in asserting its independence from pressure by patrons or the Crown than by any internal factional dispute. There had been resistance to the various challenges of the Commons to the Crown's authority in the office of the Clerk of the Crown, particularly by Lord Keepers, but compromises had resolved some of them. The great contests regarding elections still lay ahead, but one can discern that in this area, as in other aspects of the changing Commons in Elizabeth's later years, experienced Parliament-men were showing the will to take stands independent of royal advisers. Even though their views did not always prevail in the committee, they were often persuasive both there and in the House. The Committee for Returns and Privileges, with its investigations and recommendations,[98] provided opportunities for this influence to grow.

There is little evidence as to the method by which this committee was appointed. The nominating procedure seems not to have differed from that used for other committees of the House. The declaration years later (1624) that this committee should be excepted from the proposal that 'all who come may have voices'[99] implies that it was, relatively speaking, a select and closed committee to which, as occasion might arise, new names could be added. By 1601 its members regularly included all the Privy Councillor M.P.s, the chief legal officers of the Crown who were Members of the House, a number of other lawyers, a sprinkling of others who were royal officials or courtiers,[100] and, besides, a group of leaders within the Parliament — men who were recognized for their understanding of procedure and political manoeuvre and were identified with the reform ideas of the time. Earlier among these were Thomas Cromwell, William Fleetwood and James Morice. Later came Nathaniel Bacon, an anti-monopolist,[101] and Henry Finch, the Kentish lawyer who, after Wentworth, was often a spokesman for Puritan views.[102] Another Puritan and also an experienced Parliament-man was Sir Francis Hastings, brother of the Earl of Huntingdon.[103] Sir Edward Hoby, Burghley's nephew, a determined advocate of the Commons' claims and not always respectful, played a prominent role in the growth of the committee,[104] as did the experienced M.P. Robert Wroth.[105] Also helping to shape the committee were others who were interested in good government and in some reforms, but who were less 'radically' inclined. John Hare, though he was said to be a client of Burghley and was later clerk of the Court of Wards, spoke strongly against the abuses of purveyors.[106] George More (Sir George in 1597), following the pattern of a father who had helped develop the committee in its early stages, was both a loyal supporter of the Crown and one of the committee 'regulars'.[107] The distinguished lawyer,

George Snigg, afterwards a royal official under James I, served with the committee in Elizabeth's later Parliaments.[108] Such were the men who, as they were elected again as Members of the Commons in the time of King James, provided the nucleus from which a stronger and even more effective Committee for Privileges would grow.[109]

APPENDIX: *Use of committees on questions of privilege, membership, elections 1559–1601*

Privileges	*Membership and elections*
1559 *ad hoc* committee on lawsuit of M.P. (same committee on outlawry)	*ad hoc* committee to examine facts on M.P. charged with outlawry (same committee on lawsuit)
1563 *ad hoc* committees investigate 1566 cases of arrests, imprisonments, lawsuits	[decisions on new Members and elections decided by House, *without* committees]
1571 *ad hoc* committees on minor privilege cases	*ad hoc* committee to confer about eligibility of Members from restored boroughs
1576 *ad hoc* committee to investigate an arrest; *ad hoc* committee on Peter Wentworth	*ad hoc* committee to confer about the number of Members; decision by the House on particular Members
1581 *ad hoc* committee to search facts in Hall case	Speaker, with two M.P.s, considered outlawry question; *ad hoc* committee to consider returns and precedents regarding issuing of election writs by Lord Chancellor; House voted as committee recommended
1584– Committee for Privileges app- 1585 ointed; used during whole session for searches for precedents and examining cases	*ad hoc* committee to examine shire elections and precedents (committee comprised of government officials)
1586 Committee for examining privilege matters for the entire session; *ad hoc* committee on Cope case	*ad hoc* committee to examine Norfolk election case and Lord Chancellor's authority regarding writs; House accepted committee's finding
1589 Committee on Privileges for the entire session; *ad hoc* committee on Puleston case	*ad hoc* committee to consider election abuses
1593 Committee for Election, Returns and Privileges (combined) [concessions made to authority of Lord Chancellor]	
1597 Committee on Privileges and Returns [some decisions left to the committee]	
1601 Committee for Returns and Privileges [special *subcommittee* to search for precedents on election writs]; *ad hoc* committee for consulting with Lord Keeper	

Notes

1   Assisted by William Hakewill, John Selden and others, the Lords set up their Committee of Privileges in 1621: 'The Hastings Journal of the Parliament of 1621', ed. Lady de Villiers, *Camden Miscellany XX*, (Camden Soc., 3rd ser., LXXXIII, 1953), p.vi. Research for the present article was begun with the assistance of a Senior Fellowship of the Folger Shakespeare Library. The writer is pursuing a study of the evolution of the committee during the early Stuart period.

2   Wallace Notestein, 'The Winning of the Initiative by the House of Commons', *Proceedings of the British Academy*, XI (1924), 140–8, and Notestein's *The House of Commons, 1604–1610* (New Haven, 1971), pp. 435–43. See also J.E. Neale, *The Elizabethan House of Commons* (1949), pp. 363–4, and other comments cited in various notes below.

3   Henry Scobell, *Memorials of the Method and Manner of Proceedings of Parliament in Passing Bills* (London, 1656; reissued 1658, 1670). References are to the edition of 1670, cited hereafter as Scobell, *Mems*.

4   John Hatsell, *Precedents of Proceedings in the House of Commons* (4 vols., 1781; later edition 1818). References are to the 1818 edition, cited as Hatsell, *Precedents*.

5   Josef Redlich, *The Procedure of the House of Commons*, tr. A.S. Steintahl (3 vols., 1908); *Select Statutes and Other Constitutional Documents Illustrative of the Reigns of Elizabeth and James I*, ed. G.W. Prothero (Oxford, 1894; rev. ed. 1913: hereafter cited as Prothero, *Select Statutes*); Sheila Lambert, 'Procedure in the House of Commons in the Early Stuart Period', *E.H.R.*, XCV (1980), 760–1; *The History of Parliament: The House of Commons 1558–1603*, ed. P.W. Hasler (3 vols., 1982), I, Appendices III, VII and VIII.

6   See the chart on the chronological development of the committee which forms an appendix to this article.

7   The other traditional standing committees (on religion, courts of justice, grievances, and supply) had before the end of James I's reign become so absorbed by the committee of the whole House that they had virtually lost their separate identities. See Lambert, 'Procedure in the Early Stuart Period', pp. 759–60; and *Commons Debates 1628*, eds. R.C. Johnson *et al.* (4 vols., New Haven, 1977–), II, 30, n.6.

8   The practice was used frequently in the first Parliament of James I.

9   See the directions of 1593 about Members going to inform the committee about elections that should be investigated: *The Journals of All the Parliaments during the Reign of Queen Elizabeth*, ed. Sir Symonds D'Ewes (1682; repr. Shannon, 1973: hereafter cited as D'Ewes, *Jnls.*), p. 471, and below, p. 32. No such directions were given in 1597, 1601, or in the early years of James I at the times the committees were named.

10 Speaker Crew, who had served on the committee in earlier Parliaments, pointed out in 1624 that the proposal was contrary to precedent: Scobell, *Mems.*, pp. 10, 11; *C.J.*, I, 671. Occasionally, as in 1601, other Members were permitted to go to the committee 'should there be cause'. Scobell points out also that legal counsel of concerned parties could attend.

11 Scobell (*Mems.*, p. 10) described the committee as follows: '[It] hath alway had the precedence of all other Committees, being the first Committee appointed, and ordinarily the first day after, or the same day the Speaker did take his place. This Committee is constituted of particular members named by the House.' Scobell's chapters on the committee's functions, with his greater stress on procedures regarding elections, indicate the increasing importance of that part of its work.

12 D'Ewes, *Jnls.*, pp. 42–3. For discussions of the origin and development of these claimed privileges see G.R. Elton, *The Tudor Constitution* (Cambridge, 1960), pp. 253–74; J.S. Roskell, 'Perspectives in English Parliamentary History', repr. in *Historical Studies of the English Parliament*, eds. E.B. Fryde and E. Miller (2 vols., Cambridge, 1970), II, 296–323; John Hooker's description of privileges in *Parliament in Elizabethan England*, ed. V.F. Snow (New Haven, 1977), pp. 68–9, 165–7; J.E. Neale, 'The Commons' Privilege of Free Speech in Parliament', repr. in *Historical Studies of the English Parliament*, eds. Fryde and Miller, II, 147–9. See also J.E. Neale, 'Peter Wentworth', *ibid.*, II, 246–95.

13 Elton, *Tudor Constitution*, pp. 259–61. Having used some of the procedures of a court in hearing evidence before reaching judgment in a treason case in 1549, the Commons heard evidence before making its decision in the case of a Member's arrested servant (Smalley) in 1576 (see below). In 1585, when asking the discharge of a Member, Cooke, from having to answer a subpoena served on him out of the court of Chancery, the Lord Chancellor resisted their request, but near the end of the session the server of the subpoena was called before the House and fined for his action: D'Ewes, *Jnls.*, pp. 347, 373. In 1589 even the Speaker, attempting to bring the House to order, reminded them that each Member was 'a judge of this Court, the highest court of all other courts': *ibid.*, p. 434.

14 Sir Francis Bacon in 1593 mentioned especially the customary origin of money bills in the lower House: see J.E. Neale, *Elizabeth I and Her Parliaments* (2 vols., 1953–7), II, 300–10. Privileges of this type were usually discussed in the full House rather than being referred to a committee.

15 Roskell has pointed out that the actual number of Elizabethan Parliaments was relatively small, with 26 years of her 44-year reign having none in session (in *Historical Studies of the English Parliament*, eds. Fryde and Miller, II, 303–4). Nevertheless, the gaps between Parliaments were not long, and two of her Parliaments had more than one session and therefore continuity of membership (two sessions for the Parliament of 1563–7, and three sessions for that of 1572–83).

16 Neale and others have commented on the eagerness of men to secure seats in Parliament and on the Commons as a court: e.g. Neale's article on free speech in *Historical Studies of the English Parliament*, eds. Fryde and Miller, II, 148, 166, *passim*.

17 Between 1559 and 1586, when Elizabeth placed a temporary ban on new constituencies, the number of parliamentary boroughs was increased by 31, and the number of Members grew from 420 to 460: *Historical Studies of the English Parliament*, eds. Fryde and Miller, II, 26. Modern scholarship attributes this trend not to efforts at packing Parliaments but to the growing prestige that the service brought and the willingness of boroughs to waive the residency requirement.

18 As Elton has pointed out (*Tudor Constitution*, p. 257), questions about this privilege, one of the oldest, turned in the sixteenth century 'largely upon the manner of its enforcement'.

19 The committee consisted of Sir John Mason 'and others': *C.J.*, I, 55; D'Ewes, *Jnls.*, p. 48; Hatsell, *Precedents*, I, 80. Later cases involving M.P.s charged with outlawry occurred in 1593 (Fitzherbert) and 1604 (Goodwin-Fortescue case).

20 *C.J.*, I, 64, 65; D'Ewes, *Jnls.*, pp. 83, 84.

21 *C.J.*, I, 74, 77, 78; D'Ewes, *Jnls.*, pp. 123, 129.

22 Smalley was released from his arrest only to be sent to the Tower as a prisoner of the House: *C.J.*, I, 107–9; D'Ewes, *Jnls.*, pp. 248–58; Trinity College, Dublin, MS. N.2.12 (anonymous diary), ff. 122, 127. The case is discussed in Hatsell, *Precedents*, I, 89–90. See also Prothero, *Select Statutes*, pp. xc, 128; and Elton, *Tudor Constitution*, pp. 257–8, 271–2.

23 D'Ewes, *Jnls.*, p. 241. On the Wentworth case see *Historical Studies of the English Parliament*, eds. Fryde and Miller, II, 253–5; and Elton, *Tudor Constitution*, pp. 255–8, 277–8.

24 *C.J.*, I, 122, 123, 125–7; D'Ewes, *Jnls.*, pp. 291, 292, 295–7; Trinity College, Dublin, MS. N.2.12, f. 107v. This celebrated case is discussed in Hatsell, *Precedents*, I, 92–4; and in Neale, *Elizabeth I and Her Parliaments*, I, 407–10. Besides Privy Councillors and other royal officials who were M.P.s the committee list (4 and 6 Feb.) included the Recorder of London, Serjeant Flowerdew, Mr Norton (who had first raised the issue of Hall's book) and a number of others who were familiar with parliamentary precedents: see John Hooker's comments in *Parliament in Elizabethan England*, ed. Snow, pp. 99–101.

25 13 Feb. 1585: D'Ewes, *Jnls.*, p. 349.

26 *Ibid.*, p. 347.

27 The Members named to search for precedents were Mr Miles Sandys and Thomas Cromwell: *ibid.*, pp. 347–50. Named for the committee on 13 Feb. were London's

Recorder (William Fleetwood), James Morice and Edward Penruddock; Cromwell was added on 23 Feb. Cromwell and Morice were especially influential later in urging consideration of election cases. Morice, attorney for the Court of Wards, was one of the Puritan leaders of the period: see Neale, *Elizabeth I and Her Parliaments*, II, 194.

28   The case of Cooke, M.P. for Lymington, which had occasioned the search for precedents, ended with the submission of the subpoena server at the bar on 25 Mar.: D'Ewes, *Jnls.*, p. 373; 'Hayward Townshend's Journals', eds. A.F. Pollard and Marjorie Blatcher, *B.I.H.R.*, XII, (1934–5), 11; and Prothero, *Select Statutes*, p. 129. Sir Philip Sidney's servant was released from prison upon a motion by London's Recorder, a member of the committee (D'Ewes, *Jnls.*, p. 368); and a complicated case regarding another servant was decided on 25 Mar. 'after several examinations had by this House': *ibid.*, p. 373.

29   The 1586–7 committee, appointed on Recorder Fleetwood's motion, consisted of the Recorder, Sir Henry Gate, Robert Wroth and another William Fleetwood (D'Ewes, *Jnls.*, p. 393). The ten-member 1589 committee included (in alphabetical order after officials): Mr Comptroller, the Lieutenant of the Tower, Recorder Fleetwood, Francis Alford, Sir George Barns, Humphrey Coningsby, Thomas Cromwell, Sir William More, James Morice and Robert Wroth (*ibid.*, p. 429).

30   The four-member *ad hoc* committee named on 6 Mar. 1587 to search for precedents about the arrest of Members during a time of prorogation consisted of three privilege-committee members (Recorder Fleetwood, Cromwell and Morice) and Mr Alford. After the committee reported on 11 Mar. the House voted that the Member should have privilege: D'Ewes, *Jnls.*, pp. 412, 414. The committee appointed on 13 Mar. to confer with members of the Privy Council concerning the arrest of Anthony Cope and others consisted of all the Privy Councillors in the House and the following: Mr Beale, Sir Thomas Brown, Cromwell, Recorder Fleetwood, Sir John Hartington, Francis Hastings, Sir John Higham, Sir Robert Jermyn and Sir William More: D'Ewes, *Jnls.*, pp. 411, 412, 415; B.L., Harl. MS. 7188, No. 4, f. 95v. See also Neale, *Elizabeth I and Her Parliaments*, II, 148–64.

31   Named in 1589 to ascertain the facts on the case of Roger Puleston M.P. were six who were already on the session's privileges committee (Coningsby, Cromwell, Recorder Fleetwood, More, Morice and Wroth), as well as eight others (the Vice-Chamberlain, Francis Bacon, Mr Cook, Sir Edward Dymock, Mr [Edward] Grimstone, Mr Harris, Sir Edward Hoby and Mr Morgan). The Vice-Chamberlain, first on the list, made their report with a recommendation, but the House debated the matter further before reaching a decision: D'Ewes, *Jnls.*, pp. 431–2, 434, 435. See also Hatsell, *Precedents*, I, 103–5.

32   See above, p. 27.

33   They came from six newly restored boroughs. The Lord Steward was the official who regularly administered the Members' oaths at the opening of a Parliament. See *C.J.*, I, 63; D'Ewes, *Jnls.*, pp. 79, 80; and *O[fficial] R[eturn], Return of the Names of Every Member to Serve in Each Parliament* (2 vols., 1878). For three of the new boroughs mentioned in 1563, the lists in *O.R.* show that returns dated in December 1562 and another with no date, were actually recorded, but possibly had arrived too late for being included in the list used at the time the Parliament opened. For the other three boroughs the editors of *O.R.* have printed the names supplied from the Crown Office list, presumably entered there after the decision referred to in the text. As to what their 'warrants' or their 'letters patent' were, they may have been the certified returns that negligent officials had permitted Members to carry up themselves instead of submitting them through the correct official channels. Such cases did occur occasionally. Or they may have been letters sent by the borough officers to men who had been elected informing them of that fact. Examples of such notification from boroughs to the men of their choice occur fairly frequently among borough records, probably most often in cases of the selection of gentlemen who had no direct connexions with their constituencies. Possibly their own 'warrants' in 1563 were letters of notification without official seals, and the 'letters patent' may have included a record of election writs as well as other formal notice of the election.

34   C.J., I, 63, 64; D'Ewes, *Jnls.*, pp. 80, 83, 122. Notice regarding the vacancy was sent by
     the Speaker to the Crown Office so that a new writ could be issued. The practice had
     been used several times in Queen Mary's reign. See the note in the preface (p. xxiv) of J.
     Topham's edition of John Glanville, *Reports of Certain Cases Determined and
     Adjudged by the Commons in Parliament in the Twenty-First and Twenty-Second Years of the
     Reign of King James the First* (1775: hereafter cited as Glanville, *Reports*). An officer of
     the Crown Office testified in 1601 that in Elizabeth's early decades warrants from the
     Speaker to the Clerk of the Crown had been customary, but the procedure was
     challenged by Lord Keeper Egerton (see below, p. 35). For Henry Elsyng's comment on
     the procedure see Elizabeth Read Foster, *The Painful Labour of Mr. Elsyng* (Philadelphia,
     1972), p. 48, n.14.

35   The seven Members listed for the committee 6 Apr. included one Privy Councillor (Mr
     Treasurer) and at least two legal officers (Serjeants Manwood and Lovelace): C.J., I, 83;
     D'Ewes, *Jnls.*, pp. 156, 159.

36   C.J., I, 88; D'Ewes, *Jnls.*, p. 182. It was decided 'in open court' of the House that the
     responsibility for the election abuse lay rather with the town's corporation than with
     Long, 'a simple man and of small capacity to serve'.

37   The bill was committed to an *ad hoc* committee on 19 Apr.: C.J., I, 85; D'Ewes, *Jnls.*,
     pp. 168–71.

38   C.J., I, 104, 106; D'Ewes, *Jnls.*, pp. 244, 249.

39   C.J., I, 104; D'Ewes, *Jnls.*, p. 244.

40   For details on these developments see the preface to Glanville, *Reports*, pp. xxvi–xxx. Cf.
     Elton, *Tudor Constitution*, p. 259. Lord Keeper Bacon had died in 1579 and this
     session was the first during the time of his successor, Sir Thomas Bromley, who had
     been an M.P. several times. While he was Solicitor-General, an office which he entered
     in 1569, Bromley had been consulted about an election case in 1571 (see above).

41   On Norton see Neale, *Elizabeth I and Her Parliaments*, I, 375. The right of the new
     Members to participate in choosing the Speaker had actually been questioned the day
     before (18 Jan.): D'Ewes, *Jnls.*, p. 281.

42   D'Ewes, *Jnls.*, pp. 281–2. Speaking for the Lord Chancellor's authority were Serjeants
     Flowerdew and Fleetwood, the Comptroller (Sir James Croft), Robert Snagg and Mr St
     Paul. Flowerdew himself claimed one of the seats in question. The House had already
     yielded to the Crown in electing John Popham as Speaker although his duties as
     Solicitor-General would require his frequent attendance in the upper House: C.J., I,
     117.

43   The quoted wording is from D'Ewes. Somewhat different is that of C.J. (I, 117), which
     omits the reference to further examination and reads: '. . . if the Lord Chancellor send
     out a writ upon any suggestion to choose a new (whether the cause be sufficient or no,
     to remove the old, or whether the suggestion be true or not), if a new
     be returned, this House is not to examine the matter, but to accept the return; and the
     old person discharged, and the new to be received; and so, at last, the said new
     returned persons, in the places of others yet living, were allowed to be members of
     this House, according as they were severally returned.' In contrast with the clerk's
     record in C.J., Thomas Cromwell, who afterwards reported on a committee study of
     the matter (see below), noted regarding the admission of the new Members: 'Whyther
     this might be or no was debated *pro et contra* by diverse of the Howse, and was not
     agreed uppon in the end.' *Proceedings in the Parliaments of Elizabeth I. Volume I: 1558–
     1581*, ed. T.E. Hartley (Leicester, 1981), pp. 524–5.

44   Cromwell's diary (*ibid.*) indicates some uncertainty about the Speaker's election also, for
     he states that the nomination by the Treasurer was 'approved by some other voices, the
     rest saying nothing which was taken for consent'. Neale described the election debate
     during a 'day of leisure' as a 'field day' for the more radical Members, and commented
     that their insistence upon the Comons' right had no historical basis; but he did not mention
     the earlier developments that have been outlined above.

45   Norton told the House at this time that Lord Chancellor Bromley had refrained from
     issuing a new writ, awaiting judgment by the Commons. D'Ewes noted that this was
     different from his action regarding the seats of absentees. See D'Ewes, *Jnls.*, p. 283;

Glanville, *Reports*, pp. xxxiii–xxxv.

[46]   *C.J.*, I, 122, 124; D'Ewes, *Jnls.*, pp. 292, 294. The committee found that the outlawry charge arose from the debts of others and that Vaughan had committed no misdeads.

[47]   *C.J.*, I, 129; D'Ewes, *Jnls.*, p. 300. Those named to the committee were Mr Treasurer, the chancellor of the Duchy, Mr Treasurer of the Chamber, the attorney of the Duchy, and Sir Thomas Shirley, Sir Edward Horsey, Sir William More, Sir Henry Gate, Sir John Hibbott (*sic*), Mr Digges, Mr Cromwell and Mr Poole. Norton's name was not on the list.

[48]   *C.J.*, I, 135–6; D'Ewes, *Jnls.*, pp. 307–8; Glanville, *Reports*, pp. xxxvi–xlii. On the writ procedure see above, p. 28.

[49]   D'Ewes, *Jnls.*, pp. 337, 338, 344–5. Some question may have been raised about the Norfolk election, too (see below, n. 52), but no serious challenge seems to have been made against the two Puritan gentlemen who had won the places.

[50]   Prior to 21 Dec. the committee had conferred with the Clerk of the Crown Office and examined both his records and various statutes. Their proposal to consult with the clerk of the upper House meant that they would look into parliamentary precedents. Both Prothero (*Select Statutes*, p. xci) and Redlich (*Procedure*, II, 206–7) regarded this committee as a link between 1581 and 1586.

[51]   D'Ewes, *Jnls.*, p. 334.

[52]   A. Hassell Smith has pointed out that local as well as national politics had been involved in Norfolk, especially the actions of the deputy lieutenants whose interests the Council was supporting (*County and Court: Government and Politics in Norfolk* [Oxford, 1974], pp. 317–22). He has suggested also that the 1584 election may have been contested (*ibid.*, pp. 316–17). See also H.M.C., *Gawdy MSS.*, p. 25. For details about the two 1586 elections (26 Sept. and 24 Oct.) see D'Ewes, *Jnls.*, pp. 396–7; Glanville, *Reports*, pp. xliii–lxi. On the confusion at the opening of the session see D'Ewes, *Jnls.*, pp. 376, 392–3.

[53]   The Queen's command had been for the Speaker 'to signifie unto them that her Highness was sorry this House was troubled the last sitting therof with the matter touching the choosing and returning of the Knights for the County of Norfolk: a thing impertinent for this House to deal withal and only belonging to the Charge and Office of the Lord Chancellor, from whence the writs for the same elections issued out, and are thither returnable again'. The message added that she had ordered the Lord Chancellor to confer with the judges, to examine the returns and the sheriff about the second election, and to establish which was the 'true' return: D'Ewes, *Jnls.*, p. 393. Neale suggests that the reference in the message to 'the last sitting' was directed to conversations among the 1586 Members on Monday, 31 Oct., just before they decided to adjourn until 3 Nov. (*Elizabeth I and Her Parliaments*, II, 185). However, it could have referred to the previous Parliament and the Norfolk election of 1584 (see above, n. 52).

[54]   D'Ewes, *Jnls.*, p. 395, 396. Named to the committee were Mr Comptroller, Mr Treasurer (Sir Francis Knollys), Recorder Fleetwood, Serjeant Snagg, Mr Cromwell, Sir William Winter, Sir Henry Knyvet, Mr Thomas Knyvet, Mr Alford, Mr Drew, Mr Harris, Sir William More, Mr Morice, Mr Sandys and Mr Sanders. Besides officials and lawyers there are several who were becoming identified as spokesmen for privileges (e.g. Cromwell, Alford, Fleetwood and Morice). The Knyvets were Norfolk men who had been concerned about elections there (Hassell Smith, *County and Court*, p. 322). Eleven of those named met on 10 Nov. to examine the facts and hear the arguments on the validity of the first election. D'Ewes gives two accounts of Cromwell's report (*Jnls.*, pp. 396, 398) and at one point (p. 398) confuses this committee with the privileges committee that had been named on 4 Nov. Only Fleetwood, London's Recorder, had been named to both committees. He had served on the smaller committee for studying county elections in 1584 (see above).

[55]   Knollys had suggested sending a delegate to the Lord Chancellor as orderly procedure for securing information: D'Ewes, *Jnls.*, p. 399; Neale, *Elizabeth I and Her Parliaments*, II, 184–7. Lord Chancellor Bromley, in recognizing the first election, had again leant support to the Commons' claims regarding its membership, as he had in 1581 (see above, pp. 29 and nn. 40 and 45).

56 Neale commented that, while constitutionally jurisdiction on these matters lay with the Crown in Chancery, there was here the practical danger that the Crown, acting through Council or Chancery or both, might 'when hard driven and unscrupulous', use that power to exclude troublesome critics from Parliament: *ibid.*, p. 184.

57 D'Ewes, *Jnls.*, pp. 429, 430. When the question of replacing other ill Members came up on 10 Feb., the matter was referred to the now established committee.

58 Neale (*Elizabeth I and Her Parliaments*, II, 203) described the assignment as a kind of 'roving commission'. Hoby mentioned especially men from boroughs not regularly sending M.P.s, and 'erroneous returns'.

59 Those named, in addition to Watson, were Recorder Fleetwood, the lieutenant of the Tower, Mr Alford, Mr Cromwell, Sir Edward Dyer, Sir Edward Dymock, Mr Francis Hastings, Sir Edward Hoby, Mr Robert Markham and Sir William More (D'Ewes, *Jnls.*, p. 430). Mr Treasurer, though not named in D'Ewes, was probably appointed also, since he made the first report. Four of these men had been on the 1586 committee (Fleetwood, Cromwell, Alford and More); the same four had been named the preceding day to the privileges committee; and four were on the larger committee on the Puleston privilege case (Fleetwood, Dymock, Hoby and More; see above, nn. 29 and 31). Humphrey Coningsby, already a member of the privileges committee, was the first added Member; the other five added (10 Feb.: D'Ewes, *Jnls.*, p. 430) were Francis Bacon, Sir Henry Cobham, Mr Fane, Sir Francis Godolphin and Francis Moore. Bacon, too, had been named to the privileges committee and was soon afterwards named on the one to consider the Puleston case.

60 Three months had elapsed between the original date set for this Parliament (8 Nov. 1588) and the time of its opening, and the list of returns printed in *O.R.* shows that, while most of them were dated in October or November, as many as seven were dated in December, January, or early February. Some of the late elections may have occurred to replace ill Members, upon writs sent out under the Lord Chancellor's initiative. The House, on the day before the committee was appointed, had already acted on the replacing of two ill Members: see above and n. 57.

61 Neale, *Elizabeth I and Her Parliaments*, I, 184; II, 62, *passim*. As Vice-Chamberlain Hatton had been a member of the conservative elections committee of 1584 (see above, p. 30).

62 *Ibid.*, II, 203.

63 D'Ewes, *Jnls.*, p. 430. In *O.R.* the earlier return for Appleby, as described in the committee report, is not shown, but there is one dated 16 Feb. 1589 certifying the election of two different men. For a borough so far from Westminster, an election only five days after the vote was expeditiously accomplished.

64 21 Feb. 1589: D'Ewes, *Jnls.*, p. 436.

65 *Ibid.*, pp. 438, 441.

66 Both More and his father, Sir William More, knight for the county, were named to the committee. The father, an old Parliament-man, had served on such committees previously, and the son so served in many later Parliaments. On the Mores see Neale, *Elizabethan House of Commons*, pp. 43–7.

67 D'Ewes, *Jnls.*, p. 471.

68 *Ibid.*, p. 497. Wroth, one of the Marian exiles who had been a member of most of Elizabeth's Parliaments (Neale, *Elizabeth I and Her Parliaments*, II, 279, 304) and had spoken frequently on various issues, had been a member of the privileges committees, but not those on elections in 1586 and 1589. It has been suggested that, because Wroth's later correspondence (1598–1605) gives evidence of personal ties with both Burghley and his son, Sir Robert Cecil (n. Tyacke, 'Wroth, Cecil, and the Parliamentary Session of 1604', *B.I.H.R.*, L [1977], 120–5), he may have been their client. Wroth's speeches and actions in this Parliament and earlier, however, show clearly that he was a man of great independence. In this Parliament, for example, he, along with Beale, openly differed from Sir Robert Cecil about a committee decision concerning a conference: D'Ewes, *Jnls.*, p. 485. Despite the Queen's efforts to have this Parliament limit itself to granting a subsidy, Wentworth had conferred with several M.P.s about raising again the succession question: *ibid.*, pp. 470–1; Neale, *Elizabeth I and Her Parliaments*, II, 256–61. It seems unlikely that the appointment of the 1593 committee could have been the result of government initiative, as

is implied in Lambert, 'Procedure in the Early Stuart Period', p. 760.

[69] The mention of 'all the members' suggests that they were to attend the committee to provide information on cases under investigation 'as occasion shall serve' but not that they were to vote there. Notable among those individually named were Morice, (attorney for the Court of Wards), John Brograve (attorney for the Duchy of Lancaster), Francis Bacon, Mr Beale, Mr Coningsby, Sir Francis Hastings, Sir Edward Hoby, George More, Sir William More, Miles Sandys, Robert Wroth and Serjeant Yelverton. Morice and Beale, royal officers and Puritans, who ventured on 27 Feb. to attack the Court of High Commission, were presently by Council order 'confined' for the greater part of the session. Even Hoby, for having offended one of the Privy Councillors in committee, was imprisoned or confined for a time: Neale, *Elizabeth I and Her Parliaments*, II, 267–78; D'Ewes, *Jnls.*, p. 474.

[70] D'Ewes, *Jnls.*, pp. 479–80, 489, 490.

[71] The Queen's actions had been 'for causes best known to herself': *ibid.*, p. 497. D'Ewes noted that Wroth's motion of 10 Mar. was written but crossed out by the clerk in his official record.

[72] Another factor was that the outlawry charge was at the Queen's suit. On this well known case see D'Ewes, *Jnls.*, pp. 479–82, 502, 515–18; Hatsell, *Precedents*, I, 107–11; Neale, *Elizabeth I and Her Parliaments*, II, 313–18.

[73] The cases of Camelford and Southwark involved possible negligence by local officials; in the third case an incorrect first name had been written on the indenture: D'Ewes, *Jnls.*, pp. 479, 489, 494–5.

[74] E.g. Hoby, Wroth, and possibly Yelverton: see D'Ewes, *Jnls.*, p. 479.

[75] On the changing personnel and the character of this Parliament see Neale, *Elizabeth I and Her Parliaments*, II, 241–5. See also n. 69 above.

[76] This is the Parliament about which the Lord Keeper, Sir Thomas Egerton, former Solicitor-General and Attorney-General, wrote to Sir Robert Cecil in August 1597, saying there would be 'a new Lord Keeper, new Speaker, and new Clerk [of the Parliaments] . . . and all of us newly to learn our duties': *ibid.*, II, 327, 332.

[77] D'Ewes, *Jnls.*, p. 552. Yelverton, who had slipped up on procedure on the day of his presentation to the Queen (*ibid.*, p. 550), may have been reminded himself about the committee, since his action, according to D'Ewes, occurred after debate on other matters had started. The reminder may have come in a motion from the Westminster M.P., Thomas Knyvet, who raised a privilege question concerning himself. Knyvet was the first of the M.P.s not holding a major office to be named to the 1597 committee.

[78] They included, in alphabetical order, Francis Bacon, Nathaniel Bacon, Mr [Henry] Finch (one of the outspoken Puritans of this and the previous Parliament), Sir Francis Hastings, Sir Edward Hoby, George More, Sir William More, Miles Sandys and Robert Wroth. Among the others were several whose names appear in the rosters of this committee in later Parliaments; e.g. Mr Hubbard [Hobart], Mr Jerome Horsey, Mr Robert Knollys, Mr [Oliver] Luke and Mr [Edward] Peake.

[79] 8 Dec. 1597, John Roos (M.P. East Retford). The name is spelled 'Rosse' in D'Ewes, *Jnls.*, p. 570.

[80] 8 and 14 Nov., 8 and 12 Dec., and 16 Jan. (*ibid.*, pp. 553, 556, 570, 572, 581). Each of these reporters had been a member of the joint committee in 1593. As the session progressed, Hoby reported more frequently.

[81] The House voted to recognize Knyvet's privilege, and sent Brograve and Hoby to inform the Lord Keeper of this action: *ibid.*, pp. 553, 554; 'Hayward Townshend's Journals', eds. Pollard and Blatcher, p. 11. When a more deferential way of 'consulting' the Lord Chancellor had been suggested in 1586, the committee rejected the proposal (see above, p. 30). D'Ewes noted that, since there was no further record regarding the 1597 matter, it was likely 'the Lord Keeper did further satisfie the House'.

[82] D'Ewes, *Jnls.*, p. 554. Both of the returns from Weymouth and Melcombe Regis are shown in *O.R.*, but with no indication that one was disallowed.

[83] D'Ewes, *Jnls.*, p. 564. For two other cases mentioned as late as 16 Jan. the records do not indicate what procedure was followed: *ibid.*, p. 581.

84   *Ibid.*, p. 556.
85   8 and 12 Dec.: D'Ewes, *Jnls.*, pp. 570, 572. Hoby on 16 Jan., however, made a motion regarding a privilege case: *ibid.*, p. 581.
86   31 Oct. 1601: D'Ewes, *Jnls.*, p. 622. Again listed are the attorneys for the Duchy and the Court of Wards, the Solicitor, and two serjeants-at-law, along with Francis Bacon, Hastings, Hobart, Hoby, Horsey, Sir Robert Knollys, Thomas Knyvet, Sir George More, Peake and Wroth. Among the newer names were several who would serve on this committee's successors in the Parliaments of King James; namely, Mr Boys, John Hare, Sir Richard Knightley, Mr Lake, Mr Snigg, Sir Edward Stafford, Robert Wingfield and Mr Wiseman. Several were courtiers and others were linked with the reforming element in this and later Parliaments.
87   See D'Ewes, *Jnls.*, pp. 627–8, for its meeting on 5 Nov., at which the committee examined precedents from 1584 for the Speaker's orders for new elections. Also considered at the meeting were the election return from Cardigan and the presence of burgesses sent by two towns not customarily represented (Harwich and Newtown, I.o.W.). Newtown, however, had been sending M.P.s regularly since 1584, according to *O.R.*
88   One such case was that of George Belgrave which involved both a suit in Star Chamber and the Leicester borough election. The committee reports and the debates in the House on 7 and 17 Dec. show that opinions were much divided on this case but, on the latter date, two days before the session ended, the Commons voted to clear Belgrave in both the matter of the election and his privilege: D'Ewes, *Jnls.*, pp. 610, 614, 666, 669–70, 677, 688; *L.J.*, II, 247; Hatsell, *Precedents*, I, 119–21.
89   Hoby referred to the Lincolnshire sheriff who had been allowed to sit in 1589 and to the Southwark case of 1593: D'Ewes, *Jnls.*, pp. 436, 494–5. See also p. 31 and n. 73, above.
90   *Ibid.*, pp. 624–5; Hayward Townshend, *Historical Collections* (London, 1680), pp. 185–6. The present Speaker, London's Recorder, was John Croke, who had sat in the 1597 Parliament but not earlier (*O.R.*).
91   The position of the Speaker of the House was at stake, declared Hoby and others: D'Ewes, *Jnls.*, pp. 627–8.
92   I.e. Sir George More, Francis Bacon and even Sir Francis Hastings. More, in a manner characteristic of him on later occasions, suggested that there were special times when alterations in procedure were permissible. Hastings, usually a supporter of privileges, said that the Lord Keeper in a private conversation had told him he thought House warrants should go to him directly; and Bacon agreed with this view, arguing that there was more prestige in having a warrant go to the chief official rather than to an inferior clerk: D'Ewes, *Jnls.*, p. 536.
93   Named to go to the Lord Keeper were four courtiers, Secretary Herbert, Sir Edward Stanhope, Sir Edward Stafford and Fulke Greville. The six men assigned to search the records of the Clerk of the Crown, the Clerk of the Petty Bag, and the clerk of the House of Commons were not all listed by D'Ewes, since he gives their names as 'Sir Edward Hoby, Serjeant Harris, Sir Francis Hastings, &c.' Reporting the following day from this group were Hastings, Hoby and Sir George More: D'Ewes, *Jnls.*, pp. 637, 638. Since all of those named for the search were members of the Committee for Returns and Privileges, it may be assumed that the other two also were from the committee and that the group was therefore virtually a subcommittee with a particular task to perform.
94   Sir Nicholas Bacon was Lord Keeper 1558–79. Hoby quoted Stephen Brown, who had been an official in the Crown Office for 36 years (i.e. since 1565), as saying that in Lord Keeper Bacon's time the warrants about writs had been sent by the Speaker to the Clerk of the Crown. Brown had shown the committee 'five precedents and one order' as evidence. The committee had viewed some warrants with no directions and also several of 1581 addressed to the Clerk of the Crown: *ibid.*, p. 638.
95   Sir George More mentioned the warrant in the Fitzherbert case, which involved privilege as well as an election writ, and cited also the election cases of that year, which had been left to the Lord Keeper for final decision (see above, pp. 32–3).

[96] In the debate that followed the reports, several lawyer M.P.s pointed out that there could be different procedures for different kinds of writs. One Member argued in favour of using the Clerk of the Crown as 'our immediate officer; he is to be attendant between the two doors of the upper House and lower House; when any warrant general is reprised he is to subscribe it, to certify it, etc.' D'Ewes (*Jnls.*, pp. 638, 639) quoted the words from Townshend's diary.

[97] See D'Ewes, *Jnls.*, p. 643. Nine years later, writing about the first Parliament of James I, Egerton (Lord Ellesmere) commented again on the danger to the balanced monarchy if the Commons, 'under pretext of lawful liberty and ancient privileges', was permitted to encroach upon the regality. See Ellesmere's observations of 7 Jas. I in *Proceedings in the Parliament of 1610*, ed. Elizabeth Read Foster, (2 vols., New Haven, 1966), I, 276–7.

[98] Redlich, in his review of the development of the committee (*Procedure*, II, 205), concluded that the committee at this stage was a part of the Commons' investigatory procedure rather than an element for arriving at a decision.

[99] See above, pp. 25–6 and notes.

[100] Sir Francis Bacon, for example, was added to the committee on elections in 1589, and was named to the combined committee in 1593, 1597 and 1605: D'Ewes, *Jnls.*, pp. 430, 471, 552, 622.

[101] *Ibid.*, pp. 477, 552; Neale, *Elizabeth I and Her Parliaments*, II, 283, 353.

[102] D'Ewes, *Jnls.*, p. 552; Neale, *Elizabeth I and Her Parliaments*, II, 272–3, 282, 289, 326.

[103] D'Ewes, *Jnls.*, pp. 333, 356, 440; Neale, *Elizabeth I and Her Parliaments*, II, 154, 380, 396. Hastings's work with the committee started in 1589 and continued through 1601 and into the reign of James I.

[104] Neale, *Elizabeth I and Her Parliaments*, II, 203, 278, 359; and above, pp. 31, 34, 35.

[105] D'Ewes, *Jnls.*, pp. 392, 477, 552, 622, 646, *passim*; see above, p. 32 and n. 68.

[106] D'Ewes, *Jnls.*, pp. 448, 561, 622; Neale, *Elizabeth I and Her Parliaments*, II, 208–9, 361.

[107] D'Ewes, *Jnls.*, pp. 394, 440, 477, *passim*; and above, p. 34 and nn. 66 and 92. Like his father, Sir William, More had important connexions at court and with the Queen herself.

[108] D'Ewes, *Jnls.*, pp. 394, *passim*. Not only Snigg was active in the Parliaments of James I; others of the later committees of Elizabeth's Parliaments who served likewise under James were Jerome Horsey, Robert Wingfield and several more: see above, nn. 78, 86.

[109] Among the Committee for Privileges men of James's Parliaments who, although they had not been named to that committee under Elizabeth, had worked with its principal leaders on other matters were Nicholas Fuller, John Hext and Francis Moore: D'Ewes, *Jnls.*, pp. 556, 561, 622, 624, 645, 647. These men were active especially in the Parliament of 1604, during which the functions of the committee were expanded and its importance increased.

TRADE, THE SCOTS AND THE PARLIAMENTARY CRISIS OF 1713

GEOFFREY HOLMES

University of Lancaster

CLYVE JONES

Institute of Historical Research,
University of London

The parliamentary session of 1713, which ran from 9 April to 16 July, saw
the first major setback for the Harley ministry in the House of Commons
since its leader had taken office in August 1710. At the same time it
witnessed a serious crisis in the House of Lords, which took the ministry
to the brink of defeat. Once again a Tory administration was threatened
with loss of control over the upper House, a fate it had only escaped in
December 1711, following defeats over 'No Peace without Spain' and the
case of the Duke of Hamilton's British peerage,[1] by persuading the Queen
to make a block creation of 12 peers. And once again it was to be
questions raised by the peace negotiations with France and by the
grievances of Scotland's parliamentary representatives that placed the
government of Robert Harley, Earl of Oxford, in peril.

From the 1711–12 session of Anne's fourth Parliament the ministry had
finally emerged in triumph and its Whig opponents, both commoners and
peers, in retreat and disarray. But the opening of the 1713 session had been
many months delayed pending the conclusion of the final peace at
Utrecht, and during the intervening winter Tory nerves became stretched
and Whig morale recovered. Eventually, on the last day of March the
British plenipotentiaries, Lord Strafford and Bishop Robinson of Bristol,
were able to put their signatures on the Treaties of Peace and Commerce
with France. Three days later the treaties arrived in London, and on 7
April the Queen in Council ratified them. The making of peace was
undoubtedly part of the Crown's prerogative, and thus the final terms of
the peace treaty did not need formal parliamentary approval. Nevertheless,
Parliament did have a part still to play, for the commercial treaty with
France needed legislation to give it effect. The two crucial articles, the

eighth and ninth, could not come into force until existing anti-French pro-tectionist acts were repealed and the new articles were ratified in what would, in practice, be a money bill. Other than obstructing this bill, the only possible shot left in the Whigs' locker after their long battle against Oxford's peace was to try to persuade both Houses to withhold their blessing from the settlement as a whole in their votes over the address in reply to the Queen's Speech.

To judge by Oxford's calm and methodical preparations for the opening of Parliament, he was confident there would be no direct attack on the peace. His continuing contacts with one of the lords of the Whig Junto, Halifax, gave him a sure understanding of their now resigned attitude to the dynastic and territorial settlement. His apprehensions, if any, were focused on the signs that the Whigs might be planning to switch public attention, as soon as they judged the time ripe, to the sensitive issue of the Protestant Succession. The Queen's assurance in her speech from the throne on 9 April that a 'perfect friendship' subsisted between the courts of Hanover and St James's was plainly written in by the Treasurer with an eye to forestalling any early move by the opposition; and it appears to have been sufficient, for the time being at least, to calm the fears of the many Tories with Hanoverian sympathies.[2] With Hanover and the Whigs unable to decide for many weeks on a course of joint action, the Whigs had to wait until almost the very end of the session for their first suitable opportunity to make direct use of the Succession issue.

Balked on this front, they sought for other weapons with which to embarrass and wound the ministry; and six weeks went by before these weapons came to hand. Two issues then arose to which the government's armour suddenly appeared unexpectedly vulnerable: the cause of Scotland over the malt tax and the flaring-up of opposition to the Bill of Commerce. By exploiting them, like the seasoned parliamentary campaigners they were, the Whigs were able by June 1713 to recapture the political initiative they had lost since February 1712.

The earliest faint sign that the government might be heading for trouble was detectable in the Commons' Committee of Ways and Means on 22 April, though at the time the setback seemed relatively mild and the ministry may even have been prepared for it. The government wanted to bring the land tax down to three shillings in the pound, a one-shilling reduction on the standard wartime rate. But it was forced to yield to the pressure of the country gentlemen on the back benches, who had expected a halving of the tax and would settle for nothing more than two shillings in the pound. With a general election only a few months away, the Tory country gentlemen saw no better way of recommending themselves to their constituents than a substantial reduction of direct taxation after 11 years of unremitting burden.[3] The instinct of self-preservation proved stronger than any ties of obligation to the ministry. The Court party in the Commons, making the best of a bad job, promised to co-operate with the back-benchers in securing a two-shilling rate, while the latter undertook in return to see that the resulting shortfall of £500,000 in revenue was made up in some other way. And even at this early stage at least one Scottish Member, George Baillie, the Squadrone M.P. for Berwickshire began to voice fears that one result of this bargain would be an increase in the malt tax and its imposition on Scotland.[4]

The ministry, however, was to experience a less tractable spirit from the Commons over the field of trade regulations with France. The Treaty of Commerce provided for two major changes in Britain's commercial relations with her neighbours. It accorded to France the most-favoured-nation treatment which, since 1703, had been virtually (if not officially) enjoyed by Portugal, our ally under the Methuen Treaties. It also stipulated that the tariff on French goods was to return to the low level at which it had stood in 1664, before the protectionist policies of Colbert had inaugurated an era of bitter commercial rivalry between the two kingdoms.[5] The ministry, realizing that the legislation needed to repeal the anti-French trade laws might delay the passing of the Commerce Bill until the end of June, introduced a preliminary and interim measure, which it believed would be less controversial. The bill was designed to effect a two-month suspension of the additional, prohibitive, duties levied on French wine since 1696. Its attempted introduction on 2 May proved less encouraging than had been expected. After the Whigs, with James Stanhope as their chief spokesman, had skilfully played on anti-French sentiments, the government received a majority of only 29 on the motion to put the question and one of 40 on the question for its introduction.[6] The narrowness of the margin was somewhat disturbing, especially when it was clear that the Whigs had gained the support of some independent Tories.

The ministry now ran into opposition from the Portuguese envoy in London who delivered a memorial threatening an embargo on the import of British woollens into his country if Portuguese wines lost the preferential position in the British market which they had enjoyed since 1704.[7] The leading Whigs in the Commons made full play with the damage such an embargo would inflict on the British economy. In consequence the ministry carried the second reading of the Wines Bill on 6 May by a mere 25 votes. However, the next division on the same day on the commitment of the bill was carried by a majority of 102 after many Tory M.P.s had flocked into the House. The circumstances of the second vote strongly suggest a good deal of 'whipping'; but the scale of the success was mainly due to a concession by the ministry, in promising to reveal the terms of the Commerce Treaty before the committee stage of the Wines Bill was reached on 12 May.[8] It was doubtless seen at the time as a tactical ploy; but the Court managers were to have good cause to regret it. On 9 May the Commerce Treaty was laid before the House and Members soon saw that by the side of its more controversial articles, the Wines Bill seemed a very minor matter. The committee stage was, against the wishes of the Court, put off for a further week. On the 14th the storm broke over the Commerce Treaty and the Wines Bill was never heard of again.

The Portuguese memorial submitted earlier in the month against the Wines Bill had alarmed the textile interest in many parts of the country. Petitions began to pour into the Commons.[9] As the Commerce Bill could be expected to affect the same interests and many more besides, Whig tactics were naturally dictated by the hope of delaying its early stages as long as possible to enable maximum opposition to the bill to build up.[10] The chances of defeating the bill in the Commons seemed negligible in the light of the vast Tory majority;[11] but the more effective the rearguard action which the Whigs managed to fight in St Stephen's Chapel, the brighter, it seemed, would be the party's prospects when the measure reached the Lords. Since it was a money bill the peers would not be constitutionally entitled to amend it. But they could reject it.

On 14 May the ministry sought the Commons' approval to bring in the Bill of Ratification, and the debate, largely owing to the delaying tactics of the Whigs, lasted until 10 p.m. Although the Court put up a spirited defence of the terms of the Commerce Treaty and mustered an impressive team of businessmen to put its case, the Whigs appeared at the time to have had the better of the economic arguments.[12] On the other hand, Sir Thomas Hanmer, one of the knights of the shire for Suffolk, gave every impression of speaking for the solid body of the Tory landed interest in urging the introduction of the bill: and it is of particular note, in view of his remarkable change of opinion the following month, that at this stage Hanmer was seemingly unafflicted by doubts of any kind. When at length the question was called for, something like 40 M.P.s had already left the House since the start of the debate, ten hours before; but the Court still achieved a heavy majority, recording 252 votes against 130. The next day the Hanoverian resident, Kreienberg, was to purvey an astonishing report to his government that the minority was made up of 60 Whigs (all those of that party then left in the House, according to his information) and 70 Tories. But this is simply not credible and finds no support in any other account. On the other hand, it is clear that the Whigs managed to capture some Tory votes; and that among perhaps a dozen to 20 defectors were at least two Tory businessmen — Robert Heysham, a West India merchant, and the scrivener, Sir George Newland — who had supported the opposition from the floor of the House as well as with their votes.[13] Significantly, there were also some welcome Scottish reinforcements to the minority.[14] None the less, as both the Dutch agent, L'Hermitage, and Kreienberg reported on the following day, there was a general consensus of opinion that the bill would pass the Commons with little difficulty; and L'Hermitage felt that even in the Lords, where opposition was expected to be more effective, the Whigs could have small chance of ultimate success.[15]

However, the leading Whig, General Stanhope, in his speech on the 14th had touched upon the argument which was in the event to prove decisive for the future of the bill. He made a strong plea that the Commerce Bill should be divorced from the peace settlement, which must be accepted as a *fait accompli*. The bill should not be considered a party measure, and should be judged on its own merits in regard to its effect on the economy of the nation.[16] By this, of course, he had hoped to detach Tory Members from its support. Here again, time was a fundamental ingredient in Whig strategy: not only time to enable them to organize representations against the bill, but time to give the Tories a chance to shed their original attitudes to the treaty, based as they were largely on party bias and a general enthusiasm for the peace settlement as a whole. By a strange irony, the ministry itself, though its supporters were urging all possible speed,[17] allowed a delay of more than a fortnight to go by before the Bill was introduced on 30 May. This may have been due to difficulties in drafting the proposed Bill of Ratification. But whatever the reason the delay enabled the Whigs to orchestrate a propaganda campaign against the bill which soon produced results.[18] Meanwhile the House of Lords had begun to show a lively interest. On 18 May Lord Somers had moved for a host of papers relating to Anglo-French trade since 1696 to be laid before the House by the Board of Trade. He had carried his point without opposition, many leading ministers being absent from the House at the time. This was to be the origin of a long-drawn-out Lords inquiry into the background of the recent Commerce Treaty; and when it eventually got under way on 28 May the government made a confident and effective start. Oxford defended the treaty in 'a noble and cunning speech in answer to Wharton, Coupar [Cowper] and Halifax', promising in due course to lay his opinion before them. According to Lord Balmerino, 'Halifax was forced to say, "Nobly spoke"'.[19]

All the same, on the eve of the Commerce Bill's introduction into the Commons, some ministers were beginning to betray traces of anxiety about the future.[20] It was disturbing to contemplate the possibility that the issue might ultimately be decided not by party prejudice, which would have reacted in their favour, but by national prejudice, which was more likely to work against them. As one of them put it, 'it hath been soe long a receiv'd opinion that a trade with France is prejudicial to this kingdom that it is noe easie task to beat them out of it'.[21] Old bogies died hard.[22] The first reading in the Commons on 30 May passed off without serious alarms, despite two divisions unsuccessfully forced by the Whigs. The only portent, it seemed, was that 'in both questions all the Scots were on the losing side'.[23] Before the second reading on 4 June, however, the steady stream of petitions against the trade treaty had suddenly become a flood; no fewer than eight were laid before the House on the very day of the bill's next stage.[24] The debate on that day proved to be another marathon of nine hours,[25] and the division which took place on the motion for commitment provided clear evidence that the Whigs were gaining ground, if only slightly. The Court secured 202 votes, the opposition 135;[26] so that although there were 45 fewer Members voting, compared with the first big clash on 14 May, the opposition vote actually rose by five while the government's vote dropped by 50. There was still no suggestion that the bill could ultimately be defeated in the lower House — so far most Tories who felt uneasy about the prospect of a freer commerce with France were still tending to absent themselves rather than join forces with the Whigs.[27] But the attitude of the Scots was further confirmed, with the greater part of their Tory Members again deserting the Court,[28] and their alienation now began to look distinctly ominous. For should there be a corresponding move by the 16 representative peers when the Commerce Bill came to the Lords, the position of strength which the government had enjoyed there since January 1712 would be completely undermined.

It is doubtful whether any member of the Oxford ministry would have been prepared at the beginning of June to rule out this possibility, for it was the government's misfortune that at this particular juncture its problems had been suddenly complicated by a sharp deterioration in Anglo-Scottish relations. The Union had suffered recurrent stresses since the first year of its life, most of them over issues with parliamentary consequences.[29] But the most serious shock yet to the fabric of 1707 occurred in late May and early June 1713. The Treaty of Union had guaranteed that taxation in Great Britain would be imposed on a basis of general equity. In addition article 14, as amended by the Scottish Parliament, had granted Scotland explicit exemption from payment of the malt tax for the duration of the war. When, therefore, the Commons on 22 May passed a Malt Tax Bill which imposed a levy of 6*d.* per bushel on English and Scottish malt alike, there were instant and bitter complaints from the Scots that both provisions had been ignored. The second, admittedly, had been no more than a technical infringement: fighting was over, even though the signatures had yet to be appended to the treaties between Britain and Spain. But the first had undoubtedly been disregarded. There could be nothing 'equitable' about an act which taxed all British malt at the same rate, regardless of the fact that Scottish barley was much inferior to English in quality and commanded much lower prices. Why, then, did the Oxford ministry risk arousing Scottish hostility, especially at a time when it was engaged in shepherding a major piece of legislation through Parliament?

The fact is that the controversial clause of the Malt Bill, in the form in which it eventually passed the Commons, was not the work of the ministry at all. It was essentially a back-bench measure, forced on an unwilling Court by 'the countrey gentlemen of England'. Without doubt there was sympathy in the Cabinet with the Scottish plea for a reduction of the tax, and at the time the bill was introduced official hints were dropped that some redress would be made in committee.[30] Moreover, in spite of Lockhart's charge of insincerity,[31] the ministers do seem to have done their best to ensure that justice was done. It is true that when Lockhart himself, at the committee stage on 18 May, proposed that Scotland should be granted total exemption he got no official support; but a subsequent suggestion from the Scottish Members that a duty of 3*d.* a bushel instead of 6*d.* should be levied north of the border did receive ministerial backing, and was carried by the casting vote of the chairman, John Conyers.[32] The very next day, however, the Commons refused to accept the amendment and ordered it to be recommitted. According to one source, the opposition came from 'the Whiggs & Octr. Clubb', who overrode a combination of 'the Scots and the Court' by 125 to 100.[33] But perhaps the deciding factor was the attitude of independent Country Tories representing some of the northern, western and Welsh counties, who felt aggrieved that the Scots should receive preferential treatment while their own economically-poor constituencies had to shoulder the full burden.[34] In the second committee, on the 20th, the Court once again struggled hard to carry the reduction: but this time, though there was again only one vote in it when the committee divided on the clause, the decision went against them and the Scots.[35] On 21 May,

> upon reporting the bill [wrote Baillie] to the Commons, the 6d was agreed to 139 to 104 and upon a motion for leaving out the clause relating to Scot[land] it passed in the negative 147 to 115 so that there is nothing left to us now but to try to get the time of commencement of the duty allowed from June to December [1713].

The next day in the Commons the bill passed 'and the attempt that was made to alter the Commencement of the duty had the same fate with the rest'. Baillie's advice to his fellow Scotsmen was to 'make all the Malt they can before the middle of June'.[36]

From then on events moved quickly to a climax. On 12 May there had been a preliminary meeting, called together by Lord Balmerino on the insistence of the Scottish M.P.s, at which Balmerino had hoped for a unanimous resolution to bring in a bill for the dissolution of the Union. He pinned his faith on Ilay (still in Scotland), who would 'be more alerte on this head than many of our Lords because he is discontented'. The meeting, however, 'ended in the general opinion that it would be impossible to get free of this Malt tax . . . that ane endevour to throw the whole bill out would be in vain But our commons thought they would get some abatement'.[37] These hopes having by 22 May clearly proved illusory, on the following day a meeting of the Scottish commoners[38] was 'warmly pressed' by George Lockhart and Sir Alexander Erskine to move for a bill to dissolve the Union. Lockhart did not hold out extravagant hopes of success at the first attempt, but in view of the party divisions in England he thought it 'not improbable that some considerable party might take us by the hand and carry our business through'. That the meeting approved this startling proposal almost unanimously is indicative of the extent to which normal political differences among Scottish M.P.s had become submerged by a national sense of grievance. The Squadrone Members and the Whigs among them were placated by a promise to include guarantees of the Protestant Succession in the proposed bill, while ministeralists like Pringle, William Cochrane and Sir Hugh Paterson stifled whatever misgivings they might have felt. Robert Pringle, for one, was under no illusions as to the practicality of dissolving the Union. He was later to remark that 'theres never one knowing man in England has any such thoughts as to be free of us, whatever may be pretended at this time'; for it was clear that the Union was 'the strongest Bullwark for the Protestant Succession'. Nevertheless the meeting concluded with the Members agreeing to seek the co-operation of the representative peers.[39]

On 26 May the joint meeting of M.P.s and peers took place at the Blue Posts tavern in the Haymarket. According to George Baillie, there was no debate for there was general agreement on the course to be taken.[40] The only counter-arguments were put forward by Baillie himself, in order to gain time (he had not been at the meeting on the 23rd). He urged that the poor prospects of success at the present juncture 'would tye down the Union the harder upon Scotland and consequently defeat all hopes of success upon other occasion'; that this would increase divisions in Scotland and make it impossible for them to unite against future measures; that it was too great a step to be taken without the advice of their constituents. He suggested a constitutional obstacle too; in his view the Union could not be dissolved without the consent of the Parliaments of both kingdoms. Baillie stood alone, and the meeting came to a unanimous resolution to bring in a bill of dissolution. The Duke of Argyll, Lord Mar, George Lockhart and John Cockburn were deputed to inform the Queen. Balmerino, like others, was realistic enough to recognize no hope of success this session, but with an election in the offing, he saw the attempt at breaking the Union as a step towards endeavouring 'to have nather Lord nor Commoner chosen next parl[iamen]t who is not of this mind and who will have it in their hand to force the ministrie . . . to let us go'.[41]

In the meantime, the Treasurer, whose intelligence system was as usual working well — Bolingbroke had a meeting with several Scottish Members on the evening of 25 May — had got wind of what was afoot. Indeed he had already tried to deter the leading conspirators, without success.[42] Similar efforts by William Bromley and Hanmer were equally unavailing, and so were those of Anne herself when the Scottish deputation had their audience on 26 May, and were told by the Queen that their intentions were 'rash'. All they achieved was to convince the Scots that their chances of gaining any significant support from the Tories were slight, and therefore to persuade them to make their first attempt, at the earliest opportunity, in the House of Lords, where Whig assistance — could they secure it — was more likely to prove effective.[43] This decision was taken at a meeting on 27 May, at which Argyll and Ilay, supported by General Ross, suggested that the Scots should oppose all English parties in everything if they would not support the dissolution of the Union.[44] Baillie demurred, claiming the freedom to vote as he saw fit, particularly concerning the Treaty of Commerce which he believed would 'prove the ruin of the trade of Scot[land]'. His stand apparently gave Lord Mar and others the excuse 'to declare they would not oppose the Court in the Treaty of Commerce', a step which (Baillie claimed) 'otherwise they durst not have ventured upon, for they say if it be reasonable that Jerv[iswood] be at liberty on the one hand it is as reasonable we be at liberty on the other, supposing we think it a good Treaty of Commerce'. The general opinion of the meeting appeared to blame Baillie for thus causing a split in the otherwise united ranks of the Scots. He, however, had been playing a tactical game, and he was not displeased with the result. He had ensured that by furnishing certain lords 'with a handle not to oppose the Court' they could not join with the Whigs whole-heartedly and thus be 'more favourably stated with them than the Squadrone'. This, he calculated, would give him and his Squadrone friends 'the means to ruin their credit at the next Election by laying the blame upon them for the failing of the dissolution and at the same time might keep their ground with the Whigs'.[45]

Despite these differences, the Scots inevitably had to make approaches to the Whigs, and in order to strengthen their bid they began openly to co-operate with the opposition in the Commons, where in one division on 28 May a combination of the two inflicted a minor defeat on the Court.[46] On the same day the Earl of Findlater moved in the House of Lords for a day to consider the state of the nation. He was seconded by Lord Eglinton, and Monday, 1 June was agreed upon. Lord Treasurer Oxford, normally the most phlegmatic of men, commented acidly to Balmerino that the Scots were like a man with the toothache who was prepared to have his own head cut off in order to cure it.[47]

Everything depended now on how the Whigs would react to these developments. Their leaders were in a particularly awkward position. They could scarcely fail to appreciate the possibilities of exploiting the new parliamentary situation which had arisen; and while it was unfortunate that during the proceedings on the Malt Bill their followers had been noticeably unsympathetic to the Scottish cause,[48] a sudden change of face when the measure came before the Lords would involve no betrayal of party principle. But the future of the Union was a different matter. For the Junto lords to identify themselves now with a deliberate attempt to break it up, when seven years before they had done their utmost to bring it into being, would be both cynical and discreditable. Nevertheless, it has been the generally accepted verdict of historians that the Junto succumbed to the temptation put before them, and that they supported the demand for a bill dissolving the Union in the hope of binding the Scottish contingent to the opposition for the remainder of the session.[49] But this view is based on a misunderstanding of the events of the last few days of May, and more particularly of the crucial debate of 1 June in the House of Lords, and does rather less than justice to the integrity and sense of responsibility of the Whig leaders.

As late as 29 May, L'Hermitage still believed that the majority of Whigs, like most Tories and all the Court dependants, would positively oppose any dissolution of the Union.[50] And three letters written by Lord Halifax to Oxford, from the 26th to 28th, suggest (if they are not to be taken as deliberate pieces of deception) that his first impulse and that of several of his fellow leaders was to support the Treasurer in opposing 'the wild proceedings with which we are threatened'.[51] But concerned as they were with their failure to gain ground in the House of Lords this session, few of the leading figures in the party felt, at the eleventh hour, that they could afford wholly to ignore what seemed an ideal opportunity of winning over 'the sixteen'. The problem was, how far could they reasonably go in responding to the overtures of the Scots? Wharton, characteristically, seems to have been prepared to go farther than most; Somers to have exercised the most restraint. Ill-health had by this time drastically restricted Somers's parliamentary activities; but he still kept something of his moral hold on the party, and at a crucial Whig policy-meeting held at the Duke of Somerset's house at the end of May it was his sage counsel which prevailed, and not the more extreme course advocated by Wharton. In fact the latter's normal equanimity and good humour was so disturbed by the cautious tone of the meeting that he dissociated himself from the whole proceedings and retired to his seat in Buckinghamshire.[52]

Yet it was natural, after all, that the majority of his fellow leaders, finding themselves in this extremely delicate position, should want, and try to get, the best of both worlds: to secure the Whigs the immediate advantage of Scottish support, without doing any permanent damage to the Union, or endangering the Hanoverian Succession, which had been their main concern in championing the Union in the first place. And the only hope of achieving this, at least temporarily, was to keep the question of dissolution in play for as long as possible, encouraging the Scots with general professions of sympathy without ever firmly committing themselves to a decisive step. There seems small reason to doubt that these were the tactics finally decided on by the Whig lords, and that Burnet was justified, therefore, in claiming that 'they did not intend to give up the Union, yet thought it reasonable to give a hearing to the motion'.[53] The refusal of the Whigs to give the Scots any firm promises before the great Lords debate of 1 June is, in itself, significant enough; and it may have been this which confirmed Baillie in his own conviction that 'the Whigs were not for breaking the Union'.[54] But conclusive evidence in favour of the Whigs is to be found in their attitude during the debate itself.

The Scottish peers met at the Earl of Mar's lodgings at 10 o'clock in the morning of 1 June to discuss the wording of the motion that was to be put to the Lords, and it was agreed that Lord Findlater should seek leave 'for bringing in a bill for dissolving the Union and securing the protestant Succession as it is presently by law established'.[55] In the House, Findlater 'very copiously moved for leave to bring in the bill',[56] rehearsing the grievances that the Scots had suffered since the Union — the dissolution of the Scottish Privy Council, the Treasons Act, the barring of Scottish peers with British titles from sitting in the Lords, 'but above all our many taxes, especially the Malt tax bill, and the ruin of our trade and manufactorys'.[57] After all this fighting talk, however, the speech ended remarkably lamely.[58] It seems that at the meeting earlier that morning, Findlater had shown himself 'very unwilling or rather affraid to make the motion for disolving and therefore [in the House] ended his speech without it'. This piece of equivocal 'nonsense' had received the approval of a majority of the Scots peers at Mar's lodgings, but in the Lords 'some of the English muttering that he had concluded nothing, particularly Anglesey said so to himself, then he [Findlater] rose up and read it'.[59] The motion having been seconded by Eglinton, there followed a lengthy and — as the Hanoverian resident thought — a gloomy silence, 'la cour, je veux dire les ministres, regardant les Whighs et ceux-cy regardant les ministres'.[60] The Junto and their allies were content to go on sitting tight and leave the field to the Scots on the one hand — for whom Eglinton, Ilay, Argyll, Loudoun and Balmerino were briefed to support the motion — and the ministry on the other. The Court side at length opened their case with Lords North and Grey and Peterborough, with the latter in skittish mood.[61] Then Lord Trevor and the Lord Treasurer (the latter putting his finger on the very constitutional point that Baillie had anticipated)[62]

> attaqued us, they insisted that our grivances might be just and therefore we might desire redress but why a dissolution? We maintained that no other remedy could sett things right.[63]After two or 3 hours debeat (No English man helping us all the while) at lenth Nottingham made a long and excellent discourse.[64]

Nottingham's speech, in fact, was a curious mixture. The rebel High Tory, who had left the Court party over the question of the peace preliminaries in December 1711, began by expatiating on the natural advantages which Union ought to have brought, had each party properly carried out its share of the contract. He went on to disagree with Oxford and assert the constitutional right of the Parliament of Great Britain to dissolve the contract if it so wished, but then concluded with a motion for adjourning the debate to some future date. It was important, he claimed, to give the Lords more time to produce an effective alternative guarantee of the Protestant Succession. No one, he reminded the House, had opposed the Act of Union more strongly than he in 1707; but the second article, settling the Succession in Scotland, he had never objected to at the time, and he declined to lend his hand now to dissolving or weakening the Union without guarantees for the House of Hanover, at least as secure as those in the act. Nottingham's carefully judged contribution set the tone for the Whigs who followed him in the debate; and not surprisingly, Balmerino believed that he 'had concerted it with the Whiggs'.[65] The Whig lords and their supporters who spoke — Sunderland, Halifax, Townshend, Scarbrough, Bishop Burnet of Salisbury, Cowper, Pembroke, Guernsey — all in turn supported the adjournment and all, with the exception of Sunderland, whose speech marked him out (in Balmerino's words) as 'clear for us', hedged on the main question of whether they were in favour of breaking the Union or not.[66]

What is quite plain is that Nottingham's ploy had not been discussed beforehand with the Scots peers. The first reaction of the latter, as expressed by Mar and Findlater,[67] was to reject any suggestion of delay. It was only after Halifax's speech had made it fairly clear that they had no hope of support except on these terms that the Scots appear to have given way.[68] Only this interpretation of the Whig attitude and of the final Scottish capitulation enables us to make sense of the division on 1 June, which was not a vote for or against the Union, but in effect a vote on delaying the discussion to a later date. The technical question voted on was the previous question, called for by the Court peers, of whether to vcte on Findlater's motion for leave to bring in a bill. The Whigs opposed the question in order to delay consideration; the Scottish peers, apart from Oxford's son-in-law Lord Dupplin, who was not one of 'the sixteen', un-enthusiastically followed suit;[69] but Oxford and his colleagues, encouraged by the patent lack of understanding between the Whigs and the Scots, 'proposed to go on to the motion instantly'.[70]

The ministry, not unnaturally, was determined to try to remove all un-certainty and prevent the future of the Union being imperilled again this session at least; and the Treasurer must have calculated that, with at least nine Whigs absent from the House (some of them with proxies), the time for a show-down was there and then.[71] It seems, however, that he was more confident of success than the subsequent division warranted, for in the event the Junto's gambit only failed by a very narrow margin. At the first count, among the peers present, the two sides were exactly equal with 54 votes each, but when proxies were called for the Court motion for putting the question was carried by four votes. One of these was the proxy of the Duke of Richmond which had been procured by Lord Poulet and was cast — not very scrupulously in view of Richmond's Whiggery — for the Court.[72] This, plus the fact that two Low Church bishops with proxies in their pockets, Ely and St Asaph, left the chamber before the division at 6 p.m., proved just enough to save the day for the government: 'had they [the bishops] staid', wrote Edmund Gibson, the chaplain to the Archbishop of Canterbury, to his friend Bishop Nicolson, 'it had come to what our friends desired, namely the appointment of a day to hear the proposition on the part of Scotland with regard to the succession, that they might have taken an estimate from thence, whether they are in earnest for it . . .'[73] As it was, the government was able to go on to clinch its victory by defeating Findlater's original motion without a vote. The Scots declined to divide the House on it, well aware that if they did they would be deserted by the Whigs, many of whom had deliberately left the House before the main question was put so that they would not be forced to declare for or against the dissolution.[74] Balmerino claimed that the Whigs had deserted them because they could not 'get a Secret Capitulation with us upon a nice point . . . it is presently to bring over H[anover]'. The events of the following spring suggest that what the Junto may have had in mind was a parliamentary initiative to invite the Electoral Prince to England.[75]

The Oxford ministry had weathered its first major hazard of the 1713 session; but the storm created by the malt tax was very far from having blown itself out. The Malt Tax Bill itself had still to pass the Lords, where it was clear that, money bill or no, the opposition would fight it all the way in combination with 'the sixteen'.[76] Bolingbroke, and perhaps others in the Cabinet also, would have liked the ministry to follow up its victory on 1 June with an immediate counter-attack. It had caused some remark that Oxford's chief rival in the Cabinet had taken no part in the debate itself: indeed Kreienberg noted that he had still to make his maiden speech in the Lords since his promotion to the peerage the previous summer.[77] Now, however, the Secretary began to talk of a bill making it a treasonable offence to attempt the dissolution of the Union 'by any overt act'.[78] But this was not the Treasurer's way. His first concern was to pilot the malt tax safely through — the government simply could not afford the loss of another lucrative source of revenue after its enforced concession over the land tax — and then, if possible, to reach some sort of private compromise with the Scottish peers; for he was reasonably sure that many of the latter would remain susceptible to Court pressure provided they were not further antagonized. This analysis was given some weight on 2 June by a meeting of Scottish lords and M.P.s which decided not to move for the dissolution of the Union in the Commons, but to wait for a more proper occasion.[79]

The passage of the malt tax, however, proved hazardous in the extreme. Sunderland, representing the Junto, visited Balmerino on 4 June with the message that his friends:

> would all to a man joyn us [the Scots] if I would move to delay Committing of the bill till Munday 8 [June] and that then they would take into Consideration the state of the nation in relation to the 14th and other articles of union which relate to this tax — But he said [that] on munday when I opened the debeat I must oppose the bill not only with regard to Scotland but to England and not offer to amend it but to throw it out — I said I would agree to any motion that might retard the ruin of my Country But that amending it would throw it out, for the commons will not pass a Money bill that we amend — he said that was thrue but the other way was better — I said I should talk to my Scots friends of it – I apprehend that the Court will oppose this and get it committed in spite of all we can do.[80]

The joint opposition of the Whigs and Scots did divide the House of Lords on the bill, and each time the margin was uncomfortably narrow, but each time, as Balmerino predicted, the ministry scraped home. On 5 June, in a very full House assembled for the second reading, the ministry had a majority of only two.[81] Balmerino himself opened the debate as planned, vigorously seconded by Ilay, and the struggle lasted three hours. Besides trying to get the second reading put off until the eighth, Balmerino, who was sitting amongst the Tories, had a message from the Whigs 'to insist against the bill itself'. He and Ilay were strongly supported by Argyll, Mar and Findlater; but the best speech for the opposition came from Nottingham. Balmerino concluded that they had had the better of the debate, and the Court were so wearied that though the House consented to a commitment it was agreed not to proceed until the eighth. Though the Scots and Whigs were deserted by some Tories who had declared they were against the tax, the narrow defeat was squarely laid at the door of the Scottish peers themselves. The absence of Lord Wharton (with a proxy), Lord Derby and the Duke of Grafton was more than balanced by 'the poor old Bishop [of] London, D[uke of] Leeds and others [who] were wanting

on the Court side'. It was the Duke of Argyll who told Balmerino that the
Scots 'had lost it by Lord Duplin's being with the Court[82] for his vote
would have made us equall, and we being for the negative (not a 2d
reading) we had carried it'.[83] To cap it all the 'poor E[arl] of Home
(meaning no ill) had got his bottle over night and came not to the house
till after our vote, and that he was sent for'.[84] Balmerino and Argyll,
however, were not in possession of the full facts on the vote of 5 June.
The anxiety which Oxford felt about his prospects in the House that day
may be gauged from one extraordinary measure he resorted to in order to
make sure of his majority. On the very morning of the second reading he
bought the support of the independent Whig Earl of Warrington with a
promise that the arrears of £6,500 on the pension granted to Warrington's
father by William III, outstanding since 1694, would be paid. 'I believe
your Lordship would gladly that morning have given double that sum and
paid it down', claimed Warrington later, 'to have been sure of Carrying
that Bill at that time.'[85]

There was another long debate on 8 June, in which the Scots and the
Whigs, led by Nottingham, Sunderland, Cowper, Balmerino, Findlater,
Ilay, Mar and Argyll, were answered by Oxford, Bolingbroke, Leeds,
Peterborough and North and Grey. Oxford agreed with the Scots that the
levying of the duty would be very hard on them 'but that it was like the
exaction of it would not be strict'. Others also 'on the Court side insisted
to insinuate that it would not be exacted'. This led to a heated discussion
on the Queen's dispensing power which involved Oxford and Sunderland
swapping insults.[86] Lord North then flew off at such a tangent on the laws
of Scotland that Argyll refused to let Balmerino answer him. At 5 o'clock
in the afternoon, 'after many good and many ridiculouse speeches . . . it
was put to the votes [and] we were 56, they 64 — we did not call for
proxies knowing them to be equal — 19 to 19'.[87] Again the Court had
scraped through, and this despite the fact that the opposition was this time
strengthened by the reappearance of Wharton, whose 'zeal to do mischief',
we are told, 'got the better of him and brought him up . . . to be against
the bill'.[88] The larger majority for the Court on the eighth was largely
due, according to Kreienberg and Balmerino, to the actions of three
moderate Whigs, the Duke of Kent, and Lord Herbert, 'who had all along
been with us, [but who] deserted to the enemy, els we had only lost it by
two'; also to the unavoidable absence of Lord Guernsey (Nottingham's
brother) and the Whig Bishop Fleetwood of St Asaph.[89] A protest against
the vote was entered into the Journal two days later. Composed by
Balmerino, it was vetted by Nottingham, Sunderland and Halifax, and
signed on the 12th by 19 peers.[90] Baillie summing up the whole course of
the Malt Bill concluded that

> There has all along been something odd in this affair. It carried in the
> Committee of the house of Commons by the absence of a Scots member and a
> second reading in the house of Lords by a Scots man. If either of these had not
> happened we had bee[n] free of it. The thing itself does not trouble me so
> much as the consequences that are likely to follow upon it.[91]

It is certainly the case that more than the malt tax alone was at stake in the Lords division on 5 June 1713. The question before the House at the end of a long afternoon's debating was whether the Malt Bill should be given its second reading forthwith, or whether this stage of the measure should be deferred for several days. Both the Whigs and the Scots were in favour of delay; and both for the Whigs and for the government such a delay was of the utmost tactical importance. For the Whigs, as Oxford must have been well aware, had their eyes now not just on the defeat of the Malt Bill but on what, to them if not to the Scots, was much more important — namely, the defeat of the Commerce Bill, and until the latter reached the House of Lords — as both parties still assumed it would — it seemed essential to the Junto to keep some material hold over their Scottish allies. Hence their anxiety 'to have their turn served first, and the Scots to trust them, rather than they trust the Scots', as they would have to do once the fate of the malt tax had been decided.[92] Hence also Oxford's endeavours first to prevent the retarding of the money bill, and subsequently, as soon as it was safely through on the eighth, to bring back the straying Scots to the fold.

To get the whole political scene in clear focus, as it unfolded in the second week of June, we must remember that right through the period of crisis over the Union and the malt tax the House of Lords' inquiry into Anglo-French commercial relations, begun on 28 May, had been steadily proceeding. On the second, fourth and ninth of June, in fact, the Lords had given the greater part of their time to it. Already it was becoming clear to the Treasurer that a body of Tory opinion in the House was hardening against the new trade treaty. A list which he drew up on 13 June of the Commerce Bill's potential supporters and opponents in the Lords[93] shows that as early as this Oxford expected as many as 13 or 14 Tory peers to divide with the opposition when the bill arrived. If he lost the Scottish vote as well, the upper House would be almost certain to repudiate the treaty. Once again therefore, as in the aftermath of the Hamilton peerage case in February 1712,[94] it seemed that the Scots contingent held the key to the immediate political situation. An astounding turn of events in the House of Commons, however, was about to render these calculations irrelevant.

It was against a background of mounting public excitement and increasing strident criticism of the ministry's economic policy that the Commons began[95] on 9 June the first of five exhausting days of committee work on the Commerce Bill. It was this stage which undoubtedly determined the bill's fate. From the start the atmosphere of the House was tense and over-charged. There was a struggle over the chairmanship, which took the Court by surprise but which was eventually resolved in favour of Oxford's friend, Sir Robert Davers.[96] Next day, 10 June, spokesmen for the Levant and Peninsula trade and for the Italian merchants were allowed to present evidence, and Members on both sides became extremely heated after Nathaniel Torriano, who was speaking on behalf of merchants trading with Spain and Italy, had interspersed his economic data with some barbed political reflections on the government's competence.[97] Upbraided by Robert Benson, for the ministry, Torriano[98] was defended by the Whig Sir Peter King, who pleaded eloquently for freedom of speech for those giving evidence. Many Tories joined Lechmere, Stanhope and Smith in supporting King's appeal. The Court, disturbed by the warmth generated, and not least by a surprise intervention by Charles Aldworth, a High Tory Member for Windsor, dropped its motion to have Torriano censured: a small enough concession in itself; but one that for the opposition was to mark the turn of the tide.[99]

In the remaining committees on the bill the spirit of uneasiness which had begun to settle on the Tories became more and more noticeable. Besides the prospect of an approaching general election, which made many Tories less likely to disregard the views of their constituents — more than 50 sat for seats which had petitioned either against the Commerce Bill or the earlier Wine Bill — there were a growing number who were doubtful of the economic wisdom of the ministry's policy. In addition, and more disturbing still from the Court's point of view, the granting of most-favoured-nation treatment to France in the recent treaty had given fresh alarm and brought fresh reinforcements to that small but determined group of Tories which had for more than 18 months suspected the whole drift of the government's peace policy. The anti-French and anti-Jacobite spirit of the 'peace rebels' of December 1711[100] and of the March Club of 1712 was again abroad, and in its latest form it was proving dangerously infectious. What made the Commerce Bill opposition more formidable than its predecessors was that by the middle of June it had attracted the support of two or three men of real influence within the party, men who had sufficient pull to draw together in temporary association the diverse elements of the bill's opposition.

The most important convert in the House of Commons was Sir Thomas Hanmer. He had begun by favouring the Treaty of Commerce but during the committee stage of the bill there was a marked change in his attitude and he began to campaign strongly against it. His speech on 18 June indicated that the reasons for this change were chiefly economic. The county of Suffolk, which he represented, had some stake in the woollen industry, and like many other Tory gentlemen, Hanmer must have been affected by pressures in his locality as well as by the arguments he heard in the Commons. But at the same time, from his subsequent record as the champion of the Hanoverian Tories in the next Parliament, one can assume that already he had political as well as economic reservations about the ministry's policy.[101]

Even Hanmer's defection, however, did not appear to threaten the ministry with defeat in the Commons; although general feeling in London by 16 June was that the majority there would be small, and just a few were by now allowing themselves to think the unthinkable — that the lower House might actually throw the bill out ('il semble', Kreienberg hastily added in his report to Hanover, 'que ceux qui raisonnent ainsi, vont trop vite').[102] What continued to cause Oxford most concern was the bill's prospect in the Lords. Here the events of the past two or three weeks had alarmingly eroded much of the ground which the Court had so painfully regained since the spring of 1712. In his assessment of support and opposition, the Treasurer's first calculations produced a total of 77 votes for each side.[103] Second thoughts suggested a maximum of 79 votes for the opposition and 84 for the government, but the latter figure was based on the supposition that all but three of the disaffected Scottish peers[104] would eventually come to heel — and this, in the circumstances, was no better than a gamble. The 14 Tory peers whose allegiance Oxford considered doubtful or discounted included most of the Nottingham contingent,[105] plus Pembroke (now almost a Whig by adoption), and a prominent rebel of more recent vintage, Bishop Dawes of Chester; but there were also two significant new names bracketed with the Whigs, the Earls of Anglesey and Abingdon, the former being the more important politically. The defection of these two peers was just as damaging to the ministry as that of Hanmer; for each held office, each was an active politician, and together they enjoyed quite important connexions and influence in the Commons as well as the Lords.[106] Moreover, while Abingdon's opposition seems to have been mostly factious, possibly grounded on disappointment that he and his family had not been especially favoured,[107] it was believed that Anglesey was acting largely from anti-French and anti-Jacobite feelings, reinforced probably by self-interest.[108]

The rebellious state of the Lords, and in particular the disaffection of the Scots and the hostility of Abingdon and Anglesey, who both denounced the Commerce Treaty openly in the House on 17 June,[109] confronted the ministry on the eve of the report stage of the Commons with a most awkward decision. Should they drop the bill or carry on in the hope of a still-expected victory in the Commons which might rally some of the waverers in the Lords? Powerful pressure from loyal Tories persuaded the ministry to go ahead.[110]

On 18 June, after Davers had reported the amendments made in committee, the motion was made by the ministry that the bill be engrossed. The resulting debate lasted eight hours with no fewer than 35 speeches. A list of speakers in the debate which has survived[111] shows that of the 18 speeches made against the bill, seven came from English Whigs, one from a Scots Whig merchant,[112] one from a Scottish Court Whig,[113] one from a Squadrone Member,[114] the rest from disaffected Tories. The turning point in the debate came when Hanmer unexpectedly appealed to the 'country' instincts and to the self-interest of the Tory gentlemen.[115] The opposition cause was further helped by the fact that the supporting speeches from the Tory side came from a very fair cross-section of the party: three Hanoverian Tories in the March Club tradition, and two merchants,[116] one October Club stalwart, and one professional politician and placeman.[117] When the heads were finally counted at 11 p.m. the motion for engrossment was rejected by 194 to 185. The Oxford ministry had suffered its first major defeat in the Commons since November 1710.

The existence of a printed division list which is exceptionally precise, and the recent discovery of George Baillie's listing of the votes of the Scottish M.P.s,[118] makes it possible to analyze the various factors contributing to the government's defeat. Such an analysis reveals the extraordinary scale of the Tory rebellion against the Court. The printed list shows 76 Tories voting against the bill (there were also two Tory tellers) along with 104 English Whigs and 14 Scots opposition Members;[119] and yet in the final reckoning it was Tory abstentions, rather than hostile Tory votes which cost the government the day. The narrow margin of nine votes could easily have been made up if the Court could have polled even a fraction of the absentee Tories. But there can be little question that many of the absences were politic and deliberate. Out of the key group of 51 Tories who sat for constituencies which had petitioned against a freer trade with France, only 17 actually voted with the Whigs. Significantly, however, no fewer than 15 of the remainder did not attend the House. Both in this closely interested group and among Tory M.P.s as a whole a surprising number of previously highly active politicians — men who normally never missed a key division — were on this occasion absent; among them office-holders like Sir William Drake, Francis Scobell and Sir Simeon Stewart, and leading October men like the two Strangways, Sir William Barker and Sir Gilbert Dolben.[120]

Taking into account both the Tories who voted against the bill and the absentees, the importance of the attitude of the two High Church peers, Anglesey and Abingdon, becomes evident. At a conservative reckoning, their joint following in the Commons in the summer of 1713 was about 15 Members.[121] Of these only four failed to vote against the bill, and only one — Henry Bertie (Beaumaris) — actually supported the Court. Thus the friends and connexions of the two earls more than account for the small opposition majority. The impact of Hanmer's *volte-face* is much more difficult to assess from the lists, since like that of Speaker Bromley, Hanmer's influence in the Commons was based much more on his political authority than on a personal connexion. Many of the group of High Church Tories with whom Hanmer had been most closely associated in the past had also been associated with Nottingham, and for several of them the vote against the Commerce Bill was not their first revolt against the Court.[122] Such as it is, the evidence does appear to suggest that Hanmer's immediate influence on the Court's defeat, which later became part of political legend, may have been exaggerated.

There is some evidence to suggest that Oxford played a fairly passive role in whipping up support for the bill at the report stage.[123] He subsequently told Swift that 'he did not care whether Parliament passed the Commerce, or no, and that the next should have the honour of it'.[124] Yet it is noteworthy that the Treasurer spoke in favour of the treaty in the Lords on 17 June; also that it was his brother Edward, seconded by Vice-Chamberlain Coke, who opened the Court's case in the Commons on the 18th, expatiating at some length on the advantages of the bargain with France.[125] The testimony of at least one experienced Court Member, Josiah Burchett (Secretary to the Admiralty, M.P. for Sandwich) acquits

the ministry quite firmly of any obvious slackness in managing the proceedings;[126] and on the whole the division list supports this view.
Admittedly the names of five Tory office-holders can be found among the
ranks of the bill's opponents;[127] but this is a surprisingly small number
considering the warmth of feeling which the trade treaty had generated,
and in any case four of these five had been unreliable for some time past.
Had the head of the ministry himself been evidently negligent or even
indecisive in his attitude one would have expected this to be reflected far
more clearly in the votes of Court Members.

What do the two George Baillie lists for the votes on the Commerce Bill
on 4 and 18 June tell us about the behaviour of the Scottish M.P.s? With
the exception of the six who abstained on the fourth, only three voted
differently on the two occasions: Sir James Campbell, who had opposed
the bill on the fourth, was absent on the 18th, while Sir David Dalrymple
and Sir Patrick Johnston, absent on the fourth, opposed the bill on the
18th. The significant switch in voting was performed by the six abstainers
of the fourth who supported the Court on the later vote. The explanation
may well lie in the fact that five of the six were Jacobites (Erskine,
Hamilton, Houston, Lockhart and Paterson), and the Pretender had sent
instructions (dated 29 May/8 June, which would have arrived in England
shortly after the 4 June vote) to support the Court in Parliament.[128]
Baillie's only general comment on the voting was that 'all merchants of
our countrey members of the house both whig and tory voted against
it'.[129]

The Parliament still had a month to run, but the closing weeks of its
third session were something of an anti-climax for the Whigs after their
triumph of 18 June.[130] The Lord Treasurer, in contrast to Bolingbroke,
was as phlegmatic as ever. Lord Somers viewed the future with cautious
reserve. He realized that the defeat of the Commerce Treaty might turn
out to be the Whigs' one and only success, due to a combination of factors
which were unlikely to coincide again; 'our power', he warned his
colleagues, 'does not answer our inclinations'.[131] His prognostication
appeared to be proved right by the events of the next fortnight: the
Commons voted a 'palliative address' thanking the Queen for the benefits
of the peace treaties while the Whigs failed to prevent the voting of
£500,000 to pay off the debts on the Civil List, which the Court alleged
had been incurred before 1710.[132]

The greatest disappointment to the Junto was, perhaps, the
unwillingness of the Scots peers in the House of Lords to extend their
temporary co-operation at the time of the malt tax crisis into a permanent
political alliance. Here again Oxford's calm appraisal of the situation
earlier in the month, and his confidence that, properly handled, 'the
sixteen' could be coaxed back into their former state of dependence on the
Court, proved sounder than the more extravagant reaction of
Bolingbroke.[133] As early as 11 June the Treasurer had prudently arranged a
meeting with the disgruntled peers.[134] On the 25th he received a
deputation of Scottish peers and M.P.s at St James's Palace, and suggested

possible expedients to enable Scotland to escape part at least of the burden imposed on her by the controversial malt duties.[135] Findlater, the spokesman for the deputation, returned a guarded reply, but after a second meeting the following day the antipathy of the peers, at least, towards the Court noticeably relaxed. By early July Ralph Bridges was able to report the government's recovery of strength in the upper House: 'for last week the Wh—g grandees made an overture to the Scotch, that they would heartily joyn with them and by the first opportunity break the Union, provided they would come into their measures. But the Sc[otch] Lords refused it, and only the D[uke] of Argyle and 3 more of his Party will oppose the Court any more this Session.'[136]

The Whigs, having thereby lost the initiative in the Lords to the Court, had only one way left to them by which to maintain the momentum gained by the defeat of the Commerce Bill. This was to bring the question of the Succession at last before Parliament. For tactical reasons they chose to concentrate on a demand for the removal of the Pretender from his refuge in Lorraine, and after careful planning the 'Lorraine motions' were introduced into the Lords on 30 June and into the Commons on 1 July. The Lords' motion, introduced by Wharton, had been organized with some skill and caught the ministry off balance. It proposed an address to the Queen, begging her to use her influence with the Duke of Lorraine and with other friendly rulers to ensure that the Pretender would be offered no asylum in their territories. Oxford was wise enough to avoid being drawn into a vote, and the Whigs were sufficiently elated by their success in the debate to accept an amendment offered by Lord Paget, which thanked the Queen for the (entirely fictitious) efforts she had already made to secure the Pretender's removal.[137] In the light of all that was to happen in 1714, in the first session of the next Parliament, the bloodless success of the Lorraine motions may seem very significant. In fact, however, beyond a short-term tactical victory, they achieved very little at the time for the Whigs. The Tories, though evidently disturbed by the question of the Pretender, had contrived to evade a pitched battle and had denied the Whigs the material evidence of their uneasy consciences that would have come from dividing either House. With the dissolution of Parliament following a fortnight later, the Whigs had no immediate opportunity, at Westminster at least, to pursue the scent further.

Although the Oxford ministry, after treading dangerously for over a month and suffering one very painful fall, at length survived the parliamentary crisis of 1713, the session had held important lessons alike for the members of the government, for its supporters, for its Tory critics and for its Whig enemies. It had placed further strain on the fabric of ministerial unity, with the result that by the time Parliament rose Bolingbroke was confirmed in his decision to challenge Oxford's leadership more openly than before.[138] It had shown once again how very far from monolithic the early eighteenth-century Tory party was: and yet had not offered the Whigs any realistic hope that without numerous gains in the coming elections they would be able seriously to undermine the government in the House of Commons. The loss of the Commerce Bill had certainly been a humiliation for the administration and its loyal backers; but the issues involved had been so very special that no one believed that desertions on this scale would occur again. According to the shrewd compiler of the detailed division list for 18 June 1713 in *A Letter to a Member of the House of Commons*,[139] possibly Defoe, only 36 out of the 76 trade rebels were 'very Whimsicals indeed'. Of the rest, he commented that they were 'I hope . . . very far from lost sheep, which were hardly ever known to straggle from us but this once, and I hope never will again'.[140] Among those he listed were Sir Thomas Hanmer and several other prominent back-benchers, like Ralph Freman (Hertfordshire) and Lord Downe (Yorkshire), and there was no indication as yet that men of such calibre were likely to become committed opponents of the ministry in the last critical session of Anne's reign. As for the Junto, the session had underlined once again how far their hopes of salvation were bound up with the balance of power in the House of Lords, and how tantalizingly short they still were of tipping that balance decisively in their favour. On the other hand, the hostility to the ministry revealed in recent weeks by the Earls of Abingdon and Anglesey was the most promising shift in the situation there since December 1711. What the Junto needed next was a sustained campaign less opportunistic than the struggle over the malt tax and the Union had been, and certainly less dependent on the uncertain favour of the Scots.

One thing the 1713 session had shown very clearly was the strength and the weakness of the Scots in the British Parliament. In both Houses the representatives of North Britain formed an important bloc, with the 16 representative peers clearly the more important in view of the shakier Court majority in the upper House. Sufficiently aroused, and acting together, they had the capacity to inflict embarrassment on the government in the Commons and defeat in the Lords. The causes which agitated the Scots were nearly always domestic, and between the Union in 1707 and 1713 several such causes had arisen, the cumulative effect of which was the outburst of anti-Union feeling in May and June of 1713. The weakness of the Scots lay in their inherent inability to work together for long as a group. Divided by party, religion, clan, dynastic loyalty and economic interests they were rarely able to overcome these differences. The summer of 1713 was the closest they came to succeeding. Even here the Scottish M.P.s remained partly at odds with each other, but in the Lords 'the sixteen' did achieve a temporary cohesion. The fissiparousness of the Scots was, of course, invaluable to the ministry in restricting the political damage that might be caused by Scottish discontent. And as far as the representative peers were concerned, the government held a trump card whenever there was a general election in the offing. Influencing the elections of the Scottish M.P.s was difficult for the ministry, and at the general election in the autumn of 1713 the Whigs were to triumph in Scotland as a result both of the malt tax issue and growing fear of the Jacobites. The management of the peers' election was a different matter.

The relatively small electorate was open to various forms of pressure, and from 1710 onwards the government's 'list' for 'the sixteen' was invariably returned. Lord Ilay was to find to his cost that his opposition to the ministry over the malt tax in 1713 led to his being dropped from the list at the autumn election and to his consequent non-election.[141] One lesson the Oxford ministry (and subsequent ministries) did learn from the troubles of 1713 was the need for more assiduous management of the Scots. It cannot have been a coincidence that the post of Secretary of State for Scotland, which had lapsed on the death of Queensberry in July 1711, was revived for Lord Mar in September 1713.[142]

APPENDIX: *The voting of Scottish M.P.s on the French Commerce Treaty Bill, 4 and 18 June 1713*

The two division lists reproduced below, showing how the 45 Scottish M.P.s voted on the French Commerce Treaty Bill at the second reading on 4 June, and at the engrossment stage on 18 June, at which the bill was rejected, are from the papers of George Baillie (Mellerstain Papers, Series 1, Bundle 343). The two lists are in Baillie's hand and there is no reason to doubt that they were drawn up by him at, or shortly after, the two divisions. The list for 4 June (which is the only list known for this Commons division)[143] is set out in the form of four sections: those 'for committing the bill' (10), those 'against commitment' (15), those who 'went out' (6), and those who were 'absent' (14). The second list for 18 June is set out in three sections: 'Against engrossing the Bill' (16), 'For engrossing' (16), and those 'Absent' (13). There is a complete division list for the division on 18 June, 'An Exact List of those who voted for and against Engrossing', appended to *A Letter from a Member of the House of Commons Relating to the Bill of Commerce, with a True Copy of the Bill*, printed by J. Baker in 1713. It gives 187 names for the bill; 196 against it, of which 120 are marked 'W' for Whig and 36 'Wh' for 'whimisical', to distinguish them from the Tories (unmarked) who voted against the Court. Two other variants of this list were printed in 1713,[144] but the one printed in 'A Letter from a Member' is probably the more accurate as the figures for the vote correspond exactly with those given in the *Commons' Journals*, plus two tellers each side.[145] In fact, this list has been described as 'the most reliable division list to be published during Anne's reign'.[146] There are three differences between this printed list and Baillie's recording of the vote of 18 June. The M.P. for Dumfries Burghs is given as John Hutton, who in fact died in December 1712, and was replaced at a by-election by Sir William Johnstone (correctly given by Baillie). The printed list gives Alexander Reid as absent, whereas Baillie records him as 'pro', and Baillie records the Hon. John Stewart as 'con' while the printed list gives him as absent. Thus the printed list has two fewer Scottish M.P.s voting than Baillie's list.

The Lists

'pro' = voted with the Court; 'con' = voted against the Court; 'a' = absent from the House; 'went out' = at the House but left before the vote.

Names	4 June 1713	18 June 1713
Abercromby, Alexander	pro	pro
Baillie, George	con	con
Campbell, Sir James	con	a
Campbell, Hon. John	a	a
Carnegie, John	pro	pro
Cochrane, Hon. William	a	a
Cockburn, John	con	con
Cumming, Sir Alexander	pro	pro
Cunningham, Henry	con	con
Dalrymple, Sir David	a	con
Douglas, Sir Alexander	a	a
Douglas, Hon. George	a	a
Dunbar, Sir James	a	a
Eliott, Sir Gilbert	con	con
Erskine, Sir Alexander (Lord Lyon)	went out	pro
Gordon, Sir William	a	a
Grant, Alexander	con	con
Hamilton, George	pro	pro
Hamilton, Sir James	went out	pro
Houston, John	went out	pro
Johnston, Sir Patrick	a	con
Johnstone, Sir William	a	a
Livingstone, William	pro	pro
Lockhart, George	went out	pro
Mackenzie, Alexander	a	a
Mackenzie, George	a	a
Mackenzie, Sir Kenneth	a	a
Malcolm, Sir John	a	a
Montgomerie, John	con	con
Munro, Robert	con	con
Murray, Alexander	con	con
Murray, Lord James	pro	pro
Murray, Hon. James	pro	pro
Oliphant, Charles	went out	pro
Oswald, James	con	con
Paterson, Sir Hugh	went out	pro
Pollock, Sir Robert	con	con

Names	4 June	18 June
Pringle, John	pro	pro
Ramsay, Sir Alexander	a	a
Reid, Alexander	pro	pro
Ross, Hon. Charles	pro	pro
Smith, Thomas	con	con
Stewart, Hon. John	con	con
Stewart, John	con	con
Yeaman, George	con	con

Notes

1 For discussions of the two crises of December 1711 see C. Jones, 'The Division that Never Was: New Evidence on the Aborted Vote of 8 December 1711 on "No Peace without Spain"', *Parliamentary History* (forthcoming), and G.S. Holmes, 'The Hamilton Affair of 1711–12: A Crisis in Anglo-Scottish Relations', *E.H.R.*, LXXVII (1962), 257–82. We should like to thank the following for allowing us to use and quote from their papers: the Duke of Atholl, the Marquess of Bute, the Marquess of Downshire, Lord Binning and Sir John Clerk of Penicuik.

2 J. Macpherson, *Original Papers; Containing the Secret History of Great Britain, from the Restoration to the Accession of the House of Hanover*, (2 vols., 1775), II, 488–9.

3 Berkshire R.O., Trumbull MSS., Alphab. LI, Thomas Bateman to Sir William Trumbull, 17 Apr.

4 *Ibid.*, Add. MS. 136/3, Ralph Bridges to Trumbull, 21 Apr.; Mellerstain Letters, (Lord Binning, Mellerstain, Berwickshire), V (unfol.), [George Baillie to his wife], 23 Apr. As early as 8 April there had been a joint meeting of Scottish M.P.s and peers to discuss 'matters of the Utmost consequence': Huntington Library, LO 9116 (Loudoun MSS)., George Lockhart to Loudoun, 7 Apr.

5 *C.J.*, XVII, 333–4. For a valuable analysis of the economic background and implications of the eighth and ninth articles of the treaty, of the economic grounds of the opposition to the bill giving effect to them and of the consequences of its defeat, see D.C. Coleman, 'Politics and Economics in the Age of Anne: The Case of the Anglo-French Trade Treaty of 1713', in *Trade, Government and Economy in Pre-Industrial England*, eds. D.C. Coleman and A.H. John (1976), pp. 187–211.

6 *C.J.*, XVI, 310, 315.

7 B.L., Add. MS. 17677 GGG, f. 164, L'Hermitage despatch, 8/19 May (hereafter cited as L'Hermitage).

8 For the proceedings on 6 May, see W. Pittis, *The History of the Third Session of the Last Parliament* (1713), pp. 92–3; Berks. R.O., Trumbull Add. MS. 136/3, R. Bridges to Trumbull, 8 May; *C.J.*, XVII, 315; L'Hermitage, 8/19 May.

9 *C.J.*, XVII, 355–8.

10 L'Hermitage (f. 177), 15/26 May.

11 For a view of the optimism of the ministry see *The Wentworth Papers*, ed. J.J. Cartwright (1883), p. 333.

12 Coleman, 'Politics and Economics in the Age of Anne', casts doubt on the validity of some of their arguments. A good contemporary account of them is in Niedersächsisches Staatsarchiv, Hannover, Cal. Br. 24 England, 113a, ff. 76, 106, Kreienberg despatch, 15/26 May 1713 (hereafter cited as Kreienberg).

13 *Ibid.* For the proceedings on 14 May, see also *Wentworth Papers*, pp. 334–6; L'Hermitage (ff. 176–7), 15/26 May; A. Boyer, *The History of the Life and Reign of Queen Anne* (1722), pp. 632–3; *C.J.*, XVII, 353; Mellerstain Letters, V, [Baillie to his wife], 14 May, postscript 16 May.

14 See H.M.C., *Polwarth MSS.*, I, 10, for George Baillie's reasons for opposing the bill at this stage (especially the threat to the Scottish fishing trade).

15 L'Hermitage, 15/26 May; Kreienberg, 15/26 May.

16 See brief accounts of Stanhope's speech in Boyer, *Anne*, p. 633, and *Wentworth Papers*, p. 335.

17 Kreienberg, 15/26 May.

18 The first petition presented directly against the treaty (as opposed to the earlier Wine Bill) came before the Commons on 25 May. It was followed on the 26th, 27th and 30th by seven more (*C.J.*, XVII, 377–9, 385–6).

19 L'Hermitage (f. 182), 19/30 May; *L.J.*, XIX, 549; Scottish R.O., GD45/14/352/18 (Dalhousie MSS.), [Lord Balmerino to Henry Maule], 28 May.

20 *Letters and Correspondence . . . of . . . Lord Visc. Bolingbroke*, ed. G. Parke (4 vols., 1798), IV, 138.

21 *Wentworth Papers*, p. 331.

22 How hard, and why, in this case, is explained in Coleman, 'Politics and Economics in the Age of Anne', 196–205.

23 *C.J.*, XVII, 386; Mellerstain Letters, V, [Baillie to his wife], 30 May.

24 *C.J.*, XVII, 391–3. On 3 June the Whigs had scored an unexpected success in the Commons over the demolition of Dunkirk: *ibid.*, 390; L'Hermitage,(f. 209), 5/16 June; Berks. R.O., Trumbull MSS., Alphab. LI, T. Bateman to Trumbull, 3 June.

25 L'Hermitage (f. 210), 5/16 June; Mellerstain Letters, V, [Baillie to his wife], 4 June.

26 *C.J.*, XVII, 402.

27 This is confirmed by L'Hermitage (f. 210) who noted on 5 June that a number of Tory M.P.s were staying away from the House in order to avoid making an unpleasant choice between the political interests of the Court and the economic interests of their own constituencies.

28 *Ibid.* A recently discovered division list showing how the Scottish M.P.s voted on 4 June is printed below in the Appendix.

29 For example, over the abolition of the Scottish Privy Council (1708); the Treasons Act (1709); the depriving the Duke of Queensberry of his right to vote in the election of Scottish representative peers (see C. Jones, 'Godolphin, the Whig Junto and the Scots: A New Lords Division List from 1709', *Scottish Historical Review*, LVIII [1979], 158–74); the Greenshields case and the Hamilton peerage case of 1711, and the Scottish Toleration and Patronage Acts of 1712.

30 *Bolingbroke Corresp.*, IV, 138; H.M.C., *Polwarth MSS.*, I, 9; Mellerstain Letters, V, [Baillie to his wife], 12 May. A series of detailed arguments against the Scottish malt tax submitted to Oxford can be found in B.L., Loan 29/218.

31 *The Lockhart Papers*, ed. A. Aufrere (2 vols., 1817), I, 416.

32 Mellerstain Letters, V, [Baillie to his wife], 19 May. Conyers was the chairman of Ways and Means.

33 Berks. R.O., Trumbull Add. MS. 136/3, R. Bridges to Trumbull, 1 June; *C.J.*, XVII, 359. According to George Baillie, 'the Whigs have dealt basely by us for they either left the house or went against us' (Mellerstain letters, V, [to his wife], 19 May).

34 Pittis, *Third Session*, p. 113; H.M.C., *Polwarth MSS.*, I, 9. For some of their names see tellers for the opposition in *C.J.*, XVII, 359–73, *passim*.

35 By 132 to 131. What most of the justly aggrieved Scots overlooked, however, was that no fewer than 12 of their own number were out of town on the day in question, and a thirteenth, William Livingston (Aberdeen Burghs) was absent from the House though in London; so that to some extent the Scots contributed to their own misfortunes. See H.M.C., *Polwarth MSS.*, I, 10, Baillie to Polwarth, 21 May.

36 Mellerstain Letters, V, [Baillie to his wife], 21 and 23 May.

37 Scottish R.O., GD45/14/352/16, [Balmerino to Maule], 12 May. It was reported that Ilay, who had gone to Scotland 'upon some concert, to feel the pulses of some upon this [the dissolution]', had 'at a public entertainment, drunk a new kind of health, even to the speedy and legal dissolution of the Union!': *The Correspondence of the Rev. Robert Wodrow*, ed. T. M'Crie (3 vols., Edinburgh, 1842–3), I, 461, [Wodrow] to J[ames] H[art], 8 June and Hart to Wodrow, 30 May.

38   We are fortunate that George Baillie, whose letters are so illuminating for this session of Parliament, also compiled a memorandum on the malt tax crisis which details the political moves of the Scots and the Whigs against the ministry from 23 May to 2 June. Though written in the third person — Baillie being referred to as Jerviswood — it is in Baillie's own hand (Mellerstain Miscellaneous Papers, 1st Series, Box 4, Item 384, 'Memorandum about the Union').

39   H.M.C., *Polwarth MSS.*, I, 12; *Lockhart Papers*, I, 422; Scottish R.O., GD18/3150/3 (Clerk of Penicuik MSS.), Pringle to John Clerk, 6 June.

40   There was a meeting of the Scottish peers arranged by Lord Mar at Ilay's lodgings an hour before the joint meeting where they were 'all very unanimous and zealous to agree to the Commons proposal' (GD45/14/352/17, [Balmerino to Maule], 26 May; Huntington Library, LO 8868, Mar to Loudoun, 25 May).

41   Mellerstain 'Memorandum'; Mellerstain Letters, V, [Baillie to his wife], 28 May, in which the M.P. confessed his despair: 'I mean whither the Union is broke or continued, both must bring ruin on Scot[land]'. Balmerino reported that 'Jerviswood was full of shifts to put it off . . . but finding not one man of his mind (some I believe there were but durst not own it) he did agree' (Scottish R.O., GD45/14/352/17, [to Maule], 26 May).

42   *Lockhart Papers*, I, 424–6; GD45/14/352/17. Bolingbroke also dined with Eglinton and Rosebery on the evening of 27 May (GD45/14/352/18, [Balmerino to Maule], 28 May). John Crookshanks, comptroller-general of the Scottish customs living in London, had told Oxford on 26 May that the Scottish M.P.s were influenced by some of the peers 'for accomplishing their private views more then the publick good, and when they are satisfyed, the Clamour for the Country ceases' (B.L., Loan 29/218).

43   *Lockhart Papers*, I, 426–9, 432–3; L'Hermitage (f. 196), 29 May/9 June; GD45/14/348/3, Sir Alexander Erskine to [Maule], [2 June] misdated 2 May; Kreienberg (f. 114), 29 May (for Anne's reaction).

44   Lockhart reported that the two brothers on 27 May did 'roar and exclaim bloodily against the Union, and seem very positive that the Whig Lords would join to dissolve if our peers would help in the meantime to slap the ministry'. He went on to hint, as did another observer, that there was personal pique behind their position: National Library of Scotland, MS. Acc. 7228/1 (Newhailes Papers), [Lockhart to ? Sir David Dalrymple], 28 May [1713]; Atholl MSS. (Duke of Atholl, Blair Castle, Blair Atholl, Perthshire), 45/11/29, John Douglas to Atholl, 13 June 1713.

45   Mellerstain 'Memorandum'; Mellerstain Letters, V, [Baillie to his wife], 28 May. Lockhart described Mar, Findlater and Loudoun as being against opposing the Court for 'they believed the Whigs would be as much against us as the Court' (N.L.S., MS. Acc. 7228/1).

46   Scottish support enabled the Whigs to uphold the right of the Quakers to vote in parliamentary elections without taking the statutory oaths (*C.J.*, XVII, 385; B.L., Loan 29/45J, newsletter, 2/13 June; cf. *Bolingbroke Corresp.*, IV, 140; GD45/14/352/18, Balmerino reported that the votes were carried 'only by 19 or there about which shows how we can cast the balance'; N.L.S., MS. Acc. 7228/1, Lockhart wrote that after the defeat the confounded Court 'fell a flattering us').

47   Mellerstain 'Memorandum'. There had been a meeting of Scottish peers on the evening of the 27th to co-ordinate their moves in the Lords the following day (GD45/14/352/18). Lockhart reported that at this meeting Kilsyth and Linlithgow were against opposing the Court (N.L.S., MS. Acc. 7228/1).

48   Berks. R.O., Neville MSS., D/EN. F23/2, [Charles Aldworth to the Duke of Northumberland, 20 May 1713]; H.M.C. *Polwarth MSS.*, I, 10–11.

49   See K. Feiling, *A History of the Tory Party* (Oxford, 1924), p.449; W.L. Mathieson, *Scotland and the Union 1695–1747* (Glasgow, 1905), pp. 293–4; G.M. Trevelyan, *England under Queen Anne* (3 vols., 1930–34), III, 241; E.L. Ellis, 'The Whig Junto' (Oxford D.Phil. thesis, 1961), pp. 770–1; and, more recently, B.W. Hill, *The Growth of Parliamentary Parties 1689–1742* (1976), p. 139.

50   L'Hermitage (f. 197), 29 May/9 June.

51   H.M.C., *Portland MSS.*, V, 292–3.

52   Berks. R.O., Trumbull MSS., 136/3, R. Bridges to Trumbull, 9 June.
53   G. Burnet, *A History of My Own Time* (6 vols., Oxford, 1833), VI, 161.
54   *Lockhart Papers*, I, 45; Mellerstain 'Memorandum'; see also Atholl MSS., 45/11/25, John Flemyng to [Atholl], 8 June 1713.
55   Scottish R.O., GD45/14/352/19, [Balmerino to Maule], 2 June. Baillie and Lord Tullibardine confirm that the motion included both the ending of the Union and the settlement of the 'Succession as it is now' (Mellerstain Letters, V, [to his wife], 2 June; Atholl MSS., 45/11/17, Marquess of Tullibardine to Atholl, 2 June). Findlater was probably chosen, despite his closeness to the Court, because as the former Lord Chancellor of Scotland he had signed the engrossed Act of Union in 1707.
56   Mellerstain Letters, V, 2 June.
57   GD45/14/352/19. This list of grievances is very similar to one drawn up by the Duke of Atholl in April 1712. See Bute (Loudoun) MSS. (Marquess of Bute, Mount Stuart House, Bute), bundle A261.
58   It was reported that when Findlater concluded his speech 'It was hard to know whither, He was for dissolving yea or nott, which made all the Court to Smile, and he was likeing after all to desert our other peers, and goe in to the Courtt until Illa pelted him back again' (Atholl MSS., 45/11/24, John Douglas to [Atholl], Edinburgh, 8 June 1713, reporting accounts of the debate from London).
59   GD45/14/352/19, postscript, 2 June. There is some evidence that not only was Findlater pressurized into making the motion against his better judgment, but that he would have regarded the dissolution as 'a great loss to Scotland': Scottish R.O., GD 248/561/48/37, 42 (Seafield MSS.), J.L[orimer] to his uncle [William Lorimer, Findlater's chamberlain], London, 13 May, John Philp to William Lorimer, Edinburgh, 8 June 1713; Atholl MSS., 45/11/19, John Flemyng to [Atholl], Edinburgh, 3 June 1713, reporting a letter from Findlater.
60   Kreienberg (ff. 120–1), 2/13 June 1713.
61   Cobbett, *Parl. Hist.*, VI, 1217.
62   *Ibid.*, 1218.
63   For a more detailed report of these exchanges, see GD45/14/352/26, [Balmerino to Maule], 23 June.
64   GD45/14/352/19. The whole debate lasted 'near five hours' (Atholl MSS., 45/11/17).
65   GD45/14/352/19; Kreienberg, 2/13 June.
66   L'Hermitage, (ff. 203–4), 2/13 June; Loan 29/45J, newsletter, 2/13 June. Pittis, *Third Session*, pp. 113–21, states that Sunderland was for dissolving the Union. This is supported by Balmerino (GD45/14/352/19), who described Sunderland as 'the only honest hot whig which I know'; by Baillie (Mellerstain 'Memorandum'), who noted that the Whigs spoke 'without opening their minds as to the dissolution except the latter [Sunderland] who declared of it'; by Sir Alexander Erskine (GD45/14/348/3), who recorded that 'my Lord Sunderland was the only on[e of the Whigs] I saw seemd inclynd frankly to the dissolution'; and by James Gray (Atholl MSS., 45/11/20), who wrote that 'non of the Whigs appeared for the dissolution of the Union except Sunderland'. Only L'Hermitage states that Sunderland qualified his support of dissolution (f. 204).
67   L'Hermitage, f. 204; GD45/14/352/19. Cobbett, *Parl. Hist.*, VI, 1219 gives Mar and Loudoun.
68   'Halifax told Mar that they would not joyn us on that [Findlater's motion]', and if the Scots insisted 'they would put a question they were sure to lose, upon which Mar stood up and said, that no man was more sincere and hearty than he for the disolution and that he thought the question as he had moved very proper, yet since he found it was misconstructed he retracted and was for a delay' (GD45/14/352/19). See also Pittis, *Third Session*, pp. 119–20.
69   Kreienberg, 2/13 June.
70   *More Culloden Papers*, ed. D. Warrand (5 vols., Inverness, 1923–30), II, 34. That the Whigs did not vote against the Union on 1 June, but for an adjournment of the issue, was first spotted by Trevelyan (*England under Queen Anne*, III, 242, n.) using Forbes's letter. Sir Alexander Erskine, an eyewitness, confirms Forbes's second-hand account: 'the Whigs desynd to have tym to consider of what proposals cold be made to them

for their satisfaction [concerning the Succession] so all our peopell went in to that to hav had the delay but they lost itt by four votes and proxes' (GD45/14/348/3, to [Maule], [2 June] misdated 2 May).

71 L'Hermitage (ff. 204–5), 2/13 June.

72 Berks. R.O., Trumbull MSS., Alphab. LI, T. Bateman to Trumbull, 1 June; Atholl MSS., 45/11/24, John Douglas to Atholl, 8 June. There was also a rumour that Atholl's proxy had been left with the Lord Treasurer and thus used against dissolution, but Atholl countered by explaining that Mar held his proxy (*ibid.*, items 24–6, 29, 30, Breadalbane to Atholl, 9, 13 June, Douglas to Atholl, 8, 13 June, John Flemyng to [Atholl], 8 June; *More Culloden Papers*, p. 35). Unfortunately no official proxy records have survived for the 1713 session.

73 Bodl., MS. Add. A. 269, f. 23, 6 June. The story of the two bishops leaving, each with a proxy, is confirmed by Baillie (Mellerstain 'Memorandum'), Balmerino (GD45/14/352/19), Sir Alexander Erskine (GD45/14/348/3), and John Douglas (Atholl MSS., 45/11/22).

74 H.M.C., *House of Lords MSS.*, new ser., X, 112; L'Hermitage, f.205; Trumbull Add. MS. 136/3, R. Bridges to Trumbull, 1 June; Mellerstain 'Memorandum'. Tullibardine reported that those who were for bringing in the bill 'after they had gone without the barr, gave it up without telling, for they found it would then be lost by a greater majority then the former vote', while another stated that only Somerset and Sunderland, of the Whigs, joined the Scots in this vote (Atholl MSS., 45/11/17, 25, Tullibardine and Flemyng to Atholl, 2, 8 June; cf. *ibid.*, item 22, Douglas to Atholl, 6 June, where the number of Whigs is put at 'but three or four').

75 GD45/14/352/19. Sir Alexander Erskine thought that the Whigs would not join in the dissolution until something was done for the security of 'the Protestant Succession in the hous of hannover, whi[ch] indeed I beliv they would have proposd to bring him over' (GD45/14/348/3). See also Atholl MSS., 45/11/24, Douglas to [Atholl], 8 June, for Ilay's strong condemnation of the Whigs' tactics over this point.

76 'All this was a concerted piece of management not without Jerv[iswood]', wrote Baillie about the Whigs' tactics over voting on 1 June, 'in order to bring over the Scots peers to joyn with them against the Court in the Trade Bill and other matters . . . [but] Jerv[iswood] believed this will have little weight with many of the Scots for tho some are satisfied that the Whigs acted a right part even for carying throw the dissolution . . . yet there are others who say the Whigs have tricked them. But this they could not know there having nothing appeared like it in the management' (Mellerstain 'Memorandum').

77 Kreienberg (f. 122), 2 June.

78 *Bolingbroke Corresp.*, IV, 140.

79 GD45/14/352/19; GD45/14/348/3. According to Baillie, only General Charles Ross and Alexander Murray were for going on (Mellerstain 'Memorandum'). Murray himself, along with Lockhart, was in favour of both peers and Commoners unanimously opposing the Court in everything. For Murray's detailed reasoning in support of this action see GD45/14/364, Murray to [Maule], 2 June.

80 GD45/14/352/20, [Balmerino to Maule], 4 June.

81 All sources agree on the size of the majority but there is disagreement on the figures themselves. Cobbett, *Parl. Hist.*, VI, 1219 has 85–83; L'Hermitage (f. 211, 5/16 June) has 76–74 (the same as the official figures recorded in the Manuscript Minutes of the House of Lords); while Thomas Bateman (Trumbull MSS., Alphab. LI, 5 June) gives 77–75.

82 Though a Scot, the Viscount of Dupplin (heir to the Earl of Kinnoull, one of 'the sixteen') sat by right of his British peerage as Baron Hay of Pedwardine (one of Oxford's dozen peers of 1711/12). He was also married to Oxford's youngest daughter, and was one of his father-in-law's chief lieutenants in the Lords. See C. Jones, ' "The Scheme Lords, the Neccessitous Lords, and the Scots Lords": The Earl of Oxford's Management and 'the Party of the Crown' in the House of Lords, 1711 to 1714', *Party and Management in Parliament 1660–1784*, ed. C. Jones (forthcoming). Baillie confirms that the vote of Dupplin was crucial to the division (Mellerstain Letters, V, [to his wife], 6 June), while Forbes (*More Culloden Papers*, p. 35) states that Wharton had two proxies.

[83]   By the rules of the House in a tied vote the negatives carry the question.
[84]   GD45/14/352/22, [Balmerino to Maule], 6 June. Baillie again confirms that Lord Home's absence helped to defeat the opposition (Mellerstain Letters, V, 6 June; see also *More Culloden Papers*, p. 35). Home, one of the poorest Scottish peers, had recently been given the post of General to the Scottish Mint worth £300 a year, so his hangover may have been diplomatic. He was to be given a royal bounty of £150 in December 1713: G. Holmes, *British Politics in the Age of Anne* (1967), p. 394; *Calendar of Treasury Books*, XXVI, 85, 519; XXVII, 464.
[85]   B.L., Loan 29/127/1, Warrington to Oxford, 10, 24 Apr. 1714. Warrington had by that time received only £1,000 of his arrears (paid December 1713) and it was in an attempt to extract the remainder that he reminded the Treasurer of 'that matter of soe great consequence barely carryed by that vote soe askt by your Lordship'. For a discussion of this incident in the context of Warrington's finances see J.V. Beckett and C. Jones, 'Financial Improvidence and Political Independence in the Early 18th Century: George Booth, 2nd Earl of Warrington', *Bulletin of the John Rylands University Library*, LXV, No 1 (1982).
[86]   Cobbett, *Parl. Hist.*, VI, 1219–20 puts this exchange into the 1 June debate, but Balmerino (GD45/14/352/22, 9 June) clearly places it in the 8 June debate on dispensing power.
[87]   GD45/14/352/24,[Balmerino to Maule], 9 June. The number of proxies available had only increased by one over the vote on 5 June (Court 19, opposition 18), despite Balmerino reporting on the 6th that 'there are expresses on all hands to the country for proxies' (GD45/14/352/22).
[88]   Berks. R.O., Trumbull Add. MS. 136/1, R. Bridges, 9 June.
[89]   GD45/14/352/24; Kreienberg (f. 135), 9/20 June.
[90]   *L.J.*, XIX, 567; GD45/14/352/24, 23, [Balmerino to Maule], 9, 11 June. Of the 19 who signed, 14 were Scottish representative peers (including Kinnoull); the others were the Duke of Argyll (who was not a representative peer, but sat by right of his English Earldom of Greenwich), the Duke of Somerset, the Earls of Sunderland and Scarbrough, and Viscount Lonsdale. The two missing representative peers were Atholl, who was in Scotland (Mar held his proxy, see n. 72 above) and Annandale.
[91]   Mellerstain Letters, V, [to his wife], 8 June.
[92]   Berks. R.O., Trumbull MSS., Alphab. LI, T. Bateman, 5 June.
[93]   B.L., Loan 29/10/3, printed in Holmes, *British Politics*, pp. 422–3.
[94]   See Holmes, 'Hamilton Affair', 257–82.
[95]   A shower of petitions descended on the Commons between 4 and 9 June (see B.L., Add. MS. 31138, f. 188), while pamphlets critical of the trade treaty circulated freely. Robert Pringle complained that the treaty 'in place of makeing of advantageous to the nation, it is made an handle of parties . . . [and] that everie bodie speaks as they effect even merchants contradicting one another' (GD18/3150/3, [to John Clerk], 6 June).
[96]   *C.J.*, XVII, 411.
[97]   L'Hermitage (f. 220), 12/23 June; A. Baldwin, *The History and Defence of the Last Parliament* (1713), p. 241.
[98]   According to Kreienberg (f. 136, 12/23 June) the offender was not Torriano but the princely Portugal merchant, James Milner. For Milner, see H.E.S. Fisher, *The Portugal Trade* (1971), p. 104.
[99]   L'Hermitage (f. 220); Pittis, *Third Session*, p. 122; Boyer, *Anne*, p. 637; Berks. R.O., Trumbull MSS., Alphab. LI, R. Bridges, 15 June; (for Aldworth's intervention) Kreienberg (f. 136), 12/23 June.
[100] See G.S. Holmes, 'The Commons' Division on "No Peace without Spain", 7 December 1711', *B.I.H.R.*, XXXII (1960), 223–33.
[101] Hanmer's public motives as expressed in his speech may have hidden a more private one of his impatience with Oxford for not pursuing a thorough enough Tory policy. It is worth remembering that Hanmer's fellow knight of the shire, Davers, had played a key role on behalf of the bill, and thus was presumably immune to any pressure from the woollen interest. In any case this pressure was not as great on Suffolk M.P.s as it appears to have been on those from the neighbouring county of Norfolk, where the manufacturing centre of Norwich and its hinterland had a very considerable influence

on county elections. On these points we should like to acknowledge the help of David Hayton of the History of Parliament.

[102] H.M.C., *Portland MSS.*, VII, 144; L'Hermitage (ff. 225–6); Kreienberg (f. 140), 16/27 June.

[103] See above, n.93.

[104] Argyll, Ilay and Balmerino.

[105] Nottingham, Guernsey, Weymouth, Berkshire (whose proxy seems to have been held by Weymouth), Carteret and Hatton (whose name appears on both lists). Thanet is the one notable absentee in this group.

[106] See Holmes, *British Politics*, pp. 281–2 and n. 283 for details of Anglesey's and Abingdon's connexions in the Commons. Two of Anglesey's followers in the Lords, Mountjoy (the former M.P. Lord Windsor) and Conway, are also noted as possible opposition recruits in Oxford's list. They had for some time past maintained a 'strict connection' with the Duke of Argyll (Macpherson, *Original Papers*, II, 495) whose breach with Oxford was now virtually complete.

[107] See H.M.C., *Portland MSS.*, VII, 143 for a comment on the formation of the Abingdon 'party' since Christmas 1712.

[108] See Macpherson, *Original Papers*, II, 495–6; Holmes, *British Politics*, pp. 278–9; D. Hayton, 'The Crisis in Ireland and the Disintegration of Queen Anne's Last Ministry', *Irish Historical Studies*, XXII (1980–1).

[109] Boyer, *Anne*, p. 638.

[110] *Bolingbroke Corresp.*, IV, 165–6; Boyer, *Anne*, p. 638; J. Oldmixon, *History of England during the Reigns of King William . . . Queen Anne, King George I* (1735), p. 520; GD45/14/352/26, [Balmerino to Maule], 26 June.

[111] See Pittis, *Third Session*, p. 128.

[112] Thomas Smith, M.P. Glasgow Burghs. The English Whigs were Sir Peter King, James Stanhope, Nathaniel Gould, William Pulteney, Richard Hampden, John Smith and Edward Wortley Montagu.

[113] Sir David Dalrymple, Lord Advocate since 1709.

[114] George Baillie.

[115] For the speech and its effect see Pittis, *Third Session*, p. 127, and Berks. R.O., Trumbull MSS., Alphab. LI, T. Bateman, 19 June.

[116] Sir Arthur Kaye, Gilfrid Lawson and Charles Cholmondeley; Robert Heysham and Paul Docminique.

[117] Francis Annesley (cousin of Anglesey) and John Aislabie respectively.

[118] For details see Appendix.

[119] The Baillie list for 18 June gives 16 Scots voting against the bill (for details see Appendix). If Baillie is more accurate than the contemporary printed list, then two fewer English M.P.s must have voted against the bill than indicated on the printed list.

[120] Dolben, a judge in Ireland, had landed at Dublin on 18 June, the day of the crucial Commons' vote, to take up his duties. He may have been unable to postpone his visit, for he appears to have favoured the bill, chairing the committee on the French Commerce Treaty and on 2 June urging Sir Justinian Isham to appear in the House on the sixth 'on the account of the trade, which has many enemies, their number being increased by the total apostacy of the Scots': Northamptonshire R.O., I.C. 2791, 4735 (Isham MSS.), Dolben to Isham, 2 June, Elizabeth Baggs to Isham, Dublin, 23 June. Thomas Strangways *sr* did not stand in the 1713 general election and died in December 1713. Stewart, Scobell and Drake all seem to have been much less active parliamentarians in the 1712 and 1713 sessions (in the case of the two former after appointment to office). Barker, for whose absence no satisfactory explanation can be found, was to be returned, almost certainly through Hanmer's influence, at Thetford in 1713, though he did not subsequently take a Hanoverian Tory line in the 1714 Parliament and appears instead to have followed Bolingbroke. We are grateful to David Hayton for this information.

[121] See above, n. 106.

[122] This was certainly true of John Ward, Peter Shakerley, Sir Roger Mostyn, Heneage Finch and William Hedges. On the other hand Sir George Warburton, Ralph Freman,

Edward Duncombe and the Earl of Barrymore were, like Hanmer himself, 'first offenders'.
[123] *Wentworth Papers*, p. 338.

[124] *The Correspondence of Jonathan Swift*, ed. H. Williams (5 vols., Oxford, 1963–5), I, 375.

[125] L'Hermitage (f. 229), 19/30 June, Kreienberg (f. 115), 23 June/1 July.

[126] B.L., Add. MS. 31138, f. 199, Burchett to Strafford, 19 June.

[127] *Viz.* John Aislabie, Heneage Finch, Sir Roger Mostyn, John Ward and Dixey Windsor.

[128] Macpherson, *Original Papers*, II, 416. We should like to thank Daniel Szechi for this information.

[129] Mellerstain Letters, VI (unfol.), [to his wife], 4 July. In contrast, three days later, Lockhart reported from Scotland 'that most of all our trading people are extremly exasperated att the Loss of the Bill of Commerce' (B.L., Loan 29/15/3, [to Oxford], 7 July).

[130] As active a parliamentarian as Lord North and Grey had left London by 26 June on his way to Newmarket thinking that 'the business of Parl[iament] seems pretty well over'. Recalled by Oxford for a probable struggle over the Civil List, he was again on his travels by 3 July, believing that 'the right will prevail without my weak succor' and leaving his proxy (B.L., Loan 29/308, North and Grey to Oxford, 26 June, 3 July; Bodl., MS. North b.2, f.17, Oxford to North and Grey, 29 June).

[131] Surrey R.O., Somers MSS., 0/2/50, [Mrs Cocks] to her brother, [end of June 1713].

[132] For the proceedings on the Civil List see Burnet, *History*, VI, 173–4; Boyer, *Anne*, pp. 639–40; *C.J.*, XVII, 441–7; *Wentworth Papers*, pp. 338–9; H.M.C., *Portland MSS.*, V, 467; L'Hermitage (f. 250), 30 June/11 July.

[133] See H.M.C., *Portland MSS.*, V, 300.

[134] Scottish R.O., GD220/5/309/1 (Montrose MSS.), Oxford to [Montrose], 11 June.

[135] L'Hermitage (f. 244), 26 June/7 July. The meeting had again been arranged by Oxford: GD45/14/352/26, [Balmerino to Maule], 23 June. For one of Oxford's suggestions — farming the malt tax — see GD45/14/352/25, [Balmerino] to Maule, 16 June. From Scotland, Lockhart later reported to Oxford 'in Generall that what your Lordship proposed for easing this countries of the Malt tax is very acceptable' (B.L., Loan 29/150/3, 7 July).

[136] Berks. R.O., Trumbull MSS., Alphab. LV, to Trumbull, n.d., but from internal evidence probably written a few days before 8 July. Cf. Atholl's letter to Oxford, 1 July, in H.M.C., *Portland MSS.*, V, 302; *Lockhart Papers*, I, 416–17 for Lockhart's lament on the lack of 'spirit' and 'courage' shown by the Scots peers in face of Oxford's blandishments.

[137] For the debate L'Hermitage (ff. 249–50), 30 June/11 July; *Wentworth Papers*, pp. 340, 342; Boyer, *Anne*, p. 640; B.L., Lansdowne MS. 1024, f. 420, White Kennett's journal.

[138] See G. Holmes, 'Harley, St. John and the Death of the Tory Party', in *Britain after the Glorious Revolution 1689–1714*, ed. G. Holmes (1969), p. 225.

[139] See Appendix.

[140] *A Letter to a Member*, p. 25.

[141] Ilay's brother, Argyll, was, of course, unaffected by the election — his English peerage gave him a 'safe seat'. For the election see P.W.J. Riley, *The English Ministers and Scotland 1707–27* (1964), pp. 249–50.

[142] See *ibid.*, pp. 246–7 for the appointment of Mar upon the breakdown of Oxford's system of personal management of Scottish business.

[143] See *A Register of Parliamentary Lists 1660–1761*. eds. D. Hayton and C. Jones (University of Leicester History Department Occasional Publication No. 1, 1979), p. 106.

[144] For details see R.R. Walcott, 'Division-Lists of the House of Commons, 1689–175', *B.I.H.R.*, XIV (1936–7), 35–6.

[145] The Commons figures are 194 to 185 (*C.J.*, XVII, 430).

[146] W.A. Speck, 'The House of Commons, 1701–14: A Study in Political Organisation' (Oxford, D. Phil., 1965), p. 80. In the list printed in 'A Letter from a Member', 8 M.P.s are wrongly labelled: 3 'Whimsicals' are in fact Whigs, and 5 'Whigs' are either Whimsical Tories or even Tories who in this issue voted for the first time against the Court (*ibid.*).

A BACK-BENCH MP IN THE EIGHTEENTH CENTURY: SIR JAMES LOWTHER OF WHITEHAVEN*

J.V. BECKETT

University of Nottingham

History is largely concerned with the men and women who, either famously or infamously, left a record of their success. Only recently have historians begun to delve beneath the surface in order to recreate the activities of obscure communities, and to study individuals who have passed across the stage of life virtually unnoticed. Even those who took part in the political process often remain elusive. Despite the intensive research which lies behind the pages of the *History of Parliament*[1] the entry for some M.P.s is very brief. A well documented account of an M.P.'s career in the lower House is rare, particularly if he was not a frequent speaker, or never rose to government office. So to be able to follow the activities of one such man in some detail over a 60-year period is a unique opportunity to study the role of the back-bencher. Sir James Lowther, 4th Bt. (1673–1755), landowner, industrialist and financier, first entered Parliament in 1694 when he was just 21. With only two short breaks his political career spanned the turmoil of the reigns of William III and Anne, and the relative quietude which followed under Walpole and the Pelhams. In 1748 he wrote proudly that 'I have sat longer than any in either House of Parliament now that the Duke of Somerset is dead',[2] but largely because he was not prominent in the Commons in his later years he merits only one and a half columns in the 1715–54 volumes of the *History of Parliament*.[3] Yet his career was a fascinating one, not only because of its length, but also because he changed political horses. After several years as a placeman, a windfall inheritance transformed him into an independent country Member opposed to some of the values he had earlier represented,

* I should like to express my gratitude to Professor Geoffrey Holmes who has saved me from many errors during the course of preparing this paper, and to Professor W.A. Speck for commenting on an earlier draft. The faults are my own.

and chiefly concerned with the interests of his constituents. From his voluminous correspondence many of the roles that he played as a lifelong back-bencher can be pieced together, to reveal the stresses and strains which dictated the attitude of Members of Parliament towards politics, and affected the control which could be exercised by party and faction leaders.

2

The Lowther family had been established at Lowther Hall, just south of Penrith, in Westmorland, for several centuries before a junior branch settled in the west Cumberland hamlet of Whitehaven during the 1630s. Sir John Lowther, 2nd Bt. (1642–1706), came of age in 1663, and represented Cumberland in Parliament from 1664 until 1700. His life's work was to build up the family fortunes in west Cumberland by extending his land-holdings, mining the coal deposits, and developing Whitehaven into a substantial town.[4] James, his second son, was educated at Queen's College, Oxford, and the Middle Temple. As a younger son he sought a career in his own right, and Sir John Lowther of Lowther, later first Viscount Lonsdale, head of the Lowther family, brought him into Parliament when a vacancy occurred at Carlisle in 1694.[5]

This first stage of Lowther's political career lasted until 1702, by which time he had survived four general elections and shown himself to be an able and active Member of the lower House. He was frequently to be found acting as teller, and was often appointed to committees; indeed, he claimed that Lord Carlisle's decision to support his candidature at Carlisle in 1701 was 'particularly for my great application to the business of the House'.[6] He told his father that he believed himself to be well thought of in the Commons:[7]

> I was very well satisfied before but I was unwilling to speak of it without good proof, how well I was accounted of in the House for my diligence and knowledge of the orders, and judgment I was able to make of the proceedings of the house, but by what has passed this session I am very well assured that they have as great a regard for me and look upon me as well as any unless it be the considerable speakers of the House.

However, from the time of Lord Lonsdale's death in 1700 Lowther's hold on the Carlisle seat was less sure. Lord Carlisle, who held the major political interest in the borough, offered Lowther his backing in the second election of 1701, but with the proviso that he intended to transfer his support to another candidate thereafter.[8]

This was a setback to Lowther, and it was compounded by an attack on placemen in the House of Commons. In 1696 Lord Lonsdale had secured the post of Clerk of the Delivery in the Ordnance for Lowther, and he was promoted to Storekeeper when the position fell vacant in 1701.[9] From 1692 a concerted campaign gathered steam to exclude from the lower House men who received an income from government service. Some important groups of revenue officials were barred from membership by legislation of 1694, 1700 and 1701, and the 1701 Act of Settlement provided additional fuel for the anti-placemen's fire because of the ambiguity over the wording of the place clause. This stated that 'no person who has an office or place of profit under the King or receives a pension from the Crown shall be capable of serving as a member of the House of Commons'. It was not to come into force until after the death of Queen Anne, but many people considered that it was so worded as to imply immediate effect. As a result, by the spring of 1702 almost all placemen petitioned against were excluded from the House. Thomas Stanwix, defeated at Carlisle in both of the 1701 elections, brought petitions against Lowther's return after each. Since they were well down the list for consideration neither was actually heard; even so, Lowther believed that if the second had been debated he would have been excluded. Since his position at the Ordnance became both more interesting and more demanding with the renewal of continental hostilities, he decided to resign his seat in the Commons when Parliament was dissolved in the summer of 1702. His father explained his withdrawal to the Carlisle electors as being due to pressure of London business, an excuse which must have sounded rather hollow given that he had yet to attend an election, and as late as 1700 had been unaware of the procedure to be followed in canvassing.[10] In fact, he almost lost his Ordnance place at the same time. His position was reviewed in the spring of 1702, and although he believed in June that it was secure, this was not so. Marlborough, the Captain-General, wanted him out on the grounds that he was 'of the youmer that there will be noe living with him'. He only relented in July when Lord Treasurer Godolphin expressed a rather different opinion. Lowther's patent was confirmed in August.[11]

3

In 1708 Lowther resigned his Ordnance place and returned to the House of Commons, this time for his father's old seat, Cumberland. The reason for this turn-about was a transformation in his circumstances brought about by Sir John Lowther's decision to disinherit Christopher, his eldest, alcoholic and spendthrift son. Thus when Sir John died early in 1706 James Lowther inherited the west Cumberland estates and collieries, and when his brother died childless in 1731 the baronetcy also fell to him. James Lowther's commitment to London by 1706 was such that he continued to reside in the capital for the rest of his life, visiting the estate only during the summer months, but in 1708 he decided that a change of career was necessary. He relinquished his Ordnance place, officially 'out of respect to his health and his great affairs in the country',[12] but in practice because he regarded his presence in the Commons as vital. During his earlier spell in Parliament he had always taken a keen interest when matters with a bearing on Cumberland were debated: he had argued in favour of Whitehaven being named as one of the ports open for the importation of Irish wool in 1699, and had spoken against a bill concerning tobacco imports on the grounds that it would be harmful to west Cumberland. Whilst out of the House, in 1705 and 1706, he had attempted, unsuccessfully as it transpired, to organize opposition to a bill designed to allow a pier to be built at Parton (a mile or so north of Whitehaven along the Cumberland coast). The experience taught him the importance of being in the Commons, and since by 1708 he had made up his mind to solicit legislation for extending Whitehaven harbour, he considered it necessary to resume his parliamentary career.[13]

Lowther had little affection for the hustings, as is clear from his performance at Carlisle, but he was careful to prepare his case. In April 1707 he asked his Whitehaven steward to sound out opinion as to whether or not he should stand, 'for though it is what I am not very fond of, yet if the success be probable I think myself obliged to offer my service'.[14] He also made clear his reluctance to canvass, though he did send out circular letters written in his own hand to leading local gentry. In the end no third candidate presented himself, and in a general election commonly hailed as a Whig victory, Cumberland was divided between Lowther (Whig) and Gilfrid Lawson (Tory). This split ticket continued to operate until 1722, despite serious preparations for a second Tory to stand in 1710. A similar situation arose in 1720 when Lawson decided to canvass in harness with his fellow Cumbrian Tory Sir Christopher Musgrave. They spent much of the next two years preparing for the election, whereas Lowther arrived in Cumberland only shortly before the polls were due to open. Despite spending £1,000 during the course of a hasty tour of his constituency he was not able to overhaul Lawson and Musgrave, especially as opinions of him in the county were at a low ebb because of his somewhat dubious involvement in a legal tangle over the pier at Parton. As a result he was defeated.[15] Within a year, however, he was back in the House, having been nominated for a vacancy in the Westmorland borough of Appleby. The third Viscount Lonsdale had an important interest in the constituency, and, although it cost another £1,000, Lowther was returned in a straight fight with Lord Hillsborough.[16] He returned to the county seat in 1727. Lord Carlisle threatened to nominate his son, Lord Morpeth, for Cumberland in both 1727 and 1734, but despite preparations for a contest Morpeth was not actually entered at either. When Gilfrid Lawson retired in 1734 Lowther and Lord Lonsdale jointly decided who should be asked to succeed him, and their choice fell upon Sir Joseph Pennington, a local gentleman. Such was Lowther's influence by this time that according to his cousin Sir Thomas Lowther of Holker, 'there is nobody in England has such an interest in a county as you have in Cumberland'.[17] The constituency was not contested again in Lowther's lifetime.

Largely because of the wealth which he derived from the Cumberland estate, ultimately of staggering proportions, Lowther became a figure of increasing importance in the North West. From 1714 he was a vice-admiral of Cumberland and Westmorland, a post which normally went to a peer, and in 1738 he became an alderman of Carlisle. Whenever he was physically able, Lowther spent a few days of his summer visit to

Whitehaven at the Carlisle assizes, where he generally acted as foreman of the grand jury. After the third Viscount Lonsdale died childless in 1751, Lowther was recognized as head of the family. Thus, when he called at Lowther Hall *en route* for Whitehaven in the summer of 1752, 'we had the mayor and all the aldermen of Carlisle except one at dinner there this day'.[18] Lowther also played a significant role in deciding who should sit on the commission of the peace, particularly with Lord Lonsdale's elevation to *custos rotulorum* after Lord Carlisle's death in 1738. During the 1740s the two men were more or less deciding on membership of the commission between them, their expressed intention being to strengthen the Lowther interest. Lonsdale's death forced Lowther to consider new tactics, as he explained to his steward:[19]

> My Lord Egremont [*custos*] told me he wanted to see me. He proposed to add some to the commission of the peace and if there was any I would have added they should be put in ... I could have told him if it had been proper I had provided against such a surprise by waiting upon my Lord Chancellor and getting his promise of having notice before any new commission, and I did not doubt but such as I desired would be put in as my Lord Chancellor did formerly when my Lord Carlisle opposed it.

In the last years of his life Lowther also gained a measure of influence in the two Cumberland boroughs, Carlisle and Cockermouth. It had long been accepted that Lord Carlisle had the right to nominate a candidate for one of the Carlisle seats, but rumours circulated in 1752 that the fourth earl hoped to extend his interest to the second seat. At this time, however, he was indebted to Lowther for £60,000, and his pretensions were silenced by a threat to call in the mortgage.[20] Lowther's earliest interest in Cockermouth can be dated from 1710, but it was not until 1747 that a steady policy of buying up burgages had gone far enough to enable him to mount a serious challenge to the monopoly enjoyed by the Duke of Somerset and the Lawson family. In that year he proposed his distant cousin John Stevenson for the seat, but despite considerable canvassing it became clear that the burghers were not prepared to change their representatives and no contest was provoked. Before his death, however, Lowther provided the springboard from which his successor, Sir James Lowther of Lowther, 5th Bt. (1736–1802), would launch a successful assault to close Cockermouth.[21]

4

The transformation in Lowther's personal circumstances was matched by a significant alteration of his political stance. Although a lifelong Whig, in his days as a placeman he was necessarily a Court supporter. From 1708, however, he proved to be much less reliable when Whig ministers were in office. This was not immediately anticipated; Lord Carlisle considered him to be an impeccable Whig and absolutely safe for Junto backing. Furthermore Lowther greatly respected Nicholas Lechmere, the

Junto lawyer, 'my particular friend and a very ingenious man', who sat for Cumberland and Westmorland seats as a client and nominee of the Junto's chief election manager Lord Wharton. Lowther opposed the ministerial changes in 1710 because, in Bishop Nicolson's words, he was 'very sure that the new [Tory] ministry cannot support the public credit'. The following year he supported the Whig stand of 'no peace without Spain'. He also accepted the general party line on religious toleration and the Protestant Succession.[22]

Despite such indications of general party loyalty Lowther soon began to show signs of independence, an independence born from a belief that he should stand aside from the extremism of party strife, and do all that he could to check the encroachments of the Court on parliamentary freedom of action. In effect, from 1708 he was a Country Whig; a regular attender at the House, but an infrequent contributor to debates — he admitted in 1733 that 'I dont trouble them often'[23] — and increasingly unreliable as far as party managers were concerned. The eighteenth-century Country Whig was usually a man of property with, in the words of Robert Molesworth, 'a competent, visible land estate, as a pledge to his electors that he intends to abide by them'. He was suspicious of Court influence in the Commons — hence the almost annual place bills between 1702 and 1716 — and of the executive in general; he was opposed to the growth of a standing army, and suspicious of the influence its officers commanded in Parliament; and he was concerned with the interest of the taxpayer and with moral reform.[24] Lowther shared these views, as is apparent from his political activity during nearly 50 years as a Country Member.

The first evidence to suggest that Lowther's reliability was in doubt came in 1710 when he voted against his party by supporting a place bill. A year later he backed the Tory Landed Qualification Bill, by the terms of which knights of the shire were to own property yielding a minimum of £600 a year, and borough members £300. Ironically, in view of his past career, his support or these measures reflected a belief that the Commons should be the preserve of landed men: 'there never was more need for men of estates to be chosen', he complained in 1708, 'when officers of the army and merchants of London are joustling the landed men everywhere out of their elections.' He praised General Stanhope two years later for 'promoting of bills to lessen the number of officers in the House when he himself was one, because he believed one time or another they would ruin the constitution'. Thirty years later he still believed that too many officers sat in the Commons, and he settled property on John Stevenson, a former army officer, before backing his candidature at Cockermouth in 1747.[25]

Lowther's independence did not go unnoticed. He claimed to have been 'misrepresented for my honest intentions of standing out against the violent proceedings of both parties', yet he refused to be 'tractable ... in obeying the word of command' of the Junto lords. Consequently he feared that in the 1710 election he would receive only 'cool assistance of those that are in the main of the same opinion with myself'.[26] This latter comment illustrates the width of the divide between Court and Country

Whigs in Queen Anne's reign, although this tended to shrink as the Tory threat receded in the 1720s. Whigs, whether Country or Court, remained Whigs, and if Country Whigs might be thought to have much in common with Tories they did not form a Country party as such. Such a term provides 'only a verbal blanket to cover a variety of men with few ideas or aims in common'.[27] In any case, Lowther's independence was not total, particularly whilst he still took an active interest in parliamentary proceedings. In 1715, for example, he reported from the committee of the whole House regarding the Bill for the Further Limitation of the Crown, and in 1724 he seconded the Address. In these years he may even have been considered for government office. One, probably apocryphal, story relates how Lord Sunderland considered offering Lowther a place in the Treasury, but changed his mind on discovering him to be a 'mean fellow'. Lowther himself claimed in 1717 to have been offered 'my choice of very considerable places', but if this was the case he never accepted any of them.[28]

Gradually he became less active and less reliable. He supported Walpole's move against Stanhope in 1719 by opposing the Peerage Bill, and thereafter loosely attached himself to 'the great man'. For a while he appeared to be content with the oligarchic line, soliciting places for local clients and expecting to receive his fair share of Cumberland patronage. But as his wealth grew his dependence upon patronage, although still significant, gradually became less influential in determining his political position. From 1727 he usually abstained or voted against the government in the major recorded divisions, although he and Sir Thomas Lowther were apparently persuaded by Lord Hartington to support Walpole in the division of 21 January 1742 on a motion to set up a select committee to enquire into the war. Since Walpole's majority was only three their support was vital.[29] After twice voting against the government in December 1742, once on a motion for hiring Hanoverian troops, Lowther informed his Whitehaven steward, John Spedding, that he did so because 'there is no obliging courtiers without laying aside all notions of a man's judging for himself':[30] a classic pronouncement of the country gentleman's independence. He voted in favour of Hanoverian troops in April 1746, at which point he was classed as an 'old whig'. But a year later he joined the Prince of Wales's 'new opposition'. In November 1747 he had a private audience with the Prince of 'above an hour and a half … in his dressing room alone'. He was introduced to the royal children, and, by his own account the two men conversed in 'the freest manner'. When Lowther was sufficiently ill to have a leg amputated three years later the Prince 'sent frequently and even called himself to enquire how Sir James does'. But the Prince died in 1751, from which time Lowther again acted independently. In Lord Dupplin's list, drawn up following the 1754 election, and shortly before Lowther died, he was classified as one of the 26 doubtfuls.[31]

Country attitudes are also apparent in Lowther's choice of issues on which to take a political stand. He liked to express his views on matters of a philanthropic or social nature, as in 1726 when he promoted a bill 'to hinder the poor people from being starved by people that harass and oppress them', and in 1752 when he spoke on the subject of robberies and murders.[32] In addition he saw himself as playing a watchdog role on the excesses of the business world, championing investors against the power of companies and the corruption of directors. In his opinion the latter were 'as bad as robbers', while he himself was 'looked upon to be at the head of ... the great personal estate of the nation now in the funds ... not for having a large property there so much as for having always stood up for the proprietors against the directors and stockjobbers'. He spoke in May 1732 during a debate on the Charitable Corporation, and on a number of other occasions about the 'rogueries' of companies. He even departed briefly from his own distaste for directorships in 1733, joining the board of the South Sea Company in order to champion the scheme for turning three quarters of the stock into annuities. During April and May that year he was active both in the court of directors of the Company, and in the Commons, seeing the motion take on legislative form. He claimed to 'have got great commendation and thanks in all places', but, true to form, he resigned the directorship two days after the bill passed the House of Lords.[33]

On these issues Lowther's position was clear, largely because he saw them as reflecting favourably upon himself and therefore made sure that they were appreciated in Cumberland. On other political matters, however, his letters are almost silent, with hardly a mention of foreign policy or even major issues of the day such as the Church debates of the 1730s. Only on fiscal affairs did Lowther regard himself as an authority, and he took part in the debate, both in and out of Parliament, over Henry Pelham's scheme to lower the interest paid on government debts.[34] Generally it was only when a public issue had some bearing on his constituents that Lowther recorded his opinions, as for example during the 1740s when he opposed government attempts to introduce the registration of seamen because he regarded such a move as likely to exacerbate Whitehaven's acute shortage of such labour.[35] But the area in which national and local overlap was most apparent was in taxation. Lowther's Country attitudes inevitably conditioned his support for moves to relieve the long-suffering taxpayer. At the same time he was well aware that Cumberland was one of the most lightly taxed counties in England by the eighteenth century. Generations of locally-minded M.P.s had perpetuated the image of poverty, and Lowther was no exception to this tradition. In 1732 he was much disturbed by Walpole's proposal for levying the land tax to the full value in each county rather than relying on the outdated and partial assessments drawn up during the 1690s; but his opposition to tax changes likely to prove detrimental to his constituents, though less successful, was most vehemently displayed in relation to the window tax reform of 1747: 'nobody spoke', he told Spedding, 'to show the great hardship it would be on such poor counties as ours next Scotland but myself.' He failed to prevent the bill from passing, and thereby instituting 'a most grievous tax on the poor counties'.[36]

Taxation issues were not always so clear cut, and in 1733 Lowther found himself in a dilemma. Walpole's ill-fated excise scheme was calculated to appeal to country gentlemen of Lowther's persuasion because its ultimate rationale was to abolish the land tax. At the same time, the proposed excise had serious implications for Whitehaven. Tobacco trading had become an important subsidiary commercial interest for the port by the 1730s; indeed, in the following decade Whitehaven was to stand second only to London in the quantity of its imports. Walpole's scheme threatened not only a realistic consumer tax on tobacco, but also the introduction of bonded warehouses and additional customs officials to prevent the frauds and abuses which surrounded the trade. Faced with this possibility Lowther decided that the best interests of his constituents would be served by opposing the scheme. He sent papers to Spedding to be distributed at the Cumberland quarter sessions, 'for which', according to the steward, 'every one of the justices acknowledged how vastly the country was obliged to you for informing them of the danger that threatened them'. Lowther himself claimed to have heard 'from Mr Brisco of Crofton that the county is most exceedingly alarmed at those projected excises and look on themselves highly obliged to me for giving such early notice and warning them of the danger and of taking measures to oppose them'.[37]

5

Independent he may have been, but Lowther still found it necessary to strike a delicate balance between general support for Whig administrations on principle, and in order to satisfy constituency pressure to find 'places', and Country opposition to ministerial control of the House of Commons through patronage manipulation. Sir Robert Walpole's long tenure of high office partly depended upon his ability first to bring a vast range of patronage under his personal control, and then to exploit the power which this gave him over country gentry whose local reputation depended upon their ability to obtain places for constituents. Lowther expected to receive his fair share because of the prestige that it brought him in Whitehaven and in Cumberland as a whole. As he wrote in 1736, to explain his lack of support for Walpole, 'I have no reason to sacrifice my own property and the interests of thousands to anybody, much less to one that wont give me a tidewaiter's place at Whitehaven'. He made it clear shortly after inheriting the west Cumberland estates that his steward might 'at any time recommend any of our countrymen to me', and by 1737 he believed that a combination of Sir Joseph Pennington (Cumberland's other M.P.), the Bishop of Carlisle, Sir Thomas Lowther and himself, ought to be able to acquire 'almost all the places in Cumberland for our friends'. Their cause would have been further aided, he believed, if Lord Lonsdale had displayed greater interest.[38]

For prestige reasons the most sought-after appointments were those in which the nominee actually worked in the constituency, since these provided positive signs by which electors could judge the influence of their M.P.s in London political circles. For Lowther this meant that custom-house appointments were vital; indeed, he preferred to recommend people for the excise because 'those places are much easier to get than the custom-house officers which are mightily sought for'. He complained in 1712 that 'it is a little hard that our family must have so small a share in recommending to those employments that are occasioned by their improvements when our friends are uppermost', and in 1723 he informed his steward that 'My Lord [Lonsdale] and I will insist upon filling up all [customs] vacancies with our friends'. For Lowther it was a personal insult if his candidate was not appointed to a customs post; thus in 1746 he pressed Henry Pelham 'in the strongest manner I could as that it being upon my estate I valued it more than another thing of treble the value and that the country [sic] would reflect on me if I did not get the naming to it'. Yet Lowther was well aware of a further advantage in having his candidates appointed to the customs, the inside information which could be supplied to him through having a friendly party in the service. The Treasury also appreciated such advantages, and the failure of Lowther's overtures in 1746 may have been because he did not reckon with the ad-ministration's determination to defend the bureaucratic independence of the customs in the interests of the revenue.[39]

The significance of prestige can also be demonstrated from Lowther's attitude to the important county posts of lord lieutenant and *custos rotulorum*. The death of Lord Carlisle in 1738 left the positions in both counties vacant, but as a junior member of the titled Lowther of Lowther family, Sir James could not hope to succeed Lord Carlisle in preference to Lord Lonsdale. Thus his letters to Whitehaven concentrated on stressing the important role he played in persuading Walpole to recognize Lonsdale's claims. The position changed in 1751 when Lonsdale died without leaving a direct heir. 'The whole property of the family in the two counties will be under my influence', he informed John Spedding, adding that it would also be appropriate if he were to succeed to the county positions. But for the benefit of his northern audience he exaggerated the influence that he could wield in deciding the appointment. On 11 March 1751 he wrote to the Duke of Newcastle soliciting the positions in both counties. The following day, apparently without receiving a reply, he told Spedding that 'it looks as if they would have me be lieutenant and *custos rotulorum* ... but as it is not certain it must not be whispered'. In fact, he was only offered Westmorland, Cumberland going to the Earl of Egremont who had extensive estates around Cockermouth. In disgust, Lowther turned down the post, although he claimed to have been influential in having his relation Sir William Lowther of Holker appointed.[40]

Prestige apart, Lowther had some compelling practical reasons for seeking places. One was as a means of securing land purchases. John Spedding told him in October 1742 that 'in the disposal of tidewaiter's places I shall consider how far it may have influence in getting in such lands as are convenient for you to buy', and this was the bargain struck with George Davy to secure his estate at Arrowthwaite. Political advantage was also considered. John Tiffin was active on Lowther's behalf in the 1722 election because he wanted his relation Isaac Dickinson 'to be instructed in the excise', and Lowther was prepared to try to bring this about. Tiffin also owned a number of Cockermouth burgages, and when Lowther was seriously attempting to put together a political interest in the borough during the 1730s and 1740s he periodically offered to sell them to him on condition that places were acquired for his relations. Lowther generally obtained the places but was outmanoeuvred by Tiffin who hung on to the burgages.[41]

Precisely how successful Lowther was in obtaining places cannot be documented, but he certainly found employment for constituents from time to time. With his influence Thomas Lutwidge, a local merchant, acquired the Cumberland and Westmorland farm of the wine licence in 1712. Lowther also secured places in the Leather Office in 1715 and the Post Office in 1721 and 1727, besides filling one of his own Ordnance clerkships with a Whitehaven man in 1705. In 1743 he recommended 'my cousin Fletcher's son Lowther ... to the captain of a new 70 gun ship', and ten years later he helped another of the Fletchers to an appointment as second mate on an East India vessel. Judging from the frequent references in his letters to conversations with Walpole on such matters, Lowther was active in canvassing the claims of his candidates, and his Whitehaven steward periodically sent him lists of possible nominees for recommendation, as an insurance against having no one to put forward if a post unexpectedly became vacant.[42]

6

Lowther's Country Whiggery had therefore to be tempered by the needs of his constituents, and ostensibly they were his major concern from 1708. Thus, for example, during 1740 and 1741 he steered through Parliament a private act on behalf of William Hudleston of Millom, whose financial position was such that he needed to break the entail on his estate so that he could enfranchise his customary tenants 'to raise the money to pay his debts'. In 1752 Lowther helped John Banks, co-owner of graphite mines in Borrowdale. The mines were only worked intermittently, and during the inactive periods they were easy prey for thieves. By the early 1750s the high market price of graphite (black lead) exacerbated the problem, and exemplary prosecutions by the partners failed to deter illegal digging by interlopers. The partners petitioned Parliament for legislation which would enable them to secure the mines more effectively. Lowther sat on the committee which examined the petition, and found the accusations of robbery to be true. He claimed to have been active in steering the resultant bill through the lower House.[43]

Fundamentally, however, Lowther regarded the interests of his constituents as inextricably linked with his own industrial and commercial concerns. 'I have never sought one purchase', he told John Spedding in 1728, 'but what tended to make my affairs easier at Whitehaven, my being in Parliament answers the same end.' The defence of his interests was crucial: 'all our country members are false to the interest of Whitehaven', he claimed in 1729, they 'hate Whitehaven and everything belonging to it.' Lowther was probably exaggerating the situation in order to highlight his own role, but parliamentary representation was certainly important to the early industrialists. Lowther was just one of 44 'principal industrialists' who sat in the Commons between 1715 and 1754, a group which included most of the major Tyneside coal-owners.[44] This community of interests proved useful for discussing business. When the partnership running a glasshouse at Whitehaven broke up in 1738, and the premises were left vacant, Lowther attempted to interest William Bowles in taking a lease. Bowles, described by Lowther as 'the greatest glassmaker perhaps in the world', owned extensive works in London established by his father in the later seventeenth century, and was M.P. for Bridport.[45] For many years Lowther hoped to purchase an estate at Seaton, to the north of Workington. This was rich in coal, and from 1728 he held a part-lease of a substantial colliery on the estate. During breaks in parliamentary business he took the opportunity to discuss terms with the owner, Charles Pelham of Brocklesby in Lincolnshire, M.P. for Beverley. Lowther's letters record fruitless conversations on this score in 1740 and 1742, while as late as 1753 he was complaining that although Pelham was in London he 'does not come to the house', thereby preventing further discussion.[46] Certainly the Whitehaven merchants seem to have appreciated the value of Lowther's position in Parliament, lamenting his defeat in 1722, when Spedding assured him that the merchants 'find they want you in the House'.[47]

The major interests which Lowther regarded himself as defending were the coal industry — largely financed with his own capital — its related trade to Ireland, and the subsidiary trading interests with North America, the West Indies and the Baltic. Thus in April 1739 he spoke in the House during a debate about the state of the coal trade, while the following year he was active during the passage of a bill to prevent the destruction of coal works. Wartime conditions during the 1740s affected the price of coal on the London market, and the lord mayor requested parliamentary authority to regulate it. In the absence of the north-eastern M.P.s whose constituents were most likely to be affected, Lowther 'showed the house it was a wrong method for making coals plentiful and cheap'. His apparent altruism on behalf of Tyneside coal-owners masked a fear that such legislation would be used by the lord mayor of Dublin as a precedent for controlling the price of west Cumberland coal sold in the Irish capital.[48] During his fledgling years as a Member of the House Lowther spoke in a debate during 1699 regarding the bulk importation of tobacco because the proposed new regulations were thought likely to harm the smaller ports. In 1711 he seconded a proposal to add a clause to the Lottery Bill aimed at preventing the illegal 'running' of tobacco from the Isle of Man. It failed to pass despite the fact that he 'spoke pretty fully and freely for the clause'.

At the time of the debate on ratifying the eighth and ninth articles of the French Treaty of Commerce, in June 1713, Lowther presented to the lower House a petition from the Whitehaven merchants opposing the clauses on the grounds that they would harm the woollen trade. He presented further merchant petitions in 1745 and 1748, on these occasions about the state of the Whitehaven tobacco trade, and spoke in the Commons during 1749 'in favour of the outports for laying open the trade to Hudson's Bay'. He wrote to Peter How, Whitehaven's leading merchant at this time, to apologize that indisposition prevented him from attending a debate on the tobacco trade in 1751.[49]

Such trading activities depended upon good communications, and here Lowther was particularly active. In the spring of 1709 he piloted legislation through Parliament authorizing the establishment of a board of trustees for Whitehaven harbour, and making provision for borrowing money with which to finance alterations. The act did not allow for sufficient capital to be raised for the necessary developments, and Lowther returned to Parliament for further legislation in 1712. At the first reading of this second bill, in his own words, 'Mr Manley, who is the Surveyor-General, was pleased to speak against the bill, but I answered him so fully that the House took little notice of him'. Further legislation was needed in 1740. Again Lowther took the initiative, concentrating his attentions on securing a sympathetic committee. When it finally met, he 'explained everything to their satisfaction so that no objection was made to one word that I said, everybody acquiesced'. He was also able to witness its progress through the upper House: 'I was there two hours, which I could not have been for fear of hurting my feet, but the Archbishop of Canterbury was so good as to make me sit with him on his seat almost all the time'.[50] Lowther was also interested in the small feed harbour at Parton. Although he had opposed the construction of a pier in 1705 and 1706 he soon came to appreciate its usefulness. Following its destruction in a gale in 1725 he introduced a bill to facilitate rebuilding. Again he claimed to have 'explained everything to the satisfaction of the committee', and the legislation was enacted. This was a particularly coveted victory for Lowther because he was sitting at that time for Appleby, and he had to run the gauntlet of opposition from Cumberland Member Gilfrid Lawson. He was instrumental in obtaining further legislation in 1732.[51]

Road improvements affected Lowther less directly since his main concern was with coal, which was transported by pack-horses, cartways and wagonways. Even so, as a regular traveller between London and Whitehaven, and around Cumberland during his summer visits, he was not unaware of the state of the roads; indeed, he made known his willingness both to promote turnpike bills in Parliament, and also to lend one sixth of the money needed to finance such schemes — as one of the six Members of Parliament for the three Cumberland constituencies — if the other local M.P.s would join him.[52] Local merchants, concerned about the cost of transporting goods overland, were particularly interested in improvements to the roads east from Whitehaven to Penrith, to join the

London routes through Yorkshire and Lancashire, north-east through Carlisle towards Newcastle, and the north-south axis itself. None the less, the history of road schemes in this period is riddled with rancorous argument. The four main roads around Whitehaven were turnpiked according to clauses in the third Whitehaven Harbour Act of 1740, but the other projects took longer to bring about. Despite much debate,[53] only in 1750 was a second turnpike act acquired. This affected the road between Egremont, where one of the improved roads from Whitehaven ended, and Millom in the south of the county. Lowther chaired the committee which considered the bill, as well as overseeing its passage through the Commons.[54] But he was most active in 1753 following his declaration at the Carlisle assizes in 1752 that he was ready to promote road improvement schemes for any part of the region. As a result, he was partly responsible for steering six bills through the Commons during the early months of 1753, relating to the road between Carlisle and the West Riding of Yorkshire, with an extension from Penrith into Lancashire; the road between Carlisle and Workington; the road linking Penrith and Caldbeck (a village in central Cumberland); the road between Kendal and Keighley; and the road from Kendal into north Lancashire. It was hard work, but by the time that all the bills reached the statute book Lowther could claim that 'hardly any other members attend so much as I do because of these six turnpike bills'.[55] Even if this statement was spiced with the normal helping of exaggeration, Lowther's activities were remarkable for a man of nearly 80 and in poor health.

In fact, there is some evidence to suggest that Lowther became obsessed with his role to the point where it became difficult for anyone in Cumberland to obtain legislation with which he was not in full agreement. He himself had been proud of pushing through the 1725 Parton Harbour Act in the face of opposition from Gilfrid Lawson, and he was prepared to go to extraordinary lengths to dissuade people from trying to bypass him. In 1745 he was reputed to have been annoyed at the efforts of one of Cockermouth's M.P.s, Colonel John Mordaunt, to influence county affairs, and four years later he was less than pleased with the scheme to improve Maryport because the promoters more or less ignored him.[56] However, they did at least take the precaution of notifying him in advance of their intention to apply for legislation, and in so doing they may well have been benefiting from Eldred Curwen's experience in the early 1730s. In 1728 Curwen backtracked on a verbal agreement to lease Lowther all his collieries. Instead he began to work them directly, and since his estates were located in the vicinity of Workington, and, like Lowther, he depended on the Dublin market for the majority of his sales, he considered improving the harbour facilities. His relationship with Lowther had not recovered after 1728 so that his decision to solicit legislation to this end without asking for support is perhaps not surprising. In January 1731 Lowther told Spedding,[57]

> one of the clerks of the House of Commons spoke to me the other day about having an act of Parliament for Workington harbour. I told him I had heard

nothing of it, but that if such a thing was going on I presumed I should be applied to about it.

Clearly, not informing Cumberland's senior M.P. was a tactical mistake. Although improvements at Workington might have been seen as likely to increase competition, Lowther had a colliery interest at Seaton on the north bank of the river Derwent at Workington, which could well have ensured his support for the scheme. However, once it became clear that he was not to be approached, Lowther was furious, and by the time Curwen decided to go ahead with an application to Parliament at the end of 1732, he was overtly hostile. In May 1733 he told Spedding that 'it will be proper one way or other this summer entirely to confound all prospects that Mr Curwen &c may have of getting an Act of Parliament next session by proposing scheme after scheme'. Against such opposition Curwen could not continue; a voluntary agreement for collecting money towards repairs was drawn up in 1734, and efforts to obtain legislation were indefinitely postponed.[58]

7

Sir James Lowther's parliamentary career was unusual in its length, and his extraordinary energy may have made him less than typical since regular attendance at the House was not a distinctive trait of independent Members. Even so, he represents a political type, the back-bench constituency Member about whom the official records have little to say. Eight years a placeman, and for nearly 50 an independent country gentleman, Lowther was a Whig so long as Whiggery still involved a clear political stance; a steady supporter after 1708 of Country measures such as place bills (or clauses) and landed qualifications, as much during the regime of the Junto in Anne's reign, and under Walpole, as during the Tory ministry of 1710–14; yet by no means a political maverick opposed to all administrations on principle. His industrial and commercial interests, including considerable investments in government funds, naturally conditioned him to identify with the Whig cause, and to take a personal interest in matters relating to the coal and tobacco trades; indeed, from 1708 the great majority of his active political involvement was connected with such interests, either through the direct promotion of measures affecting the constituency, or by supporting legislation of a general nature which he considered to be in the best interests of both Cumberland and himself.

Despite the ferocity of party disputes in Anne's reign, Lowther was prepared to take an independent line, even at the risk of antagonizing the Whig party leaders. With the Whig flag flying high by the 1720s the situation was much easier, the major remaining problem being to reconcile such independence with constituency pressures. Responding to one request for a place in 1726, Lowther told John Spedding,[59] you may tell any of them as you see them that I have a great number of applications but am not able to procure such places unless they will engage some other that has as good or better interest than myself to join with me, every lord in the country has half a dozen soliciting him on such occasions.

In his search for jobs Lowther appears as the staunch Whig sedulously soliciting places for local clients, to avoid the embarrassment of being unable to demonstrate his political weight in the constituency. His growing local influence in Cumberland, the influence which led him to believe by 1751 that he might even be appointed to the prestigious positions of lord lieutenant and *custos rotulorum*, was a vital factor conditioning his attitude. He believed that it was necessary to demonstrate in Cumberland that his rising importance in the county was matched in London, and the clearest means of achieving this end was through acquiring places, especially customs places. To retain his independence at the same time involved walking a political tightrope between giving sufficient support to the administration to guarantee a share of places, and following the dictates of conscience in voting. Thus in 1732 he had to refuse a request to seek a place in the Salt Office because he was opposing Walpole's reintroduction of the salt tax, abolished two years earlier. From this point of view the size of Walpole's majority was a drawback; it was far better, in Lowther's opinion, for the administration to have to buy his votes with places, since this enabled the country gentleman to follow his political principles, supporting government policy when it suited him, and at the same time making the ministers more responsive to back-bench opinion.[60]

Many other Members of Parliament, particularly those country gentlemen representing county constituencies, must have experienced the same sort of local pressures; pressures which conditioned their involvement in the political process. The image of the independent country gentleman avoiding the 'rage of party' in order to judge for himself on the great issues of the day may die hard, but if Lowther's case is at all representative, these same independents had to balance their own interests, and those of their constituents, against their natural voting inclinations. Such considerations vied with those of party in determining their reactions, and in ensuring that their scope for manoeuvre was actually relatively narrow.

Notes

[1]   *The House of Commons 1715–1754*, ed. R. Sedgwick (2 vols., 1970); [hereafter cited as *HP 1715–54*] *The House of Commons 1754–1790*, eds. Sir Lewis Namier and J. Brooke (3 vols., 1964).
[2]   [Cumbria R. O., Carlisle], D/Lons/W (Lonsdale MSS.), Sir James Lowther to John Spedding, 6 Dec. 1748. Lowther's correspondence with his father from the 1690s until 1706, and with his stewards thereafter, has been preserved in this collection. From 1706 he wrote each post-day to Whitehaven (except, of course, during his summer visit to

west Cumberland), and most of these letters, together with copies of the stewards' replies, have survived. One note of caution is needed; Lowther evidently intended parts of some of his letter for public consumption, and thus they contain an element of exaggeration. Naturally enough this was most likely to occur in relation to matters thought to have a bearing on his reputation in Cumberland, such as the political roles mentioned in this paper.

3   *HP 1715–54*, II, 226–7.

4   The Lowthers' industrial and commercial interests are examined in detail in J.V. Beckett, *Coal and Tobacco: The Lowthers and the Economic Development of West Cumberland 1660–1760* (Cambridge, 1981).

5   D/Lons/W, Sir John Lowther's letterbooks, Sir John Lowther to Sir John Lowther of Lowther, 22 Sept. 1694; D/Lons/L, memoranda-books, Lord Lonsdale's letter to his son.

6   D/Lons/W, James Lowther to Sir John Lowther, 15 Nov. 1701.

7   *Ibid.*, same to same, 8 Jan. 1702.

8   *Ibid.*, same to same, 15 Nov. 1701.

9   B. L., Add. MS. 29588, f.421; 30152, ff. 24 *et seq.*; 38703, f. 28; 38707, f. 170; 38708, ff. 18, 41,161; *C. S. P. Dom.*, 1696, p. 153; *Calendar of Treasury Books*, XVI, 331; D/Lons/W, James Lowther to Sir John Lowther, 30 Jan. 1701; D/Lons/L, memoranda-books, Lord Lonsdale's letter.

10   D. Rubini, *Court and Country 1688–1702* (1967), pp. 174–7, 283; G.S. Holmes, 'The Attack on "the Influence of the Crown" 1702–16', *B.I.H.R.*, XXXIX (1966), 49–50; D/Lons/W, James Lowther to Sir John Lowther, 15, 18, 25, 27, 29 Nov., 16, 18 Dec. 1701, 3, 5, 21 Feb., 10, 12, 26 Mar. 1702; Sir John Lowther's letterbooks, Sir John Lowther to the aldermen of Carlisle, 10 Apr. 1702, to Lord Weymouth, 19 Apr. 1702, to Lady Lonsdale, 19 Apr. 1702.

11   D/Lons/W, James Lowther to Sir John Lowther, 30 Jan., 22 Feb. 1701, 19, 21, 28 May, 29 Aug., 26 Nov. 1702, 9 Jan. 1705; *The Marlborough-Godolphin Correspondence,* ed. H.L. Snyder (3 vols., Oxford, 1975), I, 80, 88, 94, 101; II, 1036, 1047, 1096.

12   Levens MSS. (Mrs O.R. Bagot, Levens Hall, Westmorland), Christopher Musgrave to James Grahme, 30 Sept. 1708.

13   D/Lons/W, James Lowther to Sir John Lowther, 15 Apr., 2 May 1699, 27 Oct., 10, 15 Nov., 6, 27 Dec. 1705, to William Gilpin, 12 Apr., 20 Sept., 30 Oct. 1707.

14   D/Lons/W, James Lowther to William Gilpin, 12 Apr. 1707.

15   D/Lons/W, John Spedding to James Lowther, 18, 25, 29 Oct. 1710, Lowther to Spedding, 1 June 1721, 13 Jan. 1722 and subsequent letters to 28 Feb. 1722; Box 'Letters to Sir John Lowther 1698–1705', Jane Lowther to James Lowther, 10 Sept. 1720; Cashbook 1720–2; *HP 1715–54*, I, 221.

16   D/Lons/L, Checklist 16, James Lowther to Lord Lonsdale, 13 May 1722; Appleby election papers; D/Lons/W, James Lowther to John Spedding, 4, 11, 13 Apr., 30 May 1723, 23 Jan., 17, 19 Nov. 1724.

17   D/Lons/W, James Lowther to John Spedding, 29 June 1727, 27, 29 Nov., 1 Dec. 1733, 5 Jan., 9, 13 Apr. 1734, Spedding to Lowther, 28 June, 2 July 1727; Misc. Corresp. bundle 37, Sir Thomas Lowther to Sir James Lowther, 6 June 1734; H. M. C., *Carlisle MSS.*, p. 127.

18   D/Lons/W, Misc. Corresp. bundle 27a, Robert Lowther to James Lowther, 21 Dec. 1714, 8 Jan. 1715; bundle 45, Sir James Lowther to John Spedding, 11 Aug. 1738, 21 July 1752; Cumbria R.O., D/Pen (Pennington MSS.), Agents' Corresp., Joseph Herbert to Sir John Pennington, 8 May 1751.

19   D/Lons/W, Sir James Lowther to John Spedding, 24 Dec. 1751. See also the letter of 16 July 1737.

20   *Ibid.*, same to same, 4 Jan. 1752.

21   J.V. Beckett, 'The Making of a Pocket Borough: Cockermouth 1722–56', *Journal of British Studies*, XX, No. 1 (1980), pp. 140–57.

22   'Bishop Nicolson's Diaries: Part VI', ed. R.G. Collingwood,*Transactions of the Cumberland and Westmorland Antiquarian and Archaeological Soc.*, new ser., XXXV (1935), 140; 'Bishop Nicolson's Diaries: Part IV', ed. H. Ware, *ibid.*, new ser., IV (1904), 49–51, 56; *HP 1715–54*, II, 226–7; D/Lons/L, Lord Carlisle to [Lord Wharton], 13 Dec [1707]; D/Lons/W, James Lowther to William Gilpin, 5 Sept. 1710.

23 D/Lons/W, Sir James Lowther to John Spedding, 5 Apr. 1733.
24 G. Holmes, *British Politics in the Age of Anne* (1967), pp. 121–9; W.A. Speck, *Stability and Strife: England 1714–1760* (1977), pp. 5–6; G. Holmes and W.A. Speck, *The Divided Society* (1967), p. 138.
25 Collingwood, 'Bishop Nicolson's Diaries', p. 142; D/Lons/W, James Lowther to William Gilpin, 12 Feb. 1708, 7 Oct. 1710, to John Spedding, 11 Oct. 1739.
26 D/Lons/W, James Lowther to William Gilpin, 8 June 1710.
27 B.W. Hill, *The Growth of Parliamentary Parties 1689–1742* (1976), pp. 147–8.
28 *C.J.*, XVIII, 200; *The Parliamentary Diary of Sir Edward Knatchbull 1722–30*, ed. A.N. Newman (Camden Soc., 3rd ser., XCIV, 1963), p. 25; Lord Edmond Fitzmaurice, *Life of William, Earl of Shelburne* (3 vols., 1875–6), I, 34–5; D/Lons/W, James Lowther to William Gilpin, 25 July 1717.
29 D/Lons/W, Sir James Lowther to John Spedding, 15 Jan. 1736; *HP 1715–54*, II, 226–7; J.B. Owen, *The Rise of the Pelhams* (1957), pp. 30–1.
30 D/Lons/W, Sir James Lowther to John Spedding, 23 Dec. 1742. The government decision in December 1742 to finance 16,000 Hanoverian troops, as part of Carteret's plan for a composite army in Europe to defend the Low Countries, was a particularly controversial one. It was in this debate that William Pitt made his notorious reference to Hanover as 'a despicable electorate': Speck, *Stability and Strife*, p. 243.
31 D/Lons/W, Sir James Lowther to John Spedding, 29 Nov. 1746, 11 Aug. 1750; D/Lons/L, Checklist 16/39, Frederick, Prince of Wales to Lady Middlesex, n.d.; *HP 1715–54*, II, 226. The Prince of Wales had about 40 supporters when he established the 'new opposition', but his hopes rested on manipulating borough elections at the election due in 1748, in order to give himself a viable party. His efforts were forestalled when George II dissolved Parliament a year early, in the summer of 1747, but Lowther's efforts to promote John Stevenson's candidature at Cockermouth may well have been associated with this plan. See Speck, *Stability and Strife*, p. 252; A.N. Newman, 'Leicester House Politics, 1748–51', *E.H.R.*, LXXVI (1961), 577–89; and Beckett, 'Making of a Pocket Borough'.
32 D/Lons/W, James Lowther to John Spedding, 10 Mar. 1726, 14 Apr. 1752.
33 *Ibid.*, same to same, 6 Jan, 27 May, 3 June 1732; H.M.C., *Egmont Diary*, I, 275. For Lowther's activities with the South Sea Company see his letters to Spedding for March 1732, and between February and June 1733, and B. L. Add. MSS. 25544–5; *C.J.*, XXII, 129, 164–5; J.G. Sperling, 'The Division of 25 May 1711 on an Amendment to the South Sea Bill: A Note on the Reality of Parties in the Age of Anne', *Historical Journal*, IV (1961), 191–202.
34 D/Lons/W, Sir James Lowther to John Spedding, 9 Dec. 1749, 4 Jan. 1750.
35 *Ibid.*, same to same, 19 Feb., 13, 15 Mar. 1740, 3 Mar. 1741, 5 Apr. 1744.
36 Holmes, *British Politics*, pp. 125–6; W.R. Ward, *The English Land Tax in the Eighteenth Century* (Oxford, 1953), pp. 71–2; D/Lons/W, Sir James Lowther to John Spedding, 21 Mar. 1732, 20 Jan., 3 Feb. 1747.
37 Speck, *Stability and Strife*, p. 213. On the general background to the scheme see P. Langford, *The Excise Crisis* (Oxford, 1975); D/Lons/W, Sir James Lowther to John Spedding, 4 Jan., 5 Apr. 1733, Spedding to Lowther, 12 Jan. 1733; *C.J.*, XXII, 104.
38 H.T. Dickinson, *Walpole and the Whig Supremacy* (1973), pp. 74 *et seq.*; D/Lons/W, James Lowther to William Gilpin, 7 Oct. 1707, to John Spedding, 15 Jan. 1736, 6 Dec. 1737.
39 D/Lons/W, James Lowther to William Gilpin, 31 Dec. 1715, 25 Sept. 1712, to John Spedding, 4 June 1723, 10, 29 Apr. 1746; E.E. Hoon, *The Organization of the English Customs Systems 1696–1786* (Newton Abbot, 1968), pp. 202–4.
40 D/Lons/W, Sir James Lowther to John Spedding, 6, 13, 16 May 1738, 9, 12 Mar. 1751; D/Lons/L, Checklist 16/45, E. Wilson to W. Tatham, 16 Mar. 1751; B.L., Add. MS. 32724, f. 182, Sir James Lowther to the Duke of Newcastle, 11 Mar. 1751.
41 D/Lons/W, James Lowther to John Spedding, 19 Jan. 1723, 11 June 1743, 30 Dec. 1746, 7 May 1747, Spedding to Lowther, 10 Apr. 1721, 24 Oct. 1742, 5 Apr. 1745.
42 D/Lons/W, James Lowther to Sir John Lowther, 5 July 1705, to William Gilpin, 29 May 1712, 27 Aug. 1715, 14 Mar. 1718, to John Spedding, 22 Apr. 1721, 28 Jan. 1727, 3 June 1742, 6 Sept. 1743, 4 Jan. 1753, Spedding to Lowther, 6 Jan. 1744.
43 D/Lons/W, Sir James Lowther to John Spedding, 4 Dec. 1740, 13 Jan. 1741, 11 Feb.

1752; *C.J.*, XXVI, 339, 364, 369, 517.

44 D/Lons/W, James Lowther to John Spedding, 4 May 1728, 14 May 1729; *HP 1715–54*, I, 150–1. On the importance of parliamentary influence see M.W. McCahill, 'Peers, Patronage and the Industrial Revolution', *Jnl. British Studies*, XVI (1976), 84–107.

45 D/Lons/W, Sir James Lowther to John Spedding, 23 Nov. 1738; *HP 1715–1754*, I, 480.

46 D/Lons/W, Sir James Lowther to John Spedding, 11 Dec. 1739, 19 Apr., 27 Nov. 1740, 30 Mar. 1742, 3 May 1753.

47 D/Lons/W, John Spedding to James Lowther, 12 Dec. 1722. Lowther also derived personal benefits from being an M.P. For example, Members could send all letters free of charge during a parliamentary session, and for 40 days before it commenced and after it ended. This was a boon to Lowther who wrote every post-day to Whitehaven. Yet he was an extremely wealthy man, and it speaks volumes for his parsimonious outlook on life that he could write to Henry Newman, secretary of the Society for the Promotion of Christian Knowledge, and a close personal friend, in April 1734, asking that rather than forward any letters to him in Whitehaven he should retain them 'in his hands until the election is over and franking comes in again': S.P.C.K., Holy Trinity Church, Marylebone Road, London, CR1/17/12634, Sir James Lowther to Henry Newman, 27 Apr. 1734. See also K.L. Ellis, *The Post Office in the Eighteenth Century* (1958), pp. 38–43.

48 D/Lons/W, Sir James Lowther to John Spedding, 14 Apr., 22 Sept. 1739, 27 Mar. 1740. In addition, Lowther did what he could to oppose legislation affecting the coal trade passed in the Irish Parliament. Poynings's Act, which remained in force until 1782, provided that legislation drafted in Ireland could be altered, without the possibility of re-amendment by the Irish Parliament, or suppressed altogether by the King and Council in London. Lowther was not slow to make any necessary appeals to the Privy Council. E.g. D/Lons/W, James Lowther to William Gilpin, 13 July 1710.

49 D/Lons/W, James Lowther to Sir John Lowther, 2 May 1699, to William Gilpin, 2 June 1711, 9 June 1713, to John Spedding, 23 Mar. 1745, 29 Dec. 1748, 27 Apr. 1749; Misc. Corresp. bundle 44, Lowther to Peter How, 18 May 1751; *C.J.*, XVI, 656, 689; XVII, 408; D.A.E. Harkness, 'The Opposition to the 8th and 9th Articles of the Commercial Treaty of Utrecht', *Scottish Historical Review*, XXI (1924), 219–26.

50 D/Lons/W, James Lowther to William Gilpin, 18 Dec. 1711, to John Spedding, 24 Jan., 12 Feb., 11 Mar., 29 Apr 1740; *C.J.*, XVI, 28, 38, 170; XVII, 6, 7, 123; XXIII, 533, 460–1, 530.

51 D/Lons/W, James Lowther to John Spedding, 2 Feb. 1725; *C.J.*, XX, 384, 390, 467; XXI, 789, 802–3, 939.

52 D/Lons/W, Sir James Lowther to John Spedding, 4 Jan. 1753.

53 *Ibid.*, same to same, 16 Dec. 1742, 13, 20 Oct. 1744, 19 Mar. 1745, 8 Oct. 1747, 18 Mar. 1749, Spedding to Lowther, 14 Oct. 1744, 1 Mar. 1745; Misc. Corresp., bundle 44, John Peile *et al.* to Sir James Lowther, 18 Mar. 1749, Lowther to Peile *et al.*, 25 Mar. 1749.

54 D/Lons/W, Sir James Lowther to John Spedding, 15 Feb, 31 Mar. 1750.

55 *Ibid.*, same to same, 20 Jan., 24, 27 Feb., 3, 6 Mar. 1753.

56 Cumbria R.O., Carlisle, D/Lec/170 (Leconfield MSS.), John Christian to Thomas Elder, 25 Mar. 1745; D/Lons/W, Sir James Lowther to John Spedding, 6 May 1749; *C.J.*, XXV, 776.

57 D/Lons/W, Sir James Lowther to John Spedding, 30 Jan. 1731.

58 *Ibid.*, same to same, 10 May 1733, 21 Mar. 1734.

59 *Ibid.*, same to same, 22 Dec. 1726.

60 *Ibid.*, same to same, 2 Mar. 1732, 23 Dec. 1742.

PARLIAMENT AND THE FIRST EAST INDIA INQUIRY, 1767

PHILIP LAWSON

Dalhousie University

Any account of the East India Company's affairs is inextricably bound up with parliamentary history. From the day of its inception in 1600 under Elizabeth I, the Company's right to exist as a trading concern depended on the grant of a charter from the state. None of these grants were made in perpetuity, the first being for 15 years and subsequent charters for similar periods. Herein lay the core of the relationship between state and Company. The Company could operate as a monopoly enterprise with all the benefits that entailed, but if it overstepped the mark trouble could ensue. When the charter came up for renewal the government had the power to insist on whatever internal changes in the Company's structure it desired. If the Company refused to comply, the charter was withheld. There were ups and downs in this relationship, especially in the first decade of the eighteenth century when the Company's monopoly was challenged, obliging Parliament to forge a new United Company. From 1709 to the end of the Seven Years War in 1763, however, relations between the Company and the state enjoyed an unparallelled period of mutual benefit and understanding. This peace was shattered by the economic implications of the Seven Years War, which in 1766 triggered off the first serious attempt by government to interfere in the financial affairs of the Company. Though the outcome was indecisive, the episode is deeply revealing not only of relations between Parliament and the Company but also of the attitudes expressed by M.P.s to chartered property rights in the eighteenth century.

'Unless you can procure a revenue of a million per annum without new taxations and oppressions on the people, there can be no salvation arise to Israel': this was the gloomy economic picture facing Britain that William Beckford presented to the Earl of Chatham in October 1766.[1] The new administration formed eight weeks earlier had inherited an anxiety with the problems of post-war public finance common to all governments in the 1760s. But it was the first to believe that the East India Company could rescue the nation's economy by providing a new source of revenue for the Exchequer. The reasons for this conviction were twofold. In the first place the Company was in a weak position to resist the ministry's advances. It was dependent for its charter and privileges on Parliament, and would not be able to retreat behind the points of principle that had balked attempts to tax the American colonists. Secondly, no one in government doubted that the Company could afford a contribution to the Exchequer. Since 1760 it had enjoyed remarkable success. Thanks in the main to the military exploits of Robert Clive, East India stock had risen to an all-time high; by September 1766 the dividend was fixed at a record 10%; and with the assumption of the *diwani* by Clive in 1765 it was estimated that the Company's revenues would be increased by some £4 million *p.a.*[2] This meteoric success raised expectations among shareholders and government servants alike, eventually proving a temptation ministers could no longer resist. The wealth of India, as Chatham put it, would be 'the redemption of a nation'.[3]

How was the Company to be forced into accepting its role as saviour? There were two options: a private agreement between government and Company in which trading concessions would be offered in return for a contribution to the Exchequer, or a parliamentary inquiry where the Company's business would be examined by M.P.s and a policy thrashed out on the floor of the House of Commons. For motives never disclosed, Chatham had always favoured the latter mode. In 1758 he attacked the Company over the high price of tea imported into England, and the following year questioned 'whether the Company's conquests and acquisitions belonged to them or the Crown'.[4] Nothing occurred in the following nine years to change his views about a parliamentary inquiry. Only a week after the new ministry had taken office, Company directors were summoned before the Privy Council 'where notice was given them that a parliamentary inquiry would be made next session into their management'.[5] It is impossible to explain this rigid adherence to proceeding through Parliament without examining Chatham's constitutional ideas on the Company's relations with the state. There was a mixture of simple prejudice and self-righteous indignation in Chatham's view of the Company's wealth. It had expanded and become rich with the help of the state, and the time had now come for the Company to repay its debt. In common with many of his contemporaries, Chatham held a misguided impression of the Company's wealth, but he did not underestimate the strength of a campaign in Parliament that promised relief for the country gentlemen from the burden of the land tax. He also shared with many Members the conservative opinion that making vast fortunes by buying and selling stock was unethical and in some way immoral. The state, as Chatham saw it, would be justified in bringing its practitioners to heel by parliamentary action. Perhaps the diarist, Horace Walpole, best summed up Chatham's attitude when he observed that private negotiations with the Company to achieve a financial settlement were not his style — 'the multiplication table did not admit of being treated in epic'.[6]

The strategy at Westminster envisaged by Chatham was to persuade Parliament that the new possessions in India belonged of right to the Crown and not the Company. Once this principle had been established Chatham hoped to conclude a private deal permitting the Company to govern their Indian possessions in return for a large payment to the state. There was nothing subtle about this plan: 'they [ministers] propose', wrote George Grenville the opposition leader, 'to take by force what they judge proper.'[7] To Chatham the inquiry was a convenient means of raiding the Company's wealth and he forced the issue in Cabinet without any pretence of reforming zeal. A moral stand was not important for there were obvious merits in labouring the point of state over Company at Westminster. Most important, ministers could exploit the growing antipathy among M.P.s towards the Company and its servants. There were two bones of contention, arising in the main from the Company's rapid financial growth and territorial expansion in the 1760s. First, a body of M.P.s, Beckford included, viewed the Company's entitlement to so vast a territory and trade monopoly with deep distrust. They believed that its privileges concealed abuses by Company servants in India, which in turn encouraged damaging speculations in East India and other stock at home. What had previously been seen as a solid investment was now regarded as a field for rich pickings by every unscrupulous jobber on the market, especially after the dividend had been put at 10% in September 1766. The remitting of fortunes to England and destruction of native institutions through private trade and illegal property deals by its employees were seen as the evil effects of a Company that had lost control over the people under its charge.[8] Thomas Walpole, the financier, summed up the feelings of many M.P.s when he told Chatham that the government might have to take control 'of that which is too unwieldy for a subordinate body of merchants'.[9] Secondly, there was antagonism in the House, felt in particular by the country gentlemen, towards the retired nabobs. They were small in number but with their immense wealth were able to find a place in English society despite supposed handicaps of birth and breeding. Robert Clive's career provides the most striking example of Company servant turned landowner and parliamentary patron, and from 1767 on he was dogged by jealous critics at Westminster determined to see his wealth and influence reduced. In fact to all those M.P.s with an axe to grind against the Company the inquiry offered an ideal forum. Their motives may have been questionable but their support proved invaluable when Chatham's plans ran into difficulty the following spring.

The inquiry was proposed to a poorly attended House on 27 November 1766, and after a lively debate on the motion 'to inquire into the state and condition of the East India Company' was approved by 129 to 76 votes.[10] The striking feature of the day's proceedings was the fact that Beckford and not a member of the Cabinet had been entrusted with steering the inquiry through the House. This was an outward sign of a rift in ministerial thinking and it was to have serious repercussions on the inquiry. Charles Townshend, the Chancellor of the Exchequer, and Henry Seymour Conway, Northern Secretary, were the ministry's leading spokesmen in the Commons but both were opposed to proceeding with the inquiry on Chatham's terms. They favoured a private agreement with the Company in which the state waived the claim to its Indian possessions in return for a payment to the Exchequer. The inquiry, in their view, was a bargaining counter that should only be employed in the last resort. This dissension was no secret to the opposition: 'nothing could be more absurd', Townshend told one of Grenville's followers in October 1766, 'than to think of taking away any of their acquisitions, or sharing the power in India between them and the Crown.'[11] It encouraged spokesmen from the two main opposition groups under Grenville and the Marquess of Rockingham to make a stand against the inquiry from the outset. In this opening debate they embarrassed ministers by questioning Beckford's role as proposer and then endorsing the line taken by Townshend and Conway towards the inquiry. 'Never ministry made a more shameful figure', wrote Edmund Burke, the then fledgling M.P. for Wendover, 'they were beat about like footballs.'[12] It was left in fact to Townshend to rescue the government from this predicament by cleverly defending the idea of plundering the Company's treasure while disclaiming 'all the offensive parts' of Beckford's motion.[13] The original proposal for the inquiry was amended to exclude 'persons concerned in the direction or administration of the said Company', and this was enough to satisfy the majority of M.P.s present.[14]

The debate was a disappointment for the opposition. Both groups felt that an opportunity to run the ministry close in the lobbies had been squandered: 'if our friends, even those in town', Grenville told the Earl of Suffolk after the division, 'had attended tolerably well we should have carried the question which we lost by 53'.[15] Such optimism when the debate began seemed well founded. Beckford was certainly the wrong person to entrust with the inquiry. His reputation as the Company's severest critic left M.P.s on all sides of the House uneasy about the government's intentions: as Walpole put it, 'men were amazed to see a machine of such magnitude intrusted to so wild a charioteer'.[16] Furthermore Grenville and the Rockinghams believed that an appeal to defend the Company's charter or property rights against the state would win widespread approval in the House. In the eighteenth–century Commons this issue consistently attracted the crucial support of independent M.P.s, and it came as no surprise to Walpole that throughout the speeches in opposition to Beckford's motion 'the violation of property was sounded high'.[17] It was a forceful case and failure of the attack was due more to motive than content. What their argument lacked was a leading opposition Member with first-hand knowledge of India who could show the inquiry to be damaging to the Company and thus of no value to the state. In his absence opposition to the inquiry appeared factious. This was especially true of the Rockinghams, who had begun the session as supporters of the ministry. Their opposition to Beckford's motion was prompted by an argument with Chatham over Lord Edgcumbe, one of the Marquess's friends recently dismissed from his post as Treasurer of the Household.[18] Burke's passionate speech against the encroachment of the state on private property was sincerely felt, but it could not override the desire to see the inquiry proceed so that the country could reap some benefit from the Company's newly acquired wealth.

These events should have given ministers heart but in practice they produced quite the opposite effect. After a meeting on 6 December to discuss the next stage of the inquiry Conway and Townshend appeared to be on the verge of resignation. Their specific objections concerned Beckford's next motion calling for Company papers to be laid before the House.[19] Such a move, they felt, would damage the Company's credit and trading position, making the chances of an amicable agreement less likely. Chatham, with the King's solid support, would hear nothing of these objections: 'I am certain I can rely on your zeal at all times to carry on my affairs', George III told Conway, 'as I have no desire but what tends to make the happiness of my people.'[20] Support for the inquiry was to become a test of loyalty to the administration in Chatham's view: 'upon the issue of Tuesday must turn the decision of the present system whether to stand or make way for another scene of political revolution.'[21] The atmosphere was momentarily tense therefore when Beckford moved for the papers on 9 December, with speculation rife as to which way the malcontents could turn. It need not have been so, for despite Conway's statement that he '*was only a passenger*' in the administration, the government carried the day by a larger majority than that of 25 November.[22] The tone of the debate was set by Beckford who made a good speech attacking abuses in India and irresponsible speculators at home. He was well supported by Townshend and Peregrine Cust (M.P. for Bishop's Castle), who underlined the point that the state was entitled to some return for the naval protection it offered the Company.[23] This put the opposition onto the defensive and prompted a spirited reply. Burke led the way with an appeal to Chatham, delivered partly on his knees in mock prayer, not to lay bare the Company's secrets to the detriment of 'that National Credit to which he owed the glories of the late War'.[24] Washing the Company's dirty linen in public, Grenville declared in support, would only be of advantage to its competitors and the nation's enemies. They both aimed to attract the votes of the independent M.P.s and to this end 'the sacredness of charters, property and public credit' was re-emphasized at length.[25] It was a vain appeal. When the opposition proposed a three-month adjournment to allow time for a private settlement between Company and state, the motion was defeated by 140 to 56 votes.[26]

The government was now firmly in the driving seat. Opposition to the inquiry had crumbled away partly because only a handful of Rockinghams entered the minority lobby but, more important, the prevailing view in the House was that 'the money is wanted and must be had, especially for the discharge of the Civil List debts'.[27] The Company responded to Parliament's overwhelming endorsement of the inquiry on 31 December, empowering its directors to seek an agreement with the government on the best terms available. As Chatham had retired to Bath for the Christmas recess the negotiations were handled by the headstrong Townshend. They did not run smoothly. On 4 January Townsend informed Chatham that there was every hope of an 'amicable and happy issue'. His leader was not impressed; Chatham did not believe the Company's terms would be adequate and held fast to his opinion that Parliament should affirm the state's right to the Indian territories before all else.[28] The only compromise he would make was to postpone the inquiry until he had actually read the Company's proposals. This procedure took over a month, and it was to be Chatham's last serious contribution to the proceedings.[29] On his return to London from Bath on 16 February he was taken ill and the Cabinet was left to plough on with his policy as best it could. The result was confusion, with Townshend and Conway actively working for a private settlement while other members of the Cabinet sought to bring the matter before Parliament in deference to Chatham's views. To make matters worse, Beckford, who was not of the Cabinet and knew little of this rift, carried on with his preparations for the inquiry. On 22 January he announced that papers to aid the inquiry would be laid before the House, but also asked for a two-week adjournment while talks between the Company and ministers continued.[30]

The only redeeming feature of this shambles was the fact that the Commons seemed unaware of the government's internal difficulties. Beckford's statement was received without surprise or comment. In the general debate that followed on the broader aspects of East India policy, however, Grenville did query the necessity of proceeding any further with the inquiry when the Company was so willing to treat with government and a settlement appeared imminent.[31] Beckford's reply is not known but it could not have satisfied Grenville for he pressed on with his line of argument. Would it not damage the delicate negotiations, he asked M.P.s, to reveal the Company's secrets in the chamber? Grenville had touched a nerve here and risked his hand further by advising that if the government still required a decision on title to the Indian territories, this ought to be settled in a court of law and not Parliament. He did not regret the gamble, for in concluding the debate Townshend openly admitted a 'difference of opinion with Lord Chatham and his deputy Alderman Beckford'.[32] Conway was no less impressed with Grenville's logic. Two days later he informed Chatham that 'the public cause has acquired considerable strength by a declaration of Mr Grenville's', and recommended they follow his suggestion about leaving the question of right to the lawyers.[33] To his dismay Grenville was unable to press home his advantage in the debate; the Rockinghams had forsaken the issue and he dared not force a division without them.

The majority of the Cabinet knew that this was really no way to proceed on a matter of such importance; but what else could they do?

Attempts were made to elicit policy statements from Chatham in January and early February, all to no avail. Parliament must decide, was as much as Chatham would say, which suggested he had no firm policy in mind. Moreover, Townshend was in control of the negotiations with the Company and forging a policy at odds with Chatham's edict of 6 January. Partly for reasons of personal gain, Townshend would have no truck with the inquiry while there was a chance of a private settlement; and no one in Cabinet had the power or will to restrain him.[34] The internal bickering continued therefore, with the Company's proposals being submitted on 6 February only to be sent back by a divided Cabinet eight days later for further explanation. The uninformed Beckford was in a hopeless position; on 6 February he had had to postpone the inquiry without notice, and on 14 February was forced to ask Shelburne, the Southern Secretary, for guidance.[35] There was no reply. Shelburne, a loyal follower of Chatham, did in fact believe the Company's proposals of 6 February could form the basis of an agreement. On 17 February, however, Chatham told Shelburne and Grafton, the First Lord, that his views were unchanged. Parliament should settle the right and the Company's offer must also be laid before the House.[36] The Cabinet were at sea, for they had already rejected the 6 February proposals. Thus ministers had no option but to instruct the hapless Beckford to seek another adjournment of the inquiry due on 20 February.

It proved an unpleasant experience. Cabinet divisions on East India policy were no longer secret and in this debate they surfaced for all M.P.s to see.[37] So enraged was Beckford at the vacillations of his colleagues that he openly 'expressed a desire to know what had passed between administration and the directors'.[38] It was bad enough that the original mover of the inquiry did not know the state of play in the negotiations but even worse that the Chancellor of the Exchequer should deliver the answer on the floor of the House. To everyone's amazement Townshend sketched the background of the exchanges between Company and government, and concluded with the new information that the explanation demanded of the directors on 14 February was due the following day. Furthermore, the two then became involved in an argument over the terms offered by the Company, which Beckford considered insolent. M.P.s on all sides of the House viewed this altercation with unease, and opposition speakers rightly questioned the sagacity of proceeding in a manner so damaging to the reputation of the Company and its stock.[39] Indeed, sensing that the mood of the Commons was hostile to the ministry, an attempt was also made to open a new line of attack on the problem of territorial rights. Two opposition lawyers, Alexander Wedderburn and Edward Thurlow, maintained that Chatham's insistence on a parliamentary declaration of right was irrelevant to achieving a settlement.[40] The Company did not claim their possessions in India, merely a guarantee, as a basis of sharing the spoils, that the government respect their charter rights. In their view, there was a limit to the power of 'the House of Commons to interfere its authority in deciding anyway about the property of individuals'; and if the government doubted this fact it should take its case to the courts.[41] Jeremiah Dyson, the government's procedural expert, quickly refuted this argument. First, he said, the conquests in India were made by the King and not the Company, and their disposal was purely a parliamentary matter. Secondly, the Company's charter was bestowed by the House and it alone had the jurisdiction over its contents. This was a creditable response but it did not paper over all the cracks in ministerial thinking. In the end Conway was relieved to finish the debate on a point of order and secure the adjournment without a division.

The government's next move passed from comedy to farce. On 3 March the Cabinet met to discuss the Company's revised proposals, sent as promised on 21 February. It proved to be a stormy meeting and Conway and Townshend soon found themselves isolated. At the end of the evening's deliberations a vote was taken to reject the offer : '8 were present, of which 6, being the Duke of Grafton, Lord Shelburne, Lord North and Lord Camden, Sir Edward Hawke and Lord Granby were for rejecting the propositions, and 2, being Conway and C. Townshend, were against it.'[42] A strategy was then evolved to drive the Company into offering terms that the majority considered adequate. It depended for its success on persuading Parliament to censure the Company's role in the negotiations with the state. The means to this end was to be a call to print papers now before the House and a further demand for all correspondence between state and Company over the past six months to be laid before Members. The rejection of the 21 February proposals was to be kept secret however, for ministers did not want to prejudice the appearance of a spontaneous decision by the House. The plan, opened by Beckford on 6 March, was an unexpected success. The opposition was strangely lethargic. The Rockinghams certainly knew of deep divisions in Cabinet thinking and it seems fair to assume that Grenville had his suspicions too.[43] The previous week they had also defeated the government in a division on the land tax, and here was an excellent opportunity to capitalize on the victory.[44] Yet the only hiccup in the day's proceedings came from a piece of stupidity by Sir Edward Hawke, First Lord of the Admiralty. After one speaker had suggested that it might be polite to wait until the present negotiations ended before examining the papers, Hawke 'acquainted the House that at a meeting of the Cabinet Council at which he was present it was determined by a majority of which he was one to reject the propositions as unadvisable'.[45] This did little for the impression of impartiality carefully constructed by earlier speakers. Fortunately for Hawke, the opposition failed to capitalize on this slip and the government survived the debate without a division being forced.[46]

The government's luck did not hold. Failure in this debate galvanized the opposition into united action against the ministry's order to print. The motives were purely tactical, aimed to embarrass the administration on the floor of the House. To avoid accusations of opportunism, however, the attack was secretly mounted in conjunction with representatives from the

Company. It proved a clever ploy. On 9 March Robert Jones (M.P. for Huntingdon) presented a petition expressing 'apprehensions that the printing the paper would be attended with ill consequences'.[47] It was fully supported by opposition speakers who sought to have the order of 6 March rescinded. Their case rested on two propositions. First, that printing the Company's secrets would be of benefit to the nation's enemies, and second, that the ministry had been prompted into this violent measure from the disunion within its own ranks. There was more than a grain of truth in these arguments and ministers found themselves in a tight spot. Townshend was absent from the debate and it was left to Conway to answer for the government.[48] In the circumstances he made a good showing. Rather than oppose the petition outright he suggested an adjournment while he consulted directors of the Company on which papers in particular they did not want printed. It was a compromise, but a timely one : in the division on the adjournment motion the government secured an uncomfortably slim majority by 180 to 147 votes.[49] Had Conway taken any other course it is likely he would have tasted defeat.

This hasty retreat marked the end of Chatham's scheme to force the Company into unconditional financial surrender. On 11 March the government acknowledged M.P.s' hostility to continuing the negotiations in this threatening manner by rescinding the order to print the Company's correspondence and accounts.[50] Chatham's plan had been ill-thought out and executed but it was the House's unforeseen antipathy to forcing the Company to the conference table that had thwarted ministerial designs.[51] The opposition, especially the Rockinghams, had been slow to realize the potential offered by this issue, and even after the withdrawal on 11 March there was an air of disbelief about the achievement. As the opposition M.P. for Hythe, Lord George Sackville, put it, 'you will say these are strange times when Administration cannot carry such important points'.[52] Nevertheless the government was not prepared to test the ground again. The next stage in this complicated negotiation with the Company, lasting until May, was conducted in private under the management of Shelburne.[53] The parliamentary inquiry continued but it was of secondary importance to the negotiations : it was to publish no report nor make any recommendations. M.P.s were aware of this, and when the committee of inquiry began reading papers referred to it on 20 March, interest and attendance fell away dramatically. There was no immediate remedy for this. East India business held the attention of M.P.s because it provided a base for sparring between the government and opposition. To follow the committee's deliberations demanded some understanding of Indian society and customs which the majority had neither the ability nor inclination to master. Knowledge of the Indian sub-continent, apparent in newspaper articles and speeches of the time, was scant and superficial. The Commons was aware of the government's financial difficulties and broadly sympathetic to the view that the Company should aid the state. More serious investigation was left to a minority of Members with a genuine concern for the future of India and its relations with Britain.

These facts notwithstanding, valuable work was done in committee. The inquiry of 1767 foreshadowed much of the ground covered in the important parliamentary investigations of the next two decades. For those M.P.s willing to attend the House in March and early April the reward was a series of unflattering revelations about the Company's financial state and its activities in India.[54] To the fore was the exaggerated prediction of the profit to be gleaned from the territories in Bengal, following Clive's victories and the assumption of the *diwani*. The Company's annual profit of about £500,000 had changed little since the 1720s but it was now hoped to enlarge this figure with income from the new acquisitions valued at £2 million. This estimate was endorsed by several witnesses, including Rous, the deputy chairman, and Jones, secretary to the Company; and yet every speaker, these two included, also presented evidence to prove how difficult it would be to fulfil this promise. The point, as Henry Vansittart observed on 27 March, was that territorial expansion brought unforeseen costs that would eat away at the profits.[55] To keep the peace Indian allies had to be bought off and allowance made for the forces defending the new frontiers. Military costs were one of several reasons why large surpluses promised by some from the Bengal revenues were unlikely to be realized. Moreover, a larger expansion of the Company's trade, which was the only practical vehicle for remitting surpluses to Britain, could not be achieved easily. The picture painted by Rous and others was of Company resources being plundered for the fortunes of its servants, leaving little surplus to promote Indian manufactures for sale in Britain. One matter that provoked little comment in 1767 was the conduct of the Company's servants towards the native population. The most common abuse to come to light in committee was the seizure of lands by Europeans in lieu of debts or other obligations. This was the area that interested observers like Walpole felt the inquiry should cover, but he fully understood the reasons why the opposition remained silent on this issue. 'Opposition was occasioned', he wrote, 'by its having appeared on examination, that the Crown would be justifiable in seizing the acquisitions of the Company, so trying were the abuses, and so little was the Company itself master of its own servants.'[56] Nothing had gone right from the beginning of the inquiry but now the examination of witnesses had laid the foundation of a case for parliamentary intervention that M.P.s would find irresistible.

The realization of this fact was a painful experience for the opposition. In two divisions, on 7 and 14 April, the government secured majorities for conducting the inquiry on its own terms. The first arose from an unexpected move by the opposition to block an adjournment of the committee after a routine debate on witnesses to be examined at the bar. It was a tactical ploy, aimed to test feeling among M.P.s about continuing the inquiry and make some show of strength before the Easter recess. The House, as usual during the inquiry, was thinly attended and the government scraped home by a mere 14 votes.[57] Encouraged by this result, Sir William Meredith, opposition Member for Liverpool, immediately gave notice that if the administration did not bring forward proposals within the week he would move to end the committee. In this set-piece debate attendance would be high and the voting was expected to be close. As Bamber Gascoyne (M.P. for Midhurst) wrote, 'Grenville and Rockingham's party join with Townshend and Conway so the division may be respectable'.[58] It was not amiss, as he saw it, to dissolve the committee when ministers were divided over its purpose and it was of no obvious use to the private negotiations with the Company. Indeed, these arguments carried much weight in the debate of 14 April, as did that of Grenville, who observed[59]

> that if these territories were adjudged not to belong to the Company they would immediately of course rest in the Crown, and took notice of the danger of trusting such an immense revenue a year to an election in the hands of the Crown who, however he might be disposed to give them to the public, might have a Minister wicked and base enough to keep the whole or part of them.

These fears about the Crown's access to Indian patronage were to pervade debates on the Company in 1772 and 1783–4, but at this stage only Grenville gave them voice. The issue had not come to a head because the government had yet to propose any legislation. The ministry intended the inquiry to continue and gave two reasons for doing so. First, in the words of De Grey, the Attorney-General, 'this case could not be properly and completely brought to an issue in any ordinary court of justice'.[60] Secondly, why terminate the committee in the middle of its deliberations? This simple but sound point of view carried the day: in the division the opposition was beaten by 213 to 157 votes.[61] The independent M.P.s were willing to give the government more time, and, as Rockingham told his wife, 'some of our friends thought the motion precipitate and divided against us'.[62] One of these friends was Lord George Sackville, an able politician and gifted speaker in the House, who was not easily misled by the rhetoric and opportunism of his opposition allies. He commented on the move to end the committee thus: 'I must say the motion was not very regular, as the examination of evidences finished but the night before', adding the interesting rider that 'Mr. Beckford desired only till the earliest day after the holidays to propose the resolutions which he said would be grounded on the evidence'.[63] Doubt has been cast on the notion that the hearings in committee would be the springboard for legislation, but Sackville believed this to be the case and events over the next month proved him correct.[64]

M.P.s could have been forgiven for believing that they had now washed their hands of the East India business. The House adjourned for the Easter recess with ministers enjoying a free hand in negotiations with the Company. By the end of the month a deal seemed imminent. On 1 May, when the committee of inquiry reconvened, Henry Crabb Boulton, a director of the Company, told M.P.s that negotiations were almost complete. Conway and Townshend also expressed 'their hopes and indeed expectation that this treaty would end in an agreement' and the committee was adjourned for six days.[65] All that remained now was for the General

Court to approve the settlement worked out by the government and Company directors. It did not oblige. On 6 May the proprietors not only rejected the proposed agreement but took the provocative step of raising the dividend to 12½%.[66] It was a premeditated move by elements within the Company eager to push up the price of stock before a final agreement with the state was reached, and the response by government was no less incisive. On 7 May the Company was ordered to lay further papers before the committee of inquiry along with an account of the proceedings in the General Court. The following day the chairman, Rous, was examined at the bar, and after hearing his statement Jeremiah Dyson gave notice of a bill to regulate the raising of dividend on East India stock.[67] In six months' hard slog this was the first piece of legislation to emerge from the committee of inquiry.

The bill was warmly received on all sides of the House. The proprietors had gone too far on 6 May: 'the indecency and insult of this proceeding raised high resentment in the House of Commons.'[68] Even the opposition leaders Grenville and Dowdeswell (M.P. for Worcestershire) tactfully expressed 'an approbation of the motion'.[69] For once ministers exploited this mood of hostility towards the Company and pushed through three further pieces of legislation under discussion by the committee of inquiry before the end of the session. Two were formed from resolutions presented to the House on 23 May.[70] There was the agreement with the Company itself. This was limited to two years' duration from 1 February 1767 and required the Company to pay the state £400,000 *p.a.* The pill was sweetened by the fact that the Company was confirmed in its territorial possession — a repudiation of Chatham's original motive for the inquiry. There was also an act allowing the Company concessions on the duty and drawback on tea. These were proposed primarily to head off objections to the duty levied on colonial tea in Townshend's American legislation.[71] The third, approved on 16 June, was an attempt to reform voting procedure within the Company by outlawing the abuse of splitting stock prior to an election.[72] Previously, possession of £500 worth of stock had been the voting qualification, allowing large shareholders to divide stock and create faggot votes right up to the time of an election. This was amended to make it necessary to have held £500 worth of stock for at least six months before an election. It was not a success: what had been done immediately before voting took place was now done six months earlier. Nevertheless all three pieces of legislation passed the House with little opposition, and the committee of inquiry appeared to be drawing to an unexpectedly triumphant close.

The only blur on the horizon was threatened opposition to the Dividend Bill. This did not transpire during the first and second readings.[73] The tide of parliamentary opinion was running so strongly against the Company that objections to the legislation required two weeks of careful preparation. The focus of the opposition attack, concerted between Grenville and the Rockinghams, was the government's proposed reduction in dividend to 10%. As Lord George Sackville explained later, two points were at issue : 'the proprietors did impertinently in voting themselves an increase of dividend whilst the bargain was settling between them and the public, but there was no illegality in it, as I conceive, and therefore the interposition of Parliament is most improper, and as it only fixed the dividend at 10 per cent till the meeting of the next session of Parliament, it by no means cures the stock jobbing.'[74] Assistance in this campaign was offered by the General Court who petitioned the House on 19 and 20 May against a reduction; and on 21 May George Dempster, a leading proprietor and opposition M.P. for Perth, requested an adjournment 'to instruct the counsel and to get some papers necessary for the purpose of showing that the Company could afford a dividend of 12½ per cent'.[75] On 25 May the committee on the Dividend Bill heard the legal case against the 10% limit, and the following day, after opposition speakers had expressed their objections to the bill, the claim for reducing the dividend was put to the vote. In a straight rejection of the charge that government was unlawfully interfering in the affairs of a private company, the opposition was defeated, by 151 to 84 votes.[76] The defection of Conway and Townshend had had no discernible effect on the outcome.[77] The attack failed for two reasons: first, many of the opposition's independent supporters had not returned to Westminster after the Easter recess; and second, Grenville and the Rockinghams had misjudged the degree of antipathy to the Company's behaviour in the House.

This vote ended Commons resistance to the government's East India legislation. Yet it was another month before ministers could relax, for the opposition continued the fight against the Dividend Bill in the Lords. This followed the pattern set in the lower House. The opposition groups concerted strategy with representatives from the Company, urged on by the expectation of running the government close in a vote.[78] On 3 June the Duke of Bedford presented a petition from the Company against regulating the dividend at 10%, and from that moment on the opposition lords worked hand in hand in committee to thwart the bill's progress. Their efforts went unrewarded, for they too were unable to surmount hostility to the Company with a series of legal niceties. There were two votes in committee and the government secured majorities in each, on 17 June by 73 to 52,[79] and on 25 June by 59 to 44 votes.[80] A week later the Dividend Bill was approved and received the royal assent.

In this manner the government's tortuous search for an agreement with the Company was completed. At its inception the idea of an accommodation between state and Company was based on nothing more than financial gain. The inquiry and Chatham's vain insistence that Parliament declare the new territories in India a possession of the Crown were the means to this end. Even the reforms, embodied in the legislation regulating voting qualifications and limitation of dividend, were incidental to this main objective. Nevertheless the inquiry left its mark. In the first place it provided Parliament with a model of procedure for dealing with the Company on future occasions. When Lord North tackled the renewal of the Company's charter in 1773 he took care not to repeat Chatham's mistakes. No less important, the issues of sovereignty and territorial rights that were to dominate relations between Company and state for the next 25 years had been given their first public airing. Members of Parliament hitherto ignorant of the problems posed by the Company's rapid expansion now had some inkling of the difficulties facing the state when it came to exercising some restraint over the Company's servants. Last, the right of Parliament to interfere in Company affairs was now established. This did not imply that future administrations could sweep away the Company's chartered rights. On the contrary the clearest message to emerge from the events of 1767 was that M.P.s would fight tooth and nail to defend the property rights of a private citizen and public companies. The right of interference was limited, and it was Edmund Burke who best explained the line drawn by the inquiry of 1767. 'We always agreed it', he said, 'to be the Province and Duty of Parliament to superintend the affairs of this Company', but superintendence did not mean a radical change in the Company's structure or relationship with the state.[81] Charter rights remained sacred for many years to come, as Fox and North found to their cost in 1783.

Notes

[1]   P.R.O., Chatham Papers, 30/8/19, f. 91. Beckford was M.P. for the City of London.
[2]   Clive himself made the original estimate in a letter to his friend and political associate George Grenville on 30 Sept. 1765: National Library of Wales, Clive MSS., 222, f. 20. The *diwani* was the grant of territorial revenues from three Indian states : Bengal, Bihar and Orissa.
[3]   *Autobiography and Political Correspondence of Augustus Henry, Third Duke of Grafton*, ed. Sir William R. Anson (1896), p.110.
[4]   Quoted in *The Life of Robert, Lord Clive: Collected from the Family Papers Communicated by the Earl of Powis*, ed. Sir John Malcolm (3 vols., 1836), II, 125.
[5]   *The Grenville Papers: Being the Correspondence of Richard Grenville, Earl Temple, K.G., and the Right Honourable George Grenville, their Friends and Contemporaries*, ed. W.J. Smith (4 vols., 1852–3), III, 312.
[6]   *Memoirs of the Reign of King George III*, ed. G.F.R. Barker (4 vols., 1894), II, 307.
[7]   Huntington Library, ST 7 (Grenville MSS., Letterbook, Vol. II) [hereafter cited as 'Grenville Letterbk.'], Grenville to Thomas Whatley, 9 Oct. 1766. I am indebted to the Trustees of the Huntington Library for permission to quote from the manuscripts.
[8]   The shortcomings of English rule in India at this time are discussed in more detail by P.J. Marshall, *Problems of Empire: Britain and India 1757–1813* (1968), pp. 58–65.
[9]   *The Correspondence of William Pitt, Earl of Chatham*, eds. W.S. Taylor and J.H. Pringle (4 vols., 1838–40), III, 62.
[10]   *C.J.*, XXXI, 25.
[11]   *Grenville Papers*, III, 334. It is worthy of note, however, that Townshend invested in East India stock and had personal reasons throughout the inquiry to oppose measures that might depress its value. See Sir Lewis Namier and J. Brooke, *Charles Townshend* (1964), pp.159–60, 167.
[12]   *The Correspondence of Edmund Burke*, ed. T.W. Copeland *et al.* (10 vols., Cambridge, 1958–78), I, 281.
[13]   *Chatham Corresp.*, III, 144, n. See also the report in B.L., Add. MS. 32980, ff. 74–5.
[14]   *C.J.*, XXXI, 25.
[15]   Grenville Letterbk., 27 Nov. 1766.

16 *Mems.*, II, 279–80.
17 *Ibid.*
18 F. O'Gorman, *The Rise of Party in England : The Rockingham Whigs 1760–82* (1975), pp. 189–92.
19 This took place on 9 Dec. 1766: *C.J.*, XXXI, 42.
20 *The Correspondence of King George III 1760–83*, ed. Sir John Fortescue (6 vols., 1927–8), I, 423.
21 *Grafton Autobiog.*, p. 110.
22 Walpole, *Mems.*, II, 289.
23 *Ibid.*, 287–8.
24 *Burke Corresp.*, I, 286.
25 Walpole, *Mems.*, II, 289.
26 *C.J.*, XXXI, 42.
27 This is taken from a summary of the events in November and December by Lord George Sackville: H.M.C., *Stopford-Sackville MSS.*, I, 117.
28 This exchange can be followed in *Chatham Corresp.*, III, 154–8.
29 Chatham rejected two offers by the Company in three weeks, the details of which can be found in Lucy S. Sutherland, *The East India Company in Eighteenth-Century Politics* (Oxford, 1952), p. 159 and J. Brooke, *The Chatham Administration 1766–8* (1956), pp. 87–92.
30 *C.J.*, XXXI, 63.
31 The account of this debate is taken from (a) Grenville's letter to the Earl of Buckinghamshire, 27 Jan. 1767: Grenville Letterbk.; (b) Horace Walpole's letter to Sir Horace Mann, 22 Jan. 1767: *Letters of Horace Walpole, Fourth Earl of Orford*, ed. Mrs Paget Toynbee (16 vols., Oxford, 1905), VII, 81 (misdated as 21 Jan. 1767).
32 Grenville Letterbk., 27 Jan. 1767.
33 *Chatham Corresp.*, III, 175.
34 Brooke, *Chatham Admin.*, pp. 90–2.
35 *C.J.*, XXXI, 139 and Sutherland, *East India Co. in 18th-Cent. Politics*, p. 161.
36 *Chatham Corresp.*, III, 214–15.
37 The account of the debate on 20 Feb. that follows is taken from three sources: (a) 'Parliamentary Diaries of Nathaniel Ryder, 1764–7', ed. P.D.G. Thomas, *Camden Miscellany XXIII* (Camden Soc., 4th ser., VII, 1969), p.332; (b) *Selections from the Family Papers Preserved at Caldwell*, ed. W. Mure (Maitland Club XXI, 3 vols., Glasgow, 1854), pt. 2, II, 107–8; (c) Walpole, *Mems.*, II, 303. Quotations are as noted.
38 'Ryder Diaries', p. 332.
39 It was a pertinent observation; once it became known that Chatham's henchman did not favour the Company's latest proposals 'stock fell 15 percent in an hour': *Caldwell Papers*, pt. 2, II, 108.
40 Wedderburn was M.P. for Ayr and Thurlow M.P. for Tamworth.
41 *Caldwell Papers*, pt. 2, II, 108.
42 'Ryder Diaries', p.334. Chatham was in London but, secluded in his apartments, refused to take part in these deliberations. His only contribution to the proceedings was an abortive attempt to replace Townshend as Chancellor of the Exchequer.
43 See, for example, Rockingham's letter to the Duke of Newcastle on 5 Mar.: B.L., Add. MS. 32980, ff. 207–8.
44 Conway was certainly not relishing the prospect of a division: *Corresp. of George III*, I, 458–9.
45 'Ryder Diaries', p. 334.
46 *C.J.*, XXXI, 207–8.
47 'Ryder Diaries', p. 335.
48 The reason for Townshend's absence is not known.
49 This is from Ryder's figure of 180–147. *C. J.*, XXXI, 211, wrongly has 140 for the minority. For confirmation see B.L., Add. MS. 32980, ff. 246–8; Walpole, *Mems.*, II, 307 and A. and H. Tayler, *Lord Fife and His Factor: Being the Correspondence of James Second Lord Fife 1729–1809* (1925), p. 40.
50 This took place after hearing statements from the chairman of the Company and his deputy: B.L., Add. MS. 32980, f. 276.

51 Grafton later heaped all the blame for this on Chatham alone : 'Lord Chatham did never open to us, or to the Cabinet in general, what was his real and fixed plan' (*Grafton Autobiog.*, p. 110).
52 H.M.C., *Stopford-Sackville MSS.*, I, 121.
53 The negotiation is explained in depth by Sutherland, *East India Co. in 18th-Cent. Politics*, pp.162–71.
54 There are two main sources for oral evidence in the East India committee of inquiry and the account that follows is taken from these: (a) B.L., Add. MS. 18469; (b) Warwickshire R.O., CR136/B2624A/8–13 (Newdegate MSS.): I am indebted to Mr Humphrey FitzRoy Newdegate for permission to quote from these manuscripts.
55 Warws. R.O., CR136/B2624A/8.
56 *Mems.*, II, 319.
57 'Ryder Diaries', p. 338 and Walpole, *Mems.*, II, 319.
58 Essex R.O., T/B 251/7 (Strutt MSS.), Vol. I. I am indebted to the Hon. Charles Strutt for permission to quote from these manuscripts.
59 'Ryder Diaries', p. 339.
60 *Ibid.*
61 *C.J.*, XXXI, 306.
62 Sheffield City Library, Wentworth Woodhouse Muniments, R[ockingham Papers] 156–14, Rockingham to Lady Rockingham, 16 Apr. 1767. I am indebted to Earl Fitzwilliam and his trustees for permission to quote from these manuscripts.
63 H.M.C., *Stopford-Sackville MSS.*, I, 122–3.
64 Sutherland, *East India Co. in 18th-Cent. Politics*, p. 108.
65 'Ryder Diaries', p. 341.
66 There is an account of this stormy debate in Walpole, *Mems.*, III, 33.
67 This was moved in the committee of the whole House on the East India Company: *C.J.*, XXXI, 348.
68 Walpole, *Mems.*, III, 16.
69 'Ryder Diaries', p. 341.
70 *C.J.*, XXXI, 382.
71 P.D.G. Thomas, *British Politics and the Stamp Act Crisis* (Oxford, 1975), p. 354.
72 *C.J.*, XXXI, 408.
73 On 11 and 12 May: *ibid.*, 352, 355.
74 H.M.C., *Stopford-Sackville MSS.*, I, 124. For an endorsement of this view see also B.L., Add. MS. 32982, ff. 248–9.
75 'Ryder Diaries', p. 349.
76 This is Ryder's figure for the division. It is in dispute, however, the result given by Charles Jenkinson to Sir James Lowther being 152–86: B.L., Add. MS. 38205, f. 174.
77 They carried only three other government supporters into the minority: *ibid.*
78 See for example the Duke of Newcastle's letter to Rockingham c. 22 May: Wentworth Woodhouse Muniments, R1–789.
79 *Corresp. of George III*, I, 490–1.
80 'Private Journal of John, Fourth Duke of Bedford ... 19 October 1766 ... to ... 28 December 1770', *Sir Henry Cavendish's Debates of the House of Commons during the Thirteenth Parliament of Great Britain*, ed. J. Wright (2 vols., 1841–3), I, 604.
81 *Burke Corresp.*, II, 385.

THE MANY FACES OF REFORM: THE REFORM BILL AND THE ELECTORATE*

JOHN A. PHILLIPS

University of California, Riverside

In one of a great many lugubrious predictions of England's fate if Parliament passed the Reform Bill proposed by Lord Grey's administration, the Duke of Wellington remarked that 'in a short time ... nothing will remain of England but the name and the soil'.[1] Conversely, a year before Grey's replacement of Wellington, the Whiggish editor and publisher of the *Maidstone Gazette*, Richard James Cutbush, commented that if reform were *not* instituted, 'we tremble for the consequences'.[2] Macaulay, in a brave statement from someone sitting for a pocket borough, Calne, gave fuller expression to the fears voiced by Cutbush when he told the Commons that if reform were not forthcoming, 'I pray to God, that none of those who concur in rejecting it may ever remember their votes with unavailing regret, amidst the wreck of laws, the confusion of ranks, the spoilation of property, and the dissolution of social order'.[3] The incendiaries at work in many counties, the widespread unrest caused by bad harvests, and the outpouring of public opinion in favour of reform in such quantity as to 'consume 2,000 sheep just for the making of parchment for reform petitions', seemed to give considerable credence to Macaulay's remarks.[4]

The subsequent debate concerning both the passage of the Reform Act and the effects of Reform has raged almost continuously, with the

* Major support for this research was provided by a University of California Regent's Faculty Fellowship and a research grant from the Committee on Research of the Academic Senate, University of California, Riverside. I am particularly indebted to the Institute of Historical Research and the University of London Computer Centre, and the Laboratory for Historical Research at the University of California, Riverside. Without the computer assistance of Dr Charles Wetherell the Northampton data would have been unavailable for analysis.

scholarly community often emulating the bitter polemics of the original protagonists. That the debate and serious disagreement should at times take on a vituperative tone is not surprising; at stake is an issue of fundamental importance to the political and social history of nineteenth-century Britain. Although the continuing controversy has been nothing if not complex, two principal areas of disagreement stand above the rest: the reasons underlying the ultimate passage of the bill and the effects of the act, whatever the intentions of Parliament. Several interpretations of the reasons behind the bill's enactment have been in conflict for more than a century. In the eyes of a moderate and relatively contented 'radical' like W.N. Molesworth, whose history of the act appeared in 1865, 'the nation ... triumphed after a desperate struggle over the most powerful aristocracy in the world, and tore from them the rights which they [the aristocracy] had not the wisdom to concede'.[5] A less radical view was quickly adopted by many, however, that pointed to the decision in a more positive and less confrontational fashion. J.R.M. Butler's famous study concluded that the Whigs intended the act as a concession to the demands of an increasingly articulate political nation, and G.M. Trevelyan agreed, pointing to the 'statesmanlike conviction' of Lord Grey, the 'wisdom of Russell', and the 'will of Durham' as the primary reasons for the bill's passage.[6] Norman Gash refined this theme further by accepting the act as a concession to the nation but also noted the intention of the Whigs to prevent even more radical, possibly revolutionary, change by disengaging the more respectable middling orders from any possible alliance with their less respectable and much less trustworthy fellows among England's working orders.[7]

The antithesis of these optimistic views of the genesis of Reform was suggested by Karl Marx a decade before the publication of Molesworth's history. In Marx's genuinely radical and *discontented* view, the Reform Act was, 'by a series of the most extraordinary tricks, frauds, and juggles ... calculated not for increasing middle-class influence, but for the exclusion of Tory and the promotion of Whig patronage'.[8] In a slightly altered format, and with the conservative landed M.P.s replacing the Whigs as the real moulders of the bill, D.C. Moore has attempted a revival of Marx's conservative retrenchment thesis with an added sociological thrust. According to Moore, 'the Bill was not a "concession" ... but an effort to impose a conservative "cure"'.[9] Neither Marx nor Moore has gained wide acceptance. As Richard Davis has observed recently, 'most historians of the period would now agree that Professor Moore ... is wrong about Whig intentions'; the concessional view of the act's passage seems to have re-emerged as a relatively solid consensus.[10] Clearly it is impossible 'to say categorically what the Whigs wanted' since considerable diversity existed within the Whig party leadership as well as among the ultimate supporters of the bill, Whig or Tory. Much of what was said by all of those concerned was conditioned by (if not determined by) the audience to which it was addressed.[11] Nevertheless, the work done by a number of scholars lends credibility to Davis's verdict and to Milton-Smith's conclusion that the Whigs' 'prime object was to satisfy demands and to make necessary concessions'.[12]

The second area of contention has not produced any such consensus and is on the whole even more complicated since the effects of the act can (and must) be measured in several ways. This discussion ignores much of the debate over topics like changes in the composition of the Commons, but even within the narrower focus of the popular impact of the bill consensus cannot be found. The range of opinions, in fact, mirrors those expressed in explanations of why the bill was passed. Predictably, many accounts of Reform have credited the bill with an immediate elevation of popular politics out of the mire of the unreformed system. D.C. Moore's revisionist thesis, on the other hand, includes a characterization of post-Reform politics as merely a continuation of older modes of behaviour, a survival of the 'politics of deference'.[13] Moore's most recent statement of this thesis is much the same as his original statement. He continues to emphasize the primacy of deference in the electorate and the continuation after 1832 of traditional modes of behaviour on the part of England's voters, old *or* new. Moore stresses the pre-eminence of the county electorates even though almost 20% of the counties remained entirely unpolled and another 60% rarely contested general elections prior to the passage of the Reform Act. Despite the relative inactivity of counties after 1832, Moore argues that 'when the continued existence of the traditionally structured deference communities and deference networks was ... threatened, steps were taken to perpetuate them and thus to perpetuate the roles and status of the traditional elites'.[14] Far from being a concession to popular opinion, the Reform Act, in Moore's view, was a successful effort to prevent the intrusion of the public into the ranks of the politically potent and the intrusion of urban voters into the sphere of county politics. As Davis has noted, 'some may suspect that Moore is also at least in part wrong about the electoral system which grew out of the Act. That, however, has yet to be proven'.[15]

One such doubter is John Cannon. Though disturbed by the quality (and quantity) of some of the evidence Moore cites (such as Moore's reference to 'all the voters' in Lowick voting Tory in 1835 when *all* referred to a grand total of four men) Cannon does not dispute Moore's contention that the public opinion expressed in 1831 was the opinion of the landed classes as a whole. He has instead challenged Moore's emphasis on the degree of urban influence in county elections before 1832. If Cannon's calculations are correct, this lynchpin of Moore's framework disappears. A more destructive critic is J.R. Fisher. While agreeing with Moore about the deferential behaviour of many of England's county voters, Fisher has challenged the adequacy of Moore's general hypothesis by pointing to the other influences affecting the choices of voters *even among the county electorates,* where Fisher admits, 'it was almost impossible to find farmers voting against the wishes of their landlords'. Ignoring as irrelevant the inaccuracy of some of Moore's extremely rare percentages (Moore offers remarkably long tables of raw numbers usually in lieu of statistical analyses), Fisher argues that if the independent electors of South Nottinghamshire were able to command one county Member until the reforms of the 1880s in one of England's most aristocratic counties, certainly independent electors cannot be so easily disregarded in other counties.[16]

Moore's argument ostensibly is limited to the county electorates and the period before the Reform Act of 1867, but it has been vastly extended both spatially and chronologically by Patrick Joyce. Rather than ending, as Moore argues, with the second Reform era as new influences such as class began to redefine voting groups, Joyce has adopted an attitude much like the one expressed in *Vanity Fair* in 1873: 'counties are naturally the appanage of the landowners and the cities of millowners and merchants.'[17] In a direct expansion of Moore's self-imposed limitations, Joyce concluded that 'in industrial Lancashire at least, for decades after 1867, class lines had not become "too sharp" and interest groups "too jumbled", nor had social and economic categories "ceased to overlap" '. In his scenario, Moore's 'politics of deference' was also an urban, post-1867 phenomenon.[18]

Rather than pursuing a test of the impact of Reform upon England's often somnolent county voters, this analysis like Joyce's assumes an urban focus, concentrating on three boroughs, Maidstone, Northampton and Lewes. Both before and after the first Reform Act, most electoral activity took place in urban settings, and the lion's share of the politically active electorate resided in towns. This assessment of voting behaviour in the Reform era employs a limited data base and cannot adequately answer many of the questions that must be posed. It does, however, reveal some of the dangers inherent in the 'deferential' thesis of reformed politics and the denigration of the changes that accompanied the Reform Act of 1832.

2

The question of the impact of the Reform Act on the nation at large can be answered in a variety of ways. Much attention, for example, has been given to the physical changes wrought in the electorate by the act, beginning with its size. Lord John Russell expected Reform to double the number of voters in the country, but Charles Seymour estimated the actual increase as approximately 50% for county and borough electorates alike.[19] John Cannon's more recent estimate would place Lord John nearer the mark than Seymour allowed; Cannon's figures suggest an 80% increase overall and perhaps a doubling of the county electorate. Even relatively minor points like this one concerning the degree of change in the qualified electorate cannot be resolved easily, though, since the size of the electorate before 1832 can be estimated only crudely. This is particularly true for the counties and for some boroughs where elections were seldom contested to the point of a poll of the voters.[20] Comparisons with the post-Reform electorate are also hampered by the varying levels of voter registration across the country and obstacles in the registers themselves including duplicate, erroneous, and incomplete registrations.[21] This aspect of the popular impact of Reform is tangential to the thrust of this analysis of voting behaviour in three borough constituencies, but in addition to pointing to the pitfalls at virtually every turn in dealing with the Reform Act, it also allows Maidstone, Northampton and Lewes to be properly placed in a relatively important context.

Whatever the change in the size of the electorate overall, Seymour was almost certainly correct in noting that in the boroughs newly enfranchised voters usually constituted a majority in reformed electorates. His estimate gave the £10 householders some 60% of the urban vote, and Cannon's figures would probably increase the new voters' percentage share. Two of the three boroughs examined here, however, proved to be exceptions to this rule. Experienced voters contributed a solid majority to Northampton's electorate after 1832 because Northampton was one of seven towns in which already enfranchised inhabitant householders were allowed to retain their votes. Northampton's electorate actually shrank steadily for a number of years after 1832 as the number of newly enfranchised £10 householders failed to offset losses among the old inhabitant householders from death, physical mobility and the like. Lewes's electorate only increased by approximately 25% in 1832; the 177 additions to the electorate (partly the product of Lewes's expanded political boundary) were outnumbered by the 690 resident scot and lot payers who had held the franchise in the unreformed system and retained it. The Maidstone electorate was expanded by approximately 25% as well, but there, unlike Lewes, the relatively small overall increase masked a fundamental change in the composition of the borough's electorate. The disfranchisement of hundreds of non-resident freemen was more than offset by the enfranchisement of a massive number of £10 householders who carried the preponderant electoral weight in the town from the beginning. Maidstone then, fell precisely into the situation described by Seymour as typical of the older 'freeman' constituencies. In Liverpool, where a similar situation left the freemen of the town in the minority, the pollbook of 1832 noted, 'the privilege [of voting] was to a great extent thrown into entirely new hands. How these new electors would act was now the question'.[22]

The question posed in this investigation remains fundamentally the same as that asked in Liverpool in 1832, but with the large number of experienced voters in Maidstone and the majorities in Lewes and Northampton the question becomes: how did the new *and* old voters act under the new system? The prolonged focus on the Reform era has not led to the formulation of a satisfactory answer to this question, no doubt partly because any discussion of the behaviour of the reformed electorate has been and is hampered by the severely maligned reputation of the *unreformed* electorate. An evaluation of the behaviour of voters after 1832 can best be accomplished by a contrast with the behaviour of voters before the act was passed; accounts of unreformed behaviour have until recently been so uniformly and overwhelmingly damning that comparisons invariably were coloured. The standard account of the unreformed system is still the 1903 work by the Porritts, and virtually any political system would be appealing in comparison to the one described by them as reeking with undiluted corruption, unmitigated coercion, and unequalled chicanery of virtually every imaginable kind.[23] The Porritts' detailed chronicle of these excesses of the unreformed system painted an image of such unrelieved vileness that only recently has any serious attention been given to the unreformed electorate.

The besmirched reputation of the unreformed voter has been restored to a semblance of virtue over the last several years; the efforts of W.A. Speck, John Money, Norma Landau and others have shown that corruption, coercion, and chicanery notwithstanding, England's voters could and occasionally did play an effective and integral part in the political processes of the nation before the passage of the Reform Act.[24] Yet even with this renewed interest in the unreformed voter, our knowledge of the unreformed system is inadequate and remains a hindrance to a fully informed discussion of the reformed electorate. Far more serious than the lack of data regarding the size of the unreformed electorate is the absence of comparative data on voter turnout, partisan behaviour at specific elections, partisan attachments over time, and other such basic topics. This analysis partially compensates for these gaps in the available data by examining, as well as the surviving data allow, the behaviour of electors in these three towns *across* the Reform era, and by focusing on towns about whose politics a good deal is known.

3

The expectations raised among many Englishmen by the passage of the Reform Bill clearly were grandiose. Cobbett felt that it would be 'the means of removing our poverty and misery and delivering our country from this mass of crime and disgrace'.[25] The 263 petitioners for reform in Lewes in 1831 were hardly less enthusiastic. They believed that 'the great distress at present existing among all the productive classes of the community ... may in great manner be attributed to the corrupt state of Representation', and expected prompt passage of the bill to alleviate these manifest problems accordingly.[26] Molesworth's 1865 account recognized how widely the bill had been misperceived by many of England's *menu peuple*, yet he felt that its effects had been tremendously beneficial: 'no doubt they [the ordinary citizens] greatly exaggerated the effects which that measure would produce, and overlooked many causes of distress which it would not remove, but still they were right in their belief that it would tend to ameliorate their condition, as the event has abundantly proved.'[27] Thirty years earlier, however, only two general elections after the act's passage, the Whig *Westminster Review* was much less sanguine about its effects. In an eloquent plea for the introduction of the secret ballot, the *Review* argued that 'as it is, the representative system is utterly defeated ... if bribery and intimidation are not effectually restrained, the Reform Bill will prove worse than a nonentity — a positive curse'.[28]

The dominant interpretation of recent years is one akin to the *Review*'s although it is worded less stridently. Partly in reaction to the regular denunciation of the unreformed electoral system, and partly in response to the standard glowing Whiggish accounts of the later nineteenth and early twentieth centuries, much emphasis has been given to continuity in popular politics after the passage of the act. Richard Davis has shown a considerable degree of continuity in voting among the electors in Aylesbury in the 1820s and 1830s generally and the elections of 1831 and 1835 specifically, but Davis's continuity, in contrast to much that has been written on this topic in recent years, is more a favourable assessment of popular politics before 1832 than it is a denunciation of continuing sins. Buckinghamshire politics contained local party activity before and after the Reform Act, yet Davis does not maintain that the links were too strong or that the political preferences of individual electors were necessarily maintained across the Reform era.[29] More typically, the emphasis on continuity in Norman Gash's magisterial studies has been largely negative. Focusing on the unbroken influence of political patrons, the many unaltered local political climates in which electoral violence and corruption still flourished, and the continuing influence of the Court in elections, Gash's careful work corrected the tendency to whitewash the post-Reform system. Undeniably, the 'post-1832 period contained many old features which it inherited from the past', and the survival of many of these can only be deemed unfortunate. Gash is careful *not* to dismiss the Reform Bill as completely ineffectual, but the benefits he attributes to the act relate primarily to party activity at the national level. When Gash focused locally, his evidence tended to minimize the impact of Reform. Thus in Berkshire, even by the mid-1840s, 'party was still only a vague and half-recognized element' in local politics that divided along other lines. More to the point, Gash reported Greville's conversation of 1 January 1835 with 'an informant', by whom he was told that Maidstone's reformed electorate was 'if possible worse than the old'. Gash went on to say 'this was not simply the after-dinner conversation of two cynical men of the world with a prejudice against the Reform Act and all that it stood for'.[30] What Gash says about these two men is certainly true in one sense; neither had a prejudice against the Reform Act. Greville's informant was none other than A.W. Robarts, Whig M.P. for Maidstone since 1818 and soon to be returned as an M.P. for the last time at the election held twelve days after the reported conversation with Greville. Robarts's relationship with his Maidstone constituents had been degenerating rather badly as a result of his absolute refusal following the passage of the Reform Act to condone or allow any form of bribery on his behalf. The important point, though, is not the obvious existence of bribery in Maidstone that apparently damaged the liberal cause after it was withdrawn, but the fact that Robarts was elected *twice* without the least reliance on bribery and in the face of wholesale bribery or attempted bribery by the Tories. Maidstone even returned *two* liberal reformers in 1832 without their paying for the privilege. Robarts refused to stand again in 1837 and lost his effort to regain his seat at the by-election in 1838 (even after his first loss was declared void due to Tory bribery). Robarts was staunchly pro-Reform, and could not be accused of prejudice against the act, but as he told Greville, he supported Reform because what he dreaded most was 'collision' i.e. revolution, what he desired most was 'quiet', and what he considered the best means of achieving this end was 'non-resistance'.[31] In short, by the time of his 1835 conversation with Greville, Robarts was a cynical, tired man who had 'grown grey in the service of Maidstone's voters'; his opinions about his constituents, valuable as they are, were undoubtedly coloured by this long association. Instead of relying solely on his opinions, or those of Cutbush (the Whig editor of the *Maidstone Gazette*), John Vine Hall (the recently converted Conservative editor of the rival *Maidstone Journal*), or even Greville, it would be beneficial to look at the behaviour of the Maidstone voters themselves, as well as the behaviour of their fellows in Northampton and Lewes.

In fact, Robarts's evaluation of Maidstone's voters is not supported by an examination of their political behaviour at the elections in question. The votes cast by Maidstone's 907 voters in 1835 were quite different from those cast by the unreformed Maidstone electorate. Applying any standard of 'improved' behaviour, the reformed electorate, while somewhat tainted by recurring venality, ranks far above the unreformed freemen. Maidstone returned two M.P.s before 1832, as did virtually every other English county and borough constituency, and by avoiding Schedules A and B, Maidstone continued to return two M.P.s after the passage of the Reform Act. Accordingly, Maidstone electors had two votes to cast at each parliamentary election both before and after 1832, though they were not under any obligation to cast *both* votes and could choose to plump (cast only one) if they wished to do so. Plumping was not a popular practice, however; reformed and unreformed electors alike seem to have been loth to waste a vote. Their ability to cast two votes meant that two parties could be supported simultaneously at an election, or one party with two candidates could be accorded less than full support. This double vote was a potentially severe stumbling block for any party, even in the best circumstances, and at these elections the best circumstances seldom prevailed.[32] Very few of the contested elections in Maidstone (or in Lewes and Northampton for that matter) pitted two full slates of candidates for the two available seats. When each of Maidstone's parties proposed two candidates, split-voting could occur easily enough; in all but one of the elections in Maidstone between 1818 and 1841, only *three* candidates contested the two seats. In seven of the eight elections in which this kind of lop-sided contest occurred, two candidates of one party (or two with similar political convictions) stood against a single candidate of the other party. Only in 1818 were the political stances of the three candidates sufficiently vague to permit confusion, and even then the single 'Purple' (Tory) candidate was fairly easily distinguishable from his two 'Blue' opponents. Normally, then, some Maidstone voters were confronted with a difficult decision. If their party proposed only one candidate, they either had to split their support between the two parties or plump for the lone candidate and discard their other vote. In one 1797 municipal election, that vote allegedly was worth £15 and a 'squeaker' (a pig fattened on brewery waste).[33] The stories of the 'squeaker' election of 1797 may well be apocryphal, but the pollbooks provide undeniable evidence that prior to the Reform Act Maidstone voters were either extremely reluctant to discard a vote even when political considerations dictated a plumper, or they were simply indifferent to partisan demands. As indicated in Table 1, a third of Maidstone's voters split their votes between the two parties as late as the election of 1830.[34]

TABLE 1: SPLIT-VOTING AT ELECTIONS IN LEWES, MAIDSTONE AND NORTHAMPTON (%)

Election year:	1818	1820	1826	1830	1831	1832	1835	1837	1841
Lewes	4.2	NC	49.3	52.9	NC	NC	26.4	5.0	2.9
Maidstone	68.1	58.2	15.9	33.2	5.9	8.7	7.1	9.6	1.0
Northampton	21.2	40.9	36.4	43.0	15.3	12.3	12.0	7.6	9.8

NC = election not polled

Most of the electorate refused to support the arch-Tory, Wyndham Lewis, and one of the Blue candidates in 1826 when Lewis ran for the first time, but on the whole the level of split-voting before 1831 was extremely high. The 1826 contest was also by far the most one-sided election of the era, which tended to reduce the number of split votes. Wyndham Lewis managed to win just over 100 votes while his two Whig opponents received more than 350 votes each. In sharp contrast, the level of split-voting fell to less than 6% at the 1831 Maidstone contest. Since the 1831 election was the only genuinely four-man election of the nine fought between 1818 and 1841, the 6% split-vote is less impressive than the reduction in the number of voters casting split-votes at the elections following the passage of the Reform Act. Fewer than 9% of the voters split their support between the Blues and Purples in 1832, despite the reappearance of a three-man election, and the level of split-voting at the three subsequent elections never exceeded 10%. By 1841, virtually every Maidstone elector voted a party ticket and disregarded the deficient slate on the part of the Whig party; a negligible 1% of the 1152 voters split their support.

At the same time, and of course directly related to the decline in the number of split-voters that began with the election of 1831, the Maidstone electorate exhibited another unmistakable sign of altered circumstances at the election of 1830 (Table 2). The level of 'necessary' plumping at the eight three-man contests between 1818 and 1841 rose from less than 9% at the elections before 1830 to more than 30% at each contest after 1830. Necessary plumping is a crude and potentially distorted measure of voting behaviour since it is inextricably tied to only one candidate or one party. The apparently strong trend evident across these elections demands careful interpretation.

TABLE 2: NECESSARY PLUMPING AT ELECTIONS IN LEWES, MAIDSTONE
AND NORTHAMPTON (%)

Election year	1818	1820	1826	1830	1831	1832	1835	1837	1841
Lewes	26.2	NC	1.3	6.3	NC	NC	24.1	4 MAN	4 MAN
Maidstone	8.6	1.2	7.5	32.3	4 MAN	38.9	48.2	35.9	31.8
Northampton	33.8	4.7	11.0	28.8	23.5	4 MAN	42.6	40.1	47.9

NC = election not polled
4 MAN = four candidates at election

For example, the low level at the 1818 election cannot be taken too seriously since the three candidates conducted a much less visible campaign than normal in Maidstone. Nor can the elections of 1832 and 1835 necessarily be seen as valid indications of any new pattern of genuinely partisan behaviour. At both contests the extremely wealthy Tory candidate, Wyndham Lewis, stood alone and spent thousands of pounds to improve his chances at the hustings; therefore, the astonishing 48% of the voters who plumped for Lewis in 1835 must be viewed with a somewhat jaundiced eye. These elections aside, however, the pattern in Maidstone remains undeniably strong. As early as 1830, Maidstone's voters were willing to plump for the one genuinely pro-reform candidate, A.W. Robarts, despite the fact that Robarts spent comparatively little money in the course of the campaign. This behaviour was in striking contrast to their unwillingness to give Wyndham Lewis more than a handful of plumpers in the previous contest even when tempted by pecuniary considerations. Moreover, Maidstone's allegedly incurably venal voters continued to plump for the sole Whig/ Reform candidate at the elections of 1837 and 1841 despite the noticeable absence of bribery on the part of the Blue party. Unfortunately, the Maidstone Blues' relative honesty was only partly the result of principle; much of the absence of Whig bribery after Robarts's withdrawal from the fray stemmed from a general lack of funds. Finding *any* Blue candidate proved difficult after Robarts's 1837 withdrawal and his subsequent defeat at the two by-elections in 1838. Finding a Whig candidate willing to do more than simply offer himself as an object of their support proved impossible; consequently, the Blues found themselves out of office only six years after their overwhelming victory at the 1831 election. In 1831, Robarts jokingly referred 'to the late contest — or rather, to distinguish it more properly, the late farce'; in 1837 the Blue candidate imported from London fell short of the imported Tory candidate, Benjamin Disraeli, by more than 100 votes.[35] Yet despite this drastic decline in their overall strength, and despite their increasingly obvious inability to control even one seat, Maidstone Whig voters proved extremely loyal. More than a third of the entire electorate plumped for the Whig, T.P. Thompson, in 1837 (providing almost 80% of his total vote), and almost a third of the electorate plumped again in 1841 for David Salomons (providing almost 90% of his total support) even though his candidacy was hampered by a lack of time and by his heritage. The Whig *Gazette* admitted the problem in finding a candidate and seemed happy enough to get Salomons 'literally at the tenth hour'. The Tory *Journal* commented six days before the poll and four weeks after the Tory canvass had begun, 'Well, the Blues have found a man — at least a Jew'.[36] Such determined plumping in the face of such daunting odds and against almost all hope, particularly when the other side would pay so well even for a single vote, is an impressive indication that Maidstone politics after the Reform era were *not* as they had been. What role the act itself played in this transformation, however, remains unclear from this look at Maidstone. The major shifts in both the level of split-voting and the level of necessary plumping at Maidstone elections took place prior to the actual passage of the act. The reformed elections merely continued, or perhaps reinforced, a trend begun slightly earlier during the agitation surrounding the possibility of parliamentary reform.

Turning away from splitting and plumping but continuing the focus on Maidstone's electorate, Robarts's comment to Greville might be tested in another way. Greville asked specifically, 'What were the new constituency?', and it was to this question that Robarts replied 'If possible, worse than the old'.[37] If Robarts's answer is interpreted as a reference limited to Maidstone's newly enfranchised voters (which it probably is not), his judgment was no less mistaken. Maidstone's remaining freeman voters were initially and then increasingly outnumbered by the newly created £10 householders at post-Reform elections. A substantial minority of freemen did continue to play a role in elections, and if apparent susceptibility to bribery or apparent indifference to Reform is the standard applied, Maidstone's new voters were not by any means 'worse than the old'. The pollbook for the election of 1832 did not distinguish freemen from householders, and the nominal linkage techniques employed in this research could positively identify as freemen only those who had participated in previous elections. Most of the voters making their initial appearance in 1832 were newly created householders, but some undoubtedly were freemen who for one reason or another had not participated at elections previously.[38] Yet even taking into consideration an inevitable degree of error resulting from the imprecision of the identification of new voters, the old freemen were much more likely to vote Tory than their newly acquired fellow voters. In a relatively close election that polled more voters than ever before, approximately three quarters of the freemen plumped for the Purple candidate, Wyndham Lewis, while well over half of the new voters doubled for the two Blue reformers, A.W. Robarts and C.J. Barnett. It could be argued, of course, that the freeman-Tory alliance was based on principle. Some of the freemen were vehemently opposed to the Reform Act on 'principle', arguing in 1830 and 1831 that it represented an attack on their 'birthrights'. On these grounds, a majority of the freemen formally protested against Robarts's vote for the Reform Act in 1831.[39] The weight of evidence, however, argues against a strongly principled stand by the freemen even if the birthright argument is accorded the status of principle; their Tory affinities beginning in 1832 were more likely the result of the 'under-current of Tory gold running in a narrow and dirty channel' through their ranks than genuine affection for the Purple banner.[40] The disparity between freemen and householders continued at the 1835 election where differential voting choices *can* be identified positively from the pollbooks (Table 3).

TABLE 3: VOTES OF MAIDSTONE'S £10 HOUSEHOLDERS AND FREEMEN (%)

Election year	1835				1837				1841			
	WD	WS	TS	SP	TD	TS	WS	SP	TD	TS	WS	SP
Freemen	21.1	9.3	67.3	2.3	65.3	2.5	22.0	10.2	72.4	—	24.8	2.6
£10 householders	45.8	6.9	41.1	6.7	41.5	4.5	38.1	15.9	65.1	—	32.3	2.6

WD = Whig double vote
WS = Whig single vote
TD = Tory double vote
TS = Tory single vote
SP = split vote

In 1835, more than two thirds of the old freemen plumped for Lewis while only 21% cast double votes for the Whigs. Forty-one per cent of the householders gave Lewis plumpers as well, and far more householders split their support than did the freemen, but the freeman Tory vote stands out nevertheless. Wyndham Lewis's guineas (perhaps as many as 10,000 of them) won more votes than his vapid attacks on the new Poor Law, the Russian-Dutch loan, the Greek loan, and the West Indian compensation money, all of which he raised briefly during the course of his canvass.[41] However 'alive to public affairs' Maidstone's voters may have been, and they do indeed seem to have been as aware and highly active as Robarts claimed, the recondite platform ostensibly adopted by the Tories in 1835 certainly exceeded the limited comprehension of most voters in Maidstone; the freemen were simply less reluctant to be purchased. Again in 1837, the proportion of Tory voters among the freemen was far larger than among the 'mushrooms' (£10 householders).[42] This continued Tory loyalty among the freemen in 1837 resulted in the return of two Tory Members and is a classic example of the power of the purse, particularly among the freemen. Lewis's newly acquired partner, Benjamin Disraeli, did *not* canvass in Maidstone dressed in a 'black velvet coat lined with satin, purple trowsers with a gold band running down the outside seam, a scarlet waistcoat, long lace ruffles falling down to the tips of his fingers, white gloves with several brilliant rings outside them, and long black ringlets rippling down upon his shoulders', but his candidacy was met with considerable incredulity and merriment in the Blue camp.[43] Asking 'Who is Mr. B. D'Israeli?', the *Gazette* quickly launched a series of vicious attacks contending that if Disraeli were returned, 'the people of Maidstone would deservedly be considered the scum of the earth'.[44] Disraeli and Lewis did not anticipate a canvass at all, assuming that the last minute withdrawal of Robarts would discourage the Blues from mounting a resistance even with Disraeli's reputation; the late appearance of a radical candidate, T.P. Thompson, ex-M.P. for Hull, editor of the *Westminster Review,* and admitted member of 'Mr. Hume's party' in the Commons, gave the freemen a chance to demonstrate the efficacy of a timely application of Wyndham Lewis's gold among them.[45] Thus Robarts's opinions, weighed against the evidence of the votes, are not persuasive. Measured as a whole, the Reform era generally and the Reform Act specifically had a beneficial impact on the Maidstone electorate. Measured as freemen against 'mushroom', the effect of the act was equally striking.

The impact of the events of the early 1830s on Northampton's voters was remarkably similar to that found in Maidstone (Tables 1 and 2). The ordinarily large number of splitters in the Northampton electorate began to disappear before the passage of the Reform Act with the general election of 1831, fell to a level not attained in the four elections before 1831, and continued at the severely reduced rate of approximately 10% (Table 1) for the remainder of the elections examined. Though the extremely low levels of the split-voting achieved in Maidstone (and Lewes) elections were not found in Northampton, the pattern was much the same and was supported by a concomitant rise in the number of necessary plumps cast by voters at Northampton's usual three-man contests. One substantial instance of necessary plumping occurred early in Northampton. Just over a third of the Northampton electorate plumped for the sole Whig candidate at the 1818 election, Sir George Robinson, but this anomalous situation may have been influenced as much by a reaction against patronage and corruption as by party. The Marquess of Northampton's son, Earl Compton, was returned along with Sir Edward Kerrison in 1818 after a sharp contest with the decided Whig, Sir George Robinson. At this 'riotous and disgraceful election' during the course of which the mayor was twice forced to read the Riot Act, Robinson lost by a mere 27 votes (2%) of the almost 1,300 cast.[46] Partisan feelings may have accounted for much of Robinson's plumper support, but the great exertions made by both sides in the form of treating and bribery for four solid months prior to the three-week long poll had little connexion with political principles, and the meaning of the poll is accordingly obscured. Following this expensive election, necessary plumping fell to extremely low levels in 1820, when Sir George Robinson and W.L. Maberley easily unseated Earl Compton. It continued at a reduced rate in 1826 when the city's closed and notoriously corrupt corporation contributed £1,000 from the city's purse to help finance the Tory candidate, Sir R.H. Gunning.[47] Neither of these single Tory candidates was capable of mustering the undivided support of more than a small fraction of the unreformed Northampton electorate. On the other hand, relatively respectable levels of necessary plumps were amassed in the two subsequent elections by Tory candidates. Almost 29% of the total votes cast in 1830 were singles for Gunning, resulting in his joining Robinson briefly in Parliament, and almost a quarter of the electorate plumped for Gunning again in 1831 as he vainly attempted to maintain control of his hard-won seat. Yet, despite these relatively high levels of plumping at Northampton elections in advance of Reform, the first three-man contest *after* Reform witnessed a striking departure from pre-Reform standards. More than 40% of the reformed electorate plumped when necessary at the Northampton elections of 1835 and 1837, and nearly half the electorate plumped in an effort to return the sole Conservative candidate, Sir Henry Willoughby, in 1841. The apparent Tory inability to attract plumpers from the unreformed electorate ceased to be an obstacle after the Reform Act even though inhabitant householders whose franchises predated the act comprised the majority of the reformed electorate.

The political background to the altered behaviour of the Northampton electorate resembled Maidstone's, though not as closely as indicated by voting patterns in the two towns. Partisan political considerations were conspicuous by their absence in later eighteenth-century Northampton elections, and party politics did not immediately accompany the 1818 reappearance of contested elections. Political labels can be assigned easily enough to the participants in the 1818 contest, and the single Tory candidates in 1820 and 1826 are readily discernible. Party dialogue, on the other hand, appeared only at the end of the 1820s. The formation of a Whig Club in 1827 was followed by the formation of a Tory Oak Club in the 1830s (after the failure of a King and Constitution Club attempted in 1823).[48] With the formation of these two clubs, Northampton's voters joined the ranks of the politically aware, just as Maidstone's voters seem to have been doing at approximately the same time. After decades of Blues versus Purples at Maidstone elections, a formal anti-reform party, the Inflexibles, was organized by the freemen in 1831 and followed in 1832 by a new pro-reform Inflexible Society, two Tory groups called the Conservative Committee and the Constitutional Society, and two Whig/Liberal clubs known as the Loyal True Blue Club and the Maidstone Political Union.[49] The drastic changes in Maidstone voting habits that occurred along with the formation of these political clubs have been demonstrated, and the changes in Northampton are equally apparent. The altered pattern in Northampton, however, is more surprising. By 1830, Maidstone's voters were already accustomed to active parliamentary politics and wide-open borough political battles that often rivalled the fervour which accompanied many of the general elections and that must have made the transition to national awareness easier. Northampton suffered from a lack of both. Parliamentary elections passed almost unnoticed for 22 years between 1796 and 1818, and municipal elections were unknown in Northampton until the reform of the city's corporation as a result of the 1835 Municipal Corporations Act. Employee coercion by politically aware owners of shoemaking establishments may have accounted for some of the changes in Northampton despite unfavourable local conditions, but Northampton's electorate was not composed entirely of politically or economically susceptible shoemakers.[50] The emergence of partisan voting in the elections after 1831 cannot be explained away so easily. However, the demise of the corrupt corporation *did* have a measureable impact on the borough; as indicated in Table 2, the level of necessary plumping that had risen to a respectable level in 1830 and 1831 actually doubled at the three elections held after the elimination of the old city government.

Unpolled elections in 1820, 1831 and 1832 reduce Lewes's utility in a comparison of split-voting in these towns, and two successive four-man contests at the last elections in this survey almost eliminate Lewes's comparability for levels of necessary plumping. Nevertheless, to the limited degree possible, much about Lewes's development over the Reform era conforms to the pattern noted in Maidstone and Northampton even though Lewes's voters exhibited signs of political sophistication somewhat earlier. Lewes's electorate participated in several elections with strong ties to national political issues at the very beginning of the nineteenth century after some experience in strictly local partisan activity at the end of the eighteenth.[51] The 1818 election continued that focus on national affairs begun over a decade before. After a two-time Whig candidate withdrew at the very last moment rather than risk a third defeat, the Lewes Whigs managed to recruit a candidate from London, Thomas Erskine, son of the famous Lord Erskine.[52] At this heavily partisan election, fewer than 5% of Lewes's voters split their support between the parties, and more than 26% cast necessary plumpers for Erskine, disregarding his arrival one day before the polling began (Tables 1 and 2). The Whig candidate fared so badly that he resigned early on in the second day of the poll, closing the hustings with at least 100 votes outstanding. Immediately before the premature closure, the Whigs put forward a fourth candidate in order to have two men available in the event of a successful election petition against the Tories. This last-minute candidate *in absentia*, Henry Baring, garnered only 27 token votes, and the Whigs eventually dropped the idea of a petition alleging Tory bribery, leaving the Tories in possession of both seats.[53]

Such overtly partisan behaviour on the part of local political leaders and rank-and-file voters in Lewes lapsed before the next election, not to be revived until after the election of 1830. A brief, dismal canvass by a potential Whig candidate led to an uncontested election in 1820. The general elections of 1826 and 1830 provoked virtually identical contests and polls, but each proved the continuing susceptibility of the unreformed Lewes electorate to the non-partisan politics of personality and illustrated the reluctance of local candidates to adopt overtly partisan electoral techniques. Amidst a flurry of advertising and traditional electioneering, Alexander Donovan prepared to present a united Whig front by standing with T.R. Kemp.[54] Sir George Shiffner, an incumbent Tory, chose to withdraw, leaving the other incumbent Tory, Sir John Shelley, to stand alone. Kemp seems to have recognized Shelley's popularity, and instead of canvassing with Donovan, he formally denounced all 'Coalitions' (the name used by Lewes's late eighteenth-century local party) and stood alone. For his part, Shelley denied any national party ties and offered himself 'without regard to party'.[55] Virtually half the Lewes electorate split their votes and returned the split ticket of Kemp and Shelley. Almost none of the voters bothered to plump for Shelley. The election of 1830 simply repeated these events except for Donovan's foreknowledge of the necessity of standing alone. Again half the electorate voted for a Whig and a Tory simultaneously, and Kemp and Shelley left Donovan 100 votes behind.

Two unpolled elections followed the apolitical elections of 1826 and 1830, but the lack of a poll in both instances masked the existence of a highly politicized electorate seething alternatively with hope and fear as the Reform Bill was proposed and defeated. The citizens of Lewes petitioned the Commons, the King, and the Lords at various points during 1831 expressing their determination that the bill should pass. Intense pro-reform agitation persuaded Shelley to give up his plans to contest the borough in 1831.[56] His resignation led to a Whig/Reform representation from Lewes in 1831 and again with no contest in 1832. Lewes voters wanted 'the bill, the whole bill, and nothing but the bill', and no one could be found by the Tories to waste both time and money challenging the obvious Whig majority. No doubt related to the fervour of 1831–2 (and the genesis of political clubs à la Maidstone and Northampton), voters greeted the resumption of contested elections in 1835 with behaviour much more like 1818 than the two non-partisan elections that immediately preceded the Reform Act.[57] A quarter of the electorate still split their votes in 1835, but another quarter more properly plumped for the solitary Tory candidate (Tables 1 and 2). This return to partisan behaviour continued at the two subsequent elections. Split-voting dropped to 5% in 1837 and dropped again to 3% in 1841. Each of these contests pitted two Tories against two Whigs and therefore were less severe tests of partisanship than those experienced by the voters in Maidstone and Northampton. Even so, Lewes's reformed electorate had undoubtedly adopted a strongly partisan stance.[58]

Cross-sectional analyses of voting behaviour such as those in Tables 1–3 point to many of the changes that accompanied Reform in these three towns. Cross-sectional measurements also seem particularly appropriate for a study of English voting habits since so many accounts of modern British elections seem obsessed with the equally cross-sectional concept of 'swings' in the electorate. Unable to examine individual voters without considerable effort, commentators and analysts focus on changes in aggregate voting totals and create the illusion of movement with a series of static assessments. The levels of split-ticket voting and plumping reported in Tables 1 and 2 are based on individual-level data and therefore do not suffer from many of the flaws inherent in unsupported aggregate data, but they indicate nothing of the behaviour of individual voters over time.[59] Faced with several opportunities to exercise a new franchise, or new conditions under which to continue to use an old franchise, how did individual voters respond? As importantly, how did the voting choices of specific electors change over the Reform era, if at all? As a group, electorates in Maidstone, Lewes and Northampton behaved in a more partisan manner after 1830 than before, but how did they react as individuals? Questions like these are among the most difficult to answer with quantitative data; answers require linked data files containing all the information available concerning each voter in a single record. Fortunately, linked files for these voters allow a glimpse at their reaction to Reform.

The political stances of the two major parties, whether distinguished as Whig *v.* Tory or Liberal *v.* Conservative, were quite stable over the years between the end of the Napoleonic wars and the early reign of Queen Victoria. The True Blues of Maidstone spoke to the point when urging: 'Let not names mislead you. Whig, Liberal, Radical all have a Common Enemy — the determined Tory.'[60] In some ways, the split between the two parliamentary parties still resembled the days of the Fox-Pitt disputes at the end of the eighteenth century, and certainly no major departures from traditionally defined positions were identifiable at the nine general elections in question. Given this stability on the part of the men contesting the elections, and the reasonably close link between national issues and local elections in these towns even before the Reform Act, political consistency would be expected of most politically aware voters. Unless an elector experienced some major personal political transformation, a vote for one party at a given election should have been followed by a vote for the same party at the subsequent election. As revealed in Figure 1, however, the unreformed electorate often failed to behave in this fashion. Conversely, most of the voters in the three reformed electorates behaved exactly in accordance with this expectation. The 'uncertainty coefficient' simply measures the degree of improvement in predicting an elector's choice of parties contributed by knowledge of his previous vote using a scale of 0 to ±1. If knowledge of an elector's Whig vote at the election of 1831 invariably allowed a correct prediction of his casting a Whig vote in 1832, the uncertainty coefficient would reach a perfect +1; alternatively, a Tory vote inevitably following a Whig vote would yield a perfect −1. Scores of less than ±.2 are not significant under most conditions, while scores greater than ±.4 indicate a substantially improved predictability.[61] Applying this test to the voters of Maidstone, Lewes and Northampton produces a remarkably similar pattern in two instances and a relatively close fit in the third. Prior to 1830, voters in Maidstone and Northampton did not normally follow a party vote with another, similar party vote. They improved on this record noticeably in 1831 and 1832, and at the elections following 1832, their behaviour was consistently partisan from election to election. A party vote at one contest usually meant that the elector would vote for the same party at the following election. Lewes's voters followed a somewhat different path; their tendency to repeat a partisan vote was greater than +.3 in 1826 and jumped to +.42 in 1830 before falling back to only +.26 in 1835 after the gap of five years without a contested election. After this deviation, however, the Lewes electorate joined the voters of Maidstone and Northampton with pronounced (+.55 and +.59) inter-election partisan loyalties between 1835 and 1841. Under the often less than optimal conditions of these elections,

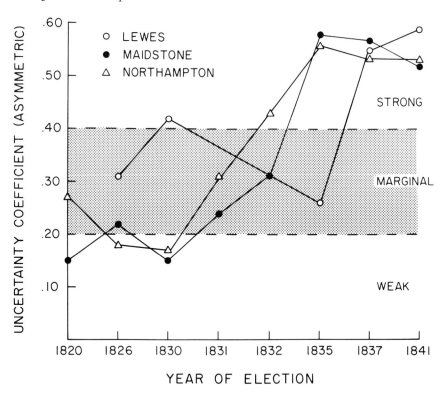

FIGURE 1: CONSISTENT PARTISAN BEHAVIOUR ACROSS ELECTIONS

particularly in Maidstone, this determinedly persistent loyalty shown by the voters argues against the negative assessments of their behaviour and for a substantially altered political climate as a result of the Reform era.

Notes

1   *Three Early Nineteenth Century Diaries*, ed. A. Aspinall (1952), p. xxxi.
2   *Maidstone Gazette*, 2 Feb. 1830.
3   Hansard, *Parl. Deb.*, 3rd ser., II, 1205 (2 Mar. 1831). For Calne see C. Seymour, *Electoral Reform in England and Wales ... 1832–1885* (New Haven, 1915), p. 54 and N. Gash, *Politics in the Age of Peel* (1953), pp. 75, 214–16.
4   *Maidstone Gaz.*, 15 Apr. 1831.
5   W.N. Molesworth, *The History of the Reform Bill of 1832* (1865), pp. 1–3, 337–40.
6   J.R.M. Butler, *The Passing of the Reform Bill* (1914); G.M. Trevelyan, *Lord Grey of the Reform Bill* (New York, 1920), pp. 350–1. Turberville maintained that 'the Whigs were essentially aristocrats and one of their dominant motives in espousing the cause of

parliamentary reform had been the persuasion that it was inevitable if they were to insure
the permanent influence of their own order': A.S. Turberville, *The House of Lords in the
Age of Reform 1784–1837* (1958), p. 396.

7   Gash, *Politics in the Age of Peel*, pp. ix–xxi, 3–33: *idem, Reaction and Reconstruction in English
Politics 1832–1852* (Oxford, 1965), pp. 1–59.
    K. Marx, 'Lord John Russell', *Karl Marx and Frederick Engels on Britain* (Moscow, 1962),
    pp. 451–4.

9   D.C. Moore, 'Concession or Cure: The Sociological Premises of the First Reform Act',
    Historical Journal, IX (1966), 44–5.

10 R.W. Davis, 'Toryism to Tamworth: The Triumph of Reform, 1827–1835', *Albion*, XII
    (1980), 132.

11 J. Cannon, *Parliamentary Reform 1640–1832* (Cambridge, 1973), p. 243.

12 J. Milton-Smith, 'Earl Grey's Cabinet and the Objects of Parliamentary Reform',
    Historical Jnl., XV (1972), 55–74. This essay ignores questions like those addressed by
    S.F. Woolley, 'The Personnel of the Parliament of 1833', *E.H.R.*, LIII (1938), 240–62.

13 At the five general elections prior to 1832, between 22% and 28% of the counties were
    polled, as opposed to between 31% and 40% of the boroughs (calculated from figures
    in Cannon, *Parliamentary Reform*, pp. 278–89). Almost half of the new county
    constituencies went to the poll once or less between 1832 and 1841. The proportion of
    contested county elections dropped from a high of 66% in 1832 to 28% in 1841
    (calculated from figures in F.H. McCalmont, *Parliamentary Poll Book* [Nottingham,
    1879]).

14 D.C. Moore, *The Politics of Deference* (Hassocks, 1976), p. 15.

15 Davis, 'Toryism to Tamworth', p. 132.

16 Examples of Moore's tables can be found in *Politics of Deference*, pp. 65–79 and 114–27.
    J.R. Fisher, 'Issues and Influence: Two By-Elections in South Nottinghamshire in the
    Mid-Nineteenth Century', *Historical Jnl.*, XXIV (1981), 155–65.

17 *Vanity Fair*, 29 Mar. 1873, p. 97.

18 P. Joyce, 'The Factory Politics of Lancashire in the Later Nineteenth Century', *Historical
    Jnl.*, XVIII (1975), 528.

19 Seymour, *Electoral Reform*, pp. 77, 83–5; Cannon, *Parliamentary Reform*, pp. 258–9, 290–
    2.

20 See J. Prest, *Politics in the Age of Cobden* (1977), pp. 1–9.

21 Moore, *Politics of Deference*, pp. 247–9, 472–6. The pollbooks for post-Reform elections
    in Northampton, Maidstone and Lewes attest to the care with which the registration lists
    were used. Duplicate registrations, deaths and other alterations were duly noted in
    making the final tally.

22 *The Poll for the Election of Two Burgesses* (Liverpool, 1832), p. 1. For boundaries, see J.H.
    Philbin, *Parliamentary Representation 1832 ...* (New Haven, 1965), pp. 193–4.

23 E. and Annie G. Porritt, *The Unreformed House of Commons* (2 vols., Cambridge, 1903).
    See also J. Grego, *A History of Parliamentary Elections and Electioneering ...* (1892) and
    T.H.B. Oldfield, *The Representative History of Great Britain and Ireland ...* (6 vols., 1816).

24 W.A. Speck *et al.*, 'Computer Analysis of Poll Books: A Further Report', *B.I.H.R.*,
    XLVIII (1975), 64–90; J. Money, 'Birmingham and the West Midlands, 1760–1793:
    Politics and Regional Identity in the English Provinces in the Later Eighteenth Century',
    Midland History, I (1971–2), 1–19; Norma Landau, 'Independence, Deference, and Voter
    Participation: The Behaviour of the Electorate in Early Eighteenth-Century Kent',
    Historical Jnl., XXII (1979), 561—83; J.A. Phillips, 'Popular Politics in Unreformed
    England', *Journal of Modern History*, LII (1980), 599–625.

25 *Cobbett's Twopenny Trash*, II, No. 2 (1832), p. 241.

26 *The Town Book of Lewes 1702–1837*, ed. Verena Smith (Sussex Record Soc., LXIX,
    1972–3), pp. 270–90. Lewes petitioned both the King and Parliament on several
    occasions. The petition quoted was addressed to the Commons on 26 Jan. 1831.

27 Molesworth, *Reform Bill*, p. 3.

28 A.B., 'Bribery and Intimidation at Elections', *Westminster Review*, XXV, No. 2 (1836),
    pp. 485–513.

29 R.W. Davis, *Political Change and Continuity 1760–1885* (Newton Abbot, 1972), pp. 15–
    105.

[30]   Gash, *Politics in the Age of Peel*, pp. x, 320, 125.

[31]   *The Greville Memoirs*, eds. L. Strachey and R. Fulford (8 vols., 1938), III, 133. Greville said of Robarts, 'what he dreads most is collision [revolution], and most desires is quiet, and he thinks non-resistance is the best way'.

[32]   Northampton and Lewes also returned two M.P.s throughout this period. Statistics on all three are closely comparable as a result, particularly with their common trait of three-man contests. For a further discussion of the implications of the double vote, see J.C. Mitchell, 'Electoral Strategy under Open Voting', *Public Choice*, XXVIII (1976), 1–26 and T.J. Nossiter, *Influence, Opinion and Political Idioms in Reformed England* (Hassocks, 1975).

[33]   H.C. 116, pp. 751–70 (1835). XXIV, 91–110; *Maidstone Gaz.*, 17 Apr. 1838.

[34]   The voting patterns reported for Maidstone and Northampton are based on an analysis of letter-cluster samples of approximately 40% of the relevant population. A full discussion of this method and the reasons for it can be found in J. A. Phillips, 'Achieving a Critical Mass While Avoiding an Explosion', *Journal of Interdisciplinary History*, IX (1978–9), 493–508. The Lewes electorate was examined in its entirety due to its relatively small size at the beginning of the period. The individuals in these samples were linked across elections, producing a 'panel' survey. For a description of the method employed see J. A. Phillips, 'Nominal Record Linkage and the Study of Individual-Level Electoral Behavior', *Laboratory for Political Research* (Univ. of Iowa, 1976), pp. 1–17. The percentages reported and the statistical measurements used in this analysis are therefore subject to a small sampling error that cannot be precisely estimated.

[35]   *Maidstone Gaz.*, 10 May 1831. Disraeli was recruited as a Conservative candidate through the auspices of the Carlton Club: W.F. Monypenny and G.E. Buckle, *The Life of Benjamin Disraeli* (6 vols., 1910–20), I, 376–7.

[36]   *Maidstone Gaz.*, 28 June 1841; *Maidstone Journal*, 29 June 1841.

[37]   *Greville Mems.*, III, 133.

[38]   Linking the pollbooks of 1831 and 1832 created two distinct sets of electors for 1832. Those *with* previous voting records definitely were freemen, but those *without* previously recorded votes were only likely to be £10 householders. Any freeman not voting between 1818 and 1831 would also be contained in the second group. The comparative figures for 1832 freeman and householder voting, therefore, are subject to additional error.

[39]   *Maidstone Gaz.*, 19, 26 Apr. 1831, 4 Dec. 1832.

[40]   Monypenny and Buckle, *Disraeli*, I, 376–8. Disraeli had considerable trouble paying back his loan from Wyndham Lewis. The quote actually appeared in the 1841 election but was equally appropriate in 1837: *Maidstone Gaz.*, 6 July 1841.

[41]   *Maidstone Gaz.*, 6 Jan. 1835. Lewis also attacked the new Bankruptcy Act.

[42]   E.M. Menzies, 'The Freeman Voter in Liverpool, 1802–1835', *Transactions of the Historical Society of Lancashire and Cheshire*, CXXIV (1973), 88, 95. Menzies demonstrated a similar tendency for the Liverpool freemen to vote Tory and the householders to support the Liberals.

[43]   O.F. Christie, *The Transition from Aristocracy 1832–1867* (1927), p. 227. Christie's description is of an appearance in 1833.

[44]   *Maidstone Gaz.*, 11 July 1837. Cutbush commented after the contest: 'it is with narrow-souled people as it is with narrow-necked bottles; the less they have in them the more noise they make in pouring it out' (*Maidstone Gaz.*, 12 Dec. 1837).

[45]   *Lord Beaconsfield's Correspondence with His Sister*, ed. R. Disraeli (1886), pp. 69–70; *Maidstone Gaz.*, 25 July 1837; R. Blake, *Disraeli* (New York, 1967), p. 147.

[46]   *The Late Elections; An Impartial Statement of All Proceedings* (1818), p. 244. The second Earl Spencer was no longer active in politics and certainly did not support Sir George Robinson since Spencer was a Tory, but Robinson's image may have been tied to the remaining 'Whig' Spencer interests in Northampton; Lord Althorp was returned for Northampton-shire at the same election. See *Memoir of John Charles Viscount Althorp, Third Earl Spencer*, ed. D. Le Marchant (1876), pp. 91, 181.

[47]   H.C. 158, pp. 3–29 (1826–7). IV, 343–69; H.C. 116, p. 1973 (1835). XXV, 567; *The Records of the Borough of Northampton*, eds. C.A. Markham and J.C. Cox (2 vols., Northampton, 1898), II, 510–11. The case brought in King's Bench was dismissed, but the corporation lost another £350 in costs.

[48]   V.A. Hatley, 'Some Aspects of Northampton's History, 1815–51', *Northamptonshire Past*

and Present, III (1960–5), 243–53.
49   *Maidstone Gaz.*, 19 Apr. 1831, 14 Aug., 20, 27 Nov., 4, 11 Sept., 4, 11 Dec. 1832.
50   A fuller discussion of unreformed Maidstone politics and coercion generally can be found in J. A. Phillips, *Electoral Behavior in Unreformed England* (Princeton, 1982), Chapters 3 and 4. An advertisement issued during the 1826 Northampton election offered shoemakers employment if they were discharged for voting Tory: Northampton Public Library, Collection of political handbills, 43/1818, 15/1830, 21/1826, 27/1841.
51   W.H. Hills, *The Parliamentary History of the Borough of Lewes 1295–1885* (Lewes, 1908), pp. 35–40.
52   East Sussex R.O., Shiffner MS. 305; *Lewes Town Book 1702–1837*, p. 221.
53   E. Sussex R.O., Shiffner MS. 170.
54   *Sussex Advertiser*, 10 Oct. 1825, 15 May 1826.
55   E. Sussex R.O., Shiffner MS. 826; *Sussex Advertiser*, 5 June 1826.
56   The citizens of Lewes sent a letter of congratulation to the people of France for defending their rights 'in opposition to the Ordinance of their late imbecile Ruler': *Lewes Town Book 1702–1837*, p. 267. Also see Meta Zimmeck, 'Chartered Rights and Vested Interests: Reform Era Politics in Three Sussex Boroughs' (Sussex M.A. thesis, 1972), pp. 49–67.
57   A Liberal 'Bundle of Sticks', and Conservative 'Constitutional Pruning Society' emerged in Lewes during the 1830s: H.C. Sessional Pprs., 1835 (7), pp. 400–19.
58   See C.E. Brent, 'The Immediate Impact of the Second Reform Act on a Southern County Town: Voting Patterns at Lewes Borough in 1865 and 1868', *Southern History*, II (1980), 129–78. Brent includes the voting distribution for 1841 but sees 1847 as a more important, 'realigning' election.
59   *Quantitative Ecological Analysis*, eds. M. Dogan and S. Rokkan (Cambridge, Massachusetts, 1969).
60   *Maidstone Gaz.*, 25 Nov. 1834.
61   W. Buchanan, 'Nominal and Ordinal Bivariate Statistics', *American Journal of Political Science*, XVIII, No. 3 (1974).

THE ORGANIZATION OF
THE CONSERVATIVE PARTY, 1832–1846*
PART I : THE PARLIAMENTARY ORGANIZATION

NORMAN GASH

The Conservatives between 1832 and 1841 were the first example in British parliamentary history of a party which organized itself for electoral victory and forced its leaders into office against the wishes of the Crown by winning a majority in a general election. In that process an important role was played by such new features as the Carlton Club, the constituency associations, and a central party electoral expert (F.R. Bonham) who except in 1835–7 was not an M.P. But the more traditional and conventional parliamentary organization of the party[1] also contributed to the growing effectiveness of the Conservative opposition. Though by its nature it was not so susceptible to striking innovations, the reorganization and improvements which took place in the parliamentary management of the Conservative Party during the 1830s were part of the general consolidation which prepared the way for the great victory of 1841.

The men concerned in this development were Peel and Wellington, the party leaders in the two Houses, a small inner advisory group of past or future ministers, the chief whips and their assistants, the election committees, and a miscellaneous number of M.P.s who from position, taste or experience, were drawn into the work of management. Two persons call, however, for special comment since their functions were connected with no special office and took place largely behind the scenes. The first was F.R. Bonham; the second Lord Granville Somerset. Of

---

* This article was written some years ago and for a different purpose. The justification for printing it now is, first, that it offers a comprehensive description of party organization in this period not, as far as I know, attempted elsewhere; second, that along with much that will be familiar to experts in this field, it includes some original material that has escaped the eye of subsequent researchers.

Bonham I have written fully elsewhere.[2] Granville Somerset, however, deserves more than a passing mention. His activities were of a kind which are rarely publicized or well documented.[3] But he clearly occupied a position in the party hierarchy as influential as it was ill-defined. He was the eldest brother of the seventh Duke of Beaufort, M.P. for Monmouthshire for nearly 32 years, chairman of quarter sessions, and a well known sportsman. His social status was unchallengeable; his experience and authority unique. From the start he was an active politician. Returned for Monmouthshire by his father's influence at a by-election in 1816, he was appointed a junior Lord of the Treasury by Liverpool in March 1819. Resigning when Canning became Prime Minister in 1827, he was reinstated by Wellington in 1828. He was one of the small group of men who worked to keep the party together during the difficult years of the Reform crisis of 1830–2; and in the crucial decade from 1832 to 1841 he acted virtually as chief of staff to the Conservative Party. After Wellington he was the first man with whom Peel discussed the political situation on his return from Italy in November 1834; he was given office as First Commissioner for Woods and Forests in the 1834–5 ministry; he was present at the inner consultations of the party leaders which preceded the overthrow of the Whig government in 1841.

His services and his rank not unnaturally led him to expect Cabinet office when Peel formed his second ministry. But he suffered from two handicaps in the pursuit of a more public career. He had a physical deformity and his manners were brusque. His deformity debarred him from the post he wanted of Chief Secretary for Ireland, since this would have exposed him to merciless attacks in the Irish newspapers. His manner made Peel also decide in the end not to reappoint him to Woods and Forests as originally intended, since this involved close relations with the court and was not in any case an office for which he had much enthusiasm. Instead he was offered and took the chancellorship of the Duchy of Lancaster, despite the disappointment that this did not carry with it membership of the Cabinet. In 1844, however, when Hardinge went to India as Governor-General, Granville Somerset was promoted to the Cabinet vacancy, though he declined the accompanying offer of Hardinge's post of Secretary at War. This was perhaps due to the relative inferiority of that office rather than to any dislike of departmental work. He was generally recognized to be an excellent man of business; but his abilities were perhaps more those of a party manager than a parliamentary leader. The young Gladstone commented that 'Lord G. Somerset affords I think a remarkable instance of a very good tempered and good humoured man with unconciliatory modes of proceeding in business; and I confess also that he seems to me scarcely a statesman, but that he has abundant talents for administration, and a mind quick in finding objections and consequently of great use in the department of intercepting what is crude and rash'.[4] His death in 1848 at the early age of 55 brought to a premature close a career which was of greater political significance than might be inferred from the general lack of attention given to it by historians.[5] Few men worked harder or devoted themselves more single-mindedly to the management of the Conservative Party in the decade of recovery after the Reform Act.

2

In its narrowest sense, the object of parliamentary organization was to secure unity of policy and efficiency in action. For a parliamentary party to be effective, it had to be present in force at important debates and above all at important divisions, and when its members mustered their strength, it was desirable that they spoke with the same voice. That did not always happen, but it was the function of the parliamentary organization to see that it happened as often as possible. The actual result necessarily depended on the efficiency of the organization, the temper of the party, and the nature of the occasion.

One of the regular methods of resolving individual vagaries and discontents in this period was to hold meetings where differences could be aired and a common resolution achieved. 'Our people', wrote Granville Somerset on one occasion, 'will not be curbed unless it is by previous consent. During the remainder of the last session [1835] they were tolerably obedient to Peel's wishes — so they would be now if he would give them an idea of them beforehand and demonstrate to them that he means to continue actively at their Head and recognize them as his party on all main points.'[6] The remedy for this, he considered, was for Peel to hold a meeting of the party to settle their future conduct. The principle thus laid down was of course applicable to both parties. Indeed the Whigs had been the first to realize that the large but heterogeneous and fluctuating majority of 'reformers' that provided the government with its legislative basis after the Reform Act needed more than the infrequent and purely informative meeting which characterized the relations between ministers and supporters before 1830. Accordingly party meetings were held more often, there was more interchange of opinion between leaders and the rank and file, and the notion of consultation with the party began to emerge.[7] To the young Gladstone of the '30s, it seemed in fact as if party meetings were primarily designed for dissentients. In January 1837, for example, he asked Bonham whether he need attend the party meeting at Peel's house before the start of the session since 'I think such assemblages are more intended for those who may be likely to offer opinions different from those of the mass or the leaders than for such as you, may I say, or I'.[8]

For the control of Members of the House of Commons, preliminary meetings were of particular importance. The numbers in the Commons were greater; debates in the lower House usually preceded those in the House of Lords; and the rank and file of the party, some new to Parliament, others drawn from the wide mass of the country gentry, would probably be less known to the party leaders and managers than those members of the upper House who took a permanent interest in politics. Yet although previous discussion and agreement within the party was felt by many to be a powerful aid to unity and discipline, there was still no regular practice of calling party meetings before the start of the parliamentary session. Such meetings were often held but each needed a separate decision and they had clearly not yet been established as part of the routine management of party, as far as the Conservatives were concerned. In December 1835, for instance, Granville Somerset was consulting Goulburn on the propriety of urging Peel to hold a meeting of the party before the approaching session in order to assert his personal leadership and enable his followers to come to some agreement on their future policy. It was duly held at Peel's house on the morning of the King's Speech.

One practical advantage of these eve-of-session gatherings was that they would bring the bulk of the party to town before the real business of Parliament started. Before the beginning of the 1837 session Clerk suggested that a meeting of the party should be held on the morning of the King's Speech and Hardinge supported the proposal on the ground that it would be the best method of ensuring a good attendance at the opening of the session. He recommended the issue of letters written in the third person requesting Members to be present. 'Such is the sluggish folly of many of our supporters', he told Peel, 'that the ordinary note *earnestly* requesting their attendance in the Hse of Commons will have very little effect.'[9] This was by no means the only occasion when the party meeting was used to reinforce the efforts of the hard-worked whips. In March 1835 Greville recorded a meeting of the Tories at Bridgewater House for the purpose of securing better attendance. This gathering had been called not by Peel but by Lord Francis Egerton in an individual attempt to impress on the party rank and file the weakness of the ministry's position. Peel declined to take any part, in view of his previous warnings to his followers, and the meeting was not a success. Ellice and Duncannon went down to see for themselves the nakedness of the ministerialists and counted only 127 that attended.[10] No doubt the social attractions of the London season thinned the ranks of the Conservatives more than those of the Liberals with their leaven of radicals, Dissenters, and Irish nationalists.

Another type of meeting was that held to discuss specific questions of legislation or policy. Three days before Chandos brought forward his malt tax motion in March 1835, Peel held a meeting of the party to ensure that the ministerialist attitude would be known and supported. It was, he told the King, well attended and the general temper good.[11] In August 1835, when the Tory peers were prolonging the battle over the Municipal Corporations Bill, Peel called a meeting of his supporters in the House of Commons and advised them not to make any attempt to recall any Members who had already left for the country. He told them that he himself would shortly be leaving town and made little pretence at concealing his opinion that it would be best if they did the same.[12] A few years later when the Conservative leaders were perturbed at the prospect of an alliance between some of their followers and the radicals to attack the government over the Canada question, it was to the party meeting that they turned to enforce discipline. 'I am much disposed', wrote Peel to Wellington, 'to have a meeting of twenty or thirty persons on Saturday next for the purpose of hearing the opinions of the leading men who usually take a part in debates. I would afterwards have a meeting of the whole party, and try to persuade them to agree generally to what might be proposed.'[13] Meetings such as these, held during the parliamentary session, were clearly a useful means of restraining the rasher elements in the party and giving an explicit lead to those Members who on difficult matters were unable to come to any more precise conclusion than a deter-mination, as one of them expressed it, 'to work on Peel's view, whatever it may be'.[14] The actual meeting-place varied according to convenience. Some were at Peel's house; others at the Carlton; others again at the town houses of the wealthier and titled members of the party.

Peel's own preference perhaps was not for a general meeting of the party or even the House of Commons element of it, but for the confidential gathering of principal leaders and debaters who formed the cutting edge of the party's parliamentary activities. Over the China question in 1840, for example, and again in the summer of 1841 before the final attack on the Melbourne administration, there were a series of such meetings. It is to be doubted whether in Peel's view these inner meetings formed the 'shadow Cabinet' of later practice although the term has sometimes been applied to them. Nevertheless the youthful Gladstone seemed to have had his hopes raised by inclusion in some of these 'confidential councils', and possibly Disraeli too; though when the Conservative ministry was formed in 1841 Gladstone did not receive Cabinet rank and Disraeli did not get office at all.[15] In all probability Peel was more concerned with ensuring co-ordination between the small group of Conservatives who provided the vocal element in debate and were thus the representatives of the party views in the public eye. But spokesmen and ministers were not necessarily the same and there is no evidence that Peel regarded these gatherings of what he once called 'the most intelligent and discreet of our friends' as his future Cabinet.[16]

The meetings of the Conservative peers were held in much the same way and for much the same purpose. A discernible difference, however, was that the peers were more independent and self-willed and met as often to decide policy among themselves as to accept a ruling from their nominal leader. The Duke of Wellington possessed immense personal prestige; but he was dealing with a difficult body of men and the contacts between the parties in the two Houses of Parliament were too slight to afford him much access of authority from below. The peers usually met at Apsley House, the duke's residence, but their host and leader scarcely seemed more than a *primus inter pares*. In August 1834, for example, when the Conservative party was stirring out of its inaction under Grey's ministry, a meeting was held to discuss general policy. Wellington exhorted them to keep together for the remainder of the session and obtained their general agreement to remain in town until the close of

Parliament. On points of policy, however, he was vague. He stated that he wished to ascertain the feeling of the party and that on the question of the Irish Tithe Bill, which he regarded as the most important issue, he would be guided by the bishops. 'This seemed', wrote Londonderry, 'to satisfy even the ultras of the meeting.'[17] At a second conference, about a week later, it was decided to reject the bill. The following year, at another meeting at Wellington's house, called to discuss the Corporation Bill, the peers decided to take a line completely opposed to that of Peel and the Conservatives in the House of Commons. 'The Falmouths, Winchelseas, Cumberlands, and so forth', wrote Peel to his wife, 'have completely succeeded...What the consequences will be I cannot foresee ... I will not be made responsible for the acts of the lords.'[18]

Organization of a sort existed but discipline among the lords was hardly to be expected. The duke performed his irksome duties with dogged conscientiousness. He held meetings, wrote letters, issued memoranda and circulars; he collaborated with Lord Aberdeen in the general management of the House. But neither the deaf and elderly soldier nor the frigid Aberdeen were perhaps best fitted to control the peers through tact and influence. There was certainly little response to the duke's attempts to unite and guide the party. At the beginning of 1834 Wellington had invited for the day preceding the opening of Parliament all the noblemen who habitually spoke in the House of Lords or whose opinion had weight. The result, he complained to Lord Roden, was that some sent not particularly civil answers; some did not answer at all; some excused themselves; and only a few promised to attend. In May 1835 he sent out a memorandum on the danger of a reactionary attitude by the peers, in terms which virtually admitted the weakness of his authority. 'I recommend', he concluded, 'these few observations to the attention of the Duke of Cumberland, the Duke of Buckingham and the Marquis of Londonderry. I cannot hope that they will induce them to alter their course. They contain the reasons for my own.'[19]

Occasionally joint meetings of commoners and peers were held when circumstances seemed to demand unusual action. Such a meeting for example was probably that summoned at the height of the dispute over the Irish Municipal Corporations Bill in 1837. It was held at Lord Lyndhurst's house on 23 April and Peel read out a memorandum on policy, particularly on matters relating to Irish affairs, which commenced with an emphatic expression of 'the evil of continual conflict between the two houses of parliament on matters affecting the peace and welfare of Ireland'.[20] But such joint meetings were apparently rare and for the most part the sections of the party in the two Houses remained distinct and independent. Agreement, where it existed, seemed to be obtained more by common Conservative opinion or by the personal influence of leaders than by any organized machinery. There was no real and permanent collaboration, in fact, even between Peel and Wellington themselves. There was naturally exchange of views and discussion of policy; but there was no regular and systematized contact between the two leaders of the party. 'I do not like to interfere in the affairs of the House of Commons', wrote Wellington in 1837, 'first because I have nothing to say to them; and next, because I really do not understand them ... I generally find that without much communication of any sort, Sir Robert Peel and I find ourselves pretty nearly on the same ground.'[21] In comparison with that may be set this extract from a letter to Peel from Lord Talbot. After inquiring what the peers were doing with the Irish Church Bill and whether his presence was desirable Talbot added, 'I am fully aware that you will naturally say, Why ask me who am not a peer? What can I know about it? But still I know that you are so well aware of all that passes that anything you may be good enough to communicate...will materially assist me'.[22] When the leader of the Conservative peers managed tolerably well without much communication with his party chief; and when the leader of the party could disclaim knowledge of the intentions of the Conservatives in the House of Lords, it would be unwise to speak too confidently of the strength of the parliamentary co-ordination between the two wings of the party.

The relatively new technique of organizing a powerful opposition in Parliament made regular meetings expedient. The greater leisure of party leaders out of office also made them easier to arrange. It was different when those leaders became ministers. The preoccupations of power and the concentration on administration clearly led to a growing loss of contact between Peel and the rank and file of his party between 1841 and 1846. One index of this was that party meetings were held less often and began to be less satisfactory. The decline can almost be plotted. In February 1842, on the opening day of the debate on Peel's new Corn Bill, an explanatory meeting of the party was held which effectively won the support of the back-benchers for what from a party point of view had seemed the most controversial of the government's fiscal measures. Over the Canada Corn Bill in 1843, which to many agriculturalists appeared to be a weakening of the tariff of 1842 under the guise of imperial preference, the ruffled feelings of the protectionists were soothed by a meeting at Downing Street on the morning of its introduction, at which Peel and Stanley described the exact nature of the measure and the justification for it. A year later the atmosphere was growing more hostile. On 13 June 1844, warned by the defection of many Conservatives over Ashley's factory resolutions the previous March, Peel convened a meeting at his own house to ensure support for ministerial policy against Miles's wrecking motion on the sugar duties. All it did however was to demonstrate the strong feelings of the protectionists and the impossibility of preserving a united front. It was, Peel told his Cabinet afterwards, 'the most unsatisfactory meeting he had ever known'.[23] Nevertheless, though the party split disastrously and the government was defeated, the episode was startling enough for an independent meeting of some 200 Conservative M.P.s to pass a subsequent resolution of confidence in the ministry and an expression of regret at the report of their intended resignation. In 1846, however, over the repeal of the Corn Laws, the breach had become so great that Peel seems not even to have considered summoning a party meeting to explain his policy. When Brougham subsequently suggested that the disruption of the party could have been avoided if Peel had taken leading members into his confidence and called a general meeting, Peel merely observed to Aberdeen that if he had done so, he would have failed in his object of carrying the repeal of the Corn Laws — and 'I was resolved not to fail'.[24] No stronger proof is needed of his realization that repeal could not be carried by the ordinary processes of party government.

3

If it was the function of the party meeting to secure agreement on policy, the task of translating that agreement into attendance at division and at debate lay with the whips. The Whigs, being in office and able to provide position and salary for their party officials, maintained about five or six whips in the period up to 1841, the chief whip being almost invariably the senior or parliamentary secretary to the Treasury, more usually known as the patronage secretary.[25] The Conservatives appear to have kept a smaller staff. Their usual number in the House of Commons was three, one chief and two assistant whips. In the slack years of 1833 and 1834, when the fortunes of the party were at their lowest ebb, there may not even have been as many as that; while after the return to office in 1841 there were probably others who assisted in the work. The Conservative whip in the House of Lords at the beginning of this period was Lord Rosslyn[26] who despite his age was a keen party politician. He died in January 1837 at the age of 74 and was succeeded by Lord Redesdale.[27] In view of the doubtful temper and numerical majority of the Tory peers, the task of the Conservative whip in the upper House was probably more to restrain than to incite his followers. In 1839 Lord Falkland, one of the Whig whips in the House of Lords, told Hobhouse that the Tory majority against the government was 130 and that Redesdale had agreed with him to act 'upon honour', that is to say, refrain from any snap divisions or other tricks of the whip's trade.[28]

The office of chief whip was important both for the distinction it conferred on the individual and for the effect it had on the party as a whole. 'I say nothing', wrote Goulburn to Peel when a vacancy arose in 1837, 'of the importance of having a good Whipper-in. You know that as well as I do and have probably thought on the subject long since.'[29] The qualities demanded of a whip were many; the number of men from whom the appointment could be made was small. In theory the chief whip had to be a good man of business as well as a good politician; discreet in his utterances and sound in his views; popular among his fellow Members and yet capable of exercising discipline over them; accustomed to moving familiarly through the world of clubs and drawing-rooms and yet prepared to devote long and trying hours to the requirements of his office. He had to be of sufficient wealth and rank to command the respect of the hot-headed gentry under his control, and yet not so elevated as to regard the position of whip as beneath his dignity. In short, it was a post which in the words of Disraeli 'requires consummate self-control'. The same qualities though in a lesser degree were requisite for his assistants.

Indeed, if we are to judge from the engaging description by James Grant in his *Random Recollections* of parliamentary life in this period, not only moral but physical attributes were needed by the whip who sought to impose discipline in the early nineteenth-century House of Commons. The famous Billy Holmes, for instance, reckoned in the pre-Reform years as one of the most efficient and assiduous of the government whips, would restrain his Tory Members by force, if he knew them well, from going out of the House when he wanted them for a division. The most unpleasant part of a whip's job, according to Grant, was

> the squabbles, sometimes conflicts, he is often obliged to have with honourable members on their seeking to leave the house. He has to watch them in the lobby, for the purpose of keeping all in that are in; especially when he suspects that some of them are inclined to 'bolt', as Mr. Holmes used classically to express it. As soon as such suspicious persons open the door of the House, he must spring upon them like a tiger, and seizing them by the breast of the coat, authoritatively tell them they must not stir a foot till the impending division is over.

With such encounters as the *ultima ratio* of his authority, it was not to be wondered at that

> to be five feet ten inches in height, and to be more than the average breadth, coupled with considerable muscular energy, are qualifications which would contribute to the efficient discharge of the duties of the office.[30]

But there were other, less athletic, aspects to the work of the whips. They sent out letters and circulars to secure a full attendance at the opening of the session and on all important issues. They were responsible for the tactics of debate and the mustering of forces at critical divisions. Usually they acted as tellers at all divisions on which the parties were squarely opposed or, in the case of the ministerial whips, where the government was directly concerned. Thus on Russell's crucial Church of Ireland motion in April 1835 the Whig tellers were Stanley and Wood, the Conservatives Fremantle and Clerk. They arranged for their absent men to be paired off; they endeavoured to keep up the party numbers in those lethargic weeks towards the end of the session when the weather grew warm and Members' thoughts turned from the stifling atmosphere of St Stephen's to fresh air and country pursuits. Above all it was their duty to keep the party together by those unspectacular but essential arts of management; by recognizing and conversing with the humblest Member so that he might not feel he was without importance in the party; and by directing and informing opinion in the House or at the club by a judicious remark or an authoritative statement. On the other hand it was also their duty to keep the leaders accurately and continually informed of the temper and opinion of the party; to be prepared with expert advice on the probable voting strength of their followers on any specific line of policy; and to glean intelligence of the enemy. All this, in an age when the result of a general election could never be exactly known until the first critical division, and when the fate of a first-class measure was a common subject of wager, demanded great skill, much parliamentary experience, and a continual perception of all the cross-currents that agitated the parliamentary assembly. Moreover the discipline which the whips endeavoured to exert on their party rested less on the official status with which their actions and speeches were invested than on their personal per-suasiveness and the obvious exigencies of the situation. There was no inherent authority in the whips' circulars that made the unwilling Member obey.

The whip's central position among the party managers rendered him liable to various duties not directly concerned with the House of Commons. An extension of his work which was perhaps peculiar to the Conservative Party under Peel was that he was sometimes required to act as the channel of communication between the party and the press. Croker in December 1834 suggested that Herries would be the best man for such a purpose. A Cabinet minister was desirable and Herries had considerable experience of party and press matters; as Secretary at War, moreover, he was probably not over burdened with official duties.[31] But nothing appears to have been done. At any rate *The Times* soon had cause to complain and Lyndhurst expressed the fear that unless some positive ar-rangement was made the party would lose its powerful ally. He therefore asked Peel to appoint 'some *confidential person* to be in regular communication with *The Times*'. Peel thereupon named Sir George Clerk, the chief whip, as the member of the government who would 'readily communicate with any confidential person who may be sent for the purpose by the *Times*'.[32] Clearly it was Peel's intention to make the chief whip the only official source of information for the whole Conservative press. The same situation and the same solution occurred in 1841 when the Conservatives again took office. There were renewed complaints then of the neglect and lack of co-ordination in the way in which the various government departments sent out information to the press. Accordingly Peel suggested to Fremantle in December 1841 that 'it would be much better that each office should send to you what it has to communicate. If each acts independently there will be constant complaint'. The chief whip agreed. 'I think it will be expedient', he replied, 'to constitute some one the depositary of newspaper intelligence with authority to dole it out among the conservative newspapers as he thinks fit or according to such directions as you may be pleased to give him.'[33] But the fact that it was necessary to discuss the matter again in 1841 suggests the absence of any satisfactory permanent arrangement earlier. It is even doubtful whether the system approved by Peel in 1841 was strictly enforced. Thus Sir George Clerk, when financial secretary to the Treasury, gave permission in 1842 for the London correspondent of the *Edinburgh Advertiser* to call on him if he wanted any information, provided the matters he raised would 'admit of no impropriety'.[34] Perhaps the Scottish members of the administration made an exception in favour of their own newspapers. But even without any additional press duties, the work of the chief whip was arduous and important, when it is recollected that he was also responsible as patronage secretary for the supervision of a great deal of government patronage.

The last Tory chief whip in the unreformed House of Commons had been William Holmes who had first entered Parliament in 1808 as a Member for Grampound and had been Treasurer of the Ordnance from 1818 to 1830. In 1829 he nearly lost his office by voting against the government on the Catholic Emancipation Bill. But Wellington, not usually indulgent to acts of insubordination (and Holmes, too, had served in the army) was unwilling to harass still further the outraged susceptibilities of the King by any public act of severity towards the official opponents of the measure.[35] Holmes retained his post therefore up to the end of 1832. In the winter of 1831–2 he was corresponding with Peel over the summoning of the party. Writing on 12 January 1832, he expressed his horror at finding, after having arranged for the party to assemble on the 20th, that Peel was not proposing to come to London till after that date. 'Pray do let me know soon, they all look up to you, and if you are not here to guide us, I shall be obliged to run out of town on the 17th to avoid the questions and angry looks of those I have summoned to town when they find that their chief is not here.'[36]

In the general election of 1832 Holmes took some part although his position by that time was rivalled if not already overshadowed by that of Bonham, as far as electoral management was concerned. Dawson, who was anxious to get into Parliament, told Peel that he wrote to Holmes to ascertain whether there was any likely place for him in England but received no satisfaction from him. At the same time Holmes was receiving little satisfaction from his party leader. 'I heard the other day from Sir Robert Peel who has a small party at Drayton', he wrote to Mrs Arbuthnot on 10 September, 'he did not say one word about politics, nor did he ask even a question about the elections; he merely asked me to go down there which I declined.'[37] Whether this uninterest was accidental or indicated any real coolness on Peel's part is not clear; but in any case Holmes's inability to secure a seat in the new Parliament put an effective term to his activities as chief whip. 'I think it right to mention to you', he wrote to Peel in November, 'that I have abandoned all hope of coming into Parliament, unless something unexpected turns up at the Eleventh Hour. The fact is, I am not able to encounter the expense of a contest, but you may rest assured that whatever assistance an individual out of Parliament can give to a party will be constantly at your service.'[38] The long reign of 'Billy' Holmes thus ended in 1832; though his reputation was such that it was not immediately obvious to the public at large that he was no longer the party whip.

It is true moreover that he still remained in politics, though no longer in Parliament, and his peculiar talents and connexions were occasionally used by his party. At the time of Ingilby's malt tax motion of April 1833, for instance, it was Holmes who acted as Peel's messenger to inform the government, through Ellice, that he would support them in rescinding the resolution.[39] Or again, in April 1841, Fremantle passed on to Peel intelligence of the government's intentions over the question of dissolution which Holmes had gleaned from Ellice as they had gone home from the House the previous evening. Holmes's intimacy with the Whigs, and especially with Edward Ellice, who had been the rival chief whip in the critical years of 1830–2, was in fact both an asset and a defect. If the Conservatives learned something of their opponents' plans from Holmes's cross-bench connexions, they were also left to speculate how much information went back to the Whigs in the same way. The value of a man with a tent in each camp had obvious limitations. These misgivings among Holmes's own party would scarcely have been allayed had they seen a letter to Ellice from Joseph Parkes, the Whig election agent, written at this time. 'I met Holmes in the Treasury the other day', Parkes wrote on 12 September 1833, 'who told me he was coming down to join you. He is a good companion, as I knew in Cornwall, has the rummiest assortment of blaggard stories I ever met with by land or sea ... I always liked him, not that he has any calibre of mind, but he is a good political telescope — the helm he could not hold in a Thames wherry.'[40]

Who actually succeeded Holmes as Conservative chief whip is not clear. Indeed, with the weakness and confusion of the party in the Parliament of 1833–4, it is possible that no one was formally appointed. Peel's mind was very far from thoughts of party organization at that juncture. Besides Holmes, both Sir George Clerk and Planta, who were otherwise eligible candidates for the post, had failed to gain re-election; Bonham had been defeated at Rye in 1831 and did not stand for Parliament again until 1835. But Fremantle was in the House and so was Charles Ross, and if any whipping-in was done, these were as likely as any to have done it. Only with the formation of the Peel-Wellington ministry in 1834 did the parliamentary organization of the party begin to take shape. Fremantle was appointed financial secretary to the Treasury and Sir George Clerk as chief whip and patronage secretary, with Charles Ross[41] a Lord of the Treasury, and Bonham, Storekeeper to the Ordnance, as his two assistants.

Many years afterwards this arrangement was severely criticized by Disraeli. 'The party', he said with the rhetorician's contempt for accuracy of detail,[42]

> had been managed in opposition [*sc.* 1833–4] by two gentlemen, each distinguished by different but admirable qualities. One was remarkable for the sweetness of his temper, his conciliatory manners, and an obliging habit, which gains hearts oftener than the greatest services; he knew every member by name, talked to all sides, and had a quick eye which caught every corner of the House. His colleague was of a different cast; reserved and cold, and a great parliamentary student; very capable of laborious affairs, and with the right information always ready for a minister. Sir Robert appointed the man of the

world Financial Secretary of the Treasury, locked him up in a room or sealed him to a bench; and entrusted to the student, under the usual title of Patronage Secretary of the Treasury, the management of the House of Commons.

This dramatic contrast between Clerk and Fremantle owed as much perhaps to Disraeli's literary fantasy as to any basis of fact. At the time the appointment of Clerk seems to have attracted no adverse comment. Nor did Fremantle appear to observers misplaced as financial secretary. The author of *Random Recollections* described him as 'a man of excellent business habits' whose favourite subject was the miscellaneous estimates — 'he is expert at figures, and seems to have a partiality for them'.[43] Differences of style in the two men certainly existed; but the passage in the *Life of Lord George Bentinck* from which the quotation is taken was inserted by the author not only to adorn his tale but to point a moral; the moral being that Peel was a poor judge of men. When Disraeli's book appeared 17 years later, G.C. Lewis wrote to Graham, 'I should have thought Peel was a good judge of men and his [*sc.* Disraeli's] example of Fremantle being Financial Secretary of the Treasury in 1836 [*sic*] does not prove much, for he was made whip when Peel came back again'.[44]

There was in fact a personal difficulty about Fremantle in December 1834 when Peel was hastily forming his first ministry. The Duke of Buckingham, on whom Fremantle depended for re-election, was at that moment sulky and disaffected. Because of his patron's hostility towards the government Fremantle felt constrained to refuse the first offer of a secretaryship of the Treasury that Peel made to him. When a few days later he hinted that a change in the duke's temper might make it possible after all to accept, Peel replied discouragingly that he had already made an approach to someone else. In any case, he added, 'it would pain me to have the decision upon an appointment, so confidential and so important as that which I mentioned to you, dependent upon the *humour* of the Duke of Buckingham'. It was only by chance therefore that Peel was able subsequently to renew the offer. Whether he originally had it in mind to make Fremantle patronage rather than financial secretary to the Treasury is not known since the distinction was popular rather than official. What is certain is that there was some political embarrassment in appointing Fremantle to any office in 1834.[45]

When the party went out of office in April 1835, Clerk, Ross, and Bonham continued in their functions. The general election of 1837, however, enforced a further set of changes. All three of the whips were defeated and it was necessary, in Granville Somerset's cavalry phrase, to 'remount the establishment'. To the general embarrassment of the party, Holmes, an obvious but undesirable claimant to the office, had been returned for Berwick. This stroke of fortune he owed to his friend and patron, Lord Lowther. Shortly before the election Lowther had written to Peel pointing out that Holmes would be certain to get in for Berwick but the expense would be about £1,200 which he was in no position to meet. The Lowthers were therefore raising a private subscription for him among their friends and Peel was invited to contribute. Whatever his private views, it was not a request which Peel, as leader of the party and one of its richest men, could easily refuse to one of the party's most influential electoral magnates. He duly sent Lowther £50 and so helped to ease the way for Holmes's return to Westminster.[46]

There was little inclination, however, to allow Holmes to resume his former position in the party hierarchy. Long before the election the Duke of Wellington had told Arbuthnot that Holmes was 'the most difficult person to deal with he knew... he took good care not to tell him anything which ought to be secret'.[47] The duke was not alone in this opinion and as soon as the election was over two men whose word carried weight with Peel hastened to warn him against the new Member for Berwick. Granville Somerset wrote on 9 August to draw Peel's attention to the problem of appointing a successor to Clerk 'in the situation of a Whipper-in to our Party'. He continued,[48]

> I am the more desirous that you should determine this as soon as possible, as it is quite sure that Holmes will put himself forward, and I cannot conceal from you that altho' he is very much looked up to by the Lowther *set*, the great bulk of our friends would not tolerate him. The natural man is Sir Thomas Fremantle, who is universally liked and I think your opinion of him coincides with mine as to his Discretion and Straightforwardness. To him, Henry Baring and Cecil Forester would be most valuable assistants, but they would not (more especially the former) have anything to do with Holmes. For it is in vain to conceal that there is a somewhat general feeling that Holmes' love of communication and desire of being considered in the secrets of the other party by means of Ellice, makes him by no means trustworthy — a more uncharitable construction indeed has been put upon some parts of his Conduct and I for one should be *very* sorry to make him acquainted with any matters of real Delicacy. It will be in vain to keep him entirely out of the Whipping-in, or indeed would it be advisable to try to do so, but he should be made *use* of under the superintendence of a discreet person like Fremantle ... I have written to you thus early lest Holmes should constitute himself as a matter of course our Muster Master & it would then be more difficult to entrust another with the Business.

A week later Goulburn wrote on the same subject. Holmes's success at Berwick and Planta's at Hastings, he pointed out, put them both in a position to resume their former occupations. As regards the first the Lowther party and some others would strongly desire to see him restored but on the other hand a large number of the party regarded him with distrust and considered that he was unable to refrain from divulging information to Ellice. His appointment would not therefore be popular. But it would need careful handling by Peel not to hurt his feelings or those of his backers. As for Planta, though there was nothing against his integrity and honour, yet it was doubtful whether he had the requisite energy and activity for the office. If Fremantle would take the post, it would solve many difficulties, and the fact that he had been Secretary to the Treasury would be an answer to the *frondeurs* in other interests. He would do business well; he was popular and agreeable; lived a great deal in society; and his appointment would be generally acceptable.[49]

Before this letter was written, however, Peel had already accepted Granville Somerset's suggestion and empowered him to write to Fremantle. The latter, after a show of diffidence, accepted the appointment and on 17 August Granville Somerset was able to report to Peel that all was arranged. He had no doubt, he added, that Fremantle would do the business well and in fact he could not think of anyone else with the required qualifications 'unless it were those who from their Rank could not well undertake it'.[50] The decision on the two assistant whips was probably postponed until the new chief whip could be brought into the discussion. But Henry Baring certainly, and probably Cecil Forester, were eventually appointed. Hobhouse has an amusing if perhaps exaggerated story of a demonstration against the Whig ministers on the occasion of the presentation to the Queen of the Lords' address against the government's educational scheme in July 1839. There was a crowd at the gates and some hissing. 'We saw Cecil Forrester on horseback evidently directing the populace; and it was said that Messrs. Henry Baring, Bonham and Ross were there, but I did not see them.'[51] More evidence than this however would be necessary to convict the whips' office of mob-raising even for the pleasant purpose of baiting the Whig ministers. (George) Cecil Weld Forester, M.P. for Wenlock, was the brother of Lord Forester of Willey Park, Shropshire. He was an army officer (a lieutenant-colonel in the army and a major in the Royal Horse Guards) and his address in 1835 was officially given as Knightsbridge Barracks. Of rather more consequence was his colleague, Henry Bingham Baring. He was nephew to Lord Ashburton who had been President of the Board of Trade in Peel's short ministry of 1834–5, and to Sir Thomas Baring, 2nd Bt., and was thus a member of one of the largest and most influential parliamentary families of the day.[52] He sat for Marlborough and like Forester was of military rank though at one remove lower, being a major in the army and a captain in the Life Guards. At the 1837 election he had been an active and zealous subordinate to the party managers and allowed it to be generally known at the Carlton that he would like to be employed in the whips' office. Goulburn reported that though his manners were rough, he evinced a promptitude of decision on various points which arose that was useful and striking. Granville Somerset, who had seen more of him, told Peel that he had been '*most* useful and *most* active, and if Zeal, Quickness & activity with a fair share of discretion are useful requisites for keeping us together, I sincerely believe he would be a most useful assistant to Fremantle'.[53]

In the establishment thus set up the vicissitudes of the 1837–41 Parliament made few changes. Clerk was returned in 1838 as Member for Lord Exeter's pocket borough of Stamford but Fremantle had shown himself so fitted for his post that there was no question of moving him. When at the end of 1838 it seemed probable that Abercromby would retire from the Speakership, there was some discussion at the party headquarters of putting up a Conservative candidate to succeed him. Fremantle because of his general popularity was among those considered, though Bonham for one regretted the prospect of removing him from his obvious destination as parliamentary secretary to the Treasury. However the occasion allowed him to bring to Peel's notice J.M. Gaskell as 'a young man whose talents, zeal and industry wd. render him a valuable addition to that department with the addition of that general confidence & personal popularity which render Fremantle so inestimable. In fact to you I may say in confidence that he is not so much a man of fashion & pleasure as Baring (who has however many advantages) or of intrigue as people are disposed to charge on Holmes'.[54] In the end no doubt Peel concluded that a good whip was preferable to a Conservative Speaker. When in May 1839 Abercromby finally resigned the Chair Goulburn, who in many respects was a less popular candidate, was the Conservative choice to succeed him. However, the Whig majority prevailed; Shaw Lefevre succeeded Abercromby and Fremantle stayed at his post.

This disposition was not altered by the general election of 1841. When Peel formed his ministry in that year, he put Clerk as financial secretary and Fremantle as parliamentary secretary in the Treasury, thus reversing the roles of 1834–5. Baring, appointed one of the Lords of the Treasury, was chief assistant whip to Fremantle and throughout their period of office the two men seem to have been outstandingly assiduous in their parliamentary duties. At virtually every government division of any consequence at all Fremantle and Baring appear as the tellers for the administration. Mindful perhaps of Bonham's recommendation Peel also put Gaskell into the Treasury and it is possible therefore that he was brought into the whips' work. By a coincidence he was the parliamentary colleague of Cecil Forester in the representation of Wenlock. But though again returned to Parliament, it is clear that by this time Forester was no longer an official member of the whips' staff even if he had once been so. Holmes had been defeated at Stafford and so was no longer a problem. James Milnes Gaskell, who was possibly therefore the new assistant whip, was a son of Benjamin Gaskell of Thornes House, Yorkshire, M.P. for Maldon for many years, and a nephew of Daniel Gaskell, the first M.P. for Wakefield after the Reform Act. He had married in 1832 a daughter of that prominent Welsh Tory, the Rt. Hon. Charles Watkin Williams-Wynn. He was also friend and cousin of a man of very different type, Richard Monckton Milnes, and had been a contemporary with Gladstone as a leading speaker in the Oxford Union. He had other qualifications as whip. When Monckton Milnes visited him on the occasion of the famous Oxford and Cambridge joint debate in December 1829, he found his cousin already possessed of a minute knowledge of parliamentary personalities. 'He offered to repeat me the tellers in every debate for the last sixty years', wrote Milnes to his mother in justifiable admiration, 'and suggested a most amusing game, which consisted in each person telling the name of a borough and of the persons who represent it, and whoever stopped first paid a forfeit! "My father and I", he said, "played at it nearly a whole day without stopping".'[55] Such specialized talents deserved the recognition of a seat on the Treasury bench.

In May 1844 Fremantle was promoted Secretary at War and was succeeded as patronage secretary and chief whip by John Young,[56] the Conservative Member for County Cavan. This was the last major change in the party organization before the crisis of 1846. Young, together with Baring who stayed on as assistant whip to the end, was thus in charge of the ministerial supporters all through the difficult sessions of 1845 and 1846; and the two of them were the government tellers in the final division on the Protection of Life (Ireland) Bill on 25 June which marked the end of Peel's period of power. Two days later Bonham wrote to suggest to Peel that if it was possible for the latter to recommend Mrs Young for any vacancy among the Women of the Bedchamber, it would be a graceful recognition of the hard and unpleasant session through which her husband had just passed. Alone among the official men Milnes Gaskell had thought it his duty in January 1846 to resign from the Treasury because of the Corn Law policy of the ministry.[57]

It was a symptom of the peculiar nature of the Conservative disruption in that year, in fact, that not one of the leading party officials went over to the protectionists. Fremantle, at Peel's earnest request, had taken the Irish Secretaryship in January 1845 when Lord Eliot was removed to the upper House. But his experiences in the post had not been happy and in February 1846 he left politics to become deputy chairman (and later chairman) of the Board of Customs. Sir George Clerk, who had been appointed Master of the Mint in 1845, remained in parliamentary life for one more session. Though his seat at Stamford was impossible after the Corn Law split, he secured election as a Liberal for Dover in 1847 and retired from public life in 1852. Henry Baring stayed on in Parliament as a Peelite. Bonham, though outside the House, remained the unofficial agent and adviser of the Peelite party until the '60s. Young, the last chief whip of the united Conservative Party, continued to act as the Peelite whip until 1852.[58] Granville Somerset, too, despite his early misgivings over the repeal of the Corn Laws, remained faithful to Peel and retained his seat for Monmouthshire as a Liberal-Conservative in 1847 despite having to fight the election against two Protectionists, one of them his own kinsman.[59]

4

The work of the whips in holding the party together and directing its energies was to some extent assisted by a division of the party on a geographical basis. The English, the Scots, and the Irish Members were recognised as three distinct groups and these territorial associations were used to supplement the normal party connexion. The English Members, being the largest element, were left to the care of the ordinary party managers. Their affairs were dealt with by the whips and such men as Granville Somerset, Rosslyn and Hardinge. The other two groups came under a more precise form of leadership. The Scottish Conservative Members were led by the Duke of Buccleuch and Sir George Clerk, the latter of whom was not only a recognized leader but also took an active part in organization and management. In 1838 the Duke of Buccleuch retired from politics owing to illness and Aberdeen, at the request of Peel and Wellington, took over the 'general charge of Scotch conservative matters'.[60] The small group of Irish Conservative Members was led by Frederick Shaw,[61] M.P. for Dublin University, in whose hands rested almost exclusively the management of Conservative Party affairs in the second island of the United Kingdom. The author of the *Random Recollections* described Shaw as foremost and almost alone among Tory Members interested in Irish affairs for their own sake, and as the oracle of the small Irish Conservative party. As an orator he was characterized more by party zeal than eloquence but there was no doubt of the high position he held in the party councils. A generation later Gladstone related an episode which bears witness to Shaw's influence and the firm control he exercised in his own domain.

> Nearly thirty years ago, my leader, Sir R. Peel, agreed in the Irish Tithes bill to give 25 per cent of the tithe to the landlord in return for that 'Commutation'. Thinking this too much ... I happened to say so in a private letter to an Irish clergyman. Very shortly after I had a note from Peel, which enclosed one from Shaw, his head man in Ireland, complaining of my letter as making his work impossible if such things were allowed to go on. Sir R. Peel indorsed the remonstrance, and I had to sing small. The discipline was very tight in those days, (and we were in opposition, not in government). But it worked well on the whole, and I must say it was accompanied on Sir R. Peel's part with a most rigid regard to rights of all kinds within the official or quasi-official corps, which has somewhat declined in more recent times.[62]

This territorial division was obviously based on the personal relationships which might be expected to exist between men from the same part of the kingdom as well as on their specialized knowledge, and was probably of some administrative use in subdividing the physical work involved in the routine management of the party. Thus in December 1835, when the question arose of calling a party meeting before the commencement of the session, Granville Somerset suggested that the enormous clerical work which this summons would entail could best be accomplished by dividing it between the various leaders and managers, Shaw for Ireland, Clerk for Scotland, Granville Somerset and others for England. In that way he hoped that letters would be sent to nearly all the Conservative Members.[63]

The letters and circulars issued by the whips were almost invariably requests for attendance either at specific meetings or generally in Parliament. The normal parliamentary session in this period ran from January or February to July or August with a long recess of five months. But even so it was found difficult to secure full attendance either at the beginning of the session or at the end. In December 1839 Fremantle emphasized to Peel the reluctance of their followers to attend in force on the first day of the session unless they believed they would be needed for a division on the Address. This was but a repetition of similar arguments used by the party managers before the start of the 1839 session when they also wished to hold out hopes of an amendment on the Address. But Peel had emphatically refused to authorize any expectation of such an event 'for such an object as that of persuading a few idle men to come to town earlier than they would otherwise do'.[64] It was for the same reason that the party managers were constantly recommending eve-of-session meetings, though Peel again was apt to disapprove of such devices unless there was a particular purpose for them.[65] In the absence of a special meeting the whips could only rely on the usual summons to Parliament. There was a conventional form for these although the detailed wording varied according to circumstances and policy. Fremantle kept a book of precedents when he was chief whip which enabled him to furnish at short notice circulars to fit most parliamentary occasions. Here, for example, is a specimen submitted for Peel's approval before the start of the 1840 session.

> The meeting of Parliament being fixed for Thursday the 16th. of January next, your attendance at the House of Commons on that day is *most earnestly and particularly* requested as it is expected that business of great importance will be brought forward at the commencement of the Session.

This was the usual nondescript circular which conveyed no pledge of a division on the Address and merely referred to the start of the session. When finally approved by the head of the party the circular was lithographed and copies sent out through the post by the chief whip and his assistants some two or three weeks before the opening of Parliament. As such it was not calculated to secure very comprehensive obedience; and in 1838 and 1839, if not in other years, the Conservative whips found it necessary to follow up the circular with a private letter to each of the party members. A letter, being more personal, might be expected to have a greater effect than a circular and had the additional advantage of being the vehicle of any last-minute information on the party's tactics at the opening of the session on which the party leaders had agreed.

These were not the only occasions when a written summons to attend Parliament was sent out. According to O'Connell cards were sent out from the Carlton Club to its members urging particular attendance in the House of Commons on the days when the election committees were chosen.[66] This was of course in the period before 1839 when the committees were still ballotted from the Members of the whole House behind locked doors. Written reminders were also necessary on occasion towards the end of session. At the end of the protracted session of 1835 which lasted until 10 September, Bonham, Hardinge and Granville Somerset wrote to the party members in the vicinity of London to muster in strength on 31 August when the Lords' amendments to the Municipal Corporations Bill were due to be considered. However they were unable to hold out the prospect of Peel being in attendance on that day and Bonham did not reckon in those circumstances on getting more than a hundred Members.[67]

On the other hand, if Members did not pay very much attention to the whips' letters and circulars, the fact of receiving them was the only certain and visible proof of party 'membership'. It should be borne in mind exactly what that signified. It meant no more than that the party leader gave formal recognition to those who by their own words and actions had recognized his leadership. The whips' circular was still in form a personal request from the leader of the party and thus implied a degree of confidence in the person so addressed. Cardwell, for instance, reported as a matter of some interest in November 1847 that Tufnell, the ministerialist whip, had not sent circulars to the 'Radicals'; though he was unable to discover more precisely what exclusions had been made.[68] Abstention from sending circulars to an individual therefore implied a loss of confidence which might in certain circumstances have an adverse effect on the political career of the person concerned. But the time was still far distant when there could be any talk of 'expulsion' from the party. 'Membership' of a party did not in fact exist in any technical sense; and therefore 'expulsion' could not exist either. It is interesting for example that not until 1912 was it definitely laid down in the rules of the Carlton Club that new members should belong to the Conservative and Unionist Party.

Politicians in the age of Peel still preferred to talk of supporting or giving a fair trial to Her Majesty's Ministers, occasionally, though less often, of opposing them; they spoke of 'the gentlemen with whom I usually act' or more informally of 'our friends'. But they did not as a rule talk of being members of a party; and they strove to give the appearance of being independent and unfettered in their parliamentary conduct. Under these conditions the sending or receiving of the whips' circulars betokened little more than mutual confidence between leader and follower. This is made clear by the well-known incident in 1844 when, after consulting his party leader, Fremantle refrained from sending the usual letter to two of the Young Englanders, Smythe and Disraeli, because of their hostile attitude the previous session. When Disraeli discovered that his failure to receive the customary summons had been deliberate, he wrote in protest to Peel. He made it clear in his letter that he regarded the exclusion as the termination of a 'public tie' and as a 'painful personal procedure which the past by no means authorized'. But the more interesting part of the correspondence is the section of Peel's answer in which he explained and vindicated his decision not to send a personal summons to Disraeli.

> My reason for not sending you the usual circular was an honest doubt whether I was entitled to send it — whether towards the close of the last Session of Parliament you had not expressed opinions as to the conduct of the Government in respect to more than one important branch of public policy, foreign and domestic, which precluded me, in justice both to you and to myself, from preferring personally an earnest request for your attendance.

Even more striking is the fact that Peel was formally prepared to accept Disraeli's assurances and to revoke that decision.

It gives me, however, great satisfaction to infer from your letter — as I trust I am justified in inferring — that my impressions were mistaken, and my scruples were unnecessary.[69]

The basis of the party whip is here seen to be a matter of punctilio rather than of discipline. The question was not whether a Member's conduct had justified 'expulsion' but whether it had invited or at least justified a personal request for support from a recognized party leader.

[*To be concluded.*]

Notes

[1] See A. Aspinall, 'English Party Organization in the Early Nineteenth Century', *E.H.R.*, XLI (1926), 389–411, for party organization earlier in the century.

[2] 'F.R. Bonham: Conservative "Political Secretary", 1832–47', *E.H.R.*, LXIII (1948), 502–22; *Politics in the Age of Peel* (1953, 2nd edn. 1977), Chapter 15.

[3] Neither the brief notice of his death in *The Times* nor the obituary in the *Gentleman's Magazine* refers to his party activities.

[4] H.M.C., *Prime Ministers' Papers: W.E. Gladstone*, II, 260.

[5] But see G. Kitson Clark, *Peel and the Conservative Party* (2nd edn., 1964), pp. xxii, xxv.

[6] B.L., Add. MS. 40333, f. 346.

[7] Aspinall, 'English Party Organization', p. 394.

[8] Add. MS. 44110, f. 154.

[9] Add. MS. 40314, f. 174.

[10] Aspinall, 'English Party Organization', p. 395. Cf. Add. MS. 40419, ff. 186–90, where a figure of about 200 is suggested for the attendance at this meeting.

[11] Add. MS. 40303, f. 61.

[12] *The Private Letters of Sir Robert Peel*, ed. G. Peel (1920), pp. 153–4.

[13] C.S. Parker, *Sir Robert Peel from his Private Papers* (3 vols., 1891–9), II, 366.

[14] Lord Francis Egerton in 1838 (*ibid.*, II, 359).

[15] J. Morley, *Life of Gladstone* (3 vols., 1912), I, 181; W.F. Monypenny and G.E. Buckle, *Life of Disraeli* (6 vols., 1910–20), II, 89.

[16] Parker, *Peel*, II, 319.

[17] Duke of Buckingham, *Memoirs of the Courts and Cabinets of William IV and Victoria* (2 vols., 1861), II, 115.

[18] Peel, *Private Letters*, pp. 153–4.

[19] Sir Herbert Maxwell, *Life of Wellington* (2 vols., 1899), II, 295, 307.

[20] Add. MS. 40423, f. 176.

[21] Maxwell, *Wellington*, II, 315.

[22] Add. MS. 40403, f. 266.

[23] H.M.C., *Prime Ministers' Papers: W.E. Gladstone*, II, 261.

[24] *Memoirs of ... Sir Robert Peel*, eds. Lord Mahon and E. Cardwell (2 vols., 1856–7), II, 324.

[25] Aspinall, 'English Party Organization', is particularly full on the Liberal Party organization in this period.

[26] Sir James St Clair Erskine, *b.* 1762, *suc.* his uncle, Alexander Wedderburn (the famous lawyer), as Baron Loughborough and Earl of Rosslyn in 1805.

[27] John Thomas Freeman Mitford of Redesdale, Northumberland, *b.* 1805, *suc.* his father as second Baron in 1830, chairman of committees in the House of Lords 1851, *cr.* Earl of Redesdale 1877, *d.* 1886.

[28] Lord Broughton, *Recollections of a Long Life*, ed. Lady Dorchester (6 vols., 1910–11), V, 219.

[29] Add. MS. 40333, f. 372.

[30] James Grant, *Random Recollections of the House of Commons 1830–35* (1836), p. 234; *idem*,

Random Recollections of the Lords and Commons (2 vols., 1838), II, 46–8.

[31] Add. MS. 40321, f. 28.

[32] Add. MS. 40316, ff. 164, 166.

[33] Add. MS. 40476, ff. 84, 86. Fremantle's reply is printed by A. Aspinall, *Politics and the Press c. 1780–1850* (1949), App., p. 433.

[34] Scottish R.O., Clerk Papers, Francis to Clerk, dated 16 Feb. but no year given. The letter is with a bundle of 1842 correspondence and it is unlikely that a journalist would be greatly concerned to secure information from Clerk unless he had been a member of the government at that time.

[35] Aspinall, 'English Party Organization', p. 397.

[36] Add. MS. 40402, f. 183.

[37] *The Correspondence of Charles Arbuthnot*, ed. A. Aspinall (Camden Soc., 3rd ser., LXV, 1941), p. 162.

[38] Add. MS. 40403, f. 98.

[39] *Ibid.*, f. 239.

[40] National Library of Scotland, Ellice Papers.

[41] M.P. Northampton 1832–7, a West India proprietor, son-in-law of Earl Cornwallis.

[42] *Life of Lord George Bentinck* (1872), p. 226.

[43] *Random Recollections of the Lords and Commons*, II, 77–8.

[44] Graham MSS. (Sir Charles Graham, Bt, Netherby, Longtown, Cumbria), 29 Dec. 1851.

[45] Add. MS. 40405, f. 295; 40406, ff. 65, 67, 240.

[46] Add. MS. 40423, ff. 285, 310.

[47] Add. MS. 40341, f. 1 (June 1836).

[48] Add. MS. 40424, f. 47.

[49] Add. MS. 40333, f. 372. The Holmes incident seems to have been misread by R.L. Hill, *Toryism and the People 1832 1846* (1929), p. 63. There is no evidence that the criticisms of Holmes implied an attack on the strict discipline imposed by Peel. Indeed the facts point the other way. The criticism came from the official men in the party; and if there were genuine grounds for criticism of the party management, it would have been directed against the whips appointed since Peel had taken over the leadership of the party, whereas Holmes had not been in the House of Commons since 1832.

[50] Add. MS. 40424, f. 82.

[51] Broughton, *Recollections*, V, 216.

[52] In the 1835 Parliament for example there were no fewer than five Barings in the House of Commons as well as Lord Ashburton in the Lords. All were descendants of the famous London merchant Francis Baring who founded the family fortunes in the latter part of the eighteenth century. Francis Thornhill Baring (M.P. Portsmouth) differed from the rest of his family in being a Whig.

[53] Add. MS. 40333, f. 372; 40424, f. 47.

[54] Add. MS. 40425, ff. 381–4.

[55] T. Wemyss Reid, *Life … of Richard Monckton Milnes, First Lord Houghton* (2 vols., 1890), I, 78.

[56] M.P. Co. Cavan 1831–55; *b.* 1807, *suc.* his father as second Bt 1848, *cr.* Baron Lisgar 1870. He should not be confused with G.F. Young, M.P. Tynemouth, who acted as a kind of whip for the Stanley party in 1835.

[57] Parker, *Peel*, III, 334.

[58] He was appointed Chief Secretary for Ireland under the Aberdeen ministry.

[59] He could indeed be said to have been a martyr to his loyalty over the repeal of the Corn Laws. His death from a heart attack on 23 Feb. 1848 was attributed to the excitements of his contested election and the annoyance of the petition brought against his return (*The Times*, 24 Feb. 1848).

[60] Lady Frances Balfour, *Life of George, Fourth Lord Aberdeen* (2 vols., 1922), II, 24.

[61] Rt. Hon. Frederick Shaw, *b.* 1799, second son of Sir Robert Shaw, first Bt and M.P. Dublin 1804–26. He married the youngest daughter of the Hon. George Jocelyn, grand-daughter of the first Earl Roden, and was Recorder of Dublin 1828–76, M.P. Dublin Univ. 1832–48.

[62] Morley, *Gladstone*, III, 87.

[63] Add. MS. 40333, f. 346.

64   Parker, *Peel*, II, 376.
65   Add. MS. 40427, f. 331.
66   Hansard, *Parl. Deb.*, 3rd ser., XLI, 108.
67   Add. MS. 40421, f. 35.
68   Add. MS. 40599, f. 393.
69   Add. MS. 40476, ff. 345–6, 349; Parker, *Peel*, III, 144–7.

NOTES AND DOCUMENTS

PROXY RECORDS OF THE HOUSE OF LORDS
1510–1733

J.C. SAINTY

House of Lords

The value of the proxy records of the House of Lords as a means of illustrating its history has been fully recognized in recent years.[1] However, their utility has to some extent been limited by the lack of any published lists indicating the extent of their survival.[2] The object of this note is to supply this want. The sources are of two kinds: the Journals of the House and the sequence of proxy books. Details of the information contained in these sources from 1510 to 1733 are to be found in the appendices.

An examination of the printed *Lords' Journals* indicates that it was the practice for proxies to be entered in them from session 1510 to session 1629.[3] Before 1552 the proxies were in some sessions recorded as part of the proceedings on the day on which they were entered; in others they were grouped together in a consolidated list prefixed to the proceedings of the session.[4] After 1553 the latter course was invariably adopted. The reason for the discontinuation of the practice of entering proxies in the Journals after 1629 is not entirely clear. No doubt one of the considerations was the fact that by then there was in existence a parallel series of proxy books recording the same information.

The earliest surviving proxy book is that for the session of 1626. It may be that the series was introduced as a result of the Standing Orders made during the course of that session for the regulation of the use of proxies. Three of these provided: that no lord might hold more than two proxies; that only a lord spiritual might hold the proxy of a lord spiritual and only a lord temporal that of a lord temporal; and that the presence of a lord in the House had the effect of cancelling his proxy.[5] It is significant that the entries in the proxy books are so framed as to enable the clerk to ensure that these provisions had been complied with.

After 1733 it was the practice to enter the proxies for each session in a single volume. The sequence is complete from that date until the session of 1864, the last for which proxies were entered.[6] Before 1733 the position is less satisfactory as the table in Appendix 2 shows. The entering of proxies or at least the method of record-keeping is not particularly systematic. Thus volume 1 in the series contains entries for sessions 1626 and 1660. There are no entries for sessions 1629, 1640 or 1661–2. Volume 7 covers the whole period from 1685–1733, omitting entries for ten sessions. The entries for one of these sessions, the first of 1714, are bound up separately in volume 8.

APPENDIX 1:*Entries in Lords' Journals 1510–1629*

Date of session	Number of proxies entered	Reference
1510, 21 Jan.–23 Feb.	4	*L.J.*, I, 4(2), 5, 6.
1512, 4 Feb.–30 Mar.	9	*Ibid.*, 11(3), 12(4), 13(2).
1512, 4 Nov.–20 Dec.	Journal wanting	—
1514, 23 Jan.–4 Mar.	Journal wanting	—
1515, 5 Feb.–5 Apr.	25	*Ibid.*, 19(18), 20(2), 22, 23, 24, 25, 33.
1515, 12 Nov.–22 Dec.	4	*Ibid.*, 43, 44, 45, 47.
1523, 15 Apr.–13 Aug.	Journal wanting	—
1529, 4 Nov.–17 Dec.	Journal wanting	—
1531, 16 Jan.–31 Mar.	Journal wanting	—
1532, 15 Jan.–14 May	Journal wanting	—
1533, 4 Feb.–7 Apr.	Journal wanting	—
1534, 15 Jan.–30 Mar.	22	*Ibid.* 58(22).
1534, 3 Nov.–18 Dec.	Journal wanting	—
1536, 4 Feb.–15 Apr.	19	N.H. Nicholas, *Report on the Barony of L'Isle* (1829), pp. 424–6.
1536, 8 June–18 July	7	*L.J.*, I, 83–4
1539, 28 Apr.–28 June	6	*Ibid.*, 103.
1540, 12 Apr.–24 July	5	*Ibid.*, 128.
1542, 16 Jan.–1 Apr.	4	*Ibid.*, 164.
1543, 22 Jan.–12 May	no entries	—
1544, 14 Jan.–29 Mar.	12	*Ibid.*, 266.
1545, 23 Nov.–24 Dec.	12	*Ibid.*, 267.
1547, 14–31 Jan.	2	*Ibid.*, 291.
1547, 4 Nov.–24 Dec.	no entries	—
1548, 24 Nov.–1549, 14 Mar.	13	*Ibid.*, 316, 317, 318, 319, 321 (3), 326, 330, 332, 338, 339(2).
1549, 4 Nov.–1550, 1 Feb.	28	*Ibid.*, 355(14), 356, 357(3), 358(2), 359, 360, 361(2), 362, 372, 376, 378.

Date of session	Number of proxies entered	Reference
1552, 23 Jan.–15 Apr.	17	*Ibid.*, 394(4), 396(3), 397(2), 398, 405, 407, 408, 409, 410 (2), 412.
1553, 1–31 Mar.	13	*Ibid.*, 430.
1553, 5–21 Oct.	Journal wanting	—
1553, 23 Oct.–6 Dec.	Journal wanting	—
1554, 2 Apr.–5 May	24	*Ibid.*, 447.
1554, 12 Nov.–1555, 16 Jan.	23	*Ibid.*, 464.
1555, 21 Oct.–9 Dec.	15	*Ibid.*, 492.
1558, 20 Jan.–7 Mar.	20	*Ibid.*, 513.
1558, 5–17 Nov.	2	*Ibid.,* 536.
1559, 25 Jan.–8 May	37	*Ibid.*, 541.
1563, 12 Jan.–10 Apr.	25	*Ibid.*, 580.
1566, 20 Sep.–1567, 2 Jan.	33	*Ibid.*, 624–5.
1571, 2 Apr.–29 May	17	*Ibid.*, 667.
1572, 8 May–30 June	21	*Ibid.*, 703.
1576, 8 Feb.–15 Mar.	10	*Ibid.*, 729.
1581, 16 Jan.–18 Mar.	21	*Ibid.*, II, 20.
1584, 23 Nov.–1585, 29 Mar.	24	*Ibid.*, 61.
1586, 29 Oct.–1587, 23 Mar.	11	*Ibid.*, 113.
1589, 4 Feb.–29 Mar.	12	*Ibid.*, 145.
1593, 19 Feb.–10 Apr.	16	*Ibid.*, 168.
1597, 24 Oct.–1598, 9 Feb.	16	*Ibid.*, 191.
1601, 27 Oct.–19 Dec.	22	*Ibid.*, 226.
1604, 19 Mar.–7 July	25	*Ibid.*, 263.
1605, 5 Nov.–1606, 27 May	29	*Ibid.*, 355.
1606, 18 Nov.–1607, 4 July	36	*Ibid.,* 449.
1610, 9 Feb.–23 July	27	*Ibid.*, 548.
1610, 16 Oct.–6 Dec.	21	*Ibid.*, 666.
1614, 5 Apr.–7 June	16	*Ibid.*, 686.
1621, 30 Jan.–19 Dec.	46	*Ibid.*, III, 4–5.
1624, 19 Feb.–29 May	31	*Ibid.*, 205.
1625, 18 June–12 Aug.	37	*Ibid.*, 431.
1626, 6 Feb.–15 June	52	*Ibid.*, 491.
1628, 17 Mar.–26 June	43	*Ibid.*, 685.
1629, 20 Jan.–10 Mar.	21	*Ibid.*, IV, 3.

APPENDIX 2: *Proxy books 1626–1733*

Date of session	Number of proxies entered	Proxy book number
1626, 6 Feb.–15 June	58	1
1628, 17 Mar.–26 June	35	2
1629, 20 Jan.–10 Mar.	missing	—
1640, 13 Apr.–5 May	missing	—
1640, 3 Nov.–1649, 30 Jan.	101[7]	3
1660, 25 Apr.–29 Dec.	14	1
1661, 8 May–1662, 19 May	missing	—
1663, 18 Feb.–27 July	41	4
1664, 16 Mar.–17 May	22	4
1664, 24 Nov.–1665, 2 Mar.	25	5
1665, 9–31 Oct.	18	5
1666, 18 Sept.–1667, 8 Feb.	48	5
1667, 25–29 July	1	5
1667, 10 Oct.–1669, 1 Mar.	34	5
1669, 19 Oct.–11 Dec.	18	5
1670, 14 Feb.–1671, 22 Apr.	73	5
1673, 4 Feb.–20 Oct.	24	5
1673, 27 Oct.–4 Nov.	3	5
1674, 7 Jan.–24 Feb.	27	5
1675, 13 Apr.–9 June	29	5
1675, 13 Oct.–22 Nov.	41	6
1677, 15 Feb.–1678, 13 May	74	6
1678, 23 May–15 July	14	6
1678, 21 Oct.–30 Dec.	40[8]	6
1679, 6 Mar.–27 May	11	6
1680, 21 Oct.–1681, 10 Jan.	7	6
1681, 21–28 Mar.	1	6
1685, 19 May–20 Nov.	24	7
1689, 22 Jan.–21 Oct.	34	7
1689, 23 Oct.–1690, 27 Jan.	31	7
1690, 20 Mar.–7 July	14	7
1690, 2 Oct.–1691, 26 Mar.	12	7
1691, 22 Oct.–1692, 12 Apr.	34	7
1692, 4 Nov.–1693, 14 Mar.	32	7
1693, 7 Nov.–1694, 25 Apr.	19	7
1694, 12 Nov.–1695, 3 May	25	7
1695, 22 Nov.–1696, 27 Apr.	16	7
1696, 20 Oct.–1697, 16 Apr.	55	7
1697, 3 Dec.–1698, 5 July	69	7
1698, 6 Dec.–1699, 4 May	missing	—
1699, 16 Nov.–1700, 11 Apr.	missing	—
1701, 10 Feb.–24 June	missing	—
1701, 30 Dec.–1702, 25 May	7	7
1702, 20 Oct.–1703, 27 Feb.	1	7
1703, 9 Nov.–1704, 3 Apr.	missing	—
1704, 24 Oct.–1705, 14 Mar.	60	7
1705, 25 Oct.–1706, 19 Mar.	28	7

Date of session	Number of proxies entered	Proxy book number
1706, 3 Dec.–1707, 8 Apr.	29	7
1707, 14–24 Apr.	missing	—
1707, 23 Oct.–1708, 1 Apr.	missing	—
1708, 16 Nov.–1709, 21 Apr.	missing	—
1709, 15 Nov.–1710, 5 Apr.	missing	—
1710, 25 Nov.–1711, 12 June	84	7
1711, 7 Dec.–1712, 8 July	197	7
1713, 9 Apr.–16 July	missing	—
1714, 16 Feb.–9 July	172	8
1714, 1–25 Aug.	19	7
1715, 17 Mar.–1716, 26 June	300	7
1717, 20 Feb.–25 July	115	7
1717, 21 Nov.–1718, 21 Mar.	137	7
1718, 11 Nov.–1719, 18 Apr.	142	7
1719, 23 Nov.–1720, 11 June	158	7
1720, 8 Dec.–1721, 29 July	152	7
1721, 31 July–10 Aug.	1	7
1721, 19 Oct.–1722, 7 Mar.	61	7
1722, 9 Oct.–1723, 27 May	110	7
1724, 9 Jan.–24 Apr.	missing	—
1724, 12 Nov.–1725, 31 May	58	7
1726, 20 Jan.–24 May	29	7
1727, 17 Jan.–15 May	31	7
1727, 27 June–17 July	5	7
1728, 23 Jan.–28 May	17	7
1729, 21 Jan.–14 May	25	7
1730, 13 Jan.–15 May	27	7
1731, 21 Jan.–7 May	46	7
1732, 13 Jan.–1 June	77	7
1733, 16 Jan.–13 June	118	7

Notes

1 J.C. Sainty and D. Dewar, *Divisions in the House of Lords: An Analytical List 1685 to 1857* (House of Lords R.O., Occasional Publication No. 2, 1976) p.11, n.44. G Holmes, *British Politics in the Age of Anne* (1967), pp. 382–403.
2 For a general description of the proxy records in the custody of the House, see M.F. Bond, *Guide to the Records of Parliament* (1971) pp.175, 282.
3 In order to remain valid proxies had to be renewed each session see *L.J.*, IV, 10–11.
4 In the case of the session of 1544, however, the consolidated list is inserted at the end.
5 H.M.C.,*House of Lords MSS.*, new ser., X, 8.
6 Proxies were last used during this session; their use was suspended in 1868; see Sainty and Dewar, *Divisions*, p. 11, n. 35.
7 Last entry dated 23 Nov. 1642.
8 A memorandum states that all the proxies so far entered for this session were made void by the Test Act which received the royal assent on 30 Nov. 1678.

RECORDED DIVISIONS IN THE HOUSE OF LORDS, 1661–1680

RICHARD W. DAVIS

Washington University, St Louis

In their excellent *Divisions in the House of Lords: An Analytical List 1685 to 1857* (House of Lords Record Office, Occasional Publication No. 2, 1976), J.C. Sainty and David Dewar simply note the dates of 16 more divisions that took place between 1660 and 1685 (p.4). The list which follows includes those 16, but gives full details, and also includes further divisions recently found. This new compilation contains the 31 divisions which are known to have taken place between 1661 and 1680.

The reasons for this listing are the same as those that prompted the earlier effort. Divisions are a useful index of the level of political activity, and the numbers who participated, of its extent. They are not, of course, an infallible guide. The first two divisions noted, the first on a judicial case, the second on a private bill, appear to be without any political implication; and there are a few other non-political divisions interspersed thereafter. By and large, however, the list faithfully reflects the rising and lowering political temperature; specifically, the political storms that arose around the activities of Clarendon in the '60s, Danby in the mid–'70s, and finally those, real or imagined, of the Duke of York at the turn of the decade.

It would be unsafe to say that the list is exhaustive. Sainty and Dewar relied on divisions noted in the Manuscript Minutes preserved in the House of Lords Record Office. I have found others, the source being indicated in a footnote. Still others will doubtless be unearthed as time goes on. But it is unlikely that a great many more will be, or that they will much change the picture of politics suggested by those already known.

Divisions were certainly the exception, not the rule. The most common way of determining questions was by voice vote. Only rarely were the lords 'told'. Usually on these occasions, tellers counted those voting, with the Contents standing and the Not Contents remaining seated. In 1675 the practice began of the Contents withdrawing below the bar of the House, though it was not always used until after this period. The old method, in which the clerks told the lords in reverse order of precedence, was already confined to formal votes, such as those in trials.

In the list that follows, the first number indicates those present and voting, the second the proxies (when called for), the third the total vote on either side of the question. After the total vote, the number of proxies is noted in parentheses. (Of the 1661–2 vote, it was simply noted that the lords were told.) An asterisk denotes those divisions noted by Sainty and Dewar. They only record one division on 20 November 1675, whereas two actually took place. In the division on 4 April 1678 on the question of Lord Pembroke's guilt, the Manuscript Minutes record that six voted him guilty of murder, 40 guilty of manslaughter, and 18 not guilty. Thus the total number of lords voting was 64, but the verdict of guilty of man-slaughter was carried by a majority of 22, the six 'guilty of murder' votes not counting towards the final verdict.

APPENDIX

Date	Subject	Question	Contents	Not Contents	Total	Majority
11 July 1661[1]	Lord Oxford's case for the Great Chamber-laincy	errors assigned by Oxford's counsel	27	41	68	14
*6 Feb. 1661–2	Earl of Derby's Bill	3rd reading	—	—	—	(passed)
*22 Oct. 1666	Irish Cattle Bill	whether to go into CWH	28+5=33	28+5=33	66(10)	0
*23 Nov. 1666	Irish Cattle Bill	3rd reading	53+10=63	31+16=47	110(26)	16
5 Feb. 1666–7[2]	Viscount Mordaunt's impeach-ment	whether to grant a confe-rence	29+9=38	34+15=49	87(24)	11
29 Nov. 1667[3]	Claren-don's impeach-ment	whether to com-mit Clarendon to the Tower	12	60	72	48

Date	Subject	Question	Contents	Not Contents	Total	Majority
19 Dec. 1667[4]	Anglo-Scottish Trade Bill	3rd reading	24+10=34	27+3=30	64(13)	4
★17 Mar. 1669–70[5]	Lord Roos's Bill	1st reading	41+15=56	42+6=48	104(21)	8
★19 Mar. 1669–70[6]	Lord Roos's Bill	whether to commit	48+16=64	44+6=50	114(22)	14
★28 Mar. 1669–70[7]	Lord Roos's Bill	3rd reading	42	35	77	7
★22 Jan. 1673–4	Hallet *v.* Kendall	whether witnesses mentioned at the bar should be heard	24+5=29	26+4=30	59(9)	1
★21 Apr. 1675	Danby's Test Bill	to reject	27	61	88	34
23 Apr. 1675[8]	Danby's Test Bill	to refer question of privilege	38	39	77	1
26 Apr. 1675[9]	Danby's Test Bill	to commit	53	37	90	16
★20 Nov. 1675	address for a dissolution	previous question	43+7=50	32+16=48	98(23)	2
★20 Nov. 1675	address for a dissolution	main question	41+7=48	34+16=50	98(23)	2
★4 Apr. 1678	trial of Earl of Pembroke	guilty of murder	6 (murder) 40(of man-slaughter)	18	64	22 (for man-slaughter)
6 June 1678	Bill against Pedlars	1st reading	25	37	62	12
15 Nov. 1678[10]	Test Bill	transub-stantia-tion	39	33	72	6
29 Nov. 1678[11]	removal of Queen from Whitehall		11 (minority)	— (no figures given)	—	— (defeated)
26 Dec. 1678[12]	Disband-ing Bill	amend-ment to pay money into Ex-chequer	44	35	79	9

Date	Subject	Question	Contents	Not Contents	Total	Majority
27 Dec. 1678[13]	Danby's impeach-ment	whether to com-mit Danby to the Tower	37	49	86	12
4 Apr. 1679[14]	attainder of Danby	3rd reading	39	36	75	3
10 May 1679[15]	lords in the Tower	to app-oint a commit-tee of both Houses on trial of	52	52	104	0
*27 May 1679	bishops	voting in capital cases	65	36	101	29
*27 May 1679	habeas corpus	to give a confer-ence 'presently'	57	55	112	2
*15 Nov. 1680	Exclusion	to reject on 1st reading: previous question	61	32	93	29
*15 Nov. 1680	Exclusion	to reject on 1st reading: main question	63	30	93	33
23 Nov. 1680[16]		joint com-mittee on state of the king-dom	32	40	72	8
*6 Dec. 1680	Viscount Stafford's trial	previous question on adjour-ning for judgement	42	42	83	0
*7 Dec. 1680	Stafford's trial	guilty	54	32	86	22

Notes

1 Bodl., MS. Carte 109, ff. 313–17.
2 House of Lords R.O., Draft Journal.
3 K.H.D. Haley, *The First Earl of Shaftesbury* (Oxford, 1968), p. 197.
4 Bodl., MS. Rawl. A 130.
5 *The Life of Edward Montagu, K.G., First Earl of Sandwich*, ed. F.R. Harris (2 vols., 1912), II, 323.
6 *Ibid.*
7 *Ibid.*, p. 332.
8 Haley, *Shaftesbury*, p. 375.
9 *Ibid.*
10 Bodl., MS. Carte 81, ff. 3, 380. See also A. Browning, *Thomas Osborne, Earl of Danby and Duke of Leeds 1632–1712*, (3 vols., Glasgow, 1944–51), III, 127–9.
11 Bodl., MS. Carte 81, ff. 3, 387.
12 *Ibid.*, ff. 3, 358. See Browning, *Danby*, III, 130, n.
13 Bodl., MS. Carte 81, ff. 3, 405. See Browning, *Danby*, III, 130, n.
14 Bodl., MS. Carte 81, ff. 4, 588; Browning, *Danby*, III, 148–9, n.6.
15 Browning, *Danby*, III, 134–7.
16 Bodl., MS. Carte 81, ff. 4, 669.

HANOVER, PENSIONS AND THE 'POOR LORDS', 1712–13

EDWARD GREGG

University of South Carolina

CLYVE JONES

Institute of Historical Research,
University of London

Foreign diplomats in London during the War of the Spanish Succession regarded political inconsistency as a peculiarly English sin: it was generally assumed that such inconstancy was the product of venality. Memories of Louis XIV's successful bribery of Members of Parliament during the reign of Charles II were still strong; yet by the accession of Queen Anne, foreign rulers had become reluctant to subsidize British politicians. Furthermore Anne's last political manager, Robert Harley, Earl of Oxford and Lord Treasurer, raised the use of promises of places and pensions, or the non-payment of past arrears, to a fine art. During his ministry, 1710–14, the Whig opposition and their dissident Tory allies had little to offer as inducements for 'voting right', other than the hope of future preferment under the heir presumptive to the throne, Georg Ludwig, Elector of Hanover (later George I), an avowed opponent of Oxford's schemes for a separate Anglo-French peace.

Two documents preserved in the Niedersächsisches Staatsarchiv at Hanover list some of the 'poor lords' — a collection of impoverished peers — and possible pensioners during the last years of Anne's reign. In both 1712 and 1713, Marlborough and his friends in the Whig party pressed the Elector to pension some impoverished peers in order to try and ensure a Whig majority in the House of Lords. The first list (Appendix 1) mentions 15 names, the second (Appendix 2) 13. Seven names (Lincoln, Radnor, Colepeper, Fitzwalter, Stamford, Sussex, Yarmouth) appear on both lists, while the two Lords Willoughby of Parham were uncle and nephew. The first Whig proposal, made in 1712, called for pensions amounting to £10,600; a year later, the requested sum was reduced to £7,900, although an additional four or five thousand pounds was asked to influence elections to the common council of the City of London.

The two crises in December 1711 in which the Oxford ministry had been defeated, on 'No Peace without Spain' (7 and 8 December)[1] and on the attempt of the Scottish Duke of Hamilton to take his seat in the Lords by right of his British dukedom of Brandon,[2] had convinced the Whigs that their position in the upper House was the place from which they could defend the Protestant Succession, particularly if the Elector of Hanover could be persuaded to support their party openly. The Whig party, and, as the Whigs claimed, Hanover's prospects of succession were endangered when the Queen, hoping to ensure parliamentary ratification of the Tory peace schemes, created a dozen new peers on 30 December 1711–1 January 1712 (o.s.). The Duke of Marlborough, who was simultaneously dismissed from all his offices, immediately proposed to the Hanoverian envoy in London, Bothmer, that the Emperor Charles VI, the most ardent opponent of the Anglo-French agreements, should award annual pensions amounting to £10,600 to 15 lords for the duration of the war (Appendix 1).[3] This proposal, which envisaged financial support for several suspected Jacobites (Yarmouth, Winchilsea, Denbigh, Plymouth, Stawell, Saye and Sele) was rejected out of hand by the Emperor's special envoy to London, Prince Eugene.[4]

The second proposal was made after the 1713 session of Parliament, in which Oxford had barely weathered a second major Anglo-Scottish crisis over the malt tax and the possible repeal of the Union, and also the defeat of the French Commerce Bill.[5] The overwhelming Tory victory in the 1713 elections for the House of Commons had rendered the House of Lords, in the opinion of the Whigs, the only arena where they had any hope of sustaining Hanover's rights. In the autumn of 1713, Baron von Schütz was sent to London by the Elector with instructions to canvass all supporters of the Protestant Succession; only after he had established his liaisons with the opposition was he formally to notify the government of his appointment as envoy.[6] Schütz, reared in England where his father had for a long time been Hanoverian envoy, wrote an unsigned, undated memorandum (Appendix 2) concerning possible pensioners sometime between his arrival in London in September and Christmas of 1713. This list was probably compiled in October by Lieutenant-General William Cadogan, Marlborough's closest associate, and Charles, Earl of Sunderland, the Duke's son-in-law.[7] Indeed, although Schütz's list of suggested pensioners is written in the first person, it seems likely to have been Sunderland's composition, rather than that of the Hanoverian envoy.

Although the Whigs consistently represented the plight of the 'poor lords' as the one article which Hanover should not fail to neglect, and while Marlborough promised a loan of £20,000 (at interest) to the Elector for such subsidies,[8] Georg Ludwig rejected these proposals both in 1712 and 1713. Generally reputed to be the richest of the minor princes of Europe, Georg Ludwig was not only parsimonious but also exceedingly cautious politically. After the passage of the Act of Settlement in 1701, he attempted to appear publicly as a neutral in British party politics. Not only was he poorly equipped to enter into financial competition with Oxford, who controlled the vast patronage resources of the British government, but also any open support for the Whig party would have alienated the Tories and thereby rendered Hanover's prospects even less certain. Cautiously refraining from handing the ministry any excuse for breaking publicly with Hanover, the Elector declined to contribute to Whig causes beyond a few small *douceurs* to those who rendered special services (the Whig journalist George Ridpath, the Dutch resident L'Hermitage). While declining both the embarrassment and the burden of paying such pensions, the Elector sought to strengthen Whig pecuniary interest in Hanover's succession by encouraging Whig potentates to finance such pensions themselves, promising them prompt repayment with adequate interest as soon as he came to the throne.[9] As a mark of his good faith, the Elector reimbursed Sunderland for £300 which the latter had loaned to Lord Fitzwalter, while paying a further £300 direct to the indigent peer.[10]

Not all the peers on these two lists can strictly be called 'poor lords'. All of them were far from wealthy, but peers such as Chandos, Grantham, Stamford and St Albans were not in the same class as the two Lords Willoughby of Parham who feature in these lists. Members of a cadet branch of the family, they were small-scale farmers from Lancashire who unexpectedly succeeded to the title in 1680 and who had been granted a pension of £200 a year by the Crown to enable them to maintain the dignity of their peerage.[11] Peers were expected to have a sufficiently large income to keep up a standard of living corresponding to their rank in the peerage. Marlborough's wife had wanted to refuse the dukedom bestowed in 1702 because her husband lacked the financial resources to go with it. The problem was solved with a state pension of £5,000 a year.[12] The Duke of St Albans had a pension of £1,000 and his salary from several offices, but his wife considered that the total, especially when fitfully paid, was inadequate to support the dignity of a duke who was, as a bastard of Charles II, a member of the royal family.[13] The majority of the peers on these lists, however, were under severe financial embarrassment, particularly when expected to attend Parliament regularly, which was often a substantial drain on their resources.[14]

The Elector's rejection of the proposed subsidies could have affected the overall party balance in the Lords in 1712–14. This assumes, however, that those peers receiving pensions from Hanover would have turned up regularly and voted with the Whigs. Oxford's experience was that many of the government's pensioners were unreliable.[15] Moreover, of the 15 men mentioned in Appendix 1, Winchilsea and Willoughby of Parham (who had never attended the Lords after 1703) were to die by early 1713, while five were strong Whig supporters in any case. Therefore only eight votes could have been captured by Hanoverian pensions. Many of these were committed Tories. If a few could have been bribed to desert their principles, the Whigs would still have made no impression on the Peace votes of late May and early June 1712 when Oxford's majorities were 28 and 45 respectively, but might have been able to defeat the ministry in June 1713 over the malt tax and Union crisis, when Oxford had majorities of only two, four and eight. Of the 13 peers mentioned in Appendix 2, nine were committed Whigs who voted against the ministry, leaving only four pro-ministry votes to capture. Even this could have made some difference in the 1714 session when Oxford's ministry on some occasions scraped home by small majorities of one and two (13 and 17 April, and 30 June).

Pensioners (of whom the 'poor lords' formed an important group) were an important element in the management of the House of Lords. Along with other groups, most notably the Scots and those employed by the Crown — the Queen's servants — they formed 'the party of the Crown' in the upper House.[16] While he commanded the resources of government, Oxford was able to outbid any counter-offer that the Whigs might make for the loyalty of that small group of non-party peers whose financial circumstances laid them open to pressure. The Whigs, under the Hanoverians, were to extend his system of office and pension and many of those on the two lists printed here did in fact later receive government money to support the ministry of George I.[17]

APPENDIX 1: *N.S.A., Cal. Br. 24, England 109, f. 119: Bothmer to the Elector, 15/26 Jan. 1712.*

[All cypher:] Mylord Radnor[18] mille livres Sterling. Mylord Stamfort[19] mille livres Sterling. Lincoln[20] six cent. Culpeper[21] quatre cent. Ces susnommez sont desja bons mais pauvres et ont besoin d'assistance pour estre conservez.

Mylord Winchelsea[22] mille livres Sterling. Dambigh[23] mille. Mylord Pleymouth[24] mille. Stanwel[25] six cent. Willoughby-Pasham[26] trois cent. Mylord Yarmouth[27] six cent. Candos[28] six cent. Sussez[29] cinq cent. Say-and-Seal[30] quatre cent. Hundson[31] quatre cent. Fitzwater[32] douze cent Livres [i.e. £1,200] Sterling.

[Robethon's notation:] Summa 10,600 livres Sterling.

APPENDIX 2: *N.S.A. Hanover 91, Schütz I, ff. 101–2: [Schütz's hand, undated]*

Lords who allways will be right out of Principle, butt are in the lowest Condition & therefore ought to be Consider'd both in Justice to them, & to encourage others.

Duke of St. Albans,[33] turn'd out of every thing, for his voting. 1000 *lib* a year.

Earle of Lincoln nott paid a farthing of his Pension, as one of ye Prince's Servants[34] & has hardly bread. 1000 a year.

Earle of Radnor turn'd out of his teller's Place, for voting right.[35] 1000 a year.

Earle of Grantham,[36] 1000 a year.

Lord Colepeper has nott in the World above 200 a year, & that incumbered; 4 or 500 a year.

Lord Haversham[37] perfectly honest, & very poor 500 a year.

Lord Willoughby of Parkam. The Poor man who was a Carpenter, & upon The title falling to him, last year, was offer'd by The Treasurer, under his own hand 1000 a year, which he refus'd, & came up to town & voted right, & allways will do so,[38] he has nott above 150 a year, last year Monsieur Kreimberg[39] promis'd him 300 a year & the expences of his journey which has nott been yett paid, butt upon all accounts ought.

Lord Fitswalter had a Pension from the Court of 600 a year, which for his voting was taken from him;[40] Monsieur Bothmar promis'd he should have the like sum continued to him, which he had last year [i.e. 1712], at Christmas next there will be a year due. As I was a kind of guarantee that this should be Continued, I must entreat, it may be paid & without it, there might be very ill consequences.

Lord Herbert never fail'd butt one vote, is Poor, & may be thoroughly fixed for 500 a year.[41]

Earle of Stamford I have been told, has something from Hannover, if not he should.

2. The following lords are such as vote with the Court, but may be had for money.

Lord Howard of Escrick,[42] 500 a year.

Earle of Sussex, 500 a year.

Earle of Yarmouth, 500 a year.

Severall others might be nam'd, if the ministry of the Elector were empower'd to do, what he should judge necessary. Severall of the Scotch Lords without doubt, might be had.[43]

The first Part of this Paper, would secure the numbers we allready have and encourage others. The latter if prudently manag'd would give a majority in spight of the Court.

The whole Summ here propos'd comes butt to between 8 or 9000 a year.

As for the Election of the Common Council for this year, 4 or 5000 would do, & That would nott be wanted a second time.

Notes

1. See C. Jones, 'The Division that Never Was: New Evidence on the Aborted Vote in the Lords on 8 December 1711 on "No Peace Without Spain"', *Parliamentary History* (forthcoming).
2. See G.S. Holmes, 'The Hamilton Affair of 1711–12: A Crisis in Anglo-Scottish Relations', *E.H.R.,* LXXVII (1962), 257–82.
3. Niedersächsisches Staatsarchiv [hereafter N.S.A.], Hanover, Cal. Br. 24, England 109, ff. 98–101, Bothmer to the Elector, 1/12 Jan. 1712.
4. *Ibid,* ff. 115–23, Bothmer to Elector, 15/26 Jan. 1712; *Feldzüge des Prinzen Eugen von Savoyen* (21 vols., Vienna, 1876–92), 2nd ser. V, supp., pp. 20–21. Cf. Sir Winston Churchill, *Marlborough: His Life and Times* (4 vols., 1933–8), IV, 500, n.1.
5. For a discussion of this major crisis for the Oxford ministry, see G. Holmes and C. Jones, 'Trade, the Scots, and the Parliamentary Crisis of 1713', *supra,* pp. 47–77.
6. N.S.A., Hanover 91, Schütz 1, ff. 34–9, 'Premier Mémoire de S.A.E. Monseigneur l' Electeur, pour le Baron de Schutz', 28 Aug. 1713.
7. J. Macpherson, *Original Papers; Containing the Secret History of Great Britain, from the Restoration to the Accession of the House of Hanover* (2 vols., 1775), II, 506, 507. On 10 Nov. 1713, n.s. Schütz wrote to Robethon that the Whigs feared a loss of six or so 'poor lords' by their accepting Court expenses or by being absent from the Lords (B.L., Stowe MS. 225, ff. 264–5). For the roles of Cadogan and Sunderland, see E. Gregg, 'Marlborough in Exile, 1712–14', *Historical Journal,* XV (1972), 596–8.
8. Macpherson, *Original Papers,* II, 519–30.
9. *Ibid.,* 580.
10. *Ibid.,* 471.
11. For details see P.J. Higson, 'A Neglected Revolution Family' (Liverpool Ph.D. thesis, 1970), especially pp. 333–50.
12. *The Marlborough-Godolphin Correspondence,* ed. H.L. Snyder (3 vols., Oxford, 1975), I, 142.
13. See her letters to Oxford in B.L., Loan 29/307–8. For a discussion of the problems of

inadequate finance and the social standing of a peerage see J.V. Beckett and C. Jones, 'Financial Improvidence and Political Independence in the Early Eighteenth Century: George Booth, 2nd Earl of Warrington', *Bulletin of the John Rylands University Library* LXV, No. 1 (1982).

[14]   See e.g. Lords Denbigh and Home, in G. Holmes, *British Politics in the Age of Anne* (1967), pp. 391, 394.

[15]   See notes on individual peers, below, Appendices 1–2.

[16]   For a discussion of Oxford's attempt to create a 'party of the Crown' see C. Jones, '"The Scheme Lords, the Neccessitous Lords, and the Scots Lords": The Earl of Oxford's Management and 'the Party of the Crown' in the House of Lords, 1711 to 1714', *Party and Management in Parliament 1660–1784*, ed. C. Jones (forthcoming).

[17]   The sources from which the information has been derived on pensions and voting behaviour, given below in the notes to the two Appendices, will be published in detail in Jones, 'The Scheme Lords'.

[18]   The second Earl of Radnor was a Court Whig, whom Oxford had regarded as a doubtful supporter in October 1710. Despite frequent approaches by Oxford and a bounty of £1,200 granted in 1710 (of which only £500 was paid in 1711) he usually voted against the ministry, though he did support the Court on 7 June 1712 over an address to the Queen on the Peace. He was to be granted a pension of £1,000 a year in 1718 (*Calendar of Treasury Books*, XXXII, 548).

[19]   The second Earl of Stamford was a Whig, whom Oxford regarded as a possible opponent in October 1710, but who in fact consistently opposed the ministry.

[20]   The seventh Earl of Lincoln was a Court Whig, regarded as doubtful by Oxford in October 1710 but who consistently opposed the ministry. In January 1711 Kreienberg, the Hanoverian resident in London, reported that Lincoln was one of the peers unable to survive without their pensions, and in December that Lincoln had risked his pension by opposing the Court over 'No Peace without Spain'. Granted a pension of £600 in 1711, he received £250 in 1711, £600 in 1712 and £300 in 1713.

[21]   The third Lord Colepeper, a Whig, regarded as a doubtful supporter by Oxford in October 1710, voted against the ministry. He was granted a pension of £600 in 1718 (*Cal. Treas. Bks.*, XXXII, 545).

[22]   The fourth Earl of Winchilsea (*d.* Aug. 1712) was a Tory who supported Oxford despite his cousin Nottingham's joining the Whigs over the Peace proposals in December 1711. Seriously embarrassed financially by attending the Lords, he had informed Oxford in January 1711 that without aid he would be forced to retire to the country. In 1712 he claimed that his subsequent appointment to the Board of Trade was not enough to 'mend [his] circumstances' (Holmes, *British Politics*, pp. 393, 516).

[23]   The fourth Earl of Denbigh, a Tory who consistently supported Oxford, received a £500 pension from the ministry in 1711. From 1712 to 1714 he failed to gain the arrears due to him. He also found attending Parliament a heavy burden (Holmes, *British Politics*, p. 391). He was appointed a teller of the Exchequer in 1713. His successor was granted a pension of £600 in 1718 (*Cal. Treas. Bks.*, XXXII, 230).

[24]   The third Earl of Plymouth was a Tory whose only vote against the ministry was in the Hamilton peerage case in December 1711.

[25]   The third Lord Stawell was a Tory whose only vote against the ministry was also in the Hamilton peerage case. He received a bounty of £1,000 in November 1712 to enable him to attend Parliament.

[26]   The twelfth Lord Willoughby of Parham (*d.* Aug. 1712).

[27]   The second Earl of Yarmouth was a Tory who consistently supported Oxford. He was given a bounty of £400 in 1713.

[28]   The eighth Lord Chandos was a Tory who voted consistently with the ministry. Having married a merchant's daughter, he had been closely involved in both the Levant and the Old East India Companies. He had had as much as £9,500 invested in the latter company in 1689, though this slumped to £102 by 1699: B.L., Add. MS. 22185, ff. 12–13; India Office Library, Home Misc. 2 (unfol.).

[29]   The first Earl of Sussex, a Tory, whose only vote against the ministry appears to have been on the questionable unparliamentary attempt of Oxford on 8 Dec. 1711 to reverse

the ministry's defeat on the Peace proposals of the previous day. A pension of £1,200 was granted in 1712, but only £500 was paid. Sussex claimed the arrears in 1713 and 1714, and received £200 out of Oxford's own pocket in September 1713.

30   The fifth Viscount Say and Sele consistently supported Oxford's ministry and was granted a bounty of £250 in 1712.

31   The eighth Lord Hunsdon was a Court Tory who consistently supported Oxford. In January 1711 Kreienberg reported that Hunsdon was unable to survive without a pension; in July he was granted a bounty of £200, and later the same year he used the crisis over the Peace votes on 7 and 8 Dec. to force a bounty of £1,000 out of the ministry for his support (Holmes, *British Politics*, pp. 385, 515, n. 8). He was granted a pension of £600 in 1718 (*Cal. Treas. Bks.*, XXXII, 546).

32   The fifteenth Lord Fitzwalter was a Whig whom Oxford had regarded as a supporter in October 1710 but who had usually voted against the ministry. He was listed as a supporter in the Hamilton peerage forecast made by Oxford, but abstained on the actual vote on 20 Dec. 1711. He did, however, vote for the Court on 2 Jan. 1712, despite the Junto's opposition to an extension of the adjournment sought by Oxford. He received £300 both from Hanover and Lord Sunderland in the winter of 1712–13. He was also granted a pension of £600 in 1718 (*Cal. Treas. Bks.*, XXXII, 545).

33   The first Duke of St. Albans, a Court Whig, considered doubtful by Oxford in October 1710, voted against the ministry. His annual pension of £1,000, granted him as a bastard of Charles II, was irregularly paid under Oxford (£750 in 1710 and 1711, nothing in 1712, his arrears of £2,500 in 1713, and £2,500 again in 1714). He was dismissed from his post of captain of the Gentlemen Pensioners in January 1712, but retained his hereditary post of Master Falconer, and the post of Master of the Register Office. In 1713 he was paid £3,400 arrears on two and a half year's allowances as Master Falconer.

34   Lincoln had been a Lord of the Bedchamber to Prince George of Denmark in 1708, the year of the Prince's death. For the complaints of a fellow servant of the Prince over non-payment of salary see Delawarr's letters to Oxford: B.L., Loan 29/307.

35   Radnor himself was never a teller of the Exchequer. His uncle Francis Robartes (*d.* 1718) held a tellership from 1704 to October 1710, and was succeeded in this lucrative post by Russell Robartes, Radnor's younger brother, who, despite his strong support of the Whigs until 1710, thereafter strongly supported the ministry. Russell Robartes confessed to Oxford in September 1713 that despite Radnor's previous support of the ministry and his financial obligation to Oxford, he 'had not answer'd, what I think in honor he ought to have done both to the Queene and your Lordship' (Holmes, *British Politics*, pp. 49, 402).

36   The first Earl of Grantham was a Court Whig whose pension had been unpaid since December 1711. Apart from his support of the Court in the Hamilton peerage case on 20 Dec. 1711, he voted with the Whigs.

37   The Whig second Lord Haversham had succeeded his Tory father in November 1710. Despite being canvassed by Oxford, he opposed the ministry.

38   The fourteenth Lord Willoughby of Parham succeeded his brother in April 1713. The thirteenth Lord Willoughby had been awarded a pension of £400 by Oxford in March 1713, only £100 of which had been paid before he died. The fourteenth Lord, described by L'Hermitage, the Dutch envoy in London, as a weaver (B.L., Add. MS. 17677 GGG, ff. 229–30, despatch 19 June 1713), was a client of the Junto and accepted the patronage of Wharton and Sunderland (Holmes, *British Politics*, p. 402). The fifteenth Lord (*b.* 1714, *suc.* 1715) was granted a pension of £200 in 1718 (*Cal. Treas. Bks.*, XXXII, 550).

39   Kreienberg, Hanoverian resident in London November 1710 – July 1714.

40   The Elector of Hanover had reimbursed Sunderland for the £300 he had lent Fitzwalter in the winter of 1712–13 (see above, p. 175). There is no evidence that he had a pension from the Oxford ministry.

41   The second Lord Herbert of Chirbury was a Junto Whig, who because of his parlous financial circumstances was to support the Court in 1713–14, and received £500 from Oxford's own pocket between March and May 1714 (Holmes, *British Politics*, pp. 393, 516, n. 36–8). The vote he had failed on was probably his support of the Court on 7 June 1712 over an address to the Queen on the Peace. He also supported the Court on 8 June

1713 on the Malt Bill and was regarded by Oxford in the same month as a possible supporter of the French Commerce Bill. He was granted a pension of £600 in 1718 (*Cal. Treas. Bks.,* XXXII, 546).

[42] The fourth Lord Howard of Escrick, a staunch supporter of Oxford, gave only one recorded vote against the ministry on 8 Dec. 1711. This listing of Escrick may be a mistake for the sixth Lord Howard of Effingham, who was a Court Whig 'poor lord' in receipt of a pension from Oxford (£600 in 1711, 1712, 1714, and £300 in 1713), and who had been regarded as 'doubtful' in October 1710. However, he usually voted against the ministry, though he did support Oxford on 7 June 1712. It was he, rather than Escrick, who was awarded a pension of £800 in 1718 (*Cal. Treas. Bks.,* XXXII, 546).

[43] Stories concerning the venality of the Scottish peers were widespread and exaggerated. While on average they were less well off than their English counterparts (see Holmes, *British Politics,* pp. 393–4), and a few were downright poor, none the less only nine of the 23 representative peers to sit in the Lords 1710–14 received pensions or annuities. They were an important constituent of 'the party of the Crown' in the upper House, especially after the election of 1710, when for the first time the Crown's full list of peers was returned. Their not infrequent opposition to the Court was usually over strictly Scottish matters and when they received satisfaction or realized their cause was hopeless they returned to the Court. Only Lord Ilay followed his brother Argyll into permanent opposition in 1713, for which he lost his seat at the 1713 election. His case proved the ultimate dependency of the Scots on the Court. In 1714 only Loudoun (a Hanoverian Tory) showed any sustained opposition.

THE EARLY STUARTS AND PARLIAMENT: OLD HAT AND THE *NOUVELLE VAGUE*

J.H. HEXTER

Washington University, St Louis

About five years ago, in 1976, a convulsion seized the historiography of seventeenth-century England. It happened in the form of an article by Conrad Russell, 'Parliamentary History in Perspective, 1604–29', in *History*.[1] Shortly after the publication of Russell's article came a series of minor quakes, lesser pieces by lesser historians reinforcing and supplementing Russell's. Then again from Russell himself there came a second major but less spectacular shock, *Parliaments and English Politics 1621–1629* (Oxford, 1979). According to those nearest the epicenter — English historians of seventeenth-century England between the ages of 30 and 45 — these convulsions registered 8.5 on the historiographical Richter scale.[2]

This article is about the set of historiographical phenomena just sketched. I hope it will do several things. *1.* It will show that there really were such tremors a few years back. *2.* It will suggest that 5 on the historiographical Richter scale is a more realistic estimate than 8.5. As usual, those nearest the epicenter overestimated the violence of the event. This is a natural result of actually feeling the quaking underfoot and seeing a couple of big statues totter on their pedestals. *3.* It will distinguish between the jerry-built structures that suffered irreparable damage from the quake and the solid ones in danger of being unwarrantedly abandoned by the Chicken-Littles of the profession who took the cries of doom at 8.5 too seriously. That is, it will try to combine a damage assessment with a cost-benefit analysis. *4.* Finally it will have to look into the broader and deeper historiographical implications of the quake. To come through on these somewhat pretentious commitments I will have to sketch in, rather more elaborately than is usual, the pre-existing historiographical structure on which the convulsions seized.

2

S.R. Gardiner

The England of the early Stuarts was singularly fortunate in the nineteenth-century historian who chose to make it the object of his lifelong inquiry. No period in the modern history of England found a historian more patient, more ready to pursue archival research at home and abroad, more possessed with both the desire to be fair and with the temperamental inclination to active fairness than Samuel Rawson Gardiner.[3] Taking it as his goal to write the history of what he thought of as the Puritan Revolution, the tumultuous decades of the mid-seventeenth century, Gardiner felt that he must seek its roots in what happened in England after the accession of James I. 'It seemed to me', he said, 'that it was the duty of a serious inquirer to search into the original cause of great events.'[4] This view of his goal rendered it certain that Gardiner would see the events from 1603 to 1642 as the pathway if not the highway to civil war. He began his intensive studies in about 1856. In 1863 he published his first volumes, starting from the Stuart succession to the English throne. His sixteenth volume — the last in his history of the Protectorate — came in 1901. Those tomes were milestones in Gardiner's steady, measured, learned, 45-year progress through 53 tumultuous years of English history, a march the whole of which no historian will ever again make with the persistence, the skill and the thoroughness that marked Gardiner's lifelong effort.[5]

Gardiner saw the 1640s as a time of strife between Puritans and Churchmen, between King and Parliament. And here a perspective more remote from the beginning of the seventeenth century than the English Civil War took over — the perspective of Gardiner's own lifetime. It was a time when in Europe the conflict between 'absolute' monarchy and popular self-rule parallelled the conflict between authority and liberty. At the end of Gardiner's own days that conflict had not yet come to Armageddon. A reading of the auspices that saw the conflict as headed toward the universal victory of liberty and representative government was not as patently wrong-headed in 1901 as it had become by 1941. It was Gardiner's own reading. He told his story in an only occasionally interrupted chronological sequence, year by year, moving deliberately and majestically forward to his pre-appointed goal, catching in particular the recurrent clashes between the liberty of the subject and the prerogative of the Crown, the aspirations of Puritans and the dominance of episcopacy. What gave form to the story was the succession of Parliaments from the first of James I to the last of Charles I. They were a set of nodes or junction boxes along the route, in which separate lines of development — foreign policy, domestic government, taxation and finance, religion — converged momentously for a time and then spread out again. It was in the succession of Parliaments that the meaning of the flow of events as Gardiner saw it became clear. In Parliament the most vigorous defence of the liberty of the subjects against the King's prerogative took place in the House of Commons. In a sense, when we read Gardiner we see history unroll from a seat in the House of Commons. When historians have referred, usually pejoratively, to the 'Whig interpretation' of the early Stuart era, consciously or not they have had Gardiner's outlook in mind.

3

Wallace Notestein and after in America

The Gardiner view of history from 1603 to 1640, the view that took with deep seriousness the importance of what happened in the House of Commons under James I and Charles I, received its next sharp stimulus *in* England but *from* an American. The vision of Parliament that English historians of early seventeenth-century England subsequently adopted took its shape if not its meaning from the Raleigh Lecture — 'The Winning of the Initiative by the House of Commons' —

that the American, Wallace Notestein, delivered before the British Academy in 1924.[6] For half a century such thought as the leading English historians of seventeenth-century England gave to the early Stuart House of Commons rested on Notestein's work in two ways. First, those historians based their conclusions about Parliament on the historical support that 'The Winning of the Initiative by the House of Commons' provided. Second, they used the magnificent editorial work conceived by Notestein and partly executed by him and his students for data to shore up their version of reality.

Although before Notestein developed his conception bits and pieces of the surviving accounts of early Stuart Parliaments had been edited and published intermittently for three centuries, no one had his heroic idea of searching out *all* the surviving accounts of the proceedings in the House of Commons of the early Stuarts and preparing scholarly editions of those accounts Parliament by Parliament.[7] For the past 60 years all the major scholarly editions of the abundant records of the Parliaments that Gardiner made the centrepiece of his great English story have been the work not of Englishmen but of Americans — Notestein himself, his collaborators, his students, students of his students (in one case a student of a student of a student) – and scholars who indirectly came under his influence.[8]

In his British Academy lecture Notestein had set himself a lively problem. In Elizabeth's day the traffic of business in the House of Commons appeared to be mainly under the direction of the Crown acting through the Speaker and those members of the Privy Council who were also Members of the House. By 1640, however, in legislative matters the Privy Council no longer had the initiative nor the Speaker control of the agenda. It had fallen into the hands of leading Members of the House who had no place in the central government. The problem was to discern the process of this shift in the initiative and to understand its implications for the balance of power between King and Commons, to lay bare the roots of the decline of government domination *of* the lower House and show the basis for what ultimately became the domination of the government *by* the lower House.

According to Notestein economic ills and the abuses of James I's officials put the initiative in the hands of men concerned about both. When James neglected to place major Councillors in the House, an extremely competent opposition took over. The government lost the electoral support of the peers who moved toward the opposition. In Notestein's essay opposition was so distinct, indeed, that he conferred on it the individuality of a capital O.[9] A new committee-system, keyed on the committee of the whole House in its many forms, 'reduced the power of the Speaker, by replacing him in the chair during major debates'. The committee of the whole also cut away the power the Privy Councillors had held over select committees. James I's failure to manage elections to the House of Commons and his alienation of the majority of English peers by favour to the Scots further weakened the King's position. The leaders of the opposition were an aggressive body of men dominating the Commons, controlling legislation and demanding a role in policy. As against the Privy Council which emphasized supply on behalf of the Crown, the new leaders of the House emphasized grievances and their redress through legislation. The drafting of bills also passed from the hands of the King's judges working with the Lords to those of opposition lawyers in the lower House. Consequently instead of looking as formerly to the King's Privy Council for the redress of their grievances Englishmen came to look to the House of Commons. And of course as the country came to look to the House for redress of grievances, the House turned its ear to the country (as against the court) for its agenda. Thus slowly emerged a more active House of Commons, certain in time to demand power. Finally Notestein makes explicit the historical vision that informs his perception of the details that he examines. 'Far back through creeks and inlets comes slowly flooding in the main.'[10] Liberty and government of the people by the people, democratic self-government gradually broadening down from precedent to precedent — such, to make a local application of the title of a general work of 1920, was 'the evolution of Parliament.'

For a half-century Notestein's Raleigh Lecture did much to direct the line of inquiry of American students of early Stuart history.[11] It either dominated the foreground or threw a large deep shadow across the background. Early, it dominates the foreground of *The Privy Councillors in the House of Commons, 1604–1629* (1940), by David Willson, one of Notestein's students; late, it looms in the background of *The Court and the Country* (1969) published three decades later by Perez Zagorin, *not* one of Notestein's students. The latter instance suggests a significant point. The larger part of American writing about early Stuart history has been done by scholars who were not students of Notestein. Almost all of it, however, from my own *The Reign of King Pym* (1941) to Zagorin's *The Court and the Country*, Robert Zaller's *The Parliament of 1621* (1971) and Robert Ruigh's *The Parliament of 1624* (1971) bears the unmistakable mark of Notestein's influence. As all these historians see it, Parliament stands at the centre of early Stuart politics. It also stands at the centre of attention of the historians themselves. The most important thing happening is the conflict of the House of Commons with the King and the developing will and power of the House to sustain that conflict. Or putting it another way, all these scholars saw the early Stuart era with the eyes of Gardiner refracted through the lenses Notestein supplied them.

Before we turn our attention back to English historians of England, one further observation is worth making about a particular cluster of the Americans. In their work several of them show the impact of the habit of thought of a scholar-thinker quite different from Notestein. As a result of having done their graduate work at Harvard rather than at Yale before or shortly after the Second World War, they came to see the England of James I and Charles I as one of their teachers, Charles Howard McIlwain, the constitutional historian and historian of political thought, saw it; that is, they did not see it as merely the superficial political manifestation of the basic socio-economic realities or as a struggle for power confined within the framework of a single important political institution, the English Parliament. Rather, with varying consistency and intensity they saw it in the broader framework of the coeval political institutions of the realms of central and western Europe, and of the constitutional ideas and political themes that had focused the thoughts of European men since the Protestant Reformation — obedience, obligation, prerogative and sovereignty; property, law, liberty and resistance. Among the scholars so oriented were George Mosse, myself, and particularly Margaret Judson. In England, her *The Crisis of the Constitution* (1949) was denied the close consideration it merited.[12] It lost out because of the intense attention it gave to what men in the mainstream of English life and thought between 1603 and 1640 said about those matters of law, liberty and constitution that had mainly concerned Professor McIlwain.

Such matters were wholly unfashionable among the new English historians of England at the end of the Second World War;[13] but then so too was the history of the early Stuart Parliaments as Gardiner had told it. Yet to them Notestein's 'The Winning of the Initiative' was warmly welcome, and Gardiner was indispensable. To understand this apparent paradox we shall need to return our attention briefly to the writing on the history of the Stuart period in England at the beginning of the present century.

4

From Golden Age to Old Hat

When S.R. Gardiner died the burden of his heroic undertaking fell on the shoulders of Charles Harding Firth, who carried it through *The Last Years of the Protectorate* (1909). In 1910 Firth published *The House of Lords during the Civil War (1603–1660).* That study is notable for something besides its solid scholarship. It is a boundary marker. Gardiner's work had seemed to establish the early seventeenth century as the epoch in which England's Parliament became the sole effective preserver of that tradition of free representative institutions which later became the political model for the western world. Positioned by Gardiner's pioneer work, up to 1910 the English Parliament sat squarely in the mainstream of seventeenth-century English historiography where he had put it 50 years earlier.

From 1910 to 1978, however, no English historian of England wrote a major book which centred its attention on Parliament and its role between the accession of James I and the meeting of the Long Parliament.[14] This graveyard scholarly silence about what for Gardiner was the very heart of the matter in early Stuart England is the more remarkable since during most of this interval — from 1926 to 1966 — the early Stuart era itself was at the focus of extraordinary historiographical excitement.[15] For those who considered historical writing a species of gladiatorial combat and who revelled in the outpouring of scholarly gore, those years and especially the decade 1946–56 were the best of times, a golden, or perhaps a crimson age. They brought to the fore several lively historians whose outstanding shared trait was a voracious appetite for mutual mayhem. In the minds and the writings of these combatants, however, Parliament — central in Gardiner's epic tale — mattered in substance scarcely at all between 1604 and 1640, or any other time actually. When English historians of England casually paid attention to parliamentary doings in those days it was only in quest of symptomatic signs of important realities that were manifested elsewhere than at Westminster.

Given the unusually high quality and sober thoughtfulness of Gardiner's work, the absorption of more than a generation of English historians of early seventeenth-century England in the pursuit of a 'reality' which merely skirted that work requires explanation. We cannot account for the casual attention these scholars paid to Gardiner without indulging in some very general remarks about a coeval general transformation of the views of historians in both England and America on the very nature of the science of history.

The transformation was from 'positivism' to 'realism'. The first wave of nineteenth-century historicism had been generated by the naïve faith that the objective neutral accumulation of historical facts would render accessible to mankind all historical reality. Gradually this faith evaporated among the more intelligent members of the profession. The loss of faith came rather more slowly in England than elsewhere,[16] but by the 1920s it had happened even there. The indiscriminate quest for the facts of history gave way to the discriminating search for the scientific laws of history, the simple dynamic structures that underlay and accounted for the clutter of mere events of the past. All such searches started from the assumption that these events, particularly political, religious and constitutional events — the very substance of Gardiner's history — were epiphenomenal, accidental, casual in the philosophical sense, superstructural. Underlying this too abundant actuality lay the 'hidden' reality from which the superstructure emerged. The serious business of historians was to lay bare that reality, what *really* happened, what underlay the events that overtly and manifestly did happen.

Under the impulse of this scientific perspective and of a strange and hideous turn in the political actualities of their own world, in the 1930s English historians of early Stuart England, at least the more lively among them, arrived at a shared vision of what was really going on in the time they were looking into. In that time, they agreed, the bourgeoisie began to displace the aristocracy as owners of the instruments of production. This displacement transformed the dominant mode of production from feudal to early capitalist. The English Revolution, misnamed by Gardiner the Puritan Revolution, was a symptom of that process. The process involved the irresistible liquidation of the superstructural elements which the trans-formation of the socio-economic base that had begun in the sixteenth century or earlier had left without a foundation. Not only the manifest turbulence of the middle decades of the century, but the earlier constitutional disturbances — that is, the demands for liberty, and the opposition to the Stuart monarchs — and the earlier religious disturbances — that is, the rise of Puritanism and the hostility both to Romanism and the religious middle way of the Anglicans — exemplified what happened in the superstructure when a profound secular shift in the material base of human existence broke through the thin and not infinitely flexible surface of things that overlay it.[17]

So pervasive did the rudiments of this science of history become that even historians scarcely aware of the culture or soup of ideas that nurtured the appropriate clichés nevertheless osmotically absorbed the clichés themselves. The rise of the middle class and the decline of the feudal order became the universal ingredients of all their historical perceptions. Given their particular ideological vision of the underlying historical reality, chasing after the day-to-day doings of Parliament, working out the mere sequence of political actions, *à la* Gardiner, did not attract them. In the Golden Age after the Second World War the English historians of the early Stuarts, like the mentor of most of them, R.H. Tawney, were happy to leave the Gardiner legacy of political history intact and were pleased to add to it what might be called the Notestein codicil. In their view the Gardiner formulation could be put something like this:

> During the decades from the accession of James I to the outbreak of the Puritan Revolution, Parliament ceased to be a body dominated by the King and his Privy Council aided and abetted by the House of Lords. It became a body in which the House of Commons was willing and able to challenge that ascendancy. During the early seventeenth century the lower House laid the foundations for building its own eventual dominance over Crown and peerage. Correlatively the structure of religion underwent a parallel process. The King as Supreme Governor had ruled the Established Church through the episcopal hierarchy. That rule was challenged from below by the Puritans, lay and clerical. Their instruments were their partisans in the House of Commons. In the Civil War, when push came to shove, the Puritans of the House of Commons destroyed royal episcopal church government, abolished the House of Lords and brought the King to the block.

Such a view of the course of events was most highly welcome to Tawney and his followers. It was all to the good that a class rising from below, from-under-up, should break the grip of the aristocracy and the King on the levers of power. In 1941 in a truly seminal study, 'The Rise of the Gentry 1558–1640', Tawney sketched the process by which the new class achieved the growth in socio-economic power that in his view had to have preceded the attainment of political power by that class in the English Revolution of the mid-seventeenth century. The process was the adoption of middle-class or capitalist methods and attitudes by a rising class of middling landowners, the gentry. Out of James Harrington's *Oceana* Tawney extracted the seventeenth-century aphorism that provided his followers with their methodological imperative for accounting for the upheavals of the 1640s and 1650s. 'The dissolution of this government caused the war, not the war the dissolution of this government.'[18] This was taken to direct inquiry away from the effects of the long Civil War itself on men's readiness to accept, as a pure given, the social order as they had formerly known it. Instead historians were to look to *prior societal* pathology for the aetiology of the overt conflict that erupted in 1642. The general social analysis to which English historians were predisposed in the 1940s pointed them directly towards what they should look for — the underlying or basic transformations and disruption that a society undergoes when in the dialectical process of historical change one ruling class displaces another, trans-formations that are antecedent to the political disorders or revolution of which they are in fact the cause. Of such changes what happened in politics — the Gardiner legacy — is merely symptomatic.

And here the Notestein codicil reinforced the effects of the Gardiner legacy. Much concerned with war, foreign policy and the personalities of politics, Gardiner left the impression that the decisions and actions of individual persons — Sir Edward Coke and Sir John Eliot, John Pym and Sir Thomas Wentworth, James I and the Duke of Buckingham, Charles I and Oliver Cromwell — might have been consequential rather than merely symptomatic, might actually have affected the course of events during their lifetimes and therefore the subsequent course of what happened in history. This suggested that the doings of such men ought to be investigated for their intrinsic rather than their symptomatic significance. Here the Notestein codicil cleared away the 'personalistic' flaw in Gardiner. For the historians of the Golden Age it was good to know that the representatives of a rising class in the House of Commons took over the direction of the House itself and afterwards by means of the House gained power over all Englishmen. It confirmed their view that the movement of history was not mainly from the past to the future, from-the-back-forward, but from-under-up.

What the Notestein codicil, 'The Winning of the Initiative', showed or was taken to show was that the first step in this essentially class process was made not by individuals but by the political incarnation of the rising class, by the House of Commons itself. Historians could therefore with good conscience turn away from doubtlessly worthy but rather boring close inquiry into the actual doings of the House of Commons, the House of Lords, and the King, and turn to the more congenial tasks of transforming the latter two into the feudal class in one move and the former into the gentry and thence into the middle class in two. This would make the conflict between King and Lords on the one hand and Commons on the other into a right class war between Feudalism and Capitalism and put the ructions of the mid-century in their due place in the series of proper Marxian Revolutions, and then everything would be hunky-dory.

Having sealed off Gardiner and Notestein like two flies in amber, highly visible but, so to speak, motionless, the English historians of the Golden Age could afford to pay them homage as ancestral totems without having to worry that they would interfere in current scholarly operations. One does not need to worry about flies in amber because they are quite dead, and historiographically so were Gardiner and Notestein. For they had assumed that in the rubs between the early Stuarts and the House of Commons some sorts of constitutional principle were at stake, and that both King and Parliament knew it, so that to explain the course of events it would not be a gross impropriety to invoke a struggle over principle. Obviously this was nonsense since the course of political events was determined not at the political level but from–under–up by the transformation of the social economy.

After the Second World War the Golden Age historians, then, went happily about their work, little ruffled by a faint though not terribly belated transatlantic warning that their claims for the middle class, their identification of the gentry with that class, and their writing off of the aristocracy were perhaps precipitate and excessive.[19] And the work of those historians was lively indeed. It reached its apogee in that splendid *histoire totale* of the English ruling class from the accession of Elizabeth to the outbreak of the Civil War, Lawrence Stone's *The Crisis of the Aristocracy 1558–1641* (1965).

Yet this *maximum opus* was an oddly ambiguous monument to the achievements of Stone's generation of English historians of Stuart England.[20] What should have been a festive celebration of the ideological view on which that generation had taken its stand turned out to be its *pompes funèbres*. During a two–decade exploration of the archives and of everything in print that provided evidence for his major work, Stone had lost his faith in the shared Marxist historical vision which had moved him to his relentless endeavours and many of his contemporaries to theirs.

He made that loss of faith explicit in his next important study of the century from the Reformation to the Revolution, *The Causes of the English Revolution 1529–1642* (1972). There he lists among the assumptions underlying his analysis the view that 'the class-war theory of the Marxists has only limited application to the seventeenth century'.[21] He balanced his partial lapse into infidelity to his beginnings by a round reaffirmation of a major item of his early credo. Reiterating the quotation from *Oceana* that we can take for the epigraph of the *sequelae* of Tawney, Stone asserts that in any quest for 'the causes of the English revolution' historians who assume that society was disrupted as a *consequence* of the Civil War will 'miss the essential problem [of] why most of the established institutions of State and Church — Crown, court, administration, army and episcopacy — collapsed so ignominiously' two years or more *before* the Civil War broke out (p. 48). Summing up a masterly survey of the precondition of the English Revolution, which is also a survey, as compact as it is intelligent, of the new learning gathered by the lively efforts of his generation of historians, Stone says (pp. 114–15),

> new social forces were emerging, new political relationships were forming, and new intellectual currents were flowing, but neither the secular government nor the Church was demonstrating an ability to adapt to new circumstances. Thanks to the growth of the national product, the changing distribution of wealth, the spread of higher education, the decline of aristocratic political dominance of local affairs, the formulation of new religious and secular ideals, and the consolidation of new administrative organizations, in the century after 1540, there appeared a growing body of men of substance, rich property owners, professionals and merchants. These men — the leading figures among the county squirearchy, the successful London lawyers, the more eminent Puritan divines, and the urban patriciates that dominated the cities — were steadily enlarging their numbers, their social and economic weight, and their political independence. Behind them loomed far larger numbers of yeomen and artisans, the respectable, industrious, literate, Bible-reading, God-fearing lower middle class, many of whose aspirations these leaders shared, represented and articulated.

Here, just before the *Nouvelle Vague* that Russell represents and that in large measure he generated washed over it, is the historiographical structure about to be rendered Old Hat, a view that sees history from–under–up and that therefore despite Stone's renunciation of Marxist views still sees Parliament as epiphenomenal.

Stone replaced a Marxist theory of the causes of the English Revolution with the theory that it was the consequence of 'multiple dysfunction'. This does not just mean that when lots of things are out of whack there is likely to be a blow up; it means more specifically that things are out of whack because of 'some new and developing process as a result of which certain social subsystems find themselves in a condition of relative deprivation' (p.9). When the ruling *élite* fails to respond to the dysfunction flexibly, revolution becomes likely. Then a secret organization, a charismatic prophet, or a military disaster can precipitate upheaval (p.10). Stone probes the condition of England during the reign of Elizabeth and finds that a pleasing universality of dysfunction and disarray penetrates the whole fabric of society. In a drumhead court martial, Lawrence Stone, Esq., a fierce prosecutor, hauls the structures of society — central administration, local government, military organization, fiscal apparatus, religious institutions, economic institutions, cultural aspirations and habituations, *etc.* — up before the Hon. Lawrence Stone, a hanging judge. Out of hand the judge declares them collectively guilty of multiple dysfunction, and of creating among the *élite* the preconditions for a revolutionary disruption of the social body.

The preconditions for a revolution are not themselves however, a revolution, and Stone, immune to his earlier habits of youthful enthusiasm, knows it.[22] What *precipitated* a revolutionary situation out of the preconditions was the intransigence of the political regime between 1629 and 1640 in the face of evidence of the dysfunction of all the indispensable organisms of social order. And finally what *triggered* the English Revolution in the revolutionary situation of 1641 and 1642 was the boundless duplicity of Charles I, who time after time in those years annulled the effect of his concessions to reform, by plots, often discovered and always rightly suspected, against the reformers. In the end, true to his origins Stone accords but a small place to Parliaments in the process he describes.

Having stashed his former naïve Marxism in the lumber-room, Stone had reason to expect a younger generation of historians warmly to embrace his broader-gauged, more ecumenical, more sociological account of what brought the English to their decades of political, social and religious turmoil in the mid-seventeenth century. If he actually did expect that, he must have been gravely disappointed. His broadening of the already broad perspective in which his contemporaries had seen the early Stuart age found no takers, no disciples. Ecumenism was out among the younger generation, and broad views a drug on the market. They were Old Hat. Why? What had happened?

5

From Old Hat to the Nouvelle Vague

If in an apocalyptic mood one were inclined to think that there was a revolution of the historiography of the early Stuart period in about 1975, one would have to note that environmental forces had begun to wear away the standing orthodoxy, turning it into Old Hat, a good bit earlier. Before we proceed to inquire into the revolution of 1975 we need to examine these forces. They were (1) the Lord-Lookers (2) the Nay-Sayers (3) the Provincials. Each of these groups needs to be dealt with because each not only weakened the fabric created in the Golden Age of the 1940s, each also contributed a significant component to the historical outlook formulated by Conrad Russell between 1975 and 1978.

The Lord-Lookers. Neither from the perspective of Gardiner and Notestein nor from that of the 1940s was intensive concern with what the peers did individually in politics or what the House of Lords did collectively appropriate to an up-to-date historian.[23] Over the four decades prior to the historiographical convulsion of 1975 however, several historians did pay some attention to the peers in a political context. For reasons wholly obscure to me, most of these historians have been American, and most have been women. Early on, Violet Rowe wanted to understand how a clientage structure worked in parliamentary elections. To do so she inquired into the electoral use of their patronage apparatus by the Herbert brothers, William and Philip, who were successively Earls of Pembroke (1601–30, 1630–50).[24] Frances Relf made amends for neglect of the House of Lords in her collaboration with Wallace Notestein by editing *Notes of the Debates in the House of Lords . . . 1621, 1625, 1628*.[25] In order to grasp the nature of the issues, the manoeuvres in the House of Commons in 1624, and the sides M.P.s took on hot issues such as war with Spain and the impeachment of Middlesex, as well as to understand the differences among clusters of peers, Robert Ruigh regarded it a matter of consequence to sort out politics in the House of Lords in that Parliament.[26] Corinne Weston had her eyes turned to the House of Lords by her discovery of the King's curious answer to the Nineteen Propositions that the two Houses sent him when England stood on the brink of civil war in 1642. That answer assigned to the House of Lords a position in the English constitution separate from but equal to the position it assigned to King and Commons. Her inquiry into this phenomenon led her in her book, *English Constitutional Theory and the House of Lords, 1556–1832* (1965), to cast her eyes back as well as forward from her starting point, and both ways she looked, the House of Lords loomed large. It loomed large for Vernon Snow too. In 1970 Professor Snow wrote *Essex, the Rebel*, about Robert Devereux, second Earl of Essex. It was the first modern scholarly political biography of an early Stuart peer who was also a county magnate.[27] It told of a man powerful in his region who was also a force in Parliament, a man whose influence leaders both at court and in the House of Commons bid high for.

Jess Stoddart Flemion has devoted three articles to demonstrating what she takes to have been the decisive influence of the House of Lords at crucial moments in the history of the Parliaments of 1626 and 1628.[28] Finally, Elizabeth Foster edited the sources on a Parliament, that of 1610, in which the surviving record of the proceedings of the House of Lords was two-thirds as extensive as that of the House of Commons. It may have been this that moved her to keep an eye cocked to the upper House. She has now completed a full-scale study of procedure in the House of Lords that should enable scholars to reassess the nature and importance of the role of the peers under the early Stuarts. (Unfortunately, at the time of writing, the press that will publish Professor Foster's book has no version available for examination.) In any case the cumulative effect of this widespread American scholarly activity over a long span of years suggested that the political decline of the peerage implicit in Gardiner, explicit in the followers of Tawney, was affirmed on the basis of ideological commitment rather than on that of historical evidence. Their propensity to underestimate the leverage of the House of Lords in the balance of political forces in the days of the early Stuarts appeared to be a serious side-effect of myopia induced by misprescribed Whiggish spectacles. They were seeing the early seventeenth-century English peerage through one lens ground for viewing the French aristocracy in the French Revolution and another lens that gave a clearer picture when turned on Lloyd George's Parliament Act of 1911 than it gave of what went on in Parliament three centuries earlier.

The Wreckers: H.R. Trevor-Roper and G.R. Elton. The earliest and fiercest attack on the from–under–up historians, both Tawney their prophet and all his disciples, was launched by H.R. Trevor-Roper in 1953. In 'The Gentry 1540–1640', he argued that these historians had not merely gone a bit wrong; they had gone 180° off the right path.[29] The country gentry, he claimed, were not rising, they were declining. The rising folk were those attached to the King's court, nourishing themselves off the public teat. That was where the opening, both straight and strait, to power and fortune lay. Some men who aimed to reach the narrow opening missed it; some were shoved off the way to it by shrewder, tougher, or luckier contestants for the prizes. Those would-be courtiers who did not make it were the 'outs', disappointed and disgruntled. Parliaments were occasions in which they brought their backstairs struggles for a share of the spoils into semi-public view. In the House of Commons for their own self-seeking reasons they led the backwoods, backward, broke country Members in a gentry-luddite assault on the court. The country gentry had got squeezed out in the inflation of the decades at the turn of the century, and now manifested its wretchedness and desperation by declining not only into poverty and the odious religious enthusiasms of sectarianism, Catholic or Puritan, but also into chronic opposition to court government. A motley gang of these losers stumbled by way of civil war into political power that they did not want and could not manage. They soon displayed their incapacity to rule and aversion to ruling in the Parliaments of the Protectorate in which they could have been dominant, but were not. During the Protectorate they had lost their rational leaders, the old 'outs' of Charles I's day, many of whom were now 'in', supporters of the new Cromwellian court. So, leaderless, the representatives of the obsolete declining gentry naturally seized on a fantastic republican dreamship which they promptly ran aground by trying to dismantle Cromwell's power. So much for the 'rising middle-class gentry', their 'progressive revolution', and their advance toward dominance through take-over of the initiative in the House of Commons — pure illusion! Yet however sharply he took issue with his contemporaries on matters of substance, formally Trevor-Roper still saw Parliament as they did and as Gardiner did not — a body without corporate purpose or intrinsic significance acting out conflicts generated elsewhere.

G.R. Elton's way of opposing the from–under–up historians has been less frontal and head-on but more frequent and persistent than Trevor-Roper's, guerilla warfare rather than a marshalling of big battalions. Because Elton's objections to the way early Stuart history has been done from Gardiner to Stone are scattered through a great many writings we must take care not to underestimate the comprehensiveness of his assault on a century of tradition in interpreting the history of England and of English Parliaments under the early Stuarts. In 1965 a study entitled 'A High Road to Civil War?' announced his entry on to that vigorously and much fought-over field.[30] He swooped down on it from the adjacent region of the Tudors, where he had long ruled the roost. His mission was not irenic. He brought not peace but the sword to an area where already a perhaps excessive use of instruments of assault was habitual. In a few pages he dealt firmly with the underlying conviction of Tawney and his followers since 1926 — the view that society had divided in two in the century before the Civil War, preparing the way, opening wide the high road for the English Revolution. Of this view Elton said, in effect, 'hallucinatory'. If that was how things had been going since 1559 or 1604, how come that in 1640, two years before Charles I unfurled his battle-standard at Nottingham, there was not a trace of this division visible, but solidarity against their governors among the men whom the communities of England elected to Parliament, a solidarity that extended to much of the peerage? In the interim there had been no evidence of an unbridgeable gulf opening between Court and

Country (so much for Trevor-Roper and, prospectively, for Perez Zagorin), nor between Puritan and Established Church (so much for Gardiner), nor were the Members of the House of Commons in any Parliament of the early Stuarts a bourgeoisified gentry (so much for Tawney), nor was there in Parliament any intimation, any reflection, of revolutionary class conflict between middle classes and feudal classes, between any class at all and any other class (so much for Christopher Hill). Far from being polarized in their political ideas, by and large on political matters the minds of all articulate Englishmen converged rather than diverged. And as for the initiative, the House of Commons did not need to win it since the first two Stuarts simply gave it away. And much good it did the House anyway in an era in which legislation was at a low ebb (so much for Notestein). In what bears marks of clairvoyance Elton also managed to repudiate in advance any diagnosis of 'multiple dysfunction', since things were not working all that badly (so much in 1965 for Stone in 1972). To his own satisfaction, then, and (as we shall see) to the satisfaction of a good many others, Elton had shot down all the authorities in the early Stuart field from Gardiner on, a century of history writing.

Elton's purpose in perpetrating his universal slaughter was not just to clear the field of error, but after the necessary carnage to direct the errant sheep who might thereafter write about the Parliaments of the early Stuarts into the correct way to arrive at the truth about them, and thus to forestall a repetition of the Eltonian massacre. To Elton's mind the previous historiography of Parliaments under the early Stuarts had been a lamentable exercise in anachronism. From Gardiner on, all writing about England in that era had garishly misrepresented those years by viewing them in the lurid light of the Civil War. Institutions and people that did get involved in the upheaval of the mid-century — the King, the House of Commons, the House of Lords, Puritans, the Established Church, social classes — were treated as if from 1603 on they were in rehearsal for the imminent conflict. But of course they were not. People were behaving like what they were, Elizabethans and the children of Elizabethans. What they knew about was the reign of the Virgin Queen, not that of the Lord Protector.

And what was Parliament in the days of Elizabeth? Or rather first, what was it not? Most emphatically it was not a place where the Members of the House of Commons organized themselves as an Opposition to the government. That is the most pernicious illusion of all, Elton believes. It is the view propagated by Neale and by Notestein in his 'The Winning of the Initiative'.[31] According to Elton, it has been the view most generally held and therefore the one most responsible for the distortions of men's vision of early Stuart Parliaments, early Stuart politics and early Stuart history.[32]

That is what Parliament was not. What it had been under the Tudors was a most important, in some respects the most important, piece of the machinery of government. Its prime function was to make law that was binding on all subjects. It also provided the government with the money it needed in order to govern and defend the realm, and the people with the forum in which their just grievances would be heard and, when things went as they should, be redressed. Because of its importance men sought places in the House of Commons to support their local status or to satisfy their ambition for office, for place in the judiciary, at court, and even in the Queen's Privy Council.[33]

Seen in Elton's perspective the Parliaments of James I and Charles I were disastrous failures, manifestations of political pathology, a breakdown of the system of government. They made few laws, balked at supplying the ruler, rarely resulted in redress of grievances, and did not provide a principal avenue down which an ambitious man might expect to advance toward office. These failures, however, were not the superstructural manifestations of class war nor the consequences of pervasive 'multiple dysfunction' in the whole society, as the now Old Hat historians would have it. Early Stuart governments failed in their proper task of governing in general and through Parliament in particular because those 'governments could not manage or persuade, because they were incompetent, sometimes corrupt, and frequently just ignorant of what was going on or needed doing'. Of course they faced 'difficult . . . problems (every age has those)', and an 'often factious and bigoted and ill-conceived opposition . . . Certainly they had quite a job on their hands, but that is what they claimed to be there for. What matters is their repeated inability, for reasons also often factious, bigoted and ill-conceived, to find a way through their problems'.[34]

The Provincials. The Eltonian prescription has a drawback. It consigns the historians of early Stuart Parliaments to technological unemployment. It leaves them to stand at the bedside of a political order in the throes of dissolution and mutter 'sick, sick, sick'.[35] By 1642, however, the appropriate mutter is 'dead, dead, dead', and the quite reasonable question is 'What did the political order that seemed in fair health a couple of decades earlier die of?' Bigotry and misconception after all are not intrinsically threats to a government. To the contrary, it is useful for a government to propagate and strengthen among its subjects the particular misconceptions and bigotry which are its own. That will enhance popular support for it. Only divergence in bigotry and misconception between ruler and ruled is destructive of the body politic. It was precisely such a divergence that a cluster of historians of early Stuart England began to explore fruitfully and in detail about 15 years ago. Unlike the followers of Tawney they did not think that the way to account for the dissolution of the English polity was to examine changes in class structure. Unlike Gardiner they did not think that to account for that dissolution one needed mainly to heed the occasional dissonances between the House of Commons and the King, much less to imagine as he did that the dissonance had to do with principle. The divergence into which these historians, inspired by the work of Alan Everitt, believed it fruitful to inquire was the one between Court and Country. They were the Provincials.

The historiographical genealogy of the Provincials reaches back to a bright idea of H.R. Trevor-Roper, a flashing piece of insight of Peter Laslett, and a solid study by T.G. Barnes, *Somerset, 1625–1640* (1961). We have already glanced at Trevor-Roper's clever manoeuvre to stultify the followers of Tawney by reversing the values on all the pieces with which they played their game. Royal government became modern, court gentry and aristocracy became the progressive winners, the country gentry became the losers, regressive and backward pawns in the parliamentary faction-fights among courtiers, doomed to fail even when chance pressed victory into their hands. As Trevor-Roper then proceeded to extend it, his idea had a hapless future. Stretched to account for something called 'the general crisis of the seventeenth century' all over Europe, the dichotomy between rising court *élite* and declining country gentry turned out to be as contrived and dubious as the crisis it was supposed to account for. Even in the England for which Trevor-Roper originally conceived the dichotomy, his 'mere country gentry' appeared to derive from a boyhood recollection of Fielding's Squire Western rather than from any painstaking investigation of the *mores* of the early seventeenth-century English squirearchy. Still, the conflict between court and country as ways of living was more than a mere literary trope in early seventeenth-century England, and the cultural divergence it signalled might reasonably be expected to have had political consequences worthy of more attention than they got before Trevor-Roper pointed to or at least towards them.[36]

A probe by Peter Laslett in one county, Kent, indicated that while Trevor-Roper's picture of 'Country' was hilariously distorted, still his view that Court and Country were in some sense adversary or at any rate drastically divergent was sound. As a spin-off from his inquiries into Sir Robert Filmer, the author of *Patriarcha*, Laslett proposed two interesting theses with a splendid future. On the basis of his study of the Filmers of Kent he had argued that Country society was rooted in a sort of patriarchal familism so powerful that it was the controlling element not only in the lives of those who stayed down on the farm (or manor house), but also in the lives of those who left the country for the town, even if the town was London. And rejecting Trevor-Roper's dispiriting view of the idiocy of rural life, Laslett found in Kent a thriving local non-Court culture among those whom Trevor-Roper had written off as louts and noddies.[37]

Then in 1961 in his path-breaking study of Somerset an American scholar, Thomas Barnes, first showed how different Caroline England and its Parliament looked if one examined both not from the floor of the House of Commons but from the quarter-sessions of the justices of the peace of an English county. He gave a lively account of the rulers of Somerset — the lords lieutenant, their deputies, and the justices — in their dual roles as instruments of royal government and as local magnates. He told of the central government's vain effort for 15 years from the accession of Charles I to impose a national pattern and policy, civil, religious, and military, on an English county. The effort was in vain because to hold their local pre-eminence magnate families had to twist and bend royal policy to suit local sentiment. Finally Barnes shows a great 'Parliament-man', Robert Philips, at home, caught between Court and Country, concentrating his maximum effort not on Gardiner's 'constitutional issues' but on doing down his country neighbour and rival, Lord Poulett.

In the '60s Alan Everitt did the decisive things necessary to form the separate and independent beginnings of Trevor-Roper, Laslett and Barnes into a Country or Provincial interpretation of the early Stuart period. He wrote a superb case-study, *The Community of Kent and the Great Rebellion*, as a foundation for his interpretation, and then set forth that interpretation in a series of highly persuasive essays.[38] According to him the provinces, the regions of England — each county actually — were little commonwealths on their own. It was Kent, that a Kentish man, Devon that a Devonshire man had in mind when he spoke or thought of his 'country'. On the insularity of these little republics, on their diversity and conservatism, on their regional cultural networks and on their tight webs of kinship and intermarriage bounded by the county boundaries, the demands and commands, the ideas and styles from the centre, from London, impinged as external annoyances and impinged by and large without impressing. 'The impact of London . . . in most of the countryside . . . was only occasionally felt if it was felt at all.' With the death of Elizabeth the court's 'influence over the nation declined' and 'each county became more than ever before a little self-centred kingdom on its own'.[39] The view of the Provincials who followed most devoutly and docilely in Everitt's footsteps, especially of J.S. Morrill, has tended to be that the source of trouble from 1630 to 1660 was the innovative efforts of the centralizers — the Duke of Buckingham, Charles I, Strafford, Laud, Pym and Cromwell — to impose the control of the centre — Whitehall, the City, Westminster — on two score conservative 'Country' societies that would have none of it.[40]

Two peculiarities of the Provincial historians of England affected their perceptions of Parliament and those of the historians who accepted their central argument. In the first place their investigations have often taken the summoning of the Long Parliament as their base-point.[41] Such works avoid an anachronistic perception of nine tenths of the Parliaments of the Stuarts by the foolproof device of not seeing them at all. This, however, does not matter all that much because, in the second place, they have transposed Parliaments into the superstructure as effectively as did their predecessors of the Golden Age, now become Old Hat.

What was really going on in England according to the Provincials was a very complex set of conflicts. In divided counties factions struggled with each other for dominance in their 'little self-centred kingdoms'. In such a faction-fight one magnate or another might seek to bring the resources of the King's government to bear on his side, pushing the other side to adopt the same tactics.[42] In tranquil counties, where one man, one family, or one league of families enjoyed undisputed dominion, the local chiefs would expect the King's government to channel local patronage and exercise local power through them, and not to interfere overmuch in their management. When the King's government tried to extend its local control, it faced a hard fight in 40 English counties, and several more in Wales. In order to sabotage and block the execution of commands that would weaken the autonomy of the 'little self-centred kingdoms' to the advantage of the big self-centred one in London, the dominant chiefs in some counties, the 'out' factions in others, deployed all the facilities that the ancient instruments of 'self-government at the King's command' offered. On the relatively rare occasions when it was in session Parliament was an important place, but by no means the only important one, where the struggle between centre and provinces and between factions in divided provinces was carried forward. So, oddly, like the Old Hat historians whose views they believed obsolete, the Provincials thought Parliament could only be understood from-under-up. They had, however, substituted province or county or country against centre, for class against class as the key to the puzzle of Parliament.

6

Russell I and Russell II

So by the 1970s the major interpretations of early Stuart England and its Parliament, the Whig interpretation of Gardiner and social interpretations of the followers of Tawney, were under unanswered challenge. Parliament was not the arena for class conflict or constitutional conflicts or until 1640 for religious conflict. But what was it? A place where the 'ins' and the 'outs' gulled the bumpkins (Trevor-Roper)? A place where two stupid Stuart rulers screwed up a tidy bit of government machinery that the Tudors handed over to them in good shape (Elton)? One of the several *mises en scène* for the enactment of a struggle between London-based centralizers and county-based federalizers (the Provincials)? A place where the peers were up to more than they were usually given credit for? It was time that somebody put those tantalizing fragments into a new synthesis. Somebody did.

In a 1976 issue of *History*, Conrad Russell published a dense, closely argued article of 27 pages, 'Parliamentary History in Perspective, 1604–1629'. Towards the end of the article, he offers his generous estimate of the consequences that must follow if its conclusions are accepted: if they are, then 'much of the history of Parliament in this period needs to be rewritten' (p. 24). Three years later he published *Parliaments and English Politics 1621–1629*; in it he rewrote one half of that history.[43] Russell was moved to call for revision by two 'received opinions': 'that Parliament was growing more powerful in the early Stuart period and that it was divided into supporters of the "government" and "opposition".' Those two opinions were wrong. Moreover they drastically distorted the true image of the Parliaments that they reflected. The opposite opinions were correct: says Russell, 'before 1640 Parliament was not powerful', but feeble, and it 'was not engaged in the pursuit of supreme power'. Moreover in the first Stuart quarter-century, Parliaments did not contain an 'opposition'.[44]

The first proposition holds true particularly of the House of Commons, the segment of Parliament whose ascent to the position from which it was ready to challenge the King had been ascribed by Gardiner, J.E. Neale and Notestein to the four (or eight) decades before the Long Parliament. And of course that ascent was a given for the followers of Tawney, because unless it was happening there was no convenient place for a rising class to challenge a declining class or for a progressive social group to shatter a society in the throes of multiple dysfunction.

Unfortunately, however, as Russell points out, from the beginning to the end of whichever set of decades one chooses Parliaments in fact existed entirely at the will of the King; they met when he chose, and ceased to exist whenever he willed. More than that, even during their brief spans of precarious being — altogether only one tenth of the 37 years of Stuart rule before Charles summoned the Long Parliament[45] — the House of Commons, the supposedly powerful branch of Parliament, continually displayed the ultimate evidence of weakness of the popular estate in an assembly of estates: it was unwilling or unable to withhold needed supply from the Crown to force redress of grievances. Instead of exercising that power of withholding, the House often threw it away by granting supply before it even asked for specific acts of redress. Moreover it proved itself utterly impotent to prevent the King from laying on one kind of port duties, impositions, which it deemed illegal, and to stop him from collecting another kind, tonnage and poundage, which legally required the (actually ungranted) consent of Parliament.

That this feeble occasional assemblage did not have within it an 'opposition' to the King was not just a consequence of its feebleness, although it *was* feeble. Nor was it just a consequence of the incompatibility of the very idea of such 'opposition' with the contemporary view of political propriety, although the two *were* incompatible. It was rather that every serious concern which emerged in the House found sympathizers, even promoters, in the King's own Privy Council, that is, in the government itself. And what kind of 'opposition' is it that can always find support among the governors?

Still, Russell generously concedes, Parliaments held from 1604–29 were not 'models of harmony'. Why not? Not, he says, because, as Elton alleges, the first two Stuarts were clods. Rather because, *à la* Everitt, those Parliaments were enmeshed 'in a . . . permanent tension between the centre and the localities', between court and country.[46] In the *tableau vivant* that Russell presents, a weak-willed, glass-jawed House of Commons is forced by its institutional position to interpose itself between a couple of quarrelsome, mean customers, court and country, a hapless referee about to sink to the floor under a rain of blows from both gladiators. It is caught between a rock and a hard place.

Finished, then, the century-old Whig tradition of Gardiner which found in the House of Commons a heroic body of patriotic Englishmen fighting off the dangers to England's Protestantism, liberty and self-government that came from the court, and winning power in the process. Blown away even more completely, the Old Hat tradition that the House of Commons was the strategic heights that the pro-gressive middle-class gentry seized in its struggle for power with the reactionary King and peers and from which it thereafter dominated the regressive social classes. Vanished altogether the illusion that there was a high road to civil war among the traditional meandering pathways of politics of the first quarter-century of Stuart rule. None of these traditions bears examination in the cold bright light of detail that Russell threw on them both in his article and later in his book. Too many of the heroes of liberty like Coke came to oppose the threat of 'absolute monarchy'[47] only after faithful and remunerative service to the absolute King, or like Digges after an almost indecent display of readiness to engage in such service, if only invited. Too many heroes of 'opposition' in 1628 later enjoyed the blessings and rewards of place in the 'absolute' monarch's service during the years of prerogative rule. Noy, the counsel of one of the five knights who were imprisoned for refusal to pay the forced loan, as Charles's Attorney-General proposed the infamous writs of ship money; Littleton, chairman of the committee of the whole House that found its way to the Petition of Right, became Charles's Lord Chancellor; Digges, imprisoned in 1626 for maligning the Duke of Buckingham, in the 1630s finally got a place in the government that he had never stopped fishing for; and Wentworth, jailed for refusing to pay the forced loan, was raised to the peerage before the beginning of the 11 years of prerogative rule, and thereafter never looked back or down until he had risen to the top in the King's service, and even higher, to the scaffold.

In his article Russell skilfully incorporated all these perceptions, adverse to the Old Hat historians, and found places for them in his new vision of politics in the days of the early Stuarts. The stimulus of the article was intoxicating, perhaps too much so. It generated a quite extraordinary effervescence of fantastic notions among several young historians, mainly North American. Delighted at Russell's assault on the idea that there was an 'opposition' in the House of Commons under James and Charles, one of these eager acolytes of the *Nouvelle Vague* fell in love with the illusion that consensus dominated early Stuart Parliaments in theory and in fact. For evidence of such consensus he relied heavily on several contemporary tracts on procedure in Parliament; perhaps rather like deriving from Roberts's *Rules of Order* one's sense of the atmosphere and dynamics of a split local of the Boiler-makers' Union. Another acolyte with a sigh of relief jettisoned everything that inquiries from 1880 to 1975 had to say about the causes of the mid-seventeenth-century upheaval, and prescribed as a substitute for such futile investigations 'the . . . charting [of] networks of patronage, kinship, and friendship which dominated the politics of court and country'. A third, a true free spirit, eliminated the need for a good deal of such charting by a sort of oracular second sight by light of which he discovered how politics were effectively controlled from about 1625 to 1645. Blithely throwing to the wind all worldly constraints imposed by evidential requirements, he claimed that for two decades the reins of power lay in the hands of a small cluster of peers, inspired by Titus Livius, the historian of the Roman republic. Through connexions and clients they smoothly guided Parliament and country down the primrose path toward 'Livian revolution' (a phenomenon not fully characterized by its inventor) and civil war. According to another acolyte, an Englishman this time, the first Stuart quarter-century was a period of internal cohesion rather than a preface to revolution. Far from resisting the King the House of Commons displayed an appetite for lavishing grants upon the Crown that was almost indecent.[48]

Russell I, 'Parliamentary History in Perspective', appeared to have cleared the historiographical strand of the detritus left by the gradual collapse of all earlier interpretative structures. Then came the second crest of the New Wave, Russell II, *Politics and English Parliaments 1621–1629*. Russell II completed the demolition, first undertaken by others, of the sandcastles reared by his own too precipite disciples. In effect Russell I and Russell II seized the historiographical slate of early Stuart Parliaments and wiped it clean of everything but Russell I and Russell II.

What did Russell's new picture of Stuart Parliaments look like? In *form* it was an outrageously radical departure from, one might believe a calculated insult to, the Old Hat history of the early Stuart era. It was of all things a narrative, a *story* written mainly from within the *two* Houses of Parliament; it was *mainly about* things that went on outside the Houses between 1621 and 1629, but that came to the attention of the Houses.[49] In substance Russell's story was a tragifarce of two young men, Charles and George, in 1621 respectively the son and lover of a prematurely old King, James I. In 1623 the two set out to win honour in peace and glory in war on the great European stage and in five years lost both. They lost partly because the shrewd old King held them back for a while, before he died and Charles succeeded him, partly because they were gulled by some of Europe's most expert cony-catchers, including the Conde-Duque d'Olivares and the Cardinal Armand du Plessis de Richelieu. Mainly they lost because from 1624 they depended for necessary aid in their enterprises on the House of Commons in each Parliament; yet in each the House was a bungling, bumbling, miserly body, incompetent to carry out its domestic business much less to understand the European state system and the due causes and the costs of European war for those involved in it. Looking out, as it were, from a series of these incompetent concourses of men, called Parliaments, Russell watches the ridiculous sequence of pratfalls by all English members of the cast except for James I, who had the luck to die just as the farce got under way and things got out of hand. And the farce ended in sudden, shocking, real melodrama, as an assassin's knife prevented George, Duke of Buckingham, from embarking himself and his country on yet another disastrous continental enterprise. The sad, foolish tale had its appropriate epilogue in the parliamentary session of 1629. On that occasion the House of Commons gave Charles I a wholly persuasive demonstration of its own futility and its uselessness to him by passing no bills, providing no funds and passively sanctioning an assault by its own Members on its own Speaker, an action that looks less like initiative on its part than like institutional suicide.

In the eyes of many historians the Russell II story of England from inside Parliament delivered the *coup de grace*, long overdue, to the Whig interpretation of early Stuart history in its Old Hat variant and in its earlier Gardiner-Notestein form. The Parliament of the 1620s was not up to and was not playing *any* of the roles that for a century historians had assigned it. On the other hand in two ways, neither of which has been noted generally or perhaps even by Russell himself, *Parliaments and English Politics 1621–1629* can be seen as a partial justification of *both* of those older images of England in the early seventeenth century that he at first sight seems to have obliterated.

First Gardiner's way. In his book Russell looks at the England he is investigating not, like the Old Hat historians, from-under-up but from-the-back-forward. That was the way that Gardiner went about *doing* history, starting in 1603 and marching forward year by year until 1656. In accord with the practice of the time in which he started to work he did most of his research in the Public Record Office amid the archives of the central government. Therefore he never lost track of the day-to-day circumstances and contingencies of government, of the complexities, domestic and especially foreign, with which the King and his advisers had to deal, of the outcomes that were the consequence of human misinformation, human misunderstanding, human error, and those lamentable human weaknesses that often accompany admirable human strengths.[50] Although in general he did tend to hold his seventeenth-century men to a somewhat rigorist nineteenth-century standard of behaviour, Gardiner got to know his leading characters so well over time that even better than Russell he is able to discern and understand the ambiguities of their decisions and actions.[51] Like Russell, too, and unlike the historians in fashion in the 1950s, Gardiner never turned the people in his story into mere puppets moved in a pre-determined course by deep, underlying historical forces. Particularly, like Russell and unlike the post Second World War historians he understood the major role of foreign affairs in shaping the relations of King and House of Commons from the time of the Spanish match to the time of the Irish Rebellion.[52] So rather oddly, despite Conrad Russell's no doubt in part appropriate claim to innovation, he may rightly be regarded as a vindicator of Gardiner.

Even more oddly Russell may be seen as providing aid and comfort to that last, most maligned, and most ecumenical Old Hat historian, Lawrence Stone. After all, in a way Russell I and Russell II together provide a coherent and intelligible account of the utter failure of English institutions to provide the realm and its ruler with the means to take their due place in a European world in which warfare was the indispensable means of taking such a place. Luckily spending most of his reign in peacetime, James had been able to evade the necessity and cost of continental wars. Until 1629 Charles may not have had the way and certainly did not have the will to evade such wars and thereby allow his state to become a second-rate power. Much of Russell's excellent and intelligent study tells, bit by bit, of the unreadiness and incapacity of English society to provide the King of England with the means to make his land a modern warlike state like France, Spain and Austria, indeed even Sweden and Prussia. It is true that Russell does not press his analysis of this palpable deficiency of English society very far. If he had been inclined to press it, he might have had to study a good many instances of that 'multiple dysfunction' which caught Stone's attention.

This is an odd state of affairs. Gardiner has been the Whig historian *par excellence* in the eyes of both the Old Hat historians and of most of those of the *Nouvelle Vague*. And Lawrence Stone is surely the pre-eminent Old Hat historian, the historian from-under-up who has most effectively insisted on the impact of a whole range of underlying phenomena during the prior century in moving England toward civil war. What if the effect, however unintentional, of Conrad Russell's work is to re-establish and in fact vindicate the method, approach, and macrorhetoric of S.R. Gardiner? What if at the same time he points, however accidentally, to the impact of the 'multiple dysfunction' of pre-existing English structures that concerned Stone on the slide of England into civil war? Surely a historiographical quake that after a preliminary shaking leaves *both* Gardiner and Stone reasonably steady on their pedestals, asking many of the right questions though not always figuring out the right answers, is something short of cataclysmic. Perhaps a slight downward revision of the place of the Russell phenomenon on the Richter scale — to 5 maybe? 4? — is in order.

7

Russell's impact: Lockyer and Fletcher

We may reasonably choose to turn our ears from the more febrile panegyrics of Russell's work that come close to likening it to the Emancipation Proclamation if not to the Advent.[53] Still, evidence of the impact both of his writing and of his scholarly *persona* is clear to see in the footnotes of a dozen, perhaps a score of the younger historians of early Stuart England, cisatlantic and transatlantic. To judge by the steady stream of acknowledgments of his help and suggestions, he must be among the most generous as well as among the most learned of the historians in his field.[54]

Further evidence of Russell's impact comes from the two most impressive historical works on the early Stuart age published during 1981 — Roger Lockyer's *Buckingham*[55] and Anthony Fletcher's *The Outbreak of the English Civil War*.[56] By no means novices, experienced historians rather,[57] both writers pay willing tribute to Russell's book. 'A major work' says Lockyer, 'full of insights and fruitful hypotheses . . . I should like to express my admiration for his work and my . . . agreement with his argument' that war lay at the heart of England's troubles in the 1620s (pp. 476–7). Fletcher's acknowledgment is less direct but no less impressive. In the footnotes to the first *seven* pages of his book, he once expresses his gratefulness to Russell for a bit of information and cites one work or another by Russell 35 times.

Both Lockyer's book and Fletcher's will surely be heartily welcome to scholars in the field. It is time, and long past time, that without apology and without the danger of being condescended to by historians claiming to be 'on the cutting edge of historical work', Lockyer should be able to devote his talents to a reliable, intelligent, and truly learned work on George Villiers, Duke of Buckingham, a man who in all major matters had in his hands the effective, full direction of English policy for four critical years (1624–8). And the increased availability of information on the doings of the Long Parliament since Gardiner wrote sufficiently justifies Fletcher's full-scale narrative re-examination of the course of events in the agonizing two years during which the English stumbled and lurched into a long civil war.[58] Here I will deal more briefly with the excellences of these studies than I would in other circumstances choose, and say more than I ordinarily would about their few shortcomings, since those shortcomings lie especially within the purview of this article.

In his sympathetic pursuit of Buckingham, Roger Lockyer has immersed himself in the sources of the period and especially in those from 1621 on, when the sources on politics overlap those on patronage and supersede those on perversion. He has tried to see the world through the eyes of the handsome, impecunious courtier George Villiers, raised by the favour of his King and lover, James I, to the greatest wealth in the kingdom and then by the favour of Charles I, son and successor to James, exalted to quasi-royal authority. Lockyer has succeeded so well that he has truly identified with Buckingham and come to admire the man through whose eyes he sees the world of the 1620s. Indeed as an empathizer Lockyer may have been over-successful; he may see George Villiers's decade at the top of Fortune's Wheel too much as Villiers saw it and not see Villiers clearly enough as others saw him. Seen *as* Villiers saw it, the world is a great bowl of goodies to be grabbed, bitten into, swallowed or spat out, a merry-go-round offering one brass ring after another — the patronage of the English Crown, the favour of the ladies of Spain, diplomatic triumph, the chance to be the saviour of Europe from the Hapsburgs, to be the champion of Protestantism, and to be the lover of the Queen of France — all things Buckingham never managed to become. Life was a rush of days of feverish preparation for war and of nights of gambling and adultery, of patronage of the arts, and of the joys of the hunt, all in a wildly whirling cyclorama in which there was no time to set priorities and make choices, no time to weigh the possible gains of a venture against its likely costs or against the assets available to carry it out, no time even to come to grips with one stunning failure before plunging on to the next, and indeed no need, because the royal bail-out was always available. Buckingham never seems to have paused to reflect. He may have lacked the inclination, the time, the ability. Although there is no evidence that Lockyer lacks any of these traits, in his book he has modelled himself too closely on the young man in a hurry who is his hero. A little more reflection by Lockyer, on

Buckingham, a little more distancing from him, might paradoxically have enabled the reader to see him better.

Nor does Lockyer ever see Buckingham as his manifold audience saw him — as for example the Spanish first and then the French saw him — a feckless light-weight to be gulled *ad lib.*, a man who in the poker game of international politics persistently drew to inside straights because he did not really understand the values in the deck, and who did not have to worry too much about his losses because his stupid master was ready to bankroll him through each successive disaster. Nor does Lockyer see him as the Members of the House of Commons did in 1621 — a favourite so greedy of office and patronage that he threw distributive justice or the customary division of the spoils of office badly out of balance while advancing family connexions who would have been more properly provided for in Bedlam or Bridewell. Nor as the House saw him after 1624, as the man who had assumed control of English policy, who bewitched an innocent young King and led him into idiotic ventures, who in a world deeply imperilled by the triumphant counter-march of popery and tyranny, lived domestically with a popish wife and a popish mother, devoted to both if not particularly faithful to the first, as a dilettante who through corruption or incompetence could not produce the fleet for which as Lord Admiral he was responsible, who could find money for the most lavish living but not for the wretched starving sailors of his fleet nor for the defence of the coast and English shipping in the Channel. The taxes that the country and its chosen spokesmen in Parliament were loth to grant the King while the duke had the spending of them Buckingham poured down one continental rat-hole after the other, and, when the House held back on squeezing the country to subvent the disasters into which he successively plunged it, he persuaded the King against law to find the money and in doing so to violate the most fundamental liberties of Englishmen — to take their property without their consent and to imprison those who refused to give up what was rightfully theirs.

This blind area that affects Lockyer's otherwise clear and photographically detailed perception of Buckingham creates a flaw in an otherwise excellent work of scholarship. The flaw may well be the consequence of the powerful confirmation that Russell's work gave to conclusions at which Lockyer had independently arrived. In *Buckingham* Lockyer notes his agreement with Russell that 'the "constitutional" difficulties of the 1620s derive from the impact of war upon a society that was unprepared for it . . . in any . . . way' (p.477).[59] This agreement affects Lockyer's perceptions in a peculiar way, best illustrated in his summation of Buckingham's role in the proceedings that eventuated in the Petition of Right. He writes, 'Buckingham had fought a long, skilful and honourable campaign on the King's behalf, and he accepted defeat gracefully. His principal concern had always been to stop the Commons provoking Charles into a sudden dissolution, so that the much-needed subsidies could in due course be made available and the crown's credit restored' (p. 436). Buckingham was commander of the campaign on the Île de Ré. That campaign directly or indirectly consumed all the intake from the illegal levy of 1626–7, required the imprisonment of those who refused to pay, *pour encourager les autres*, made necessary the taking of free quarter for the host of poor wretches who were pressed into service and the imposition of martial law in peacetime on the military and civilian vagabonds who still had enough spirit to loot, rape and murder. In 1628 the House of Commons wanted the law against such doings to be made so clear that they could not happen again. The constitutional issue was that the House of Commons wanted binding rules against administrative imprisonment, and that the duke did not want the King to be bound by such rules and did everything in his power to prevent him from being so bound.

The constititutional issue was in fact an issue of liberty. It was on the agenda of the House not because of England's involvement in war. It was there because of the measures that Charles and Buckingham took to break out of the bind into which their war policy put them and their country. Every circumstance suggests that, with the assassin's shadow looming over Buckingham, his biographer should have taken a look at the course that brought his hero to this pass, and that he should have taken that look from a point a bit away from the inside of Buckingham's head. Such a move did not suggest itself to Lockyer, and his reading of Russell's *Parliaments and English Politics* apparently did not suggest it to him either. Both Lockyer and Russell, although successful in getting into the heads of King, favourite and courtiers were not successful in getting into the heads of the Members of the House of Commons who challenged their actions. Or, perhaps, they did not try very hard. Too bad!

Anthony Fletcher's *The Outbreak of the English Civil War* is a rich, detailed account of the events and the men that brought Englishmen who were at peace with one another at the beginning of 1641 to the widespread taking up of arms against one another by the end of 1642. Fletcher starts with several strong convictions about the situation at the time the Long Parliament assembled: England was not in any contemporary's eyes headed toward civil war; civil war was not the inevitable consequence of the rise of a social class or of a political body, the House of Commons, because these were mythical not actual events; ascription of the outbreak of the Civil War to deep structural causes is simply a Whiggish mistake. No so-called underlying cause or gradual development accounts for the actual polarization among the Members of both Houses that took place in the first two years of the Long Parliament. That polarization, however, was the indispensable precondition for the taking up of arms by Englishmen under the standard of 'the King' on one side and 'Parliament' on the other.[60]

In Fletcher's view this polarization was the work of one man, John Pym. Firmly convinced of the existence of a popish plot to destroy both the Protestant religion and liberty in England, 'King' Pym, who dominated the Long Parliament from its beginning, set out to convince his fellow Members that they stood in peril of such a plot, centred at court, embracing the King's close servants and his French Catholic wife. Charles himself had earlier conjured up this distrust by his support of Archbishop Laud's religious innovations and of clerical exalters of the King's arbitrary power during the intermission of Parliaments between 1629 and 1640. Charles's support of Laud intensified Pym's suspicions, and threw him — not all unwilling — into the arms of the more zealous Puritans. Moreover Charles actually did negotiate for help from foreign Catholic sovereigns, from the Irish Catholics, from the English Catholics, from English Catholic officers in his army. And Pym always discovered him at it. 'The deepest irony of our story', says Fletcher, 'is that the further parliament plunged into investigating and combating popish conspiracy the more the plot seemed to become a self-fulfilling prophecy' (p. xxv); the more, too, the intensified distrust between Pym and Charles (warranted on both sides) rendered impossible the peaceful, parliamentary settlement of England's difficulties that, Fletcher believes, was Pym's own durable purpose, the one for which he had long planned.

This is the central theme of Fletcher's story, a story whose value does not depend on the adequacy of its theme to account for the outbreak of fighting in 1642. Its value rather depends on the mass of detail about what was happening in the House, in the councils and the churches of the City, and in county after county between the meeting of the Long Parliament and the arming of men for civil war. By the force of the events and accidents that Fletcher tells about, Englishmen reluctantly, bewilderedly, yet as though in the grip of a destiny unintelligible, irrational, but irresistible, careered headlong into a conflict.

It will take a longer time than the present writer has at his disposal and some careful thinking to decide whether to settle for an account of the origins[61] of the English Civil War, whose author is unwilling to look for any causes back beyond the Short Parliament.[62] Two points however may be worth making. They are evident enough in Fletcher's book, even more so if one re-examines the polemic exchanges of King and Parliament in 1642–3 and the flood of petitions from the counties in 1641 and 1642. Practically all of these documents claim to seek or promise to protect the same things — the true Protestant religion, the King's prerogative, the privileges of Parliament, the liberties of the subject, the law of the land. All of these are taken to be desired and desirable ends, all are the rightful inheritance of free Englishmen. Two of them at least — the liberties and laws of the land — must go by the board. They had to be violated, they were violated by both sides during the prosecution of a civil war. For many Englishmen, which side they chose or whether they were willing to choose at all depended on their guess as to which of the current violators of their shared values would be the most trustworthy custodian of those values in case of victory. That was a matter of judgment on which men might be divided, on which in his own mind many a man might be divided. The second point is that these shared political ends were not consequent on but antecedent to the events of 1640. They were, so to speak, the big ticket items that had reached their high current value at some earlier time. To tell the story of the outbreak of the Civil War without trying to understand how these shared political ends came to mean what they did to those who shared them is to risk misunderstanding the story itself. Trying to understand these things demands that the inquirer look back to find where the lumber that went into the structure of big values came from and to look forward to see what became of the structure under the strains and stresses of change. What happened, say, to the Petition of Right and the sense of the political order that it manifested not just in the month or the year after it became law but in the next ten years and in the crunch of civil war? That is a somewhat Whiggish question. Is it wholly irrelevant to the outbreak of the English Civil War?

8

The old and the obstinate — a restoration?

It is surely a useless and foolish question in the eyes of the *Nouvelle Vague* historians. One of them, Paul Christianson, recently assessed the impact of the wave — the 'new view of early Stuart English political history'. Christianson thinks that the new view challenges 'root and branch the traditional Whig interpretation' of the period, and that in consequence 'a remarkable transformation has taken place already — by reaching a fruitful consensus the revisionists have already put together a powerful explanatory pattern' for the era. So dynamic and powerful had that consensus become that, 'by the end of the 1970s, it seemed, only the old and the obstinate resisted the search for revision'.[63]

Well, yes and no. In a way that does not quite fit Christianson's formulation Conrad Russell almost single-handed has indeed revolutionized the fashion in historical discourse about early Stuart England. Without the impact of Russell, the books by Lockyer and Fletcher we have just finished examining would probably have been written much as we have them, but on publication they would have had to encounter the arched eyebrows of the truly with-it historians, as the work of C.V. Wedgwood did a quarter-century ago. Like her work they are, alas, mere stories, not analytical but narrative. Fortunately, though, it is not stylish to say 'Alas!' any more when confronted with a mere story. By the sheer force of one highly persuasive example, *Parliaments and English Politics 1621–1629*, Russell has convinced the relevant cluster of professional historians that the best way to deal with some kinds of historical phenomena that lie within the chronological bounds of their studies — the history of Parliaments for example — is to tell a story about them, and to do it in accord with Humpty-Dumpty's prescription — 'start at the beginning, go on to the end, then stop'.[64] This is a historiographical revolution, all right; but not, I think, in the sense that Christianson and the rest of us moderns use the term. Rather it is a revolution in the old seventeenth-century sense, a re-turning, as of a point on the rim of a flywheel, to the position from which it started, a return to — of all things — the mode of historical discourse of S.R. Gardiner, though not to his opinions. It is rooted in the belief, apparently shared by Russell but not by Christianson, that the most efficient way to get a great many historical matters straight is to tell a story about them.

As to 'only the obstinate and the old resisting the search for revision', if by that phrase Christianson means to designate those who in review articles have publicly declared themselves in doubt about some of the expressed historical conclusions of the *Nouvelle Vague*, he is fairly close to the mark. Of the eight such sinners I have encountered, three on a reasonable audit are old,[65] two although not old are to my personal knowledge obstinate.[66] In mutual public combat two — Christopher Hill and I — have shown themselves to be stubborn. On the public record we are both reasonably stricken in years, so both 'old' and 'obstinate' make a fair fit for both of us.[67] Still, granting these unfortunate traits of a majority of the nay-sayers, perhaps one ought at least glance at the grounds of their dissent.

This whole cluster of writers are in agreement on one point: Conrad Russell's writings on the Parliaments of the early Stuarts are works of extraordinarily high quality in scholarship, historical imagination and persuasiveness. Moreover, in some of his contentions, they agree, Russell is right, where many previous historians have been partly in error, wholly in error, or simply oblivious of what was going on. For Russell it must be an odd experience to hear this chorus of praise as he feels each chorister exploring ever so carefully for the precise spot between his ribs in which to drive a knife home.

To deal with each critique by this most recent set of revisionists would be difficult because of their number and inconvenient because the objections of the critics tend to overlap. Fortunately, in a recent and relevant symposium *Past and Present* has published essays by Derek Hirst and Theodore Rabb under the covering title, 'Revisionism Revised', followed by the Neale Memorial Lecture for 1980 in which from his own point of view Christopher Hill summarized the controversy up to the end of 1980 with a view to putting 'the issues in a wider context than has so far been done'.[68] The *pièce de resistance* at this banquet was Conrad Russell's work, set out for convenient carving, while Provincials and lesser Russellians, already conveniently minced,[69] were served up as side dishes. Attention to these essays will therefore give us some sense of what is left of the *Nouvelle Vague* after the doubters have specified the ground for their doubts. Or, to revert to the metaphor with which we started, about where on the historiographical Richter scale the revisionist tremor falls.

In Christopher Hill's opinion the lesser acolytes of Conrad Russell, several of whom made their début as such in one issue of the *Journal of Modern History*, were promptly knocked off by one 'obstinate' and one 'old' in another issue of the same journal that followed less than a year later.[70] No wonder. After all, they were sitting ducks. The Provincials were another matter. The work of Everitt and of those who had followed his lead was serious, thoughtful, and based on careful and patient scholarship. It was their view, as we have seen, that the country was far more seriously preoccupied with local concerns than with high and Whiggish issues of political or constitutional principle, and that this former preoccupation also dominated the Country Members of the House of Commons. In Russell II as in Russell I this view of the provinces and the Country is primary.[71]

In 'The County Community in Stuart Historiography', published in 1980, Clive Holmes counters the main arguments of the Provincials about the role of the counties with extraordinary force.[72] His critique is terse, powerful, always to the point. So far it has not been answered by either the Provincials or the Russellian revisionists. It is a tough string of denials of the main affirmations of the Provincials, always buttressed by specific counter-instances. Most of the traits of the counties that Everitt singles out as differentiating them from each other were either moderated and qualified by other traits or were actually not there at all, says Holmes. The county was not a political body with a life separate from and nearly indifferent to the centre. Long settlement in one county did not necessarily result in overwhelmingly localist sentiment. In any case in most counties long-settled gentry did not predominate. The dominant major gentry in each county were not markedly endogamous; many took their wives from places beyond their county's bounds. The interests, connexions, and relationships even of gentry whose own marriages were endogamous were not because of that limited to their county. Localism was attenuated by trans-county kinships and by the extra-county education of almost all the upper gentry from all counties at the universities and the Inns of Court. During their education in what were truly national institutions the gentry forged nationwide links of friendship. There, broad contacts with both people and books extended horizons that previously may have been bounded by the limits of a youth's native shire. Nor did the gentry community's doings as governors strictly conform to county lines. Most of it was done in units smaller than the county, and when the county was the unit it was often brought into action by the agents and dominated by the purposes of the central government. County-wide assemblies mainly did the business of that government — assizes with domineering royal judges, elections of knights of the shire to royal Parliaments, service willy-nilly on royal commissions like the one for the forced loan. Nor did the county gentry respond to and resist the central government solely in terms of provincial interests — not in the matter of ship money nor of the forced loan in both of which evidence of trans-local concern is clear. Nor did the counties always choose as knights of the shire men who concerned themselves solely with the local impact of the policies of the central government. On the contrary the counties chose men dedicated to 'Church and Commonwealth'.[73] Finally no longer was the political nation just and only the gentry; men further down the social scale insisted on making themselves and their grievances heard, and aspirants to seats in the House had to listen.

Each of the points that Holmes makes tells directly against the view, that the Provincials sponsored and Russell adopted, of what was essentially going on in early Stuart England. Each is supported by concrete evidence. If these sponsors do not counter specifically and precisely, one will be entitled to assume that silence gives consent and that one prop of recent revisionism has been shot away.

In directing attention to matters that the Provincial historians did not pay enough heed to, Holmes frequently has recourse to an adjective not much heard in English writing on early Stuart history since before the Second World War. He writes of the 'constitutional issue' that the demand for the forced loan 'presented starkly to the local gentry', of the local magistrates being 'confronted . . . with a major issue of constitutional principle', of the 'novel constitutional doctrine' of the King's court, and he observes that the 'inhabitants' of England 'were well informed and deeply concerned about national . . . constitutional issues' (pp. 68, 69, 73).

And that brings us back to the recent *Past and Present* symposium on the revisionists. There the new arguments against the revisionist positions elaborated by Rabb and Hirst are backed by Hill's skilful reworking, with glosses of his own, of arguments made by others earlier. They sharply drive the ball of debate back into Russell's court — as sharply as Holmes drove it into the court of the Provincials. Unless Russell can counter-attack, his position looks badly shaken. It is not for this reason, however, that at this point I want to turn from Holmes to Rabb and Hirst. I want rather to note the frequent recurrence of the term 'constitutional' in their essays, as in that of Holmes. According to Rabb the events of the 1640s faced England with 'a constitutional crisis', but, as he shows, 'constitutional issues' had risen in earlier Parliaments. The English were then trying to cope with 'constitutional problems' encountered on the Continent as well as in England (pp. 64, 68). And, says Hirst, although 'arguments of constitutional principles were at their liveliest in times of war', 'differences about the nature of the constitution' were 'not wholly dependent on the effects of . . . wartime'. 'Fear of constitutional innovation' enabled men to grasp the 'constitutional implications' of Bate's case as early as 1608, and even more intensely in 1628 'Parliament . . . saw an upsurge of constitutional protest' (pp. 85, 87, 90, 84, respectively).

Now let us note another word our three young obstinates — Holmes, Rabb and Hirst — share. It is a proper noun — Gardiner. Said Holmes, 'challenges to Gardiner's account', have been infected with excessive localism and this resulted 'in a failure to recognize ideological divisions' (p. 55). Says Rabb, 'Gardiner was one of those inexhaustible nineteenth-century masters'. The aspiration of 'the revisionists . . . to offer a comprehensive and plausible replacement for Gardiner' is doomed. Their 'notion that the short term and the accidental' can 'match the Gardinerian mounting drama . . . as a convincing account of seventeenth-century history' is simply illusory (pp. 56, 76). And, finally, Hirst, right up front: 'Russell's argument ought not lead us to abandon the thesis of S.R. Gardiner', or to forget that 'long-running disagreements about the nature of the constitution' played 'a significant part in bedevilling not only the early Stuarts' relations with their parliaments, but also, ultimately, their ability to govern the country' (p. 81).

So, here's a pretty kettle of fish! For about a half-century we have been painfully learning that in the days of James I and Charles I constitutional issues and constitutional principles were superstructural, or did not count all that much, or were not what really mattered, or did not matter at all. And for about the same time we have been told that Gardiner missed the main point (the Golden Age historians), that as a consequence of his Whiggish myopia he did not understand Parliament (Elton), that in his concentration on the House of Commons he missed the conflict that really counted, the one between the centralizing Court and the anti-centralist Country (the Provincials), and that he sadly overestimated the importance of Parliament, especially the House of Commons, and therefore had a distorted image of what was going on not only in the House but in England between 1604 and 1629 (Russell). Just a very few years back we came into the new era. The *new*, new era, that is. It offered 'a new view of early Stuart political history,' we were told, by means of which the new revisionists not only 'challenged, root and branch, the traditional Whig interpretations' but reached a 'fruitful consensus' and put together 'a powerful explanatory pattern'.[74]

And now up bobs this gang of old and young obstinate spoil-sports. They do not proclaim the new, new, new era. Rather they say quite firmly and with an impressive set of arguments backed by solid evidence, 'Sorry, chaps, you did grab off a few good points, but you had better keep plenty of room on the bench for Gardiner and those Whigs or you are in trouble. After all there was a serious constitutional struggle going on under the early Stuarts, the Kings and the House of Commons were parties to it, and if you don't keep that in mind quite often you won't be able to account for what either King or House of Commons are doing and saying. That's the way Gardiner said it was and to an extent that you have failed to recognize he was right'.

Well, that is a very odd place to end up, but it suits me fine. My reward for marching in place all these years is to have the vanguard circle around so that it is just behind me. Still, since historians are putatively concerned with the improvement of the understanding as well as with winning historiographical brownie points, I feel impelled to do more than chortle.

It seems to me that there is a chance that we are at least on the verge of reaching a better and fuller understanding of what moved men involved in the life of politics in the early Stuart era than we have ever had before, but that if we get into the old business of overclaiming we may miss our chance. This is especially so because to arrive at that understanding we shall need to take up constitutional issues as Holmes, Rabb and Hirst have felt impelled to do. Few present-day historians, however, have had much practice in dealing with such issues; the past half-century of English history writing and teaching has not featured the study of constitutional ideas and concerns. In their essays Rabb and Hirst dealt with constitutional matters fruitfully but brashly, not bothering to unpack the term 'constitutional' in the interest of preventing confusion. But if we do not unpack it, we will create confusion, and will end up in another fruitless round of logomachy. We need to make a few fundamental distinctions.

Here are several of the central questions around which constitutional ideas cluster: (1a) What is the rightful source of political authority? What in effect legitimates the right of one man or group to command the obedience of others? (1b) Who — what person or persons — does or should possess the powers of command? (2a) What is the extent and what are the limits, if any, of the ruler's power of command over those subject to it? (2b) What are the limits on the subject's duty to obey?

These questions overlap but they are not the same. The first primarily raise questions of distributive justice: in whom should power to command and rule lie? The last two are mainly in the area of liberty: are there any limits to the authority of the legitimate ruler to command and if so what are they? When Holmes, Rabb and Hirst talk about constitutional issues under the early Stuarts, which pair of questions do they have in mind — the ones bearing on the *distribution* of authority among the rulers or those having to do with the *bounds* of their authority over the ruled? None of them tells us. From the context and tenor of their discourse, however, it seems to me that Rabb may mainly have in mind the conflicts over the distribution of authority, Hirst and Holmes the bounds of the ruler's authority.

And here it seems to me we need to tread especially carefully if we intend to talk about constitutional issues in the early Stuart period. J.S. Morrill speaks of 'the old-fashioned constitutional history which dominated the Oxford history school until the 1950s'. He says 'it looked at constitutional thought in terms of distribution of power within the state'.[75] That is, the Oxford school was preoccupied with the first pair of constitutional questions having to do with where power lay. With respect to that pair, Conrad Russell argues there really was no question and no issue between the accession of James I and the meeting of the Long Parliament. In *The Crisis of the Constitution* Margaret Judson had proved this point beyond reasonable doubt a quarter-century ago. And she is quite right, and so is Russell. Bar a handful of papists, no Englishman thought that there was any rightful political power in England independent of the King's. From James I to Sir Edward Coke to John Pym, from Archbishops Bancroft and Laud to William Perkins and John Winthrop, all agree that England is an absolute monarchy. Russell is most helpful in clearing away the debris left by the worn-out notion that anyone or anyones were challenging the royal supremacy, seeking to supplant it or intentionally encroaching on it. No one was. The erroneous 'Whig' view that Russell rejects alleges or more often unconsciously assumes that the House of Commons was in conflict with James and Charles over the locus or distribution of power, that it was seeking power or more power, that it was engaged in a struggle for sovereignty with the King. It is indeed possible that, as the King claimed, some of the things the House sought for itself seemed to him to encroach on his power; it is even possible to see these claims 'as steps on the way to power', but only if we realize that this is a retrospective view of *ours*, not a view of the House of Commons before 1640 or of any Member of the House.[76] On the face of the evidence no Member either thought that way or, more important, ever acted as if he thought that way.

Nevertheless there was conflict between the King and the House of Commons and it was constitutional conflict. It had to do with the second set of constitutional issues — with the bounds of political authority, with the relation of that authority to the rights of freemen. Repeatedly the claim was made that the privileges of Parliament *were* liberties of the subject, part of their due inheritance. Repeatedly it was alleged that actions of the government encroached on those liberties. Repeatedly it was asserted that by levying on property without the consent of Parliament, the government was abusing the royal prerogative and threatening the rights of free Englishmen. The clash at the boundaries of the King's prerogative and the subject's liberties was loud, explicit and frequent from the first day of James I's first Parliament to the day 25 years later when Charles I's consent made the Petition of Right the law of the land. To deny that Members of the House of Commons were concerned about the liberties of the subject, of which they deemed the privilege of Parliament an indispensable ingredient, one must stop one's ears to things the Members said and did in one Parliament after another, or face the problem of explaining away as insignificant or meaningless words and actions into which Members were recurrently and palpably investing heavy drafts of emotion and energy. Some of the matters concerning the liberty of the subject that were of deepest concern in the 1620s are of deepest concern to men in the 1980s — the abuse of martial law in peacetime, for example, or the detention of people by state power without bringing any charge of criminal action against them. Lech Walesa and Solidarity in Poland have recently had some experience of such things. When 'Whiggish' is used as a pejorative term, do those who use it mean that it is Whiggish to point out that in the seventeenth century for the first time men tried effectively to limit the power of the state over its subjects in many of the same ways and for precisely the same reasons as we do today? Really? If that be Whiggery make the most of it.

Notes

1   *History*, LXI (1976), 1–27.
2   The age-span is significant. With rare exceptions editors of established journals turn over the reviewing of big books to old hands — or old fogies, or old toads — e.g. in Russell's case to Professors Geoffrey Elton, Austin Woolrych and me. The old hands, fogies and toads take it as part of their role as historians and as guardians of sound tradition to make explicit the deep misgivings that they are likely to feel about rash novelties. Consequently in a case such as Professor Russell's, established journals are not likely to reflect adequately the enthusiasm of the rising generation for the major breakthrough and for the opportunity it affords that generation of doing the old hands down. At any rate it was thus with me in my youth. I assume things have not changed all that much since then.
3   There have been, for example, only two full-scale efforts since his time to go over the ground that Gardiner covered from the assembling of the Long Parliament to the outbreak of the Civil War — C.V. Wedgwood's *The King's Peace* (1955), and just a few months ago Anthony Fletcher's *The Outbreak of the English Civil War* (1981). Of Gardiner, Wedgwood says, 'Gardiner was sure he knew which side was right . . . although he tried to be fair to the characters of the men on the other side . . . His scholarship has not its equal today' (pp. 491–2). Fletcher's first acknowledgment of debt goes to Gardiner, 'the authoritative account', in these terms (p. viii): 'His was a staggering achievement. His narration only needs correction on a few points of detail.' I am not sure there is any major historian of England from before the First World War, even Stubbs, even Maitland, of whom the same can be said.
4   *D.N.B.*, 2nd Supp. (1901–11), II, 76. The prologue to Gardiner's *chef d'oeuvre* turned out longer than the play, ten volumes as against eight, when death stopped Gardiner's pen.
5   Gardiner published his ten-volume prologue in two-volume instalments from 1863 to 1882: *The History of England from the Accession of James ' to the Disgrace of Chief Justice Coke 1603–1616* (2 vols., 1863); *Prince Charles and the Spanish Marriage 1617–1623* (2 vols., 1869); *The History of England under the Duke of Buckingham and Charles I 1624–1628* (2 vols., 1875); *The Personal Government of Charles I 1628–1637* (2 vols., 1877); *The Fall of the Monarchy of Charles I* (2 vols., 1882). The completed series was re-issued as a ten-volume set between 1884 and 1886 as *The History of England from the Accession of James I to the Outbreak of the Civil War 1603–1642.*
6   *Proceedings of the British Academy*, XI (1924–5), 125–75.
7   The first yield of Notestein's vision was his edition, with Frances H. Relf, of *Commons Debates for 1629...* (Minneapolis, 1921).
8   Collaborators: Frances H. Relf, Hartley Simpson; students: W.H. Coates, Elizabeth Read Foster, Mary Frear Keeler, D.H. Willson; students of students: Esther S. Cope, R.C. Johnson; student of a student of a student: Maija J. Cole; scholars who indirectly came under Notestein's influence: Robert Ruigh, J.H. Hexter. The role of the last-named in these editorial affairs has been entrepreneurial rather than scholarly.
9   Notestein, 'Winning of the Initiative', p. 148: 'One notebook tells us of an early morning caucus of the Opposition.' The Privy Councillors were unable 'to hold their own with an extremely competent Opposition'. 'The Peers moved toward the Opposition.' Given this language, the muted reservations Conrad Russell winkles out of Notestein's article as evidence that its author was too cautious to view the Members of the House he investigated as an opposition seem too weak to sustain Russell's apologia for Notestein: Russell, 'Parl. Hist. in Perspective', p. 4.
10 Notestein, 'Winning of the Initiative', p. 170.
11 Notable exceptions were Mildred Campbell's work, *The English Yeoman under Elizabeth and the Early Stuarts* (New Haven, 1942), and several studies of Puritanism, especially William Haller's *The Rise of Puritanism* (New York, 1938) and *Liberty and Reformation in the Puritan Revolution* (1955).
12 It is for example the only major American work on the early Stuarts, except those of William Haller and Mildred Campbell, that Lawrence Stone overlooks in his *The Causes of the English Revolution 1529–1642* (1972).

[13] Indeed they remain unfashionable among the *Nouvelle Vague* of the past decade.

[14] Although of some interest, D. Brunton and D.H. Pennington, *Members of the Long Parliament* (1954) does not seem to have been such a work.

[15] I date the gingering up of early Stuart history from R.H. Tawney's *Religion and the Rise of Capitalism* in 1926, rather than from 'The Rise of the Gentry' in 1941. The former was almost certainly the meat on which as cubs the lions of the ensuing generation had fed in the 1930s.

[16] The assumptions of the historians of Gardiner's generation are stated or implied in the preface to the *The Cambridge Modern History*, ed. A.W. Ward *et al.* (13 vols., Cambridge, 1907–11), I, pp. v–viii. The knowledge of history is cumulative: 'the aim of this work is to record . . . the fulness of knowledge in the field of modern history which the nineteenth century has bequeathed to its successor' (p. v.). History calls for a narration of developmental change: 'a universal Modern History' will be 'a narrative which . . . displays a continuous development' (p. v). The goal is the final truth about the past: 'ultimate history cannot be obtained in this generation, but . . . conventional history can be discarded, and the point shown that has been reached on the road from one to the other' (p. vi).

[17] In the later nineteenth and earlier twentieth century there had been a good many different views as to the nature of the scientific essence of the fundamental reality. It was alleged to be climate, race, survival of the fittest, *etc.* In the end none had the attractiveness to historians of the Marxian version, which was enormously rich in intellectual texture and was of such scope as to be relevant to *all* the record of the past, all the doings of man. Or at least with a reasonable amount of not too conspicuous pulling, hauling and stretching, it could be made to appear so. In the '30s it had the additional attraction of apparently proving itself out on the stage of contemporary history in the fascist *Götterdammerung* of the capitalist era and the emergence of the first stage of communism in Soviet Russia.

[18] *Economic History Review*, XI (1941), 1–38, esp. p. 36.

[19] The voice was mine. It was raised in two papers — 'The Education of the Aristocracy in the Renaissance', presented to the Renaissance Club of New York in the winter of 1946–7, and 'The Myth of the Middle Class in Tudor England', read at the annual meeting of the American Historical Association in December 1948. The former paper was published in the *Journal of Modern History* in 1950. The latter was concealed rather than revealed by publication in an abridged version in *Explorations in Entrepreneurial History*, a periodical of most modest circulation, in 1950. Both essays were subsequently reprinted in *Reappraisals in History* (1961), pp. 45–116. Some of my reservations were expressed in terms of what happened in the House of Commons under the early Stuarts in 'Storm over the Gentry', which appeared in *Encounter* in 1958 and was reprinted in *Reappraisals*, pp. 117–62.

[20] Or perhaps better, of what H.R. Trevor-Roper christened 'Tawney's Century', from the accession of Elizabeth to the Restoration of Charles II.

[21] It may be proper here to pay tribute to Stone's attitude toward his calling and toward his work in it. Few historians are as ready as he to try out new conceptual frameworks and hypotheses in hope of bringing order and digestibility to the vast heaps of data that his voracious appetite for understanding impels him to ingest. Few historians are as ready as he to take pains to give what looks like a bright idea a good run. And no historian I know is so ready to drop such an idea when it does not work. Stone is far more heavily committed to his vocation than to any of the intellectual tools and gadgets he experiments with in his work in his vocation, or to a professional vanity which in his case is noteworthily slight. In his time he has been wedded to many ideas, but the union is always a *mariage de convenance*. And he must be nearly unique in his readiness to reflect on even harsh criticism of his assumptions, his evidence, his arguments and his conclusions, to accept that criticism when it seems justified, and to adjust his views to it on his next try. Thus almost uniquely among scholars he often treats seriously offered destructive criticism of his work as a benefit rather than an affront.

[22] I am not sure he knows that, supposing multiple dysfunction to be the sole precondition of revolution, every society from time immemorial has always fulfilled that precondition. Multiple dysfunction is merely an esoteric but conveniently terse epithet descriptive of the permanent condition and situation of social man. Human societies might with reasonable accuracy be defined as concourses of persons dysfunctioning in multiple ways.

Consequently Stone's allegation that the multiple dysfunction of English society before 1629 was the precondition of the English revolution cannot escape the taint of a certain *post hoc ergo propter hoc-um*.

[23] Lawrence Stone, the author of *The Crisis of the Aristocracy*, obviously does not quite fit into this taxonomic scheme. A curious accident of his youth turned his attention to the peerage. When quite young he set out to portray the *Götterdammerung* of the aristocracy that was the necessary complement of Tawney's sketch of the apotheosis of the gentry. Nevertheless, although *The Crisis of the Aristocracy* is supposed to be all about all of the peers, it is in one respect avowedly about more: it includes as aristocracy, Stone says, not only the peers but also the top layer of the gentry that was both able and willing, in the French phrase, to *vivre noblement*. It is also unavowedly about less: it is not about one aspect of the peerage — that part of their political lives that they lived collectively in the House of Lords.

[24] Violet A. Rowe, 'The Influence of the Earls of Pembroke on Parliamentary Elections, 1625–41', *E.H.R.*, L (1935), 242–56.

[25] Camden Soc., 3rd ser., XLII (1929).

[26] Ruigh, *Parliament of 1624*, pp. 91–148.

[27] This statement should be qualified by an 'as-far-as-I-can-make-out-on-hasty-reflection' and a hasty canvass of the two principal relevant bibliographies : *Bibliography of British History: Stuart Period 1603–1714*, eds. G. Davies and Mary Frear Keeler (2nd edn., Oxford, 1970) and J.S. Morrill, *Seventeenth-Century Britain 1603–1714* (Folkestone, 1980). There are of course modern biographies of Lionel Cranfield, Earl of Middlesex and Thomas Wentworth, Earl of Strafford. The former, however, was a City rather than a county magnate. Moreover his activity in the House of Lords was constricted by his impeachment when only a year into his peerage, while Strafford only got to sit in the House for a few weeks in all before his colleagues voted for his decapitation. We have just got our first competent biography of the Duke of Buckingham (see below, n. 55), and we shortly expect one on Henry Howard, Earl of Northampton, by Linda L. Peck. It is surely symptomatic of something odd that with such worthy subjects in the relevant time-span as John Digby, Earl of Bristol, Thomas Howard, Earl of Arundel, and the Herbert brothers, William and Philip, successively Earls of Pembroke, there should have been such a void. Snow's *Essex* deals with a great lord in the context of the traditions, customs and expectation of the Tudor-Stuart magnate class of which Snow sees the son of Elizabeth's last favourite as a member.

[28] Jess Stoddart Flemion, 'The Dissolution of Parliament in 1626: A Revaluation', *E. H. R.*, LXXXVII (1972), 784–90; 'The Struggle of the Petition of Right in the House of Lords: The Study of an Opposition Party Victory', *Journal of Modern History*, XLV (1973), 193–210; 'The Nature of Opposition in the House of Lords in the Early Seventeenth Century: A Revaluation', *Albion*, VIII (1976), 17–34.

[29] *Economic History Review*, Supp. No. 1 (1953).

[30] In *From the Renaissance to the Counter-Reformation*, ed. C.H. Carter (1966), pp. 325–47.

[31] 'We need to take heed of the fact that the once dominant reconstruction of the early Stuart parliaments, associated with Wallace Notestein, is crumbling': 'Parliament in the Sixteenth Century: Functions and Fortunes', *Historical Journal*, XXII (1979), 277.

[32] The errors of Notestein with respect to the Parliament of James I and Charles I are the reiterated theme of several of Elton's essays. According to him those errors are a continuation of the mistakes and a cause of the mistakes of Sir John Neale about Elizabethan Parliaments that Elton most systematically laid bare in his Neale Memorial Lecture, 'Parliament in the Sixteenth Century', *loc. cit.* The whole matter of the history of procedure in the House of Commons under Elizabeth and the early Stuarts has been subjected to intensive review by Sheila Lambert in a superb article, 'Procedure in the House of Commons in the Early Stuart Period', *E.H.R.*, XCV (1980), 753–81. Her demonstration that many of the practices which Notestein considered procedural innovations of the House of Commons under the Stuarts were already in place under Elizabeth and at that time had no constitutional significance at all seems shatter-proof. Some of these changes, however, *may* have subsequently provided shelter for actions of the House that had constitutional significance, actions that they rendered it easier for the House to take. Whether or not this is so cannot be known until someone pushes a

systematic investigation of the question, and as far as I know, no one has. In the meantime I owe Miss Lambert an apology for concealing her fine study in a footnote.

[33] G.R. Elton, 'Tudor Government: The Points of Contact: I. Parliament', *Transactions of the Royal Historical Society*, 5th ser., XXIV (1974), 183–200.

[34] *Idem*, 'The Stuart Century', *Studies in Tudor and Stuart Politics and Government* (2 vols., Cambridge, 1974), II, 161.

[35] Professor Elton made his points about the failure of Parliaments in the early seventeenth century with what I regarded as too much enthusiasm in 'Studying the History of Parliament', *British Studies Monitor*, II, No. 1, pp. 4–14. I suggested as much in 'Parliament under the Lens', *ibid.*, III, No. 1, pp. 4–15. Professor Elton replied in *ibid.*, III, No. 1, pp. 16–22 (reprinted in Elton, *Studies*, II, 13–18). The controversy was conducted jovially with the usual armament of rapier and bludgeon (mainly the latter) that Professor Elton and I have employed on each other in our engagements over the past two decades. I believe Professor Elton learned something from the exchange. I ruefully suspect and reluctantly admit that I may have learned something too.

[36] The *Ur-vater* of the Provincials was William Willcox, a student of Notestein, who in 1940 published a revision of his doctoral dissertation, *Gloucestershire . . . 1590–1640* (1940). It was the first work by a modern social historian concerned with the history of a county during the early Stuart era, that was written with an eye to the response in the county to the political developments at the centre — at Whitehall, Westminster, and the City. Willcox made the discovery — to be rediscovered much later, amid shrieks of 'Eureka!' and, 'Oh, looky!' — that country folk had a good many other things in mind than the goings-on in London, to which far-off place they paid only intermittent attention at best, and that the local big shots tended to treat orders from London as interesting suggestions to be modified or neglected according to local customs and needs, sometimes identified by them with their own interest and convenience.

[37] P. Laslett, 'The Gentry of Kent in 1640', *Cambridge Historical Journal*, IX (1947–9), 148–64 and 'Sir Robert Filmer: The Man versus the Whig Myth', *William and Mary Quarterly*, 3rd ser., V (1948), 523–46.

[38] The key works by Everitt were *The Community of Kent and the Great Rebellion 1640–60* (Leicester, 1966) and *Change in the Provinces: The Seventeenth Century* (University of Leicester Department of English Local History Occasional Papers, 2nd ser., No. 1, 1972). These studies develop and define ideas broached in *Suffolk and the Great Rebellion 1640–1660* (Suffolk Records Soc., III, 1960).

[39] A. Everitt, 'The County Community', in *The English Revolution*, ed. E.W. Ives (1968), pp. 48–9. See also his 'Social Mobility in Early Modern England', *Past and Present*, No. 33 (Apr. 1966), pp. 56–73.

[40] Notably J.S. Morrill both in *Cheshire 1630–1660* (Oxford, 1974) and in *The Revolt of the Provinces* (1976).

[41] I draw my list from the relevant local studies published since Barnes, *Somerset* (1960), and mentioned in Morrill, *Seventeenth-Century Britain*; from the dissertations Morrill lists as having been consulted by him for *The Revolt of the Provinces* (pp. 7–8); and from Christopher Hill, 'Parliament and People in Seventeenth-Century England', *Past and Present*, No. 92 (Aug. 1981), p. 102.

[42] This appears to have happened in Yorkshire in the bitter rivalry between Sir John Savile and Sir Thomas Wentworth.

[43] Except for the futile two months of the Addled Parliament in 1614. Otherwise in 'this period', 1604–39, Parliaments happened in two spurts, the six years and five sessions of James I's first Parliament, 1604–10, and the eight years of James I's last two and Charles I's first three Parliaments, 1621–9.

[44] 'Parl. Hist. in Perspective', pp. 3, 24.

[45] More precisely, a shade less than 3.9 years in the 37½ years between the accession of James and the assembling of the Long Parliament.

[46] 'Parl. Hist. in Perspective', p. 26.

[47] The phrase 'absolute monarch' has precipitated whole legions of historians, neophytes in the history of political ideas, into mistakes about where politically active Englishmen stood on the central issues of politics from the accession of Elizabeth to the outbreak of the Civil War. The short of the matter is that almost all Englishmen firmly believed that

the legitimate power of the King was 'absolute', not subject to the command of any human authority: '*rex non est sub homine . . .* the king is not under man'; but his authority is not arbitrary, not a matter of his mere will or whim; it is subject to his duty to God, all would have said, and to the law, almost all would have said. Since he is a sworn servant of both, he is both '*sub Deo et lege*, under God and the law'.

[48] There is no need to name here these young men who got things so wrong. They have already been subjected to enough vigorous criticism elsewhere by me and others. It can only be desolating to have one's beloved brainchild run over by a parade of steam-rollers.

[49] It incorporates enough well wrought connective narrative to keep readers abreast of what relevant transactions occurred in the considerable lacunae between one Parliament and the next.

[50] For example the combination of rashness and courage in the Duke of Buckingham: Gardiner, *History*, III–VI, *passim*, esp. VI, 172–99.

[51] See, for example his careful and thoughtful characterization of the eminent supporters of the Petition of Right in 1628 who early in 1631 took office under Charles — Noy and Littleton — and of the mental process by which they and others dissociated themselves from the Members responsible for the explosive close of the session of 1629: *History*, VII, 220–4.

[52] Ironically, when she published *The King's Peace*, C.V. Wedgwood, the only eminent historian of early Stuart England after Gardiner who understood and seriously looked into such matters, was summarily dismissed as unimportant and trivial, lacking in the appropriate and chic analytical concerns, interested, it was said condescendingly, in 'what' questions rather than 'why' questions. Yet surely by the criteria of the *Nouvelle Vague* hers was well away the soundest account of the origins of the Civil War in the century between Gardiner in the 1880s and the last couple of years.

[53] See, for example, Paul Christianson's review article 'Parliaments and Politics in England, 1604–1629', *Canadian Journal of History*, XVI (1981), 107–13; Morrill, *Seventeenth-Century Britain*, p. 35.

[54] To that generosity I can testify. In 1975, just before Russell's 'Parliamentary History in Perspective' rendered my argument at least temporarily obsolete, I gave the annual Neale Lecture at University College, London. Its inexplicit, archaic, Whig assumption was that the concerns of the House of Commons in 1628 were serious matters because they bore decisively on the emergence of modern liberty. After the lecture Professor Russell generously directed me toward a piece of evidence that might have been deemed to substantiate my point, prefacing his suggestion with a sceptical and perhaps monitory, 'if that is the line you want to take'. (I hope that I have remembered the episode right and that Professor Russell remembers and will repeat to me the reference, which I have lost.)

[55] *Buckingham: The Life and Political Career of George Villiers, First Duke of Buckingham 1592–1628*. By Roger Lockyer. London: Longman. 1981. xix, 506 pp. £14.95.

[56] *The Outbreak of the English Civil War*. By Anthony Fletcher. London: Edward Arnold. 1981. xxx, 446 pp. £24.00.

[57] Fletcher had previously published an excellent county study, *A County Community in Peace and War: Sussex 1600–1660* (1975). In 1964 Lockyer published a text in the field of Tudor-Stuart history, *Tudor and Stuart Britain 1471–1714*, a most successful effort that fully deserved its success.

[58] In fact all accounts of Parliaments since Gardiner have been dominantly narrative. In order of their dates of publication, Hexter, *Reign of King Pym* (1941), T.L. Moir, *The Addled Parliament of 1614* (Oxford, 1958), W. Notestein, *The House of Commons 1604–10* (New Haven, 1971), Ruigh, *Parliament of 1624* (1971), D. UNderdown, *Pride's Purge* (Oxford, 1971), Zaller, *Parliament of 1621* (1970), A.B. Worden, *The Rump Parliament* (Cambridge, 1974), C. Holmes, *The Eastern Association in the English Civil War* (Cambridge, 1975), Russell, *Parliaments and English Politics* (1979).

[59] In fairness to Lockyer it should be said that he prefaces the 'difficulties' with 'many, if not most'. As one who has himself inserted fudge words to evade responsibility for a strong statement without significantly diminishing its impact, I tend to discount such words at 90% of face value.

[60] I use quotation marks here as a reminder to the reader of two easily forgotten

circumstances. First, many Members of the House of Commons and most of the members of the House of Lords rallied to the King's standard in the end. Second, in their official pronouncements the Parliamentarians always engaged to 'maintain and defend His Majesty's royal person and estate': *The Constitutional Documents of the Puritan Revolution 1625–1660*, ed. S.R. Gardiner (3rd edn., revised, Oxford, 1906), p. 156.

[61]   I here substitute 'origins' for Fletcher's word 'outbreak.' It seems to me to do better justice to his intention. His book explicitly asserts that to explain the beginnings of actual armed conflict one *should* go back no further than Pym's assumption of leadership in the Short Parliament. Therefore the origins or roots of the Civil War must be sought in what happened after April 1640.

[62]   Or at least, only willing to explore the prior religious commitments of John Pym.

[63]   'Parliaments and Politics', pp. 107, 109.

[64]   A possible dissenter is Lawrence Stone. One of the most adept of historical trend-spotters, he has recently written an article noting a turn from analytical to narrative history. It appears, however, that it is only the turn of the trend-setting set itself, Le Roy Ladurie, Lawrence Stone *et al.*, the historiographical Talmudists, as it were, that renders kosher the hitherto *träfe* narrative history. Stone's view is a little like that of ex-Communists in my youth. When they became liberal-conservative-democrats they were as sure as they had been before that only they, not people who had been exponents of liberal-conservative-democracy all along, had anything worthy of attention to say about liberal-conservative-democracy. Even though Stone may be willing to open his arms in a somewhat wider embrace than that, they do not seem quite wide enough spread to let Russell in.

[65]   Dr Christopher Hill, Professor Austin Woolrych and myself.

[66]   My colleague Derek Hirst has for three years stubbornly resisted my frequently offered and sage advice that he quadruple-space his original drafts. Robert Zaller wrote his doctoral dissertation under my supervision and only managed to do it well by disregarding my persistent advice.

[67]   There are several even odder statistical facts about the nay-sayers. Six of them, writers of ten of the review articles out of 12, hold academic posts in the United States. Most peculiarly, one half of all the pieces dissenting from the 'new consensus' emanate from one Department of History in a relatively small private university in the American Middle West, specifically from Derek Hirst and me of the Department of History at Washington University in St Louis. Since, however, we both entered the lists in 1978 and were not then colleagues, the statistical correlation is about as significant as the fact that two thirds of the articles were written by historians whose surnames begin with H. The value to me of conversations with Professor Hirst in recent years has been inestimable.

[68]   *Past and Present*, No. 92 (Aug. 1981), 'Revisionism Revised: Two Perspectives on Early Stuart Parliamentary History': T. Rabb, 'The Role of the Commons' (pp. 55–78); D. Hirst, 'The Place of Principle' (pp. 79–99); C. Hill, 'Parliament and People in Seventeenth-Century England', *ibid.*, pp. 100–24.

[69]   Particularly by C. Holmes, 'The County Community in Stuart Historiography', *Journal of British Studies*, XIX (1980), 54–73; J.H. Hexter, 'Power, Parliament and Liberty in Early Stuart England', in *Reappraisals in History* (Phoenix edn., Chicago, 1979), pp. 163–218 and D. Hirst, 'Unanimity in the Commons, Aristocratic Intrigues, and the Origins of the English Civil War', *Journal of Modern History*, L (1978), 51–71.

[70]   Hill, 'Parliament and People', *passim*, esp. p. 105; J.K. Gruenfelder, 'The Electoral Patronage of Sir Thomas Wentworth, Earl of Strafford, 1614–1640', *Journal of Modern History*, XLIX (1977), 557–74; P. Christianson, 'The Peers, the People and Parliamentary Management in the First Six Months of the Long Parliament', *ibid.*, 575–99; C. Roberts, 'The Earl of Bedford and the Coming of the English Revolution', *ibid.*, 600–16; M. Kishlansky, 'The Emergence of Adversary Politics in the Long Parliament', *ibid.*, 617–40; J.E. Farnell, 'The Social and Intellectual Basis of London's Role in the English Civil Wars', *ibid.*, 641–60; J.H. Hexter, 'Power Struggle, Parliament, and Liberty in Early Stuart England', *ibid.*, L (1978), 1–50; Hirst, 'Unanimity . . . Aristocratic Intrigues and the Origins of the . . . Civil War'.

[71]   Literally so. It is the first substantive point that Russell makes in *Parliaments and English Politics*, p. 8.

72   See n. 69, above.
73   For example on 22 Mar. 1628, the first day of full debate on the issues that were to be before the House until the Petition of Right received the King's consent ten weeks later, the five speakers who were apologists for the government were officers in it or in the King's household. The other six in defining the issues did so in terms not of 'local' interests but of the liberties of free Englishmen. *All six* were knights of the shire.

To one who has lived all his life as a citizen of a 'federal polity' and concurrently as a citizen of one 'sovereign state' or another and one city or another, the either-or-ness of the Provincials is perplexing. This month the receipt of my St Louis tax bill, and my Missouri and United States income tax forms will serve to put me in mind sharply that besides being a citizen of no mean city, I am also a citizen of a pretty mean state and of a terribly mean federal union. Although not unduly gifted with flexibility of mind I have not found it hard at all to be successively and even concurrently concerned with all three sets of my obligations and rights as a citizen. I deeply sympathize with the inadequate seventeenth-century bumpkins who, if the Provincials are right, could only manage to care about their own counties even when the King's government was so vigorously treading on *all* their toes.
74   Christianson, 'Parliaments and Politics', p. 107.
75   Morrill, *Seventeenth-Century Britain*, p. 55.
76   At least there is no evidence of such a view.

REVIEW ARTICLES

MEDIEVAL ENGLISH PARLIAMENTS

EDWARD MILLER

The English Parliament in the Middle Ages. By H.G. Richardson and G.O. Sayles. London: Hambledon Press. 1981. 560 pp. £24.00.

The English Parliament in the Middle Ages. Edited by R.G. Davies and J.H. Denton. Manchester: Manchester University Press. 1981. x, 214 pp. £13.95.

The more or less simultaneous appearance of two major collections of essays about the English Parliament in the Middle Ages makes 1981 a year for students of this subject to remember. Between the two collections, of course, there is a substantial difference. The essays edited by Dr Davies and Dr Denton are new work, summing up the present state of our knowledge of medieval English Parliaments; the articles by Mr Richardson and Professor Sayles were published originally in the period 1925–67 and were fruits of their fundamental researches into medieval parliamentary history. They were not, of course, the only fruits of these researches. Richardson and Sayles also published English Parliament rolls and Irish parliamentary and conciliar records, as well as an extended study of Irish medieval Parliaments; there is much relevant material in the ten or so volumes which they edited, jointly or severally, for the Selden Society; and in *The King's Parliament of England* (1975) Professor Sayles endeavoured 'to place the medieval Parliament of England in its contemporary setting' with characteristic succinctness and occasional pungency. For long it was hoped that these two scholars might give us a history of the English Parliament in the Middle Ages on a grand scale; but, even before Mr Richardson's death in 1974 ruled out that possibility, they were also frequently urged to republish the articles they had scattered through a variety of periodicals in order that they might be more readily available to students. The fact that the major history never came makes their publication now doubly welcome.

The contribution made by Richardson and Sayles to our understanding of medieval Parliaments has indeed been a major one. Relentlessly they urged a return to the sources and a concern for the history of Parliament 'in its own right'. The implications of their approach were inevitably negative in certain respects. In particular they have striven to eradicate a 'national myth about the political significance of the lower House of Commons from the very emergence of Parliament in our history' and which 'regards popular representation as the focal point of interest'. The chief responsibility for the currency of this myth they attributed to William Stubbs, whose *Constitutional History* is endowed with an influence which may significantly exceed the extent to which it has been read. If Stubbs makes a somewhat antique whipping-boy and little effort is made to inquire how his attitudes may have been shaped by the intellectual climate of the Oxford of his day, the positive content of Richardson's and Sayles's work is in any case even more important than their dissipation of myths. The 26 essays now reprinted will continue to be required reading and indispensable works of reference for students of the Middle Ages. Their content is sufficiently well known to need no detailed exposition here. Richardson and Sayles read history forwards. They start with Parliaments of which the essential ingredients were ministerial and aristocratic, the essential business administrative and judicial, the essential characteristic that they were the King's occasions — summoned, organized and orchestrated by him and his agents. Access by the people generally to Parliament came initially when Edward I allowed private petitioners to approach the judicial and administrative sessions of Parliament, so that the original essence of Parliament was that it was a court set above other courts. In the years 1297–1330, however, the old order was changing, with the emergence of the parliamentary peerage as the judges of Parliament and of the Commons as petitioners in Parliament, thus ensuring their normal presence there. We must still, on the other hand, not make too much of the representative element. Even though they had in Parliament an assured place, specific functions and increasingly established ways of fulfilling those functions, they still acknowledged a position of subordination. In Richardson's words: 'in open Parliament... the Speaker rarely spoke other than acceptable things: if not always acceptable to the King, acceptable to the Lords who, for the time, were his masters.'

The consistency of the interpretation which gives unity to the collected essays of Richardson and Sayles is impressive and there can be no question that they have permanently influenced the ways in which we regard the history of medieval Parliaments. In particular, no one could now ignore the fact that, in early Parliaments and in Maitland's phrase, 'the whole governmental force of England is brought into a focus' in order to do justice and to find a solution to problems of administration. Further, we also have a far clearer understanding of how these original characteristics shaped the ways in which Parliament developed in the changing circumstances of the outgoing Middle Ages and beyond. In these and other ways the work of Richardson and Sayles has been definitive. Their approach to parliamentary history, of course, has not gone uncontested. Some have felt that, in their eagerness to strip away inessentials, they have discarded as of small account some features of early Parliaments that deserved less peremptory treatment; and others that even the antiquities of representation are a matter of legitimate curiosity even when it was of modest or occasional significance. The collection of essays edited by Davies and Denton may be said to belong to these other traditions, and appropriately so: for they are published as a tribute to Professor J.S. Roskell, historian of the fifteenth-century Commons and of the office of Speaker in the later Middle Ages. Roskell, too, has significantly enlarged our knowledge of medieval Parliaments and the review of their development offered by these essays is a fitting recognition of that fact. The review begins with representation, but with representation considered in a different framework of ideas and of government than that subsumed in much of the discussion of parliamentary development. J.C. Holt takes us back to the improvisations in the times of John and Henry III which brought representatives of the local communities before the King or his agents and their connexion with the administrative devices to secure information which had become part of the routine of government well before the end of the twelfth century. As yet, however, there was no question of these delegates representing the community as a whole: that was the role of the magnates, the purveyors of 'common counsel' and common consent. The developments considered here, at least in the light of how things turned out, belong therefore to 'the prehistory of Parliament'. Conversely, 'the formation of Parliament' was an outcome of the century which opened with the accession of Edward I. The main stages are sketched by G.L. Harriss: the ways in which Parliament provided an instrument of political and administrative accommodation in Edward I's more peaceful years down to 1294, the focus for criticism and amendment of the King's government between 1294 and 1327, and the scene of a recovery of royal direction when Edward III achieved harmony with his baronage in their joint absorption in the French war. Uncertainties, too, gave way to definition. The structure and functions of the medieval Parliament were settled in principle, including the regular presence of representatives of the counties and boroughs with a duty to bring 'common' grievances to the attention of government. The fulfilment of this last obligation is the theme of J.R. Maddicott's 'Parliament and the Constituencies', which takes us back to the beginnings of petitioning in the thirteenth century and forward to the 1370s when 'Parliament had become the chief intermediary between the Crown and its subjects'. This is an original and important essay precisely because it looks to Parliament from the angle of the local communities. J.H. Denton's study of the clergy and Parliament also deals with a topic that is too often neglected, although this time earlier potentialities were not to be realized. Under Edward I the possibility that Parliament might comprehend a clerical 'estate' seemed strong, but by 1340 it had evaporated. Negatively, at least, this was an element in 'the formation of Parliament'.

Two further studies, by A.L. Brown and the late A.R. Myers, continue the story from the accession of Richard II to the death of Henry VII. This was not a period of fundamental changes of direction. Developments there were, of course: for example, in the procedures for dealing with petitions, for law-making and for the granting of taxes. From time to time, too, peers and Commons alike took advantage of the problems and weaknesses of kings to extract concessions; while Richard II, and Edward IV and Henry VII more subtly, were moved to find new forms for the expression of the royal initiative. Consequently, as Brown puts it, the period 1377–1422 'marked a significant stage in the evolution of the classic English Parliament and... made its continuance if not inevitable at least more likely'. Myers also concludes that, by the opening of the sixteenth century, Parliament 'within its proper sphere...had an increasingly assured position which could not be ignored or by-passed'. Yet he is also properly cautious: 'all this fell short of control of the government by Parliament' or of ensuring 'an inevitable victory for Parliament in the long run'. All this brings us back to J.S. Roskell who, in a well known article, postponed until 1689 the 'great divide' marking the end of 'the power of the Crown to govern effectively without Parliament'. A final essay in this volume in Roskell's honour rubs in that lesson. In it D.H. Pennington draws our attention to the way in which the increasingly assured position of medieval Parliaments was followed by a period of intermittent Parliaments and ultimately, in the 1630s, by a time of no Parliaments at all. In this environment medieval history with its treasury of parliamentary precedents became 'a weapon in a struggle to survive'. It was a struggle, moreover, the outcome of which was anything but certain; and, had it been lost, England's experience would have been in no way unusual among the European lands.

Ultimately, of course, what Roskell called the 'medieval potentiality' of Parliament, and especially of the Commons, prevailed; and that is one good reason for seeking out even its small beginnings. The essays assembled in Roskell's honour strengthen implicitly the case for as broad, as inclusive a view as possible even of the early days when, in Powicke's phrase, 'men are doing things because they are convenient and do not attach conscious significance to them'. The age of improvisation did not end with the reign of Henry III. This is an approach which will produce some dead ends (like the representation of the clergy) and demands a constant care to avoid the temptation of anachronism. The essays reviewed here, however, are an indication that this temptation can be withstood. If there is a lack of balance in our understanding of medieval English Parliaments it is not a result of proper curiosity about the medieval Commons, to whose precedents Stuart parliamentarians clung so desperately, or of an appreciation of the role of the King's ministers in Parliament which we have learned from Richardson and Sayles. It stems rather from the much lesser intensity with which the Lords of Parliament have been scrutinized. This was a failing which Mr Enoch Powell recognized and sought to remedy; but much more work is needed before the medieval 'upper House' is known as well as it should be. In a world dominated by lordship, how the possessors of the power that lordship conferred operated in and upon Parliament is a matter crucial to our view of that institution. The essays edited by Davies and Denton were designed both to review existing knowledge and 'to open up some new lines of enquiry'. Maddicott has perhaps pointed to one, a line down into the constituencies; but surely another is a more systematic study of the Lords of Parliament. After all, if the monarchy was one compelling power during the English Middle Ages, what became in the end the parliamentary peerage was the other.

THE *MODUS TENENDI PARLIAMENTUM*

MICHAEL PRESTWICH

University of Durham

Parliamentary Texts of the Later Middle Ages. By Nicholas Pronay and John Taylor. Oxford: Clarendon Press. 1980. ix, 230 pp. £16.00.

It would be very useful to have a collection of texts which illustrate the history of Parliament in the later Middle Ages, but this volume, despite its title, serves a different, and equally important, need. The *Modus Tenendi Parliamentum* has long been the subject of controversy, but discussion has not been easy in the absence of a definitive edition of the two main versions of the English *Modus*. This volume provides such an edition, along with the text of the Irish version. Translations are given of the better English text, and of the Irish one. The *Modus* dominates the book, but it also contains an extract from the Rochester chronicle dealing with the Parliament of 1321, a diary of the 1485 Parliament kept by the Colchester representatives, and an early sixteenth-century draft of the Speaker's Protestation.

The *Modus* in its English version purports to be a description of Parliament as it existed in the days of Edward the Confessor; in its Irish version to be an ordinance for the holding of Parliament issued by Henry II. As such, the work is clearly fictional. A long list of scholars, however, such as W.A. Morris, M.V. Clarke, V.H. Galbraith and J.S. Roskell, has thought it worthy of detailed consideration. A consensus opinion developed, which saw the English version as being written in Edward II's reign, probably in 1321–2 by a government official, as a blueprint for an ideal Parliament rather than as an actual description of the institution as it existed. The treatise was seen as particularly important given its celebrated proposal for a committee of 25 to be elected in cases of discord, and its argument that shire representatives 'have a greater voice in granting and denying than the greatest earl of England'. Suggestions have been made linking the *Modus* to Thomas of Lancaster's opposition to Edward II, to the Statute of York of 1322, and to the deposition proceedings of 1327. The Irish *Modus* was viewed as a late fourteenth-century adaptation of the English text. Pronay and Taylor stand firmly in this tradition; they only depart from it in one major respect, for they suggest that the *Modus* should be seen not as a political tract, but as part of a tradition of

legal literature. They are inclined to seek an author in the common law rather than
in the ranks of government officials.

There has been one strongly dissenting view from all this. In the 1930s H.G.
Richardson and G.O. Sayles categorically stated, rather than argued, that the
Modus was late fourteenth–century in date, and that the English versions were
based on an Irish original. Little critical assessment of this view was possible, for
the work that Richardson and Sayles did was not published. Now, however, at
long last Sayles has written an important article: '*Modus Tenendi Parliamentum*: Irish
or English', in *England and Ireland in the Later Middle Ages*, ed. J.F. Lydon (Dublin:
Irish Academic Press, 1981). This was not, of course, available to Pronay and
Taylor, while equally, Sayles wrote before their edition was published. It seems
right, however, to try to set some of the various arguments on each side against
each other.

Before turning to the technical questions raised by the manuscripts, which form
an important part of the arguments of both parties, the internal evidence of the
texts should be examined. Pronay and Taylor's arguments are familiar. They draw
attention to the statement that the roll of Parliament is said in the *Modus* to be ten
inches wide, which fits Edward II's reign, as does that which explains that the rolls
were to be delivered to the Exchequer, rather than the Chancery. The absence of a
set rate of payment to representatives suggests a date prior to 1327. Pronay and
Taylor are not absolutely committed to the precise date of 1321, but they suggest
that the committee of 25 might be linked to the Parliament of that year in which
the Despensers were banished. The reference to the Chamberlain in the singular in
one version may be an allusion to the younger Despenser, who held the office
from 1318 to 1321. The fact that the Cinque Ports were not regularly summoned
before 1322 might explain why the text does not use the past tense when speaking
of the summons of their representatives, as it does in the case of other groups.

The weakest of these arguments are those which seek to place the *Modus* in 1321.
It is most unlikely that a tract written then would seek to give a position of
importance to the younger Despenser as Chamberlain, and the possible political
references are not so exact as to point unmistakably to the one year. A particular
difficulty is that this precise dating depends on the more corrupt of the two main
versions of the *Modus*. Yet the arguments which try to put the tract less specifically
in the early fourteenth century are not so easy to dismiss. Sayles, arguing for the
Irish character of the work, asks: 'When was taxation a particular concern of
English earls, and when did the English clergy grant aids in the English parliament
as distinct from their own ecclesiatical [*sic*] assemblies...?' In reply it can be pointed
out that the evidence of the negotiations between the King and the magnates in the
aftermath of Gaveston's death shows that the earls were much concerned then with
the question of the grant of a tax, although they recognized that they could not act
without wider consultation with the community. In 1295 the clergy did make a
grant of a tenth in Parliament. Yet it must be acknowledged that there are many
features of the *Modus* which do not accord with early fourteenth–century practice,
and some of these Sayles is able to link with Ireland in the later years of the
century.

One feature characteristic of Irish rather than English practice is the list of fines
to be levied upon absentees from Parliament. The *Modus* mentions two principal
clerks of Parliament: there never were two such clerks in England, but there may
have been in Ireland in the late fourteenth century. The section dealing with the
absence of the King from Parliament is connected by Sayles with the inability of
Roger Mortimer, royal lieutenant in Ireland, to attend in 1382, and the request that
Parliament should not be held in a private or secret place might fit a meeting of a

great council at Ballydoyle in 1371. The reference to a *capitalis justiciarius* does not fit English usage, for there were two chief justices, one of King's Bench and one of Common Pleas, but a single justiciar survived longer in Ireland than in England.

One obvious problem with this case is that the list of fines and the references to the two chief clerks and the one chief justice are all features of the English *Modus*, and do not appear in the Irish version. Sayles attempts to meet this criticism by arguing that there must have been an original Irish version of the *Modus* which is now lost, and from which the English texts are derived. The surviving Irish *Modus*, he suggests, was taken through a further lost intermediary from the initial Irish original. This is entering a world of unprovable hypothesis, and does not convince. Some of the other arguments can be easily met. The *Vita Edwardi Secundi*, as Pronay and Taylor point out, refers to the King failing to attend Parliament in 1313, detained by what was thought to be a feigned illness. The same chronicle records Lancaster's objection in 1320 to the King holding Parliament *in cameris*.

The internal evidence of the *Modus* may with some justification be thought inadequate for a definite conclusion to be reached as to the date and purpose of the tract. Both Pronay and Taylor, and Sayles, make much of the evidence of the manuscripts in which the *Modus* in its various versions is to be found. The problems that the manuscripts present are highly complex: if they could be resolved, however, some of the other difficulties could perhaps be discounted. The two editors and Sayles are again very much at odds in interpreting the manuscript evidence. They do agree that, as has long been established, there are two main English versions of the text, known for convenience as A and B. The most obvious difference between them is that they place the chapters in a different order, while the B tradition contains some sections which are so obviously corrupt as to be virtually unintelligible. Pronay and Taylor nevertheless consider that some of the B readings go back to an earlier version than A: Chamberlain in the singular, for example. This is possible, but it is very hard to place much trust in such a poor text. Sayles provides a very neat explanation of the difference in the chapter order: this probably arose through a simple mistake when the sheets of one manuscript were bound in the wrong order. Pronay and Taylor go further than the normal classification into A and B. They suggest that in the late fourteenth century a C version was constructed by someone making use of both previous texts. For Sayles, on the other hand, the C text is an antecedent version of the majority of B texts, B1 as against B2. The evidence is difficult to interpret, but Sayles's case is perhaps the more convincing. One so-called C version, that at Durham, is found in conjunction with the treatise on the Steward and the tract on the rights of the Marshal, a fact not noted by Pronay and Taylor. This association with two other texts links the Durham version much more closely with the A tradition, and it seems far more likely that it precedes the more corrupt B versions, rather than being a later attempt to remedy their deficiencies.

So far the argument appears to favour Sayles's interpretation, but when it comes to his case as regards the Irish *Modus*, there are probably few who will be convinced. He considers that the text is derived from the original Irish ancestor of all versions. Pronay and Taylor, on the other hand, follow Clarke in arguing that the Irish text is based on a French translation of the English *Modus*. They differ from Clarke only in suggesting that it was produced not at the end of Edward III's reign, but under Richard II, plausibly arguing that there may be a link in the form of Philip Courtenay, King's lieutenant in Ireland in 1385, for in the Courtenay cartulary there is a French copy of the *Modus*. Clarke provided five pages collating the French and Irish texts, showing a large number of striking verbal parallels. Sayles is able to show that at one rather confused point the Irish *Modus* does not follow the French. He also suggests that *in aperto loco* is not derived from *en lieu appart*: the meaning is certainly not identical, but the verbal resemblance is still close. He again argues that the similarity in pronunciation is merely coincidental when the French describes the King as *chief de parlement, commenceour et fyne de parlement*, and the Latin of the Irish text as *caput, commensor et finis parliamenti*. Much more would need to be done if Clarke's case is to be demolished: it will, for example, be necessary to explain why it is that the French version of the Courtenay cartulary and the Irish *Modus* both omit mention of the aid for knighting the King's eldest son. In general it seems abundantly clear that the Irish *Modus* is ultimately based on the English version.

Pronay and Taylor use the evidence of the manuscripts to support their argument that the *Modus* should be seen as a legal tract. The A text in particular is found in collections of legal tracts; the B in association with 'the corpus of the developing law of chivalry'. The editors certainly go too far with one example: they state that the Durham text is contained in a 'law book belonging to Durham priory', a description which in no way fits the register concerned. Pronay and Taylor are rightly cautious, and admit that their evidence is not finally conclusive. One difficulty is that the fact that the work is found in a legal context in a number of manuscripts from the late fourteenth century onwards does not prove that its original purpose was legal. It does not concentrate on the legal aspects of Parliament, and provides a very different view of Parliament from that of an undoubted, if earlier, legal treatise, *Fleta*. Pronay and Taylor are surely correct in dismissing the theory that the *Modus* was a political tract, but they do not reject from consideration either of the two royal clerks who have been proposed as authors, William Airmyn and William Maldon, and the case for seeing the work as the product of some member of the royal administration remains strong.

How, then, should the *Modus* be regarded? In spite of Sayles's arguments, it remains most probable that it was written in the early fourteenth century. Many features in it do fit contemporary practice: even the committee of 25 might be linked with the body of 26 set up in 1301, or that of 35 in the following year. At the same time, the tract was not intended as an accurate description of Parliament, and it contains much that is puzzling. The notion that an earldom was worth £400 a year (when Andrew Harclay was made Earl of Carlisle in 1322 he was granted land worth 1,000 marks a year); the large number of parliamentary clerks; the absence of any mention of the chief justice of Common Pleas; such doctrines as 'the King can hold Parliament with all the community of his kingdom, without bishops, earls and barons': all such points as these appear to be the product of imagination rather than of observation. Nor, if the *Modus* was written under Edward II, did it have any obvious influence. The inclusion of the community of the realm in the much debated final clause of the Statute of York of 1322 does not obviously reflect the extreme views of the *Modus*, and the chronicles of the period offer no hint of any such ideas. Indeed, even after the work became widely known, in the late fourteenth century, it does not seem that much practical use was made of it. Pronay and Taylor are only able to point to isolated instances, such as the one case in England when fines for non-attendance were levied, in 1454, and they had a definite resemblance to the scale set out in the *Modus*. In more general terms, however, they are able to argue that as the only treatise on Parliament that existed, it must have had a role in spreading ideas about the character of Parliament, even if actual procedure differed very considerably from that set out in it.

The other texts included by Pronay and Taylor in their volume do not require as much attention as does the *Modus*. The section of the Rochester chronicle they edit has been used by recent scholars writing on Edward II's reign, but it is very useful to have the text properly available, for it provides more detail of Bartholomew Badlesmere's devious machinations against the Despensers than any other work. It was the Bishop of Rochester who challenged Badlesmere's claim that the younger Despenser had used the *Homage et serment* declaration of 1308 against the King. The Colchester account of the Parliament of 1485 has been printed before, but not so accessibly as now. As the earliest account of Parliament written in English, and the earliest produced by Members of the Commons, it has obvious importance. The Protestation of the Speaker, almost certainly dating from 1504, is of interest in showing that what the Speaker actually said might be a good deal more muted than what was recorded on the Parliament roll.

The technical task of editing has been competently done by Pronay and Taylor. It is a pity that it was not possible to set the various versions of the *Modus* side by side for ease of comparison, but to do so would have meant altering the order of the chapters in the B text. As it is, however, it is not very easy to contrast the three different texts that are given. Nor can the translations be easily checked, as the Clarendon Press has apparently given up its former practice of putting Latin and English on facing pages. It is also irritating that the references in the notes are only to the pages of Latin text, and not to those of the translations. Disconcertingly, there is a misprint in only the third line of the first version of the *Modus* to be given, the A text, but thereafter matters improve. However, on p. 112 *Eborum* is given for *Eboracum*, and *pedern* for *pedem*: both mistakes are sufficiently obvious, and few will be confused by them. On the other hand, the editors' statement that the Durham text of the *Modus* has Chamberlains in the plural is wrong, and cannot be checked without recourse to the manuscript. There are oddities in the section of the book giving the Rochester account of 1321; it seems strange to extend H. as *H[ugh]*, and R. more correctly as *R[ogerus]*, while Roger Damory appears as Roger Samory. The translation inexplicably omits one of the two Mortimers.

It is obviously a great pity that Sayles's arguments did not appear in print before Pronay and Taylor published their book. Their edition of the *Modus* should have been the definitive word on the subject, at least for many years, but as it is their arguments will have to be set alongside Sayles's in any attempt to reach a final conclusion on a highly complex series of problems. It has only been possible in this review to outline some of the more obvious points, rather than to do full justice to both sides. If it is not possible to reach any final cast-iron certainty as to the date and purpose of the *Modus*, it is at least much easier now, thanks to this recent work, to put the different arguments together. It would have been sad, in some ways, had Pronay and Taylor succeeded in silencing such a long-lived discussion: it is to be hoped that the debate may continue to be fruitful.

VICTORIAN POLITICAL DIARIES

RICHARD W. DAVIS

Washington University, St Louis

Disraeli, Derby and the Conservative Party: Journals and Memoirs of Edward Henry, Lord Stanley 1849–1869. Edited by J.R. Vincent. Hassocks, Sussex: Harvester Press. 1978. xviii, 404 pp. £25.00.

The Diary of Gathorne Hardy, Later Lord Cranbrook 1866–1892: Political Selections. Edited by Nancy E. Johnson. Oxford: Clarendon Press. 1981. xxxviii, 908 pp. £48.00.

Namierism is like one of those creeping vines, the striking flowers of which gain them a place in a garden they then take over. Rooted out in one place, they spring up and luxuriate in another, where the process of extirpation has to be begun anew.

The problem in the historiographical garden is even greater in that, more often than not, those who tend it seem not to recognize the plant when it reappears. To a quite remarkable degree, historians of one period seem to be ignorant of work in other periods, and controversies rage in isolation. As a result, the progress of historical knowledge is to say the least an uneven one, and all the glorious battles have to be fought over again and again.

To professional historians such a situation is perhaps not uncongenial, as it militates against redundancy in one sense of that word. But for students, who are forced to take a somewhat longer view than the professional with his 'period', it is one likely to breed confusion; and it is hard to believe that the historical profession cannot find better and more profitable ways to maintain full employment. Thus it is distinctly encouraging to find two historians of a 'century' (and one which conventionally begins sometime after 1600 and ends at 1660, at that) sensitive to the broader implications of the debate in which they are engaged.[1]

If historians have left the seventeenth century strangely truncated, they have destroyed the eighteenth and nineteenth. Of the former, it is unclear whether it begins in 1714 or 1760, and equally unclear whether it ends in 1741 or 1832. As for the nineteenth century, that is discreetly cloaked under the phrase 'Victorian'.

No one would deny that there is much to be said against traditional periodization by reign and century, or that there is much to be said for newer forms. The problem with the latter is that they appear to have led to an even more blinkered view of history. Particularly, they have impeded the efforts against Namierization. First successfully attacked as applied to the reign of Anne, it was over a decade later that more or less simultaneous (though by no means co-ordinated) questions began to be raised about its application to the reign of George III and the great Reform Act respectively.[2] In both periods, neo-Whiggery would now seem to be in the ascendancy. In the seventeenth century meanwhile, Namierization has been going from strength to strength. In the Victorian period, it is triumphant and largely unchallenged.

All historical controversy to some degree deals in strawmen: those with whom one disagrees are rarely as ignorant or obtuse as one would like to pretend. There is, however, such a phenomenon as Namierism, and its broad outlines are fairly clear. Namier and his disciples distrust and de-emphasize what might be called the rational element in politics, putting their stress instead on the irrational elements. Thus ideas and principles tend to be dismissed as mere rationalizations in the struggle for power and place. Equally, this struggle is held really to be understood only by those actually engaged in it, people at the top. A good deal of what these people say about what they are doing, we are told, is aimed at keeping those over whom they rule in ignorance and subordination, and most of the rest at keeping the opposition confused and off balance. Politics is a game of sleight of hand. Politicians rarely, if ever, mean what they say and nothing is as it seems. Such are the assumptions of Namierism, and more particularly of its manifestation in recent writing on Victorian political history by the High Politics school.

The insights of that school are not entirely new, and they are far from being totally wrong. They were anticipated by Michael Hurst in method, and to a certain extent in conclusion.[3] And Robinson and Gallagher brilliantly demonstrated the largely autonomous role of the official mind in shaping foreign and imperial policy.[4] There can be no doubt that too little attention has been paid heretofore to political motivation, in the narrow and restricted sense of tactics and manoeuvre, in writing the history of the Victorian period. Nor is it any longer enough merely to ask such questions as whether an area had any actual economic potential, in order to explain the motives for imperial expansion; or how electoral politics really worked, in order to understand decisions which purportedly took them into account. The answer to such questions certainly does not cease to be important. But at least equally important as the reality of the situation at any given place or time was what politicians believed that reality to be; for it was on the basis of their beliefs and assumptions that their decisions were made.

What is more, there are certain Victorian politicians whose careers fit the High Politics analysis almost exactly. If there was ever a politician who throughout a long political career never meant what he said, and always intended something else, it was Disraeli. Another prominent example, as Roy Foster has demonstrated with great brilliance and charm in his recent biography, is Randolph Churchill.[5] Very likely Joseph Chamberlain's biographer could make an equally successful case.

Whether the formula is capable of much wider application is, however, somewhat doubtful. Maurice Cowling has questioned the validity and usefulness of political biography. Certainly if his precepts were very widely followed in the writing of biography, it is unlikely that it would be read. And not only because political manoeuvre has to be on the outrageous and grand scale of a Dizzy or a Randolph in order to be amusing — also because on the careers of most politicians, one suspects, the analytical tool is at best of indifferent utility.

It is therefore perhaps as well that the High Politics school tends to look with suspicion on biography. But if they have not done much to encourage that form of publication, they can undoubtedly take much credit for promoting another sort. If the primary explanation of politics lies in the thoughts and assumptions of leading politicians, then it is obviously necessary to know as much as possible about those thoughts and assumptions — hence the flourishing trade in publishing the political papers of eminent personages. There are great multi-nationals such as the Disraeli industry drawing in about equal proportions on Canadian wealth and hard work and Oxford influence and talent for publicity. But there is also an active domestic industry in Britain itself, largely centred in the Harvester Press. The two works primarily under review in this article emanate from Oxford and Hassocks respectively.

Both are a particular sort of political document, a sort that Professor Vincent tells us has a peculiar usefulness and validity, the political diary. There are, according to him, two main reasons for this. One is that, unlike correspondence which for obvious reasons tends to be most extensive when the political nation is not gathered in London for the parliamentary session, diaries usually cover the whole year — and therefore give us more information on that period of the year we particularly want to know about, when all the most important decisions were being made. The other main reason, Vincent holds, lies in the special validity of diaries, as opposed to letters, as evidence of true political motivation: 'a letter is a political action... an act of persuasion or deception taking place on a smaller stage.' Diaries, in contrast, apparently because they are not meant either to persuade or deceive, are more 'natural outpourings', and therefore better evidence.[6]

There is undoubtedly considerable truth in the first point. Both diaries under consideration do provide a more or less continuous narrative of the behind-the-scenes preoccupations of leading politicians during the periods they cover. Thus, as Vincent rightly contends, they fulfil a function similar to that of the medieval chronicles, providing a factual context and frame of reference against which to judge other kinds of evidence. And Gathorne Hardy particularly, perhaps because with hindsight we tend to impart different significance to the period after 1867, serves to remind us of the continuing obsession with religious questions — not only those connected with education, but with oaths, burials, and deceased wife's sisters, among others.

The special validity of the evidence provided in diaries is more questionable. If diaries were not meant to persuade or deceive, why, one wonders, did Lord Stanley in 1855, as Vincent tells us he did, sit down and rewrite his, several hundred thousand words' worth?[7] Quite clearly he had a reader in mind besides himself, and that he did not so revise his later diaries is no proof that these were 'natural outpourings' either. Few diarists probably write only for their own benefit — and no nineteenth-century political diarist that I can think of is likely to have done so. That they were writing to convince posterity, either members of their own family or a future biographer rather than other politicians, does not make the results either more 'natural' or more honest.

On the other side, neither is it sensible to dismiss wholesale the evidence afforded by letters. There are letters and letters. Some were undoubtedly meant to persuade and others to deceive. But still others were meant to give accurate or useful information, or both. The historian must treat them with care and discrimination, as he must diaries.

Given that, what useful evidence, if any, do these particular diaries give us about the politics of their period? The first thing to strike one is that neither gives much aid or comfort to the High Politics school. As Vincent rightly observes, Stanley's diaries 'show him to be a disinterested, liberal English nobleman', and once more in his editor's striking phrases, one who 'achieved his life's ambition, which was to avoid becoming Prime Minister'![8] Gathorne Hardy was never liberal and did not start his life as a nobleman, but he was equally high-minded and disinterested. He was by no means totally lacking in ambition. There is no evidence, however, that he ever let it range beyond the leadership of the House of Commons; and even here, when he was passed over for Northcote, he accepted his disappointment with modesty and good grace. Principle, and more particularly the support of the Church of England, is a good deal more important in explaining his political positions. Those who believe that politics are a perpetual jockeying for position, guided by an insatiable ambition to get to the top of the greasy pole, will not find much comfort in either of these diaries.

Or perhaps one should say that those who hold such beliefs will not get any new comfort. For both Stanley and Gathorne Hardy clearly recognized Disraeli for the unprincipled political opportunist he always was. They accepted and even loved him, partly because he was theirs, a leader whose immense talents were necessarily guided and restrained by the principles of the party at whose disposal he put them, partly because he was lovable. Though his charm, as opposed to his wit, was clearly much greater than his contemporaries are able to convey (and these are no exception), its powerful attraction cannot be doubted. And even without being able to grasp it fully, few probably if given the choice of being stranded on a desert island with Disraeli or Gladstone would choose the latter. Certainly the diarists would have had no hesitation. Stanley thought Gladstone more than a little crazy. Gathorne Hardy agreed, and found him a quite unprincipled and power-hungry maniac as well. But people are likely to find those qualities in their political opponents.

Some of the editor's other claims for the Stanley diary are doubtful. I, at least, am by no means convinced that it reveals Stanley's father as the archetypal High Politician. To affect total lack of ambition was one of the stock poses of the high Whig aristocracy from which Lord Derby came, a Foxite extravagance which has never been any more believable in him than it was in his old colleague Lord Grey. But to admit ambition in Derby is by no means to admit that it was his most important characteristic. He had always been, and remained, more burdened than most perhaps with scruples of principle, scruples which were likely to yield only to the high patriotric priority he put on service to Queen and country. His decision to carry a reform bill in 1866–7 (and Vincent is right that it was his decision, not Disraeli's) is probably a prime example. Grinding one of the great axes of the High Political school, Vincent tells us that 'Stanley's comments mostly pour cold water on the idea that ministers took demonstrators (or their leaders) seriously'. Such a contention would seem, however, to accord ill with Stanley's explanation for the key concession of the compounder franchise: 'our justification for doing what we are doing lies in the state of feeling on both sides — on the certainty of being thrown over by our own friends if we held out (in fact they are for the most part pressing us on) and in the danger of revolutionary agitation if nothing were done.'[9] The Reform Bill was partly party tactics, but it was much more than that.

But whatever one's reservations about some of the editor's contentions — or perhaps because of them — the final conclusion must be that this is both an excellent and an important book. It is also a highly readable one. Lord Stanley writes almost as well as Professor Vincent. Perhaps we need to know a little more about to whose skill we are most in debt. Vincent assures us that he has included all we need to know, but he never tells us what he has excluded. Yet it is probably quite safe to rely on his judgment and discrimination. He is, after all, the author of *The Formation of the Liberal Party*, which is without doubt the most significant challenge yet to the views of the co-author of *The Governing Passion* and of the High Politics school generally.

With Stanley one feels that one is being made truly privy to discussions behind the closed doors of the Cabinet room and to whispered exchanges on the front bench. One can, as Vincent suggests, almost hear people talking. But as he goes on to observe: 'some even of the most industrious diarists do not report speech as they should, it is true. Gladstone and Gathorne Hardy, for instance, were not shining examples.'[10] Unfortunately, this comment is all too accurate; and, while there are a number of other good reasons for reading Gladstone, it seems unlikely that any but the most dedicated will be able to stand the hard slog through Gathorne Hardy — and those could probably make their way to Ipswich. Among a number of unjustified claims by the Gathorne Hardy's editor is that the diarist throws important new light on the discussions of the Cabinet and proceedings in Parliament. Mostly Gathorne Hardy's diaries are dry reporting of topics and names. More often than not, without the editor's voluminous notes it would be quite impossible to tell what was being discussed, much less get a feeling for the discussion. Indeed, given the decision to publish, the editor has done a highly commendable job, scrupulously laying out her principles of selection and meticulously illuminating even the most minor points with thorough and painstaking scholarship. The fault lies not so much with her as with those who made the decision to publish in the first place.

Of course Gathorne Hardy provides important bits to many historical puzzles, and of course these bits will be most welcome to those who are trying to put them together. But the same could be said of the contents of countless archives. A number of recent projects seem to be based on the assumption that archival work can be rendered superfluous. That seems unlikely, and the attempt is bound to be expensive and likely to be unprofitable. Publishers probably need to exercise more discrimination. One sensible rule of thumb might be that they should publish books which can be read, as opposed to those that need to be mined. There are doubtless some remaining exceptions, but they should be truly exceptional.

Notes

[1] T.D. Rabb and D. Hirst, 'Revisionism Revised', *Past and Present*, No. 92 (Aug. 1981), pp. 55–99, esp. 57, n.
[2] For the reign of Anne, the attack was first launched in J.H. Plumb's review of Robert Walcott's *English Politics in the Early Eighteenth Century* in *E.H.R.*, LXXII (1957), 126–9 and later fully developed by Geoffrey Holmes, *British Politics in the Age of Anne* (1967). J. Brewer, *Party Ideology and Popular Politics at the Accession of George III* (Cambridge, 1976) is the first frontal attack for that period. M. Brock, *The Great Reform Act* (1973); J. Cannon, *Parliamentary Reform 1640–1832* (Cambridge, 1973); and, at the constituency level, my own *Political Change and Continuity 1760–1885: A Buckinghamshire Study* (Newton Abbot, 1972).
[3] M. Hurst, *Joseph Chamberlain and Liberal Reunion: The Round Table Conference of 1887* (1967).
[4] R. Robinson and J. Gallagher, *Africa and the Victorians* (1961).

[5]   R.F. Foster, *Lord Randolph Churchill: A Political Life* (Oxford, 1981).
[6]   p. x.
[7]   p. xiii.
[8]   p. xvii.
[9]   pp. xvi, 309.
[10]   p. x.

REVIEWS OF BOOKS

Parliamentary History, Libraries and Records: Essays Presented to Maurice Bond. Edited by H.S. Cobb. London: House of Lords Record Office. 1981. xvii, 80 pp. £3.00 (from the House of Lords Record Office).

An impressive section in *Parliamentary History, Libraries and Records* is the bibliography of Maurice Bond's own writings on Parliament. This only partially illuminates the broad range of his activities as Clerk of the Records, 1946–81, and Principal Clerk, Information Services in the House of Lords, 1974–81; but it admirably illustrates the nature of his services to the historical profession. He edited three volumes of calendars of House of Lords manuscripts. He planned and edited the splendid *Guide to the Records of Parliament*, which appeared in 1971, supplanting a series of useful handbooks. Articles on the archive at the House of Lords Record Office and its history, on the clerks and their activities, on the Lord Chancellor, and on Black Rod, on records available for the study of transport, on the nature of public and private Acts, all served to publicize the wealth of material available at the House of Lords Record Office and to make it accessible to scholars. At the same time, Bond was busy building the archive itself and providing for its care. He played a major role in the modernization of the Victoria Tower and the development there of a safe and convenient repository for the treasury of parliamentary papers entrusted to his care. He gradually gathered in as many as possible of the papers which had escaped from public custody (such as the papers of the Clerks of the Parliaments which had descended to Lord Braye) and obtained photocopies of those which could not be recovered. More recently he established a sound archive for tape recordings of both Houses, edited a catalogue of works of art in the House of Lords and discussed computer applications in the House of Lords Record Office. All reveal the breadth of his concept of the nature of the record of Parliament. The result, as those who have worked at the House of Lords Record Office know, is a first-class archive, well and efficiently run, where the scholar may carry on research with every possible aid, where he feels welcome, and where trained archivists and historians are on hand to render assistance and give advice. It has been said many times that the history of the House of Lords has been long neglected. The recent development of interest in the upper House owes much to the work of Maurice Bond and the staff he has assembled.

It is altogether fitting that the volume of essays in his honour should have been drawn from within the precincts of Parliament itself. Though many in the wider world of scholarship would have enjoyed an opportunity to contribute, this particular collection seems appropriate and right. Published simply, in the format familiar in annual reports and occasional publications of the House of Lords Record Office, it reflects the context within which Bond himself worked and the points at which he served not only the upper House but the whole Parliament. A graceful foreword by Sir Peter Henderson, Clerk of the Parliaments, outlines Bond's parliamentary career and supplies the wonderful epithet which characterizes him as a 'human beaver'. There follows a variety of essays which surely should please a man of such wide-ranging intellectual curiosity. Phillis Rogers, Curator of Works of Art in the Palace of Westminster, contributes a careful essay on 'Medieval Fragments from the Old Palace of Westminster in the Sir John Soane Museum'. Jeremy Maule, Senior Clerk, House of Lords, has provided an interesting study of assemblies, or Parliaments, in Chaucer. H.S. Cobb's survey of descriptions of the state opening of Parliament, 1485–1601, and David Johnson's 'The House of Lords and its Records, 1660–1864', are in the tradition of Bond's own writing. Each is interesting in its own right. Each will be useful to other scholars. Cobb has succeeded Bond as Clerk of the Records, Johnson is Deputy Clerk. The collection also includes essays by the Librarians of the House of Commons and the Assistant Librarian of the House of Lords. Dermot Englefield tells the story of the printing of the *Journals* of the Irish House of Commons, 1753–1802, David Menhennet of the first 16 years of the library of the House of Commons (1818–34), and David Lewis Jones of the exchange of books between the House of Lords and the Chambre de Paris in 1834. John Sainty, Reading Clerk and Clerk of the Journals, relates the sad story of one of his predecessors in office, Leonard Edmunds. Douglas Slater, Clerk, House of Lords, provides the final piece — an engaging essay on 'Beaconsfield: or Disraeli in the Elysian Fields', a study of Disraeli's view of the peerage, the upper House, and of his years in it.

   This is a modest volume. It is sound. It is wholly appropriate for the purpose for which it was designed. Like the writings of Maurice Bond himself, it shows the many fascinating facets in parliamentary history for those with imagination to perceive them.

ELIZABETH READ FOSTER
Bryan Mawr College

A History of the County of Chester: Volume II (The Victoria History of the Counties of England). Edited by B.E. Harris. London: Oxford University Press for the Institute of Historical Research. 1979. xvi, 266 pp. £45.00. *A History of Shropshire: Volume III* (The Victoria History of the Counties of England). Edited by G.C. Baugh. London: Oxford University Press for the Institute of Historical Research. 1979. xvi, 399 pp. £50.00.

The Shropshire and Cheshire volumes of the V.C.H. reviewed here, which survey local government and politics in each county, are among the most ambitious in the series, and if the pace, in going from the Middle Ages to 1974, gets a little breathless at times, this in no way detracts from the considerable feat of giving us such a long view of history in a particular part of England. The two volumes start with a valuable analysis of source material at the local level and in the Public Record Office. The administrative history of Shropshire, by the editor and D.C. Cox, covers the county government and franchises up to 1889 and the county council from 1889 to 1974. The administrative history of Cheshire, by the editor, deals similarly with the earldom of Chester, the palatinate and county government up to 1889 and the county council from 1889 to 1974, as well as including extensive tables on population.

   Steeped in knowledge of his county, its families and its traditions, J.F.A. Mason (assisted by D.C. Cox for the period up to 1629) reviews the parliamentary history of Shropshire from 1290 to 1974, comprising until 1832 six constituencies: the county, Bishop's Castle, Bridgnorth, Ludlow, Shrewsbury and Much Wenlock. Ludlow and Much Wenlock, which had been Yorkist, owed their enfranchisement to Edward IV. The names of the Members of Parliament are a roll-call of the governing families of that part of England: the Newports, Bridgmans, Corbets, Kynastons, Mores and Leightons, not forgetting the Herberts, Whitmores, Foresters and Clives who formed the nucleus of the Shropshire Whigs beloved of

Sir Lewis Namier. Amidst generations of dull country gentlemen, one of these county families, the Kynastons, produced a poet in Sir Francis Kynaston, knight of the shire in 1620, who saw the House of Commons not as many others did as a bear garden but as 'the high court of heaven sitting as angels to judge the world at the last Day'. The Civil War and Interregnum interrupted the stately procession of county families and saw the return of Esay Thomas at Bishop's Castle, of Humphrey Edwardes the regicide for the county and of Major Edmund Waring, an Anabaptist, for Bridgnorth. Later on, the 'omnipotency of gold' was much in evidence at Bridgnorth, Ludlow and, most of all, at Bishop's Castle where the Harley estates were purchased in 1718 by the great James Brydges, first Duke of Chandos 'in haste and repented at leisure'.

In dealing with the parliamentary representation of Cheshire, J.S. Morrill draws on his own admirable work on the county in the seventeenth century. He has only two constituencies to contend with until 1832 — the county itself and Chester — but Cheshire had the third largest electorate in England and a singularly independent one, since it consisted largely of tenant farmers holding long leases at low rents. Dr Morrill delineates the political divisions in the 1620s, between baronets and Irish peers at the county level, and gives an interesting account of an early example (1624) of the county meeting to choose knights opposed to the policies of the Crown, representing in Sir Richard Grosvenor's words 'the opinion and resolution of those worthy gentlemen who sit about me, upon whose careful judgement and experience the well-being of the county depended'. The stately procession of the Cheshire county families, the Breretons, Masseys, Savages, Cholmondeleys, Grosvenors, Fittons, Egertons, Leghs and Cottons was again broken by the Civil War, with the return for Chester of William Edwards, one of the few aldermen of Chester who had fought against Charles I, and of Edward Bradshaw in 1656. The political cross-currents of the bills for the navigation of the rivers Dee and Weaver are well charted. Bargains cutting across party lines were also struck in eighteenth-century elections, although the Whigs regarded the Tories as 'either incipient rebels or, at best, as men who had merely acquiesced in the Revolution', while the Tories saw their opponents as 'pseudo-Republicans and crypto-Presbyterians'. The cost of elections steadily rose as the century progressed. The financial extravagance of Robert Clive in Shropshire was matched at Chester by that of the Grosvenors, drawing on the vast wealth provided by their Mayfair, Belgravia and Pimlico estates. Despite a fairly large electorate (1,500) the Grosvenors controlled one seat without a break at Chester from 1715 to 1874 and both seats together for 42 of these years.

Neither county played a prominent part in the agitation leading to the Great Reform Act of 1832, which itself appears to have made little difference to the 'politics of deference'. Both in Shropshire and Cheshire treating and bribery carried on apace. In Shropshire Bishop's Castle was abolished, two parliamentary divisions were created and the four existing boroughs extended into rural areas: out of 46,900 inhabitants 3,510 were enfranchised. Members of the same county families continued to sit, although Benjamin Disraeli was elected at Shrewsbury in 1841 after enduring 'the most scurrilous anti-semitic abuse'. Dr Mason draws Trollopian vignettes of Shropshire politics in the 1880s: Sir Baldwin Leighton, of whom it was said that 'statistics are his forte, omniscience his foible', and the redoubtable Mrs Ormsby-Gore, the archetype of the parliamentary candidate's wife, who never left a shop without 'a promise or an insult'. County consciousness was still prevalent and the Conservatives claimed in 1892 to have 'one common cause at heart and that has been to return Shropshire men to Parliament'. In Cheshire, the 1832 act increased the number of seats from four to ten and the number of voters from about 7,000 to 10,300. Here again it lessened but did not abolish the role of the county families. The secret ballot introduced by the act of 1872 made tenants independent of their landlords, but it was the 1885 redistribution of seats, allocated on numbers and not on historic divisions, which broke the back of the old allegiances. Outside funds became available and outsiders came in. Shropshire, with its number of seats reduced to four in 1918 retained some local coherence except for the Wrekin, an industrial area where a Labour Member was elected in 1923. Jasper More, however, whose family had been in Parliament since the seventeenth century, was elected at Ludlow in 1960. Cheshire, on the other hand, was much more widely affected by industrialization, so that as early as 1906 it elected its first Labour Member, a former carpenter and a leading figure in the Co-operative movement. The old Cheshire families quickly surrendered their monopoly to the new managerial classes, as local identity was lost in the suburban sprawl of Liverpool and Manchester.

EVELINE CRUICKSHANKS
History of Parliament

Kingship and Unity: Scotland 1000–1306. By G.W.S. Barrow. (The New History of Scotland, Volume 2.) London: Edward Arnold. 1981. vi, 185 pp. Hardback £9.95; paperback £4.95.

The publishers of *The New History of Scotland* could hardly have hoped for a better volume to inaugurate their series than this most excellent introduction to the history of medieval Scotland. Professor Barrow's book is thoroughly readable and even entertaining, while it is filled with learning worn very lightly. The two main themes are the development of the monarchy, with its roots in the Scottish traditions of the west, and its strength drawn from the resources of the east of the country; and the emergence of Scotland as a nation, initially maintaining its independence from England and then establishing itself as a European power in the thirteenth century. A number of aspects receive separate treatment: the establishment of feudalism, the burghs, the church. For readers of this yearbook the few pages on the community of the realm are important reading for the early history of Parliament, in England as well as Scotland. There was, of course, in Scotland no precise parallel to the development of a representative system in England, for there were no county communities to elect Members of Parliament. Equally, Scotland lacked the trained body of royal judges who were so important in England, but in other respects the experience of the two countries was surprisingly close. Grants of taxation were not made in Scottish Parliaments, but legislation was enacted, cases were determined, and matters of state discussed. Above all, it was through Parliament that the community of the realm found expression.

It is perhaps unfair to criticize for omissions a book which packs so much into a short space. It is, however, a pity that there are only two maps. Had more been provided it would be easier for the reader to share in Professor Barrow's vast topographical knowledge, and it might not have been necessary to describe the lordship of Somerled Macgillebrigte in five lines of sonorous place-names. The principle adopted in providing footnotes is not clear: there are so few that it might have been better not to include any. There will not be many readers of this book capable of following up a reference to a work in Dutch.

Professor Barrow has a nice taste for the revealing anecdote. The story of the learned parson of Inverkeithing, who tried to revive classical Priapic fertility rites in the 1280s by persuading the village girls to dance naked round him, provides evidence of both scholarship and of the defects in the parochial system. As befits a book written for a fairly general audience, Professor Barrow lets his imagination have a rather fuller rein than in his more academic works. He expounds, for example, his views on the smell of medieval Scotland: it was probably rather unpleasant, with 'the acrid reek of peat fires, the putrid odour of rotting meat and … the stench of animal and human ordure'. This, however, Professor Barrow thinks was acceptable, unlike the 'austere squalor' of modern Scotland which attracts his outright condemnation.

MICHAEL PRESTWICH
University of Durham

Robert Winchelsey and the Crown 1294–1313: A Study in the Defence of Ecclesiastical Liberty. By Jeffrey H. Denton. (Cambridge Studies in Medieval Life and Thought. Third series, Volume 14.) Cambridge: Cambridge University Press. 1980. x, 341 pp. £17.50.

Although too shrewd and circumspect a politician to suffer the fate of his predecessor, Thomas Becket, Archbishop Robert Winchelsey was just as much a thorn in the flesh of Edward I and his son as the saint and martyr had been to Henry II. Becket's posthumous reputation as a staunch defender of ecclesiastical liberties certainly owes much to his dramatic death on the altar steps of Canterbury cathedral; and even had his votaries succeeded (in the face of considerable political opposition) in obtaining his canonization, it is hard to believe that Winchelsey would ever have come to occupy a similar place in the popular imagination. Yet his fight to maintain the social and constitutional standing of the church through the protection of clerical rights was an epic struggle in which he showed himself a formidable opponent, possessed at once of determination, integrity and total commitment to the cause of sacerdotalism. As Dr Denton so convincingly argues, the history of this struggle can best be understood when set against the wider background of practical politics, for even though Winchelsey would gladly have eschewed any involvement in the business of government, his insistence upon the church's sovereignty with regard to its own finances inevitably drew him into the political arena.

Edward I's quarrel with Winchelsey found expression in the two-fold issue of cure of souls — or more precisely the abuses of certain royal clerks and curialist bishops — and the church's right to determine when and how it should be taxed. Edward's chronic shortage of money as a result of his wars against the Scots and the French brought the second of these conflicts to a head, thus precipitating the constitutional crisis of 1297 in which Winchelsey played such a major part. Asserting that 'there can be no separation of (the archbishop's) life of personal devotion and determination from his life of public devotion and determination', Dr Denton sets out with enviable clarity and thoroughness to place his subject firmly in the general context of late thirteenth- and early fourteenth-century politics. If he does not altogether succeed in covering the historical bones of his subject with more than a token layer of flesh — for the archbishop remains a tantalizingly remote figure throughout most of this book — the author presents a compelling analysis of the growth of both clerical *and* lay opposition during this troubled period. Historians of the English Parliament rightly see the question of money supply as a leading factor in the early development of the House of Commons. The taxation of lay movables naturally occupies a special place in such studies, although as this book shows the taxation of the English church was just as important in monetary terms; and in proportion to their numbers the clergy were faced with disproportionately heavy demands. Irrespective of the ideological issues at stake, they simply could not afford to continue to meet such crippling taxes; and it is a measure of Winchelsey's success that their payments into the royal coffers fell from £60,000 (1294) and £78,000 (1295) to an average of £15–17,000 a year during his archiepiscopacy. Although undeniably helped by the promulgation of the papal bull *clericos laicos*, which forbade the taxation of the clergy without permission from Rome, Winchelsey's desire for independence forced him to steer a difficult course between the Scylla of subservience to the King and the Charybdis of papal interventionism — a course described here in fascinating detail. Yet despite the pressures thus brought to bear upon him from both court and curia he was able not only to defend the church from attack, but actually to strengthen its position with regard to the Crown. Not least of his achievements was the reassertion of the principle that the clergy would not join with the laity in discussing taxation in Parliament (an innovation made by Edward I in 1295 with signal lack of success), but that they were to be approached separately, in independent ecclesiastical councils, with control over appropriation and supply. Such freedom proved both an inspiration and an incentive to the laity, who had yet to fight their battle against royal exactions; and Dr Denton's examination of the interaction between the clerical and lay opposition, which together forced the *Confirmatio Cartarum* upon the King, provides an important and stimulating contribution to the history of Edward's last Parliaments. That Winchelsey played a leading role (perhaps *the* leading role) in forcing major concessions from the King is clearly revealed; and if he regarded himself primarily as a crusader in the cause of ecclesiastical liberty, his reform programme hardly differed from that of the laymen who wished to end arbitrary taxation. The coalescence of lay and clerical interests naturally strengthened the hand of Edward's opponents, among whom Winchelsey occupied a position of pre-eminence as befitted so shrewd and experienced a politician.

The *rapprochement* between the Crown and the Papacy which occurred after the death of Boniface VIII seriously undermined Winchelsey's position. After some preliminary sparring he was suspended from office and summoned to Rome, charged by the King with such 'injuries and shameful and despicable acts' as virtually amounted to treason. Although restored to his archiepiscopacy by the newly crowned Edward II in 1308, he was by then a sick man, and his subsequent role in national affairs was circumscribed both by illness and a genuine disinclination to speak for any cause other than the church. Whereas Tout saw him as 'the brains and policy' behind the programme of the Lords Ordainers elected in the Parliament of 1310 to curb Edward II's worst extravagances, Dr Denton is more realistic. Then, as before, the archbishop's sole purpose was to secure a lasting commitment by the Crown to the preservation of the liberties of the church. Such a single-minded policy lay behind his great triumph of 1297, and was the cause of his eventual failure. His unshakable belief that the welfare of England was dependent upon that of the church prevented him from exercising any positive influence over Edward I and his son, and in this respect, at least, his statesmanship went by default. As this book so clearly demonstrates, Winchelsey was fighting a rearguard action against new and more pragmatic elements in the English church, and to us his eventual defeat now seems almost inevitable. The history of his struggle none the less remains a subject of great importance to students of this period, and Dr Denton is to be thanked for producing so astute and scholarly an analysis of a confrontation which went far beyond the confines of the church.

CAROLE RAWCLIFFE
History of Parliament

John Russell, First Earl of Bedford: One of the King's Men. By Diane Willen. London: Royal Historical Society, Studies in History series No. 23; published for the Royal Historical Society by Swift Printers (Publishers) Ltd. 1981. xi, 145 pp. £13.00 (£7.98 for members of the Society).

Diane Willen has written a serviceable, straightforward account of the life of John Russell, first Earl of Bedford. She follows him in his career from gentleman usher at the end of Henry VII's reign to Privy Councillor and Lord Privy Seal to Henry VIII, Edward VI and Mary. No private family papers have survived, but there is a good deal of information about him in the official records. Dr Willen decided to keep the general historical narrative to a minimum and, perhaps as a consequence, has not fully exploited all the material she has found. However, in three analytical chapters she considers Russell's role in the West Country, his policies as a landowner, and his use of patronage (in which she acknowledges the assistance of the History of Parliament Trust).

Born about 1485 to a gentry family in Dorset, Russell served a long apprenticeship at court, on diplomatic missions abroad and as a military leader, losing the sight of one eye in a raid on France in 1522. His marriage to an heiress a few years later brought him his first major acquisition of land, including the manors of Chenies in Buckinghamshire — which became his country residence — and Thornhaugh in Northamptonshire. Henry VIII gave him Amersham manor in 1526 and in 1539, after creating him a baron, a long list of lands, mostly in Devon, which included the parliamentary borough of Tavistock. Early in the reign of Edward VI, Russell received the reversion to Woburn abbey as a gift from the Crown and, after the fall of Somerset, an earldom and still more lands, including a small estate in Covent Garden forfeited by the Protector. By the time of his death in 1555, therefore, he had gathered the estates which secured his family's future for centuries to come. How had he managed it?

Dr Willen concedes that Russell was not an outstanding political figure. Indeed, she ascribes some of his success to that fact: he did not aspire to decision-making and tried to steer clear of faction at court. Service, not policy, was his contribution. He worked hard, he was shrewd and, above all, loyal. He is seen as a typical new nobleman, ready to serve the monarchy, whatever its policies, out of loyalty to the dynasty — a loyalty heavily reinforced by self-interest. Russell and his like-thinking colleagues, such as Paulet, 'sprung from the willow, not the oak', acted as a stabilizing force in Tudor England. They and the kingdom together reaped the benefit.

HELEN MILLER
University College of North Wales, Bangor

The Lisle Letters. Edited by Muriel St Clare Byrne. Chicago and London: University of Chicago Press. 1981. 6 volumes. Volume I: xxviii, 713 pp., genealogy; Volume II: xviii, 705 pp.; Volume III: xv, 633 pp.; Volume IV: xv, 546 pp.; Volume V: xxi, 770 pp.; Volume VI: ix, 472 pp. £150.00.

Arthur Plantagenet, Viscount Lisle, an illegitimate son of Edward IV, was Deputy of Calais from 1533 to 1540, a period of mounting unrest which culminated in his recall and subsequent arrest on suspicion of treason. His papers were impounded and remained in the hands of the Crown. Of some 3,000 letters covering these seven years Muriel St Clare Byrne prints about two thirds, with much ancillary material designed to satisfy the 'normal curiosity' of her readers. She perhaps credits others with her own exceptional zest for knowledge, but the enthusiasm with which she presents the Lisles and their world generates the necessary will to learn about them. As she says, the letters are unique, more personal than the Paston letters and less parochial, with a sustained narrative interest. Although the substance of virtually all the letters is known from the calendared version in *Letters and Papers of Henry VIII*, the complete, modernized text expresses the personality as well as the full meaning of the writers. The vivid, natural prose of early sixteenth-century familiar writing has been neglected by scholars. Many of the letters were dictated to a scribe and preserve the speech rhythms of the time, besides words and phrases known hitherto only from later printed sources. For those who still hanker after the original spelling, Miss Byrne provides a number of literal transcripts and facsimiles. But her purpose is to meet the needs of the non-specialist, and in her commentary and supplementary documents she carefully guides the general reader through the complexities of the 1530s.

In a spirited defence of her decision to modernize the text she discusses some of the difficulties which it entails. Every word must be understood, not merely transcribed. Some of the handwriting is hard to puzzle out, but by reading the whole collection of letters Miss Byrne has been able to make the connexions which elucidate the text. She has also redated a number of letters, explaining her reasons for doing so in each case and listing all the alterations in an appendix in Volume I. Throughout she gives cross-references to *Letters and Papers*, noting the major discrepancies between manuscript and calendar. The index — 260 pages long — distinguishes between the letters and the commentary and gives reference to subjects as well as to people and places. Inevitably in a work of this scale, time has overtaken some of the comments, but it is a scholarly enterprise which has been brought to a triumphant conclusion. The six handsomely bound volumes stand as witnesses to the meticulous labour of a lifetime.

The letters are arranged chronologically with the exception of those concerning the children of the earlier marriages of Lord and Lady Lisle. The education and advancement of the young Plantagenets and Bassets provide the major themes of Lady Lisle's correspondence. By grouping these letters together in five long sections Miss Byrne allows the family, its needs and anxieties, to stand apart from the main narrative and to make its own contribution to the social history of the period. The chief value of these chapters lies in the incidental exposure of contemporary attitudes. For example, Lisle wanted to appoint his ten-year-old stepson to a benefice and approached Cromwell for a licence. He was told that Cromwell would not hear of it, 'specially when the matter is touching cure of souls; ne yet the same pertaineth unto any man within this realm but only unto my lord of Canterbury, who hath denied the same to the best of this realm'. However, Cromwell was said to be ready to help if Lisle could 'spy a prebend or free chapel' for the boy (V, 1096).

The historical interest of the correspondence as a whole is wider than might be expected. Much about Calais and its administration is revealed, naturally, but even more about the workings of the English court. Five hundred and fifteen of the letters were written by John Husee, Lisle's agent in London, who frequently reported his progress — or lack of progress — in the suits he was handling for his master. The immediacy of his writing preserves Husee's day-to-day experience of waiting upon Cromwell or on the gentlemen of the privy chamber currently in favour, catching them when they are free for a moment, listening to their promises of support so often belied by events — and, by extension, their experience of being forever surrounded by suitors, insatiable in their demands. Lisle's plea to Cromwell in 1536 'to help me to some old abbey in mine old days' (III, 653a) started negotiations the record of which remains as a case history of the manoeuvres lying behind Henry VIII's grants of monastic land. Husee devoted himself to promoting Lisle's causes, at the cost of much nervous energy. He already knew that 'it is hard trusting this wily world' (II, 323). He soon realized that 'every man here is for himself' (III, 753a) and that 'this world is queasy' and some things were better not written down (III, 792). By 1539 he was driven to pray 'God send me little ado in that Court of Augmentations!' (V, 1319). Too often he felt that his efforts were not enough appreciated. But to Husee's relief Lisle was rewarded by the King with the gift of Frithelstock priory in Devon in 1537 and in 1540, a few weeks before his recall, the White Friars in Calais.

Lisle had been warned early on that news of everything said or done in Calais was at once conveyed to the court by informers (II, 260). Any criticism of his actions he at once rebutted, claiming to have 'as good regard to his grace's town and jewel as any that was here' (II, 372). But the English bridgehead on the continent was not secure: the fact was better appreciated at Westminster than in Calais itself. By Act of Parliament early in 1536 new ordinances for Calais were promulgated and the town was given two M.P.s, one to be chosen by the Deputy and council, the other by the mayor and commonalty. The first two Members attended the Parliament which opened in June 1536. Thomas Boyes, the council's nominee, asked Lisle, through Husee, 'to send him instructions what you will have them move and motion in the Parliament House' (III, 705). Re-elected to the Parliament of 1539, Boyes at Lisle's suggestion reported to Henry VIII on the religious situation at Calais, but had to tell Lisle that at the court 'they say that the most part of Calais are heretics' (V, 1445). His fellow-M.P., Thomas Broke, reinforced this dangerous opinion, attacking the Bill of Six Articles in a long speech which, according to Husee, was badly received by the House of Commons (V, 1451). Lisle asked another of his servants to speak to Stephen Gardiner about the incident. Gardiner declared that Broke, 'being a burgess there, might well declare his mind and opinion'. Nevertheless, Lisle could rest assured that he would be 'after a more due and strait fashion examined, than he have been yet, before his departure out of the city' (V, 1459).

For all his concern to implement the King's policy, Lisle's attempt to enforce the new act on religion was frustrated by divisions within the Calais council. At his own request he was recalled in April 1540 to discuss his problems with Henry VIII. For the first time since he had gone to Calais, Lisle was free to attend Parliament when it reconvened at the end of the month. He was present in the Lords at every sitting until the Whitsun recess, apparently still high in the King's favour. A week later he was led prisoner to the Tower, a suspected traitor. Evidence had been found that one of his chaplains had visited Rome and offered to betray Calais to the Pope and Cardinal Pole. There was nothing to implicate Lisle; he was in reality a victim of the struggle for power between Norfolk and Cromwell. He was neither tried nor attainted. But it was not until March 1542 that the King could bring himself to order his release, and Lisle died in the Tower within hours of receiving the news.

John Husee's judgment on Calais was that it was a town 'like to the frogs, which can be long contented with no deputy nor governor but desiring ever new changes' (V, 1388). Its instability was accentuated by the ferocious competition for offices. The letters contain many requests for 'rooms' for friends or clients, attracted by the ease with which actual attendance was evaded: Husee himself, rarely in Calais, was a gentleman of the retinue there. The incessant squabbling provoked Henry VIII to an irritated outburst at one suitor in 1539: 'I have more ado with you Calais men than with all my realm after' (V, 1481). All the same, for Lisle himself the King seems to have felt a genuine affection. Of royal blood, he was a fitting representative of the kingdom, yet one who could pose no threat to the Crown. He apparently knew French, and quickly established friendly relations with his French and Flemish neighbours. Miss Byrne argues forcefully against the impression of historians that he was exceptionally incompetent. The office of Deputy was no sinecure. Calais was a financial liability, its income from the Staplers no longer sufficient to maintain the defences. Lisle coped reasonably well with the duties of the post. He also worried about his own financial problems, about the future of his family and the difficulty of promoting their interests in his absence from the court. By the end he was angling for a less arduous appointment nearer the centre of power and had visions of becoming Prince Edward's governor or, failing that, Lord Chamberlain to the new Queen, Anne of Cleves (V, 1388, 1593).

Lisle's hopes and plans, his strengths and weaknesses, the realities of his life are gradually revealed. The great men of the day are glimpsed in action: Henry VIII allocating gifts of venison after the hunt (IV, 1004) or showing Lady Lisle 'all the commodities of his palace' (V, 1269); the Duke of Suffolk breaking into a conversation to present the King with a brace of white greyhounds (III, 671); Cromwell wanting to be the only mediator between Lisle and Henry VIII (II, 375) and saying that 'he remembereth your lordship oftener than he hath fingers or toes' (IV, 939). *The Lisle Letters*, rich in their variety and human interest, offer a window on the living world of the 1530s.

HELEN MILLER
University College of North Wales, Bangor

The Irish Constitutional Revolution of the Sixteenth Century. By Brendan Bradshaw. Cambridge: Cambridge University Press. 1979. xi, 303 pp. £16.00.

Between 40 and 50 years ago the interest of professional historians in Irish history was centred largely on the early modern period. This was due mainly to a group of young scholars who signalized their entry into the field of academic Irish history by the publication of a number of monographs on sixteenth- and seventeenth-century Ireland. Curiously, while their expanding interests soon led them into wider pastures they left few successors to tend their original gardens. Hence the long overdue revival of interest especially in the sixteenth century has had to await the labours of a younger generation of scholars of whom Dr Bradshaw is one of the most notable and to date the most prolific. Following in the footsteps of Professor Elton, he is primarily interested in the political and constitutional aspects of his subject. His aim is to provide a conceptual framework within which the political and constitutional history of early modern Ireland can be discussed. But he is well aware that much of contemporary interest lies elsewhere and suggests that such a framework must be erected before 'the social and economic dynamics of political history and the like' may be usefully taken up.

The conceptual framework within which he sets the events of the early and middle Tudor period is in many respects a novel and arresting one. It is that a constitutional revolution was effected by conciliatory policies in the early 1540s whereby the lordship of Ireland became a sovereign kingdom under the English Crown; that this movement for change from lordship to kingdom was pioneered from the second decade of the century by a group of Palesmen and townmen inspired by humanistic ideals acquired at the English Inns of Court; that similar ideals later influenced the Irish policies of the London government and led to fruitful co-operation between the Crown and the Pale reformers. Reform policies, he shows, were vigorously pursued by Cromwell but reached their apogee under Sir Anthony St Leger, in whose first deputyship the constitutional changes were given statutory effect. Thereafter for a variety of reasons London abandoned conciliation in favour of conquest and colonization, thus putting an end to the reforming programme. This in turn led to the disenchantment of the Palesmen and their alienation from the government; and the fusion of their concept of 'commonwealth liberalism' with traditional ideas of separatism carried the seeds of an ideology of nationalism which aspired 'to unite Gaelic and Anglo-Irish alike in common devotion to the native land' and proposed as a political objective the merging of the two 'nations' into a single political community.

This framework is based on a close examination of manuscript sources in the Public Record Office in London and in other British repositories. Nothing germane to his argument appears to have escaped Dr Bradshaw; indeed, one occasionally feels that he is able to make bricks out of straws in the wind. One wonders whether the Vatican archives would contain anything relevant to his thesis, but on the other hand there is a welcome incursion into Gaelic literature. Some of the Gaelic literature he uses — all of it printed material — is of much earlier provenance than the period with which he is dealing (e.g. Gofraidh Fionn Ó Dálaigh and Gearóid Íarla) and some is later (e.g. Céitinn and Haicéad) but his aim is 'to chart political mentalities' by means of 'comparative analysis' and this requires a *longue durée*. Remembering the remark of Osborn Bergin ('all court poetry is more or less tainted by the voice of insincerity and formalism') was it wise of him to concentrate so much on encomiastic verse, in the strict sense of praise poetry, to the comparative neglect of political poetry, a *genre* he has used elsewhere? For example, he does not refer to the political poem dating from *c.* 1542–3 edited by Professor Ó Cuív in *Éigse* (XV, 261–76) which bears directly on the 'constitutional revolution'.

The Statutes of Kilkenny provide his point of departure and the prototype to which much subsequent policy and legislation are referred. Indeed the most notable feature of the work is its comparative method. Three early pieces of reform literature emanating from the Pale which he analyzes separately are compared with one another to show the development of political thought within the Anglo-Irish community. Policy making and parliamentary statutes are explained and illumined by comparison with those which preceded them. Surrey's expedition is put into perspective by a backward glance at that of Poynings; Henry VIII's and Surrey's Irish policies in 1520–2 are placed side by side; the transformation of Henry's policy as a result of Surrey's judgment of its impracticability is noted and the King's new policy described as a return to government on late medieval lines. Again St Leger's policy of 'commonwealth liberalism' in the early 1540s is contrasted with Henry's policy of 'royal liberalism' in the early 1520s and with Cromwell's 'strong conservatism' in the 1530s. Similarly the Kildare Rebellion of 1534–5 is juxtaposed with the Geraldine League of 1539–40. Seen in the context of each other the rebellion of Silken Thomas loses its aura of romantic nationalism with a 'faith and fatherland' component and becomes merely the last medieval struggle between local dynasts. The League, on the other hand, especially in its final stages, appears as a cohesive Gaelic movement of resistance to the Crown buttressed by the beginnings of counter-reform ideologies. Geographically too the same method is employed and light is shed on the administration of the Irish colony by reference to Wales and to Calais. In all this, comparisons are not odious and pay handsome dividends.

Certain themes introduced in the opening chapters recur throughout the book and help to give it coherent unity. Attention is drawn to the government's consistent resolve to keep its options open. The low priority given to Ireland in Henry VIII's overall policies and programme is repeatedly noted: 'balancing the books' was a major preoccupation. There is insistence (though with occasional qualifications) that 'racial tension of major political proportions' between Gaelic Irish and Anglo-Irish simply did not exist and that, on the contrary, there was a considerable amount of social and cultural intercourse. This needed to be emphasized. Sources of possible conflict between the two communities are seen as likely to stem, not from their different ethnic origins but from differences in constitutional and political status and especially from differences in land tenure. The problems surrounding tenurial rights and the anxiety of the Gaelic Irish arising therefrom loom large in the book and culminate in a masterly treatment of surrender and regrant. But the most original and challenging issue, introduced early, returned to frequently and forming a final set-piece to the book, is his exposition of the origin of Irish political nationalism.

As indicated earlier, Dr Bradshaw argues that this was born of the Palesmen's disillusion with the government's refusal to recognize their rightful place in the body politic following on the recall of St Leger, and that their discontent fused with an incipient separatist sentiment among the Gaelic Irish. It seems to this reviewer that he has in fact uncovered an unsuspected strand in the beginnings of Irish nationalism which becomes more apparent in the constitutional thinking of early seventeenth-century Irish lawyers, notably (and significantly) Patrick Darcy. His attribution of the reformers' ideas to humanism, however, is open to discussion. The influence of humanism on Anglo-Irish politicians and writers in the sixteenth century and beyond is now becoming a new orthodoxy among Irish historians. The idea is attractive but it is time to ask for the evidence on which the statement rests. 'The fact is incontrovertible', says Dr Bradshaw, 'that it was the influence of humanism' which lay behind reform thought and action. The internal evidence provided by his analysis of the reform literature and of the policies pursued by the reformers does not suggest an incontrovertible fact. Rather it suggests that some ideas and policies were characteristic of humanism and some were not: thoughts of conquest and colonization, for instance, were never far below the surface of the reformers' minds, though Dr Bradshaw thinks that when they surfaced they were deliberately put forward to be knocked down as being impracticable. A less charitable historian might suggest that a desire to destroy the 'over-mighty' Kildare and the lure of monastic property (with which they were to be richly endowed) also motivated the reformers' zeal. The source of their humanism he attributes to their residence in the Inns of Court. This may possibly be so, but there is nothing in the extant records of the Inns to substantiate that the Irish students moved in humanistic circles.

Dr Bradshaw argues convincingly that Cromwell in the 1530s was the real architect of Crown policy in Ireland. The reform programme, he holds, was inaugurated before the Kildare Rebellion which merely interrupted and postponed its implementation. Hence he accepts the traditional view that the rebellion was the result, not the cause, of the new policy which he ascribes to the influence of humanism and to Cromwell's master-plan of 'unitary sovereignty'. Here he parts company with the traditionalists who would attribute it to the imperatives of an aspiring Tudor despotism, the necessity of securing acceptance of royal ecclesiastical supremacy and the need to guard against Catholic invasion. Cromwell initially intended to reform, not to destroy, the house of Kildare and showed no bias against the Anglo-Irish, though he it was who first established the 'new English' in Ireland. The Dublin executive was emasculated and power centralized in London but the Irish Parliament made a remarkable recovery and Dr Bradshaw's weaving together of parliamentary enactments and current events is expertly done. The climax of the book is reached in the deputyship of Sir Anthony St Leger who with the Anglo-Irish Sir Thomas Cusack engineered the 'constitutional revolution'. Whether it was a revolution in reality or merely in conception, and whether it was a constitutional change rather than a 'constitutional revolution' will long be debated. But perhaps this is a question of semantics.

It will be clear that the book is bursting its covers with new perspectives, fresh insights and original ideas. Dr Bradshaw's careful qualifications, subtle distinctions, and especially his proliferation of categories, would do justice to a medieval Schoolman. He has an impressive power of sustained argument which he uses so fairly that he sometimes provides counter-arguments for those who may disagree with his views: for example, in the downplay of the religious element in the 'constitutional revolution'. The book will continue to tantalize and provide food for thought to historians of Tudor Ireland for many years to come and none will be able to ignore it.

DONAL F. CREGAN

King Charles I. By Pauline Gregg. London: Dent. 1981. xii, 496 pp. £12.50.

It is easy to see why Charles I has deterred serious biography. The personal materials relating to this essentially private man are relatively thin and they are well scattered. Various recent studies have all been light-weight. Nothing daunted, Pauline Gregg has undertaken a full-scale biography. There is much to commend about her book: the narrative shows that she is well acquainted with a large range of primary and secondary works; she writes easily and with nice flashes of colour; she extracts every ounce of pathos inherent in the final stages of her story. Gregg's feel for the period is largely secure but occasionally it falters. One is startled, for instance, to be told that yeomen travelled in coaches and that the inhabitants of forest areas were 'few and largely itinerant' (pp. 205, 224). The number of minor inaccuracies that occur in the chapters on 1640–2, the years with which this reviewer is most familiar in detail, is rather more serious. The Earl of Bedford becomes a duke (p. 298); William Taylor's accusation against the Commons for committing 'murder with the sword of justice' was made at Windsor not Westminster (p. 330); the Root and Branch Bill did not lie undiscussed through the spring and summer of 1641 (p. 335); the Grand Remonstrance, introduced by John Pym in November 1641, had not been 'lying on the table since the previous November', though another kind of remonstrance, to be sent to the King not published for the people, had been discussed then (p. 340); the Militia Ordinance was never cast in the form of a bill (p. 349). Such slips jolt one's confidence in the factual accuracy of Gregg's account as a whole. It is also quite maddening to be offered no citations for the vast majority of the contemporary quotations and accounts of specific incidents that appear in this book.

But what matters most about any biography is the overall sense it conveys of a man's life and character. Pauline Gregg is at her best on the private and personal side of Charles' life. She is excellent on his upbringing and she provides an intelligent discussion of many familiar aspects of his character such as his diffidence, meticulousness, determination and obstinacy. She rightly emphasizes the impact on his mind of two of his greatest continuing sensitivities: his failure to do his sister Elizabeth the right she deserved over the Palatinate and his betrayal of the Earl of Strafford. But if in some ways this is the Charles we had expected, in others it is not. Gregg's portrayal of Charles as an adventurer, a man of action who quickly grew restless with hunting, court life and debate, is particularly interesting. This enables her to make sense of and link together such apparently disparate events as the trip to Madrid, the visit to Scotland in 1641 and the campaigns of 1642–6. The portrait of the King as 'no cardboard commander' but a monarch who 'actively participated in general strategy and individual campaigns' is carefully constructed and persuasive.

What is lacking in this book is a convincing political analysis, an argument that is about the springs of Charles's political policies and activities. Thus Part III, entitled 'Personal Rule', remains ultimately less than satisfying, despite informative sections on the role of the Privy Council and the court and a sympathetic account of relations between the King and the papal envoys. Gregg is in no doubt that there was a personal rule. So far as foreign policy is concerned she clearly has a strong case and her stress, in this context, on the diplomatic and naval objectives of the ship money experiment is timely. But she fails to press home her suggestions that social policy was 'the King's great business in a more fundamental sense than the raising of ship money' and that he showed compassion for the poor. Recent work by Dr Quintrell and Dr Slack on the Book of Orders actually points in a very different direction. Charles came closer to William Laud, Gregg declares, 'in an unemotional way', but she dodges the question of how far the King himself initiated or drove on the policy of imposing the English prayer book in Scotland.

The treatment of parliamentary politics between 1640 and 1642 is often simplistic. Gregg clings to an outdated notion of a monolithic 'opposition' although she has cited Conrad Russell's account of the 1620s Parliaments with approval. She tends to see the conflict of these years as a political game in which Charles was repeatedly caught out: in April 1641 he had 'little room for manoeuvre'; in May he was 'distraught'; in Scotland later in the summer 'his faults of character were relentlessly exposed'. Gregg thinks that the abortive January coup was hatched while the King was in Scotland but she does not consider whether it was related to a wider strategy. Too many questions are left unanswered. With what objective did Charles call the Long Parliament? Did he entertain serious hopes that it might provide him with the revenue and authority which his monarchy had so conspicuously lacked in 1640? What plans lay behind his negotiations with foreign powers for men and money at this time? Was he at any stage deep in the army plot? Was he, as his letters to Secretary Nicholas strongly hint, poised ready to reassert himself in November 1641, when the Irish Rebellion blasted his carefully prepared strategy? There must be more to be said about the King's mind and policy on the eve of the Civil War. His role, it may be suggested, remains the most puzzling feature of the whole crisis.

Pauline Gregg's conclusion is emphatic. 'It was Charles's misfortune', she writes, 'that accident had placed him in the path of momentous change of one kind or another.' Her resolute determinism at the end of this long book sits oddly with her patient unravelling of a complex story event by event. It is hard to accept. All in all though there is much in this book to be grateful for. We have a clearer view than ever before of the kind of man Charles I was and what he believed in and stood for. Yet there remains another book to be written about why this King alone among English monarchs was confronted in battle by thousands of his subjects and then finally executed by a clique among those who had defeated him.

ANTHONY FLETCHER
University of Sheffield

Denzil Holles 1598–1680: A Study of his Political Career. By Patricia Crawford. London: Royal Historical Society, Studies in History series No. 16; published for the Royal Historical Society by Swift Printers (Publishers) Ltd. 1979. viii, 243 pp. £15.60 (£10.14 for members of the Society).

Denzil Holles is an example of a politician whose prominence on the public stage was considerably greater than his political talents warranted. His judgment was often wrong, and he allowed his passions to carry him into positions too extreme to serve the ends to which his rather conventional political convictions were really pointing. He made his first sensational impact on parliamentary history at the age of 30, when he helped to hold the weeping Speaker in his chair and uttered the three wild resolutions which were to be the last proceedings in the House for 11 years. Yet unlike Eliot, Valentine and Strode, his fellow actors in that scene, he made a most humble submission to the King, saying that 'it was the height of his ambition to end his days in your service'. Dr Crawford considers that he was 'not completely identified with the opposition leadership' in the early days of the Long Parliament, but after dissociating himself from the proceedings against his brother-in-law Strafford he was soon in the van with Pym and Hampden, and he fully deserved his place as one of the famous Five Members in January 1642. Nor did he show any sign of flinching at the prospect of civil war. He commanded a regiment of foot in the first campaign, and it fought well until Rupert broke it at Brentford.

Yet nine days after that defeat Holles spoke earnestly in the Commons in favour of peace, and he rapidly emerged as a leader — later *the* leader — of the peace party. Understandably, Dr Crawford has some difficlty in explaining his change of stance; her contention that 'he was probably little altered' is only half convincing. Granted that he had never had any radical religious convictions, or any vision of a new and better political order, or any part in the Hartlib-Dury circle's hopes for a vast improvement of man's estate on Baconian lines, it remains a puzzle that he parted company with Pym and Hampden so suddenly. But the evidence of how he spoke and voted at the time is faithfully assembled, and it may be a mistake to try too hard to explain his apparent change of direction; at any rate the reader is given the means to form a judgment for himself. Perhaps, as in 1629, the consequences of the extreme position that Holles had adopted dismayed him; contemporaries may have been right that he was shaken by the slaughter of his men at Brentford.

He showed his fallibility of judgment again when he personally advised Charles I in 1644 to come to London and throw himself upon the support of the citizens and the peace party. His suspected traffic with the King got him into serious trouble with the Commons, and it was a very remarkable recovery that raised him to the height of his influence over the House in 1646–7, especially as his policy depended on bullying the King into accepting the Propositions of Newcastle, which (Charles being what he was) could never be done. Since his judgment was so unreliable and his loyalty to the parliamentary cause so suspect, one may wonder how he came to exercise the ascendancy that he did, not once but several times in the course of his career. He had rank and wealth, of course, but having an earl for his father and an income comfortably counted in thousands do not in themselves explain it. He must have been a most effective orator; his memoirs, though neither candid nor attractive, are at least eloquent in their fashion. He certainly had courage, though it led him at times into recklessness, and enormous self-confidence, though it often spilled over into arrogance and aggressiveness. Above all, perhaps, he articulated the attitudes of large numbers of M.P.s at certain critical times when their feelings ran high: their distrust of Charles early in 1642, their dismay over the early reverses in the Civil War, their anxiety to get the New Model disbanded in 1647, their desire for peace with Charles I in 1648 and for the restoration of Charles II in 1660. To each situation he brought a passionate conviction, but little foresight and an indifferent grasp of the political realities. He is a classic exemplar of the difference between a politician and a statesman.

Dr Crawford has looked at Holles carefully and critically, and he emerges as a consistent and convincing character; the same pride and quarrelsomeness that marked his early parliamentary career marred his effectiveness as ambassador to France after the Restoration. She does not bring to her subject any strikingly perceptive insights or point to any major reinterpretations, but she assembles the evidence about Holles's career honestly and thoroughly, using a full range of both printed and manuscript sources. Only at the most important and controversial stage in it, the spring and summer of 1647, does one feel the need for even fuller treatment and discussion, but she was not to know how contentious this topic was to become in the light of Dr Kishlansky's work. As far as I have noted, she cites nothing published later than February 1976, and she was unfortunate in not being able to take advantage of recent important revisions of the political scene in the 1620s and '30s. Even so, her use of 'the Parliamentarians' and 'the Puritans' to refer to political groups in the '20s is really inadmissible, and some of her references to 'the opposition' in the pre-war Long Parliament are also rather loose. There is a slight tendency throughout to smooth over the complexities of parliamentary politics, but her judgment is generally sound and fair, and she wisely resists any temptation to take her subject at his own evaluation. The proof-reading could have been better; besides minor errors, the notes on p.45 are garbled, and it looks as though a line has been left out in the middle of p. 135.

AUSTIN WOOLRYCH
University of Lancaster

A Register of Parliamentary Lists 1660–1761. Edited by David Hayton and Clyve Jones. University of Leicester History Department Occasional Publication No. 1. Leicester: University of Leicester History Department. 1979. xxvi, 168 pp. £1.75.

A Register of Parliamentary Lists 1660–1761: A Supplement. Edited by David Hayton and Clyve Jones. University of Leicester History Department Occasional Publication No. 3. Leicester: University of Leicester History Department. 1982. xii, 20 pp. £1.00.

When it comes to using the method of collective biography for the analysis of parliamentary history we are all Namierites nowadays. The raw materials for this methodology include information on the behaviour of members of both Houses; whether, like the 'crook-taloned birds' of Aeschylus cited by Sir Lewis, they were of the right by nature or of the left. Without detailed knowledge concerning the position of individual peers and M.P.s on particular issues, generalizations about their political affiliations or even principles cannot be satisfactorily substantiated. For this purpose the best evidence is contained in lists which record how they actually voted in divisions. Other useful compilations are forecasts of how they would divide, lists drawn up by or for parliamentary managers to assist their activities, and attributions of individuals to groups or parties within Parliament.

Since official records of divisions at Westminster were not kept until the nineteenth century, even division lists for earlier periods are scattered and elusive. 'Management' lists must be tracked down in surviving private papers of individual managers. Although some 'group' attributions were published, many of these remain in manuscript. The editors of this *Register* and its *Supplement* have saved historians of Parliament in the period 1660–1761 endless trouble in locating such lists by gathering and collating the holdings of many repositories. The help of others, here fully acknowledged, will also be gratefully appreciated by anybody who uses these guides. In addition to printed versions, and many manuscript lists in the Bodleian and British Libraries, and House of Lords and Public Record Offices, they indicate no fewer than 39 archives holding such materials, including four outside Britain. They also record lists for the Irish and Scottish Parliaments.

Although their own diligence doubled the number of lists for the English (after 1707 British) Parliaments known a decade ago for inclusion in the *Register*, they acknowledge in the Foreword that other researchers might well unearth more, and indeed encourage them to do so. The editors and Dr Eveline Cruickshanks themselves actually turned up no fewer than ten new lists for the Lords in the period 1689–94 alone. These were discovered amongst the Ailesbury manuscripts in the Wiltshire Record Office. This collection apparently contained three division lists of peers now alas missing: one of 1705 on 'the Church in Danger'; one on the Septennial Bill in 1716; and another of the same year on amendments to the Forfeited Estates Bill. It is to be hoped that these will eventually surface. For the time being they are simply listed as 'lost division lists' in an Appendix.

Such is the rate of discovery that already a *Supplement* has been compiled, cataloguing 56 lists in addition to those in the *Register*. Fourteen of these are versions of compilations previously registered, but 42 are new. A particularly rich seam has been struck for the Scottish Parliament in William's reign from the Breadalbane manuscripts in the Scottish Record Office. Besides adding entries to the *Register*, the *Supplement* also takes the opportunity to remove two lists of peers which merely duplicated one already noted, and makes other slight amendments and corrections.

The chance survival of lists gives them a very uneven chronological coverage. Robert Harley's concern for the details of parliamentary management and the fact that all his papers appear to have come down more or less intact, alone account for the availability of 25 lists between 1693 and 1719; 14 for the Lords, 11 for the Commons. This compares with the known existence of only 66 lists all told for the years 1727–54. As the editors observe,

the predominance of lists compiled by and for parliamentary managers is reflected in the chronological spread of the lists, the lulls and peaks of activity. The absence of lists for some years can sometimes be accounted for by the lack of party conflicts in the House, as during the first four years of the Cavalier Parliament or the closing years of the Parliament of 1747–54, but they can also be the result of lacunae in the private archives of the leading politicians; the partial destruction of Sir Robert Walpole's papers and the almost complete loss of Henry Pelham's, for instance, having limited considerably the yield from four of George II's five Parliaments.

An analysis of printed lists indicates the remarkable extent to which their production was influenced by the imminence of general elections. Of the 161 for the upper House only about a dozen appeared in print at the time. This compares with some 35 lists of M.P.s out of 201 compiled in the whole period. Sixteen of them were published in election years, while many of the remainder were intended to influence voters, including the *List of those who were For and Against bringing in the Excise Bill* ... (1733). It is significant that the list of M.P.s who supported and opposed the Peerage Bill in 1719 was preserved for posterity in *A Guide to the Electors of Great Britain* ... put out at the time of the 1722 election. The use of lists as electoral propaganda presumably explains why no fewer than 16 of the 35 which appeared in print did so between 1694 and 1716 when, thanks to the Triennial Act, England was in a permanent state of electioneering. In the period before 1694 and after 1716 such publications were few and far between.

In Ireland, where general elections were even fewer and farther between, there was little interest in the publication of parliamentary lists. None of those for the Dublin House of Lords were printed, and only two of the 24 compilations of M.P.s appeared in print. The Scottish lists are distinct in that official records of divisions were kept at the time and published in the *Acts of the Parliament of Scotland*. The chronological distribution of divisions in the Edinburgh Parliament is also skewed towards those over the Union, 42 of the 77 lists being for the period 25 October 1706 — 10 March 1707. Only two of these, however, were published as broadsheets. Given the unrepresentative nature of the Scottish Parliament, and the fact that it was about to disappear anyway, their production was presumably for a wider public than the electorate.

Not that the market for published lists in England was confined to the voters. One reproduced in the *Register*, listing members of both Houses who supported Dr Sacheverell, was an elaborately produced print, with portraits of Sacheverell, Charles I, and the six bishops who voted for the doctor, together with a view of St Paul's Cathedral. This had headings and comments in four languages: English, Dutch, French and Latin.

The reproduction of this print is of indifferent quality compared with the rest of the book. Although the text copies a typescript, with unjustified right-hand margins, it is not unattractive, while plans of the parliamentary buildings in London, Dublin and Edinburgh are beautifully bold and clear.

These plans indicate that the *Register* and its *Supplement* do not merely record the whereabouts and contents of parliamentary lists. Although the editors refer for commentary to *The Parliamentary Lists of the Early Eighteenth Century: Their Compilation and Use*, edited by Aubrey Newman (Leicester, 1973), they contribute brief introductions to place the lists in appropriate contexts. Particularly valuable are the sections on voting procedures in the three Parliaments. Such considerate editorship makes these compilations of indispensable value to all parliamentary historians of the period.

W.A. SPECK
University of Hull

The Correspondence of John Locke. Edited by E.S. de Beer. (The Clarendon Edition of the Works of John Locke.) *Volume VI: Letters Nos. 2119–2664.* Oxford: Clarendon Press. 1981. vii, 798 pp. £42.50.

For the historian concerned with Parliament and national politics the interest of this sixth volume of E.S. de Beer's edition of Locke's correspondence is less immediate than that of its predecessor. In the latter the 'College' correspondence between Locke on the one hand and Edward Clarke, excise commissioner and M.P. for Taunton, and the barrister John Freke on the other constituted an invaluable source for the 1694–5 and 1695–6 sessions of Parliament; it also cast fresh light on Locke's involvement with the Great Recoinage as well as on the 'abolition' of the licensing of the press. By the time the sixth volume (which covers the period from 19 February 1697 to 27 January 1700) commences the 'College' had ceased to function as a means of passing on political information on a regular basis. In contrast to the 50 or so 'College' letters in Volume V there are only two in Volume VI, both of which seem to have been prompted by personal rather than political concerns. In this volume Locke's interests emerge primarily as philosophic and religious. There is much about the pamphlet controversy with Stillingfleet over Locke's treatment of substance in the *Essay* and of its implications for the traditional doctrine of the Trinity. Locke's religious concerns are further illuminated by the continuing correspondence with the Dutch Remonstrant theologian, Philippus van Limborch, of which de Beer provides a valuable translation to accompany the Latin originals together with an appendix containing drafts of key passages on the unity of God from Locke's papers. Another appendix contains the text of Leibniz's *Remarques* on the *Essay* from the version forwarded to Locke by Jean Le Clerc in April 1697.

As in previous volumes information about Locke's finances is plentiful. The intermittent difficulties of managing his small patrimony in Somerset as an absentee continue, though in the field of monied investments in London Locke's cousin and eventual heir, Peter King (the future Lord Chancellor), proves an increasingly helpful go-between and effectively replaces Edward Clarke and Locke's publisher, Awnsham Churchill, in this role. There are revealing glimpses of the great philosopher *en famille*, and much information is exchanged about books, old and new, especially with continental correspondents. By now Locke had achieved sufficient eminence to attract letters from complete strangers anxious to use his influence to advance their pet projects, such as the Derbyshire clergyman John Tatam who wanted an act to improve the collection of tithes. Similarly too the numbers of requests, both from strangers and acquaintances, for Locke's assistance in obtaining posts and advancement has substantially increased.

Perhaps the major correspondence of political interest in the volume is that with William Molyneux, though the full version has little to add to what was published in the *Familiar Letters* of 1708. What does throw light on this friendship, but is not alluded to in de Beer's notes, is the evidence provided by the printer's copy of Molyneux's *Case of Ireland* as to the date of completion of the pamphlet. This establishes that Molyneux's request of 15 March 1698 that 'the *Author* of the *Two Treatise of Government*' should consider 'how justly' the English Parliament can bind Ireland 'without our *Consent* and *Representatives*' was not written some five weeks after the completion of the *Case*, as the date, 8 February 1698, in the preface would suggest, but well before the work was actually finished on 26 March 1698. Furthermore, in view of the fact that some letters from the correspondence no longer survive, de Beer's categorical assertion that Locke had not at this stage acknowledged his authorship of the *Treatises* to Molyneux is surely too strong; indeed comparison of the tone in which Molyneux refers to the authorship of the *Treatises* in this letter with his earlier hesitancies in broaching the subject of Locke's anonymous works makes it extremely probable he now shared Locke's secret. Also of interest are the many references to Locke's activities at the Board of Trade, notably his comment to Clarke on 25 February 1698 as to the rejection of his poor relief project by his fellow commissioners (which does not emerge from the official journal). However it would have been desirable to have noted that Locke's scheme was taken up again by the board on 13 July 1699, embodied with a few minor changes in a formal representation of 2 October, and subsequently referred to a Commons committee discussing poor relief on 20 November 1699. Finally in February 1705 this 1699 representation formed the basis of an abortive bill introduced in the Lords. In assuming that the editor of the *Newton Correspondence* was mistaken in taking the letter from Newton of 19 September 1698 about the value of guineas (of which there is a copy in MS Locke b.3, f. 127v) to have been addressed to Locke rather than to William Popple, secretary of the Board of Trade, de Beer is indeed correct. The original of the letter, complete with notes by Popple at the foot of the page, is still among the board's papers in the P.R.O. at Kew (C.O. 388/7, f.63). Also worthy of note is Locke's suggestion to Clarke at the end of December 1697 as to the desirability of adding a clause to the bill dealing with hammered money, to force the Tellers of the Exchequer to accept it only by weight and cut counterfeit pieces in order to prevent their circulating further. Although it proved too late to amend this particular bill, which became law as 9 Wm. III, c.2, Clarke subsequently introduced a further bill dealing with counterfeit coin that provided for Locke's suggestions and which received the royal assent in May 1698, as 9 & 10 Wm. III, c.21.

PATRICK KELLY
Trinity College, Dublin

The Whig Ascendancy: Colloquies on Hanoverian England. Edited by John Cannon. London: Edward Arnold. 1981. xii, 226 pp. £12.50.

This is an unconventional book. Seven historians gathered at the University of York for the Easter weekend of 1979 to read papers to each other. Each script was then subjected to a critical examination by the other participants: but a point not made clear is whether the papers were previously circulated or whether the discussions were entirely spontaneous. The original papers are printed exactly as they were delivered, together with an edited summary of each discussion. The volume ends with a final session of general discussion, printed verbatim. The central theme of this mini-conference was 'the nature of the Hanoverian political regime', and the chief aim to provide 'some general interpretative framework' of a subject fragmented by the so-called Namier Revolution. A second purpose was to demonstrate the formulation of historical criticism and assessment. In this latter aim the book succeeds admirably: but it is disappointing in respect of the former and more important objective, perhaps because social motivations outweighed scholarly ones in the selection of participants. Their choice, four from Newcastle University, was not sufficiently representative of the range of current opinions. With the exception of Norman McCord, whose presence was somewhat of an anomaly explained by the Newcastle connexion (an evocative phrase in the context of the subject) they fell into two broad schools. Either, like Geoffrey Holmes, William Speck and H. T. Dickinson, they were former Queen Anne specialists advancing into the Hanoverian era; or, like John Cannon, John Derry and Frank O'Gorman, they were reared in the Cambridge Whig tradition. Both categories of historians tend to attach more credence to the reality of party in eighteenth-century Britain than do those who have followed the Namier path, among whom John Owen and Paul Langford were authors criticized. As deplorable as the omission of an orthodox Namierite viewpoint was the absence of any representative from among the group of historians currently seeking to rewrite the politics of George II's reign. Heavy blows were struck at the diverse views of Jonathan Clark, Linda Colley, Eveline Cruickshanks and B.W. Hill; but none of them were present to defend themselves. Perhaps even more damning was the absence of any champion of what might be called 'the E.P. Thompson school', which sees the whole scene from the different angle not of disputes within the ruling class but of the relationship between it and the rest of the population. To some extent these different viewpoints were portrayed and canvassed. The validity of 'stability' as a meaningful concept was questioned. Doubts were raised, even at this gathering, as to whether the Whig–Tory party conflict of Anne's reign might not have been a deviation from a long-term political norm of a Court-Country alignment, and Speck's paper on George II's reign verged on Namierism. But even though the participants ranged widely in approach, the fact remains that much of the argument was at second hand. A more genuine discussion would have been produced from the assembling of a wider spectrum of views. The reader is left with a misleading impression of consensus that does not exist.

Nor do the papers achieve as much as they promise. They were essentially reflections, on both the authors' own work and that of others, efforts at synthesis rather than the product of new research; and this attempt to trade 'new thoughts for old' was by and large disappointing. Holmes developed the Plumb theme of stability. Dickinson re-hashed his views on Whiggism. Speck made a brave attempt to delineate the state of politics under George II in the light of current work, most of which took a pounding. O'Gorman's survey of George III's reign was centred on the Rockingham-Fox connexion, which hardly made for originality or balance; symptomatic of a somewhat cavalier approach was his failure to distinguish between the two Dr Mitchells mentioned on pages 91 and 93. Apart from Speck, the most successful attempt at a synthesis came in Cannon's analysis of the end of this political system in the early nineteenth century. Derry's look at government between 1780 and 1830 was handicapped by the lack of sufficient detailed work on the ministries of Pitt and Liverpool. Since the earlier papers were all concerned in some way with government and politics, the final one by McCord on economic and social development during the Industrial Revolution looked quite out of place.

The book is clearly aimed primarily at an undergraduate audience, both as a deliberate revelation of how their seniors operate and as a valuable collection of short-cuts through the scholarly jungle of Hanoverian politics. Conversely it could also prove a useful source of examination questions! But it has little that is new for the specialist and assumes too much for the general reader or those previously ignorant of the subject. Better in conception than in execution must be the verdict on this enterprising and novel idea.

PETER D.G. THOMAS
University College of Wales, Aberystwyth

Ireland in the Age of Imperialism and Revolution 1760–1801. By R.B. McDowell. Oxford: Clarendon Press. 1979. vii, 739 pp. £28.00.

It is inevitable that Professor McDowell's latest book will create comment and controversy, because he has chosen to display his vast knowledge and impressive historical skills within the framework laid down over a hundred years ago by the Victorian historian W.E.H. Lecky in his five-volume *History of Ireland in the Eighteenth Century* — a monumental work which has been skilfully abridged by Professor L.P. Curtis (University of Chicago Press, 1972). It would, however, be wrong to talk of McDowell, or for that matter Curtis, as superseding Lecky. The Curtis abridgment highlights the structure and shape of Lecky's work, which tends to get lost in a great wealth of detail, while at the same time indicating the unique flavour and quality of the great historian. McDowell broadens, expands and elucidates Lecky. All three books have an essential place on the desk of any historian of eighteenth-century Ireland, and a case could also be argued for their prominence on the bookshelves of any serious historian of Britain or the British Empire and Commonwealth in the later modern period.

Like Lecky's great masterpiece, this book is very long and heavily weighted towards the 1790s. It is remarkably free of obvious errors (though there is some confusion on p. 285, where 'brother' should be substituted for 'cousin' in relation to Charles Francis Sheridan, under-secretary in the Military Department 1782–9, a relationship which is quite correctly stated on p. 317). The book has been well produced in the traditional format of the Clarendon Press, with the carefully prepared footnotes conveniently placed at the bottom of each page. Professor McDowell has obviously had the same difficulty in organizing his massive corpus of material as confronted Lecky — and every subsequent scholar who has embarked on a wide-ranging study of this field. The book is divided into 19 chapters, grouped into three sections: 'Background', 'Constitutional Conflict', 'Revolutionary Era'. The first two sections (pp. 1–351) summarize the existing state of our knowledge and do this very clearly; the important section is the third, which amounts to almost exactly the second half of the book.

Not the least of this book's many virtues is its admirable clarity; Chapter 17, 'Insurrection', contains the most succinct description of the '98 rebellion I have read, while the preceding chapter, 'The Maintenance of Law and Order', is one of the highlights of the book and displays Professor McDowell's great gift for cutting through a mass of detail to pinpoint the basic issues involved. In fact, the strength of the book probably lies in the light which it throws on the problems inherent in the application of the English legal system to Irish conditions. Professor McDowell, although writing from the viewpoint of the Anglican governing class, is particularly useful in his understanding of that other Protestant nation, the Ulster presbyterians. He highlights their influence on the organization of the United Irishmen, their belief in education, and the extent to which they were a separate strand in Irish society. Another important aspect of the book is its discussion of urban problems (pp. 21–37), and the structure of Dublin corporation, a body of considerable commercial and political importance.

It is indisputably the author's prerogative to define his field, although it might be queried why the word 'imperialism' is used in the title when the author avoids any major discussion of even the important imperial issues of the 1760s, 1770s and 1780s! On p. 53 Professor McDowell states that 'the state was hesitant to advance into the wide and controversial field of social welfare' and continues by emphasizing that private 'benevolence was a virtue which the eighteenth century held in high regard'. This latter point is quite correct, but the *Journals of the House of Commons* and the other parliamentary papers, about which Professor McDowell is very knowledgeable, do not entirely bear out this *laissez-faire* concept. Within the framework available to the eighteenth-century state, considerable efforts were made in the fields of poverty, sickness, unemployment and education. It is true that the results were frequently disastrous, but the intention certainly existed, and there was an area in which private benevolence and public intention merged, for instance in parliamentary grants for hospitals, *etc.*

On large issues there is a selective approach; for example, there is a good discussion of the modernization of the university curriculum under Provost Hely-Hutchinson after he had been 'almost stung to death by obtruding into the hive of the academics', but virtually nothing is said about education at other levels, and of other groups than the privileged undergraduates of Dublin University. On some broad themes like liberalism, radicalism and their connexion with romanticism, the book draws interesting interconnexions and makes stimulating comments. Professor McDowell also offers valuable insights into late eighteenth-century liberalism and radicalism, and it is here that the author's unrivalled knowledge of the eighteenth-century political press is best displayed. His perhaps unduly favourable interpretation of Pitt, and the implied prominence of Irish affairs in his thoughts, is a useful counterbalance to Lecky's very critical assessment of the leading British minister of the late eighteenth century.

In no part of the book is the author's individualistic approach more clearly shown than in the bibliography. In it he lists an impressive number of original sources, mainly official papers and contemporary books, pamphlets and newspapers. He then gives a list of secondary authorities which, with the exception of R.J. Coughlan's *Napper Tandy* (1976), does not list a single work published in the ten years preceding the publication of this book. It would therefore appear to be out of date as a synthesis of recent modern scholarship. However, from internal evidence, it seems probable that Professor McDowell has read a selective list from the many important monographs of the last decade, with, apparently, three major omissions: W.A. Maguire, *The Downshire Estates* (1972); A.P.W. Malcomson, *John Foster: The Politics of the Anglo-Irish Ascendancy* (1978) and *Penal Era and Golden Age*, eds. T. Bartlett and D. Hayton (1979). There is no list of theses consulted and no consolidated list of periodical articles, although there are some references in footnotes. The book is not particularly concerned with economic and social history apart from the odd comment on a specific topic, and hence there is no reference to the important new journal of the '70s, *Irish Economic and Social History*, although it is unlikely that anyone working in Trinity College would have been unaware of it.

Initially, *Ireland in the Age of Imperialism and Revolution* appears to be dated and therefore a little disappointing, particularly in the light of Professor McDowell's great knowledge of the period. I put down the book very conscious of the difficulties, particularly the organizational difficulties, which had confronted the author, but nevertheless wondering if he had done himself justice. However, it is a book which, I think, will stand the test of that ultimate reviewer, time.

E.M. JOHNSTON
Macquarie University

The Writings and Speeches of Edmund Burke. General Editor: Paul Langford. Oxford: Clarendon Press. *Volume II: Party, Parliament and the American Crisis 1766–1774.* Edited by Paul Langford. 1981. xviii, 508 pp. £40.00. *Volume V: India: Madras and Bengal 1774–1785.* Edited by P.J. Marshall. 1981. xv, 667 pp. £55.00.

Professor T.W. Copeland launched the great project of a modern edition of the works of Edmund Burke during the 1950s and conducted the first, and essential, part of it, the *Correspondence*, through to completion in 1978. Sadly he has not lived to see in print any part of the *Writings and Speeches*, the first two volumes of which (out of a projected eight) have now reached completion. Dr Langford and Professor Marshall have maintained his high standards of editing at the outset of an undertaking which, in some respects, is more testing than the *Correspondence*. For if the more familiar pamphlets — the great set pieces like the *Thoughts on the Cause of the Present Discontents* — present relatively few problems, this is far from the case with many of the speeches. Newspaper reporting of debates was carried on under such difficult conditions, and often with so little scruple, that Burke himself declared: 'they are rarely genuine; they are for the most part extremely misrepresented, often through ignorance, often through design; and very frequently the whole is a mere matter of invention.' Langford has been the more fortunate to be able to draw upon the records left by three noted parliamentary diarists, Nathaniel Ryder, Sir Henry Cavendish and Matthew Brickdale, whose reports are generally more reliable than those of any newspaper, but these are not always full or easy to follow, and only here and there are they — possibly — verbatim. In some cases it has also been possible to make use of notes and drafts surviving in Burke's papers, but this sort of material presents its own problems. It is not always apparent which is the final of several surviving drafts. Moreover, intentions set down on paper were not always necessarily pursued in the course of debate. Given all these difficulties the editors — and also the textual editor, Professor William B. Todd — deserve high praise for the skill with which they have sifted, collated, and exploited these various sources. In dealing with the speeches they have also faced formidable problems of selection. Their choice has been dictated partly by their judgment of the reliability and value of various reports, partly by their concern to present the key evidence displaying the general development of Burke's thought and beliefs on questions of substance. Both volumes contain appendices giving references to the many speeches not selected for publication. Between Burke's election to the Commons in January 1766 and the dissolution of 1774, he is known to have spoken over 230 times in the House: 39 of these speeches are included in Langford's volume. Marshall lists sources for 84 speeches on East India Company affairs between 1774 and 1785, but has selected only 11 for publication.

The presentation of the *Writings and Speeches* in two series, each of four volumes, the second of them relating specifically to Burke's concern with East India affairs, is probably preferable to a strictly chronological sequence. Nevertheless, the arrangement will present some problems to users of the series, who will have to keep in mind the need for synoptic examination of the material. Home and Indian affairs cannot be studied in this period in isolation from their common context. In particular, the preconceptions which Burke formed about the domestic political situation deeply coloured in some ways his approach to Indian problems.

Volume II covers Burke's career during years when these preconceptions were being formed, and when he was stepping into a particular role in the service of the party led by Lord Rockingham with which he had finally cast his political fortunes. Many years ago one scholar referred to him as 'the perfect butler'. This provocative description has since drawn scornful comment: nevertheless, it was not wholly wide of the mark, for at least up till the early 1780s Burke commonly deferred on matters of policy to the leading men of his party and accepted a clearly subordinate position. Between 1766 and 1774 he became the chief supporting speaker to the Rockinghamite leader in the Commons, William Dowdeswell, habitually intervening at a late stage in debate with the intention of effectively demolishing the arguments used by critics of his party; he became, as it were, 'the cavalry troop of the party's debating strength'. Langford sees the emergence of this role in an important parliamentary partnership as one arising out of the superior effectiveness of Dowdeswell in handling financial affairs (always a major topic in the Commons). But weight should perhaps also be given to the fact that Burke lacked the social prestige to attain leadership: being an Irish outsider who did not belong by family background to the charmed circle of the landed class was a handicap he was never to overcome. Langford suggests that the debating pattern set in the 1770s made it the more difficult for Burke to emerge as a leader in debate later in his career, but surely here, also, the social disadvantage loomed large. Like Sheridan, Burke was a brilliant auxiliary but could never become a chief. By contrast birth and brilliance together could carry to the top Charles James Fox, a man of far less intellectual or moral ballast; before the age Burke entered Parliament Fox had become a secretary of state.

Burke's interest in India did not begin in 1774. It seems to have long predated his entry into Parliament, and he intervened in debate on the subject on a number of occasions in 1767, 1769, 1772 and 1773. But it was in the late 1770s that his ideas on India, like those of other politicians, began to gain both depth and range, as he and they came to realize the gravity of the problems created by the East India Company in South Asia and to measure them against the keen sense of moral responsibility for human welfare engendered at that time as much by the Enlightenment as by the traditions of the Christian churches. Up till the 1770s M.P.s and ministers alike thought of the Company's growing political role simply as one which would enable it to pay substantial dues to the Treasury: no one thought about the quality of government experienced by the native populations under its sway. The idea that Indians should enjoy a rule of laws, that they should be free of oppression, that their lives, liberty and property were as deserving of protection as those of Englishmen in whose land John Locke's theories of the state had become axiomatic, took root only slowly after the passage of Lord North's Regulating Act of 1773. By the early 1780s it was becoming a matter of conviction among that minority of politicians, including Burke, who had begun to devote major attention to the question. In fact, the weight of the contents of Volume V, in which this development in Burke is traced, is almost wholly on the years 1781–5.

From the early 1770s, Burke's approach to the Indian problem was essentially coloured by the interpretation of domestic politics which he had articulated in the *Thoughts on the Present Discontents*. This affected his attitude to both measures and men.

Assuming it was necessary to strive against the corrupt effects of patronage, owing to the dangerous powers this placed in the hands of the sinister secret cabal which Burke had postulated, then this ruled out any direct administration of Indian territory by the Crown and dictated the adoption of whatever expedients might be available to circumvent this. In 1772–3 Burke and his party had accordingly pressed for a continuance of Company administration. But by 1780 the shortcomings of such a system were becoming only too apparent, and some form of closer control appeared essential. By 1783, as a result of his participation in parliamentary investigations and his personal contacts, including his kinsman, William Burke, Burke had become the most knowledgeable man on the subject in his party, and indeed perhaps in the Commons. His solution was the establishment of a commission which would take basic political decisions and impose sanctions of inquiry and punishment, while the Company remained responsible for the appointment of its servants. He was appalled by the extent of the influence awarded to the executive government in 1784 under Pitt's India Act, after the bill he had done much to frame had been buried in the ruins of the Fox-North Coalition. This same suspicion of secret influence heightened Burke's animus against individuals in India who, to save their ill-gotten gains, cultivated, or appeared to cultivate, the politicians who kept his party out of office. The development of his unbalanced attack is well revealed in the important pieces Marshall has chosen for publication, including reports of the House of Commons select committee on East Indian affairs. The cumulative effect of passionate denunciation in many of these documents and speeches tends to have an overwhelming effect. A deliberate act of will is necessary on the part of the reader to recall that Burke was sometimes misled by the malicious and self-interested testimony of Philip Francis and other witnesses; and that although much was wrong with the East India Company's activities in India, nevertheless the House of Lords in its capacity as a legal tribunal ultimately absolved the Company's chief servant, Warren Hastings, of the many charges laid against him. Parliamentary investigations in the eighteenth century could not be trusted, and were no more reliable than those who mounted them and those who performed in them would allow — a point also conspicuously clear from the use by Burke's party of parliamentary inquiries into North American affairs in the spring of 1766.

IAN R. CHRISTIE
University College, London

The English Administrative System 1780–1870. By Sir Norman Chester. Oxford: Clarendon Press. 1981. [iii,] 398 pp. £22.50.

Nineteenth-century English government may have grown under its own momentum, but the historiography of nineteenth-century English administration certainly has not. The great boom in Victorian studies so marked since the later

1960s has not extended to Victorian administration; equally, the new ways in history so enthusiastically explored in those same years have not led to a 'new' administrative history equipped with its own societies, newsletters and research centres, although in 1969 a notable colloquium seemed to foreshadow something of the sort. Yet in reality more nineteenth-century administrative history is currently being written than annual lists of publications or theses in progress immediately suggest. Not only the great departments of state, but such topics as the relations between legislative and executive or between central and local authorities have indeed been left relatively undisturbed; but the same cannot be said of such matters as the processes of making and implementing official decisions, or the changing boundaries of public action. Today it is often through work on interest groups, policy-making and many other aspects of political, economic, social and intellectual history that nineteenth-century government is becoming better understood. Urban history, to take one example, has already provided by implication a quite copious 'new' history of local government.

Nevertheless anyone who sets out to write not an interpretative sketch nor an *état des questions* but a solid, rounded history of the fundamental changes which took place in the English system of government in the century before the 1880s must still give essentially the same account as the one which could and should have been written some 20 years ago. After the Second World War historians working in this field were in broad agreement upon the major constitutional, financial and administrative developments of the years between 1780 and 1870. Authority became concentrated rather than diffused. The authority of the Crown replaced that of the King; and his servants became employees not office-holders, and moreover employees who worked within constraints imposed by political rather than legal responsibility for their actions. The hierarchical ministerial department and a permanent professional civil service came to dominate Whitehall, a unified financial system under parliamentary and Treasury control was established, and local government came to feel new pressures from without, particularly financial ones. A number of much appreciated studies of one or other of these developments appeared; but no single account was produced which connected them all, still less one which brought out not only the legal and institutional changes, but the shifts in the assumptions animating the whole system.

It is precisely this missing book which Sir Norman Chester has now given us as the first literary fruit of his retirement. *The English Administrative System 1780–1870* combines abundant factual information with an interpretation which links together each of these trends. Nor is this all. Written as it is by a distinguished member of the generation which pioneered the academic study of public administration in this country, whose own experience as practitioner, author and teacher of public administration stretches back over 60 years, this book is permeated by the intellectual tones of a world now submerged beneath the waves of specialization and expansion. In it distant echoes can be picked up of the urbane, relaxed, confident style of Bagehot, Maitland or Lowell; Sir Norman talks (he does not seem to be writing) authoritatively and diffusely to people who share his assumptions and interests, but happen to know nothing about his subject. Clear in expression, anodyne in content, his language is reminiscent of the white papers of the past (a *genre* to which Sir Norman has himself made notable contributions, and which he has used here as a staple source). It goes without saying that so distinctive a style has brought some penalties as well as bonuses. Outright beginners will prefer the business-like outline provided by G.K. Fry in 1979. The able students and mature general readers whom the book should attract may have their confidence undermined by some sweeping outdated judgments on much-studied aspects of the history of King, Cabinet and Parliament, and by the absence of a political dimension; while their patience may be tried by its combination of recondite antiquarian snippets with rudimentary constitutional law. Any knowledgeable reader under the age of 45 will be likely to think it old-fashioned in matter and manner; and every reader without exception will think the Clarendon Press should be ashamed of pages so typographically faulty and unsightly.

This is not a workaday book. It is a characterful product of an outstanding vintage, which demonstrates that among historians 'dated' ought not necessarily to be a pejorative term. Its author has never before tried to handle a past earlier than his own lifetime. Amateur history, however, can have a value which professional history cannot match, at least when it comes from an amateur who has been, in the words of the *festschrift* published in Sir Norman's honour, 'a productive and authoritative scholar, a remarkable Head of House', and an accomplished professional in so many adjoining fields.

OLIVE ANDERSON
Westfield College, London

Order and Equipoise: The Peerage and the House of Lords 1783–1806. By Michael W.McCahill. London: Royal Historical Society, Studies in History series No. 11; published for the Royal Historical Society by Swift Printers (Publishers) Ltd. 1978. x, 256 pp. £15.00 (£9.60 for members of the Society).

Having been almost completely bypassed in the current preoccupation with party ideology, elections and popular politics, the eighteenth-century House of Lords is now receiving some of the scholarly attention which it has long merited. There has been no treatment in depth since that of A.S. Turberville, who wrote in the 1920s, and even the superb volumes of the *History of Parliament* confine their analyses solely to the Commons. The sense of deprivation increases as one approaches the final years of the century, since recent revisions of the parliamentary history of that period, including detailed studies of the Foxite Whig party, have had disappointingly little to say about the Lords. The first signs of a revival of interest in the upper chamber began to appear several years ago in the pages of the learned journals, as such crucial sources as Lords' division lists gradually came to light and as the leadership of the House and the purposes of Lords' protests were elucidated. A work of synthesis to consolidate and if possible extend this modern research and to provide a survey long enough to enable the principal themes to be identified was therefore most necessary. It is this which Michael W. McCahill seeks to provide.

The choice of period emphasizes the need for his book. For the late eighteenth and early nineteenth centuries witnessed a remarkable transformation in the composition and character of the House of Lords. There was, of course, a rapid and sudden expansion in its membership, both hereditary and non-hereditary. The Hamilton judgment of 1782 allowed the Crown to confer the dignity of a British peerage, with full rights of summons to the House of Lords, upon peers of Scotland; the Act of Union with Ireland added 28 representative peers, elected for life, and four bishops, to its numbers, and the younger Pitt was responsible for almost 100 new peerage creations. It has been estimated that, excluding the royal dukes, the membership of the House of Lords grew from 238 to 358 between 1783 and 1831. At the same time there is evidence of a tightening of the aristocratic grip upon the unreformed institutions of government as the influence of the peerage in the Church, through episcopal appointments, and the House of Commons, through nomination to boroughs, perceptibly increased. It might be an exaggeration to speak of an 'aristocratic resurgence' in these years but the House of Lords undoubtedly exerted much influence in economy and society while playing a vital and sometimes decisive part in parliamentary politics.

A sensitive understanding of all these changes pervades McCahill's researches. As the author of a series of articles, notably on the Scottish peerage, he brings impressive qualifications to his task and one's expectations of a careful and thorough book are not disappointed. There are useful discussions of procedure, of proxy voting, and of the peers' attendance at and participation in debates. A particularly valuable chapter on the conduct of private business will complement the work of P.D.G. Thomas and Sheila Lambert on the House of Commons. Readers will also appreciate the convenient listing in the appendices of those peers who held government or household office and exercised parliamentary patronage. Against this background McCahill offers a competent examination of the place of the House of Lords in the constitution and presents it as the 'upholder of the equipoise'. He is at pains to stress the dominance of the House by politicians, men of business and lawyers, its essential role in times of serious ministerial instability and its effectiveness as a second chamber in the revision and correction of legislation. Nor, he argues, can the House of Lords simply be regarded as 'the scourge of reformers'; even the formidable opposition of Thurlow could not thwart the passage of relief measures for Roman Catholics and Scottish Episcopalians, while in 1806–7 the Lords consented to the abolition of the British slave trade. Two later chapters examine the growing electoral influence of the nobility and the link which industrial patronage and the promotion of local interests helped to forge between the peers and the national community. The author concludes with the claim (p.208) that their lordships 'endowed the unreformed parliament with a certain vitality by giving access to power to the nation's under-represented regions and propertied interests'.

This is an elevated view indeed and the author provides much substance in its support. That the House of Lords accorded with the national mood on many issues and that it benefited from the climate of loyalism in the 1790s cannot seriously be doubted. But in two respects McCahill comes dangerously close to overstating his case. He continually emphasizes the independence of the House of Lords, noting its 'watchfulness and exertion' (p.14) and claiming that 'national policy and important legislation were scrutinized in debates, often intelligently' (p.88). One would certainly agree that this was a far cry from Chesterfield's 'hospital for incurables'. What needs to be asked, however, is whether between 1783 and 1806 the House of Lords ever showed genuine or sustained independence of a ministry which was fully supported by the Crown. Both McCahill's examples of the way in which a collapse of support in the Lords contributed to the fall of an administration suggest a negative answer. For in December 1783 when the Lords rejected the Fox-North Coalition's India Bill the royal disapproval of ministers could hardly have been more public, while in 1804 the decline of the Addington administration began with falling majorities in the Commons and it is a considerable exaggeration to assert (p.88) that 'the House of Lords drove Addington from office'. The truth is that although the House of Lords at times clashed with the Commons it never entered into sustained conflict with a Commons majority supported by the King. This is hardly surprising. Most of its members were reluctant to resist or weaken the royal authority. McCahill constantly and rightly insists upon the conservatism of the upper House and its respect for existing constitutional practice. It follows that any 'independence' which it displayed took only one form. The Lords might have behaved independently in resisting change, but independent initiatives in a radical direction, like those of the third Earl Stanhope, were quickly swept aside.

Secondly, McCahill devotes a chapter to those elements — household officers, bishops, Scottish representative peers and newly created or promoted peers — which formed the solid predictable basis of the government majority in the House of Lords and which, in the analysis of Dr D. Large's important article, emerged as the 'Party of the Crown'.[1] But McCahill seeks to challenge their status as a party, denying that they were bound together by the ties of patronage and attributing their loyalty to the exercise of individual consciences. These peers, he insists, were the 'King's Friends', not the Crown's 'political bondsmen'. This amounts to little more than a quibble. The identity of interest shared by these groups was sufficiently strong to render a sophisticated organization unnecessary. To argue that they 'never constituted a party in the sense that the whigs were a party' (p.158) is to make an unreal comparison because the Whigs were engaged in the pursuit of electoral advantage and the management of campaigns in the Commons, exercises fundamentally different from the control of the Lords. The cynic might add that the Whig organization could not save the party from disintegration in the 1790s, while the strength of the Crown's following in the House of Lords became ever greater. Serious divisions among the pro-government peers were rare. Some of their number, particularly the Scots, were prepared to go their own way if their special interests so dictated. Occasionally the 'King's Friends' were not altogether certain as to where their personal allegiance in the Lords actually lay; at times they entertained doubts about some areas of policy. Yet these instances tend to be the exceptions which prove the rule. When the conjunction of Thurlow's removal from the woolsack and the second reading of Fox's Libel Bill in May 1792 brought the personal and political unease together, the *Caledonian Mercury* sensed an event rare enough to be newsworthy:[2]

> The division in the House of Lords on Mr. Fox's important bill for ascertaining the functions of Juries in trials for libel was very interesting to the political observer in the present curious moment. The Bedchamber Lords, with only one exception (Earl Fauconberg) voted with the Ex-Chancellor. The Marquis of Salisbury, who owes his continuance in place to Mr. Pitt, against all the influence of Lord Thurlow, and Lord Winchelsea, who is in the Queen's Household, voted against the Chancellor. And what is as marked as any of the above instances, the new Lord Dorchester, who owes his peerage directly to the King, voted with Lord Thurlow. The Marquises of Stafford and Bath withdrew before the division.

Here the followers of the Crown were faced by the divided loyalties which naturally arose when a powerful figure left office. Some of them also experienced the misgivings which seized ministerial adherents when the Lords debated a reforming measure which had won the approval or acquiescence of the government itself. But this too was a display of independence in a conservative direction and it was insufficient to defeat the Libel Bill. As long as clear leadership was provided and as long as dangerous innovations were avoided the traditional supporters of the Crown were capable of voting in a remarkably united way in support of a ministry. Dr Large's view of the 'Party of the Crown' emerges unscathed from this book and will remain a significant landmark for historians.

One's other complaints are relatively minor ones. It is somewhat confusing to be told that 'great care was taken by ministers ... to see that peers did not attend unnecessarily' (p.15) and yet that 'ministers continued to summon peers to divisions even when the opposition was numerically insignificant' (p 154) The omission from the bibliography of N. Ravitch, *Sword and Mitre* is odd, since no other work so clearly illustrates the increase in the number of bishops of noble birth during the later eighteenth century. McCahill's style throughout is rather flat and pedestrian by comparison with the crisp authority of his articles. None of this, however, should disguise the real merits of the book. Lucidity and precision are its main virtues and the author is at his best when dealing with attendance, procedure and parliamentary business. *Order and Equipoise* may not present any dramatic breakthrough in terms of new evidence or interpretation. But it is a welcome step in the process by which the late eighteenth-century House of Lords is restored to a well deserved position of academic prominence.

G.M. DITCHFIELD
University of Kent at Canterbury

Notes

[1] 'The Decline of the "Party of the Crown" and the Rise of Parties in the House of Lords, 1783–1837,' *E.H.R.*, LXXVIII (1963), 669–95.
[2] *Caledonian Mercury*, 26 May 1792.

Castlereagh. By Wendy Hinde. London: Collins. 1981. 320 pp. £16.00.

This is a well written, scholarly and useful book. Dividing Castlereagh's career into Irish, English and European dimensions, the author guides the reader through his successive administrative responsibilities with a crisp style and a convincing grasp of the options he faced and those that he chose, or was obliged to follow. There is, as far as I can tell, hardly a serious error of fact or, on the basis of the several specialist studies of his career from which the author draws quite freely, any distortion of the different contexts into which his actions have to be placed. Moreover a clear line of interpretation runs through the study: of a man of moderate intellect and ambition who was prepared to devote his considerable aptitude for administration and personal diplomacy to win the war and avert revolution. Thus as far as the Irish phase of his career is concerned she argues that his conversion from a moderate Whig in 1790 to a Pittite in 1795 was not due to opportunism but rather to the combined effect of the progress of the French Revolution, the disorder in Ireland, and the force of Pitt's personality (p. 40). Later, she takes an equally circumspect view of his conduct as Chief Secretary at the time of the Union. He is therefore portrayed as one who genuinely believed that Ireland would benefit from the measure (p. 97) and praised for advocating that it should be accompanied by three specific measures of reform: political equality for Catholics; tithe commutation; and state provision for Catholic and Dissenting clergy (p. 98). He is criticized, on the other hand, for failing to recognize that by deploying all the available means of influence to win a majority for the measure in the Irish House of Commons he might 'tarnish a worthy end' (pp. 87, 97).

Moving to the 'English' dimension, that is Castlereagh's career as President of the Board of Control under Addington and Pitt and as Secretary for War under Portland, the author draws, on balance, more critical conclusions about his administrative abilities. She praises his militia measures of 1807 and 1808 which improved upon his predecessor's attempts to raise the level of recruitment into the regular army (pp. 128–32); gives faint praise to his earlier efforts to check expansionism in India and the autonomous tendencies of the Company directors (pp. 111–15); and condemns the expeditions which he sponsored as war minister, all of which flew in the face of military opinion and proved to be failures (pp. 168–9). It is against this background that the causes and consequences of the famous duel between Castlereagh and Canning are discussed, the author confirming that although Canning's case for removing his colleague from the War Department was probably justified, his methods were underhand (p. 167).

Following an interesting chapter on Castlereagh out of office between 1809 and February 1812 (in which the point is made that his popularity rose as a reaction to Canning's duplicity) the author deals with him at the height of his career: as Foreign Secretary and leader of the Commons until his death in 1822. In the former case she distinguishes carefully between the humdrum and brilliant features of Castlereagh's diplomacy. Thus she points with the one hand to his well known reliance upon Pitt's peace plans of 1805 (p. 190); to his curious choice of Aberdeen for a mission to Vienna (p. 194); to his surprise at Harrowby's suggestion that he should travel to Europe in 1814 (p. 198); and the failure in the Vienna negotiations to check Russia's expansion through Poland (p. 228). And, with the other, underlines the novelty of his concept of a 'perpetual defensive alliance' to preserve a peace (p. 195) and the persuasiveness of his personal diplomacy at Chaumont (p. 208), Paris and, particularly in the matter of Russia, at Vienna (pp. 227–8). A similar mixed verdict is recorded as to his leadership of the Commons. He emerges, therefore, as a leader who experienced success and failure in both debate and management and, in view of the Home Secretary being in the House of Lords, as the popular scapegoat for the repressive legislation which he introduced in 1817 and 1819–20. In fact the overall impression is of a man who progresses in the service of the political and social status quo, not brilliantly, not always with success but hardly ever with personal dishonour — only to commit suicide when the strain of office and, in the author's view, the shock waves of his father's death, proved too much.

My reservations about this portrait rest more upon the scale of the work and the points of emphasis or the lack of them, than the technical execution. Thus I would question whether sufficient analysis was devoted to Castlereagh's merits as a diplomatist either as Chief Secretary or Foreign Secretary. It is true that specialist studies of these aspects of his career are in print but it sometimes seems that in omitting so much of the detail of diplomacy the author diminishes the complexities of the issues and obscures rather than clarifies the points where Castlereagh's contribution was vital. In addition, I wonder whether sufficient emphasis has been placed upon Castlereagh's debt to Pitt? The two men were a good deal closer than is suggested here and one cannot help being struck by Castlereagh's deference to Pitt's policies both before and after the latter's death. The author certainly notes most if not all the examples of deference (the scheme to reform the relationship between the state and religion was not unique to Castlereagh) but does not give them sufficient emphasis as an explanation of Castlereagh's political thinking.

Finally there is insufficient analysis of Castlereagh's qualities as a parliamentarian. The point that his performances varied considerably is certainly made but why and with what results are questions that are not answered satisfactorily. In short, although the author has written the best available account of her subject, questions remain about the qualities and circumstances which propelled an Irishman with never more than a handful of personal supporters to within an ace of the premiership.

P.J.JUPP
Queen's University, Belfast

The Seventh Earl of Shaftesbury. By Geoffrey B.A.M. Finlayson. London: Eyre Methuen. 1981. 639 pp. £19.50.

The best, or at least the most enjoyable, lives of men are written with a passion. Think of Edith Sitwell's loving defence of Pope or of Disraeli's endeavour (no doubt partly from self-seeking motives) to erect Lord George Bentinck into a hero. A biographer enjoys great freedom. No one expects logical consistency from him, since he is not, after all, pursuing an argument or analyzing a proposition. Nor can anyone justly complain that he misrepresents his subject's motives or feelings: who among us can give an adequate account of his own? Biography resembles fiction even more closely than most history books.

Biographies of politicians are, *pace* Disraeli, only marginally contributions to history. There lies the snare. Lord Ashley, the seventh Earl of Shaftesbury, compels the attention of posterity neither by his thoughts — from early manhood he lost, as, sadly, most politicians do, the habit of reading — nor by his private life. Geoffrey Finlayson wisely pays little attention to them (although he intersperses his narrative of Ashley's public career with somewhat shamefaced résumés of his subject's domestic life). Not a single letter is reproduced in full, nor, by the end of the book, are we any the wiser about the nature or extent of Ashley's private friendships. On the other hand, our understanding of nineteenth-century Evangelicalism and social reform, notwithstanding the central position Ashley occupied in both movements, is little advanced by the detailed account of his career which Mr Finlayson gives us. A more local difficulty arises from the fact that, although Ashley lived until 1885 and continued almost until his death to campaign unstintingly on behalf of the wretched of England, the point of his career, the fight for the ten-hour day in the textile mills, had largely been won by the late 1840s. Thereafter, although Shaftesbury's interest did not wane, ours does.

Mr Finlayson, casting doubts aside, has decided to give each stage of Ashley's life (except, mercifully, his childhood and youth) equal treatment. The effect is that of a flat, aerial photograph, not a relief map, but the result is a more thorough exposition of Shaftesbury's public activities than we have had before. The whole is written in a chaste prose appropriate to Mr Finlayson's method. Readers who want to know in detail Ashley's contribution to the establishment of the Jerusalem bishopric, the working of the metropolitan lunacy commission, the operation of the ragged schools or the debates on the justness of the Crimean war will be grateful to Mr Finlayson. He is a scrupulous historian — cautious, accurate, informed. Perhaps historians' debates about matters on the periphery of Ashley's concerns — Peel's handling of the repeal crisis, for instance — might have been more succinctly put or left out altogether, but the trouble, I suspect, is that Mr Finlayson is too intelligent an historian to be have been seduced by the meretricious charms of biography.

Ashley's outpourings in his voluminous, tediously repetitive, diaries reveal him in his true colours of self-lacerating self-justification. Despite his fame and the contemporary recognition of his due, Shaftesbury was an isolated figure, unloved by the public and distrusted by the Tory party. No true reformer can afford to seek love and Ashley did not shrink from giving offence by his opinions and his persistence in unpopular causes. Night after night he returned to his study, weary of the world's cupidity and indolence, to console himself with the sure knowledge that every step he took, every suggestion he made, was working God's purpose in the world. The Board of Health, he told Lord John Russell, was effecting 'all the wise, beautiful and sanitary regulations of the Levitical Code'. There was point to Pusey's plea that if Ashley would think more mildly of the Tractarians and try to love them more, he might come to understand them better. Evangelical fervour led Ashley to make rash judgments: Gladstone's Puseyism (not in itself a very subtle way to describe Gladstone's religious opinions in the 1840s) would render him 'strange and useless' throughout his life; Russell's Durham Letter, which everyone of sense and experience knew to be a piece of political opportunism, and not a very judicious one at that, was, for Ashley, the finest thing in 300 years of English history. Mr Finlayson, in the taciturn way in which he respects his readers' intelligence, lets it be seen that Ashley, clear-sighted in the particular matter at hand, allowed wishful thinking to cloud his wider vision. The Ten Hours Act of 1847 and the Public Health Act of the following year were proof that the aristocracy and the people, after a long separation, were re-approaching one another. 'Oh Cobden, Bright and all that dismal crew, you will be crushed in the friendly collision!'

Ashley was often fierce in his denunciation of the wicked, that is, of people whose brand of Christianity did not suit him (and it seems never to have occurred to him that the wayward behaviour of his eldest son, behaviour which brought Ashley much pain and sorrow, might have been caused by the father's self-righteousness). But it is one of the merits of Mr Finlayson's book that Ashley is shown not to have been an entire bigot. He could step out of his Evangelical straitjacket to serve the larger purposes of the Christian faith — to co-operate with Dissenters in missionary work in the Far East and with the Protestant Church of Prussia in the establishment of the Jerusalem bishopric.

Mr Finlayson's book makes it abundantly clear that Ashley's appetite for social reform was fed by his social conservatism. Although he came to support Free Trade, Ashley was not an anti-Peelite Tory for nothing. Since working-class discontent was the gravest threat to the social order, its causes must be removed — by better education (although Ashley sneered at the progressive, scientific temper of the age), by better housing, by better working conditions. Mr Finlayson is less forthcoming about the connexion in Ashley's mind between his Evangelicalism and his social conscience, implying (if I have not missed the argument) that they amounted to the same thing. Not only is the argument tautologous, it robs Evangelicalism of its variety and complexity.

But then, Mr Finlayson is not interested in explaining Ashley. Instead, he lays his works before us. He neither prosecutes nor defends. Whom this book will serve it is not easy to see. It is long. It is not cheap. Yet neither social nor political historians will find much in it that is new or controversial. And it is too much like an *Annual Register* account of Ashley's life to find favour among the biography-quaffing public, whose hunger for past gossip shows few signs of being sated. Perhaps, swept midst the confused pretensions of the psycho-historians and the prurient omniscience of the modern crowd of biographers, we should count our blessings.

ROBERT STEWART

British Interparty Conferences: A Study of the Procedure of Conciliation in British Politics 1867–1921. By John D. Fair. Oxford: Clarendon Press. 1980. xi, 354 pp. £20.00.

Mr Fair's thesis is that interparty conferences in the late nineteenth and early twentieth centuries alleviated political stress and that, by assisting in the operation of the party system, they were 'a major source of Britain's stability' in a period of intense political conflict. He argues that the dominant tradition in the political historiography of the period emphasizes conflict at the expense of an understanding of the mechanisms of co-operation. He thereby aligns himself with historians as diverse as Dr Morgan and Mr Cowling who have examined the behaviour of politicians working with a set of shared assumptions about party and power, of which the most important is that the political system exists to preserve as far as possible the existing structure of power and social relationships. But in method Fair's work is more narrowly restricted to leading politicians than most recent work on Victorian and early twentieth-century politics, and at the same time more convoluted and less subtle than the historical tradition we have come to know as 'high politics'. On the one hand he assumes, somewhat implausibly and certainly without adequate discussion, that the party system can be understood without reference to the social infrastructure of political allegiance. Commenting on the importance of legitimacy in the development of political institutions, he writes as though 'some semblance of a national consensus' could be created if the opposition took part in the decision about a constitutional change; but he does not feel the need to explain why or whether political parties were themselves recognized as legitimate. On the other hand he has written a whole book on the premise that politicians are men who mean what they say and say what they mean. To sustain this belief through 276 pages and 54 years of British politics is a *tour de force*. Fair's industry is remarkable, his archival work thorough; but his exposition of the interparty conference as a means of maintaining political stability, isolated both from the social basis of consensus and from the continuous febrile interaction of active politicians, makes great demands on the reader's confidence.

Fair discerns twelve occasions of interparty negotiation between the discussions over Irish Disestablishment in 1869 and the Anglo-Irish Treaty negotiations in 1921. Gatherings of between two members (the Disestablishment Conference) and 97 members (the Irish Convention of 1917) are included. The Irish Convention is included even though it was confined to Irishmen of whom only a small minority were parliamentary politicians. The Anglo-Irish Conference of 1921, which other historians have understandably seen as a peace conference between belligerents, Fair treats as a British interparty conference, though half the participants were at war with the British government and the other half were all drawn from the coalition Cabinet. While the Buckingham Palace conference on Home Rule in 1914 was unchallengeably an interparty conference, including Liberals and English

Unionists as well as Nationalist and Ulster Unionist politicians, it is straining a definition to include the discussions between Redmond, Carson and Lloyd George in 1916. To interpret the political crisis of December 1916 as an interparty conference, on the strength of the meeting at Buckingham Palace on 6 December between Asquith, Bonar Law, Lloyd George and Henderson, is quite perverse; the policy and relationships of individuals, not of parties, were at stake, and there was no clash to be resolved between government and opposition.

When the less disputable conferences are considered alone a clearer pattern emerges, not favourable to Fair's thesis. The Disestablishment Conference and the interparty discussions during the Reform crisis of 1884 evidently succeeded in defusing crises: disestablishment went through and the reform package was treated as a body of agreed legislation. These successes Fair describes as 'procedural precedents'. The twentieth-century conferences are presented in two groups: discussions over the Education Bill in 1906, the 1910 constitutional conference, the Irish conference of 1914, the 1916 Irish negotiations, and the December 1916 crisis, are treated as a set; while the 'Lloyd George Era' comprehends the Speaker's Conference on Electoral Reform (summoned under Asquith's premiership), the Second Chamber Conference, the Irish Convention, the 1919 Devolution Conference, and the 1921 Treaty discussions. If the Treaty negotiations, the Irish Convention and the 1916 meetings are excluded as not being interparty in nature, only one of these six encounters (the Speaker's Conference) succeeded in its object. Yet the regime did not fall. This is not much on which to base a theory of political stability. Fair's naïve, formalistic and very lengthy discussion of these minor episodes does not add to our understanding of early twentieth-century British politics. The persistent reader who wonders why the author thought they would add something will learn on the last page that 'the principal value of any study of interparty conferences ... stems from their revelation of the noblest virtues of mankind.' Ah, well. *C'est magnifique, mais ce n'est pas l'histoire.*

JOHN TURNER
Bedford College, London

The Campaign for Prohibition in Victorian England: The United Kingdom Alliance 1872–1895. By A.E. Dingle. London: Croom Helm. 1980. 233 pp. £12.50.

This case-study of a pressure group is as authoritative as Professor McCord's classic study of the Anti-Corn Law League. The United Kingdom Alliance, which fought for total local prohibition by the enactment of machinery for local ratepayers' referenda, was the main prohibitionist body. It was founded in 1853 (and is still going). The author passes lightly but clearly over the years 1853–72, when the Alliance concentrated on educating public opinion, in order to avoid duplicating Brian Harrison's *Drink and the Victorians*. Instead he concentrates on the period 1872–95, when involvement in party politics was greatest and success seemed nearest.

The Alliance was of course its own worst enemy. Dr Dingle explains the reasons for this. Controlled from the top downwards by a Nonconformist, manufacturing, Manchester-based (and ageing) *élite*, it was too provincial to accommodate to parliamentary values, but too rigidly rooted in respectability to reach out to the lower orders (though 172 trade union officials supported the 1895 bill). Most remarkably, perhaps, it failed to politicize more than a small fraction of the huge number of practising abstainers. Prohibitionists, Dr Dingle shows, were 'effective political agitators but poor temperance reformers'.

Useful chapters on 'The Machine' and 'Campaigning' spell this out. Details of leaders, agents, and finances show relative success, as an agitation. Membership (open to drinkers) cost one shilling; it probably reached 30,000, and was usually above 20,000. Both the national secretary and the editor of its newspapers were, surely significantly, vegetarians. By the last quarter of the century, the social and financial centre of gravity of the movement was falling, and the small donor, contrary to the usual pattern, becoming much more important. (Dr Dingle's Monash Ph.D., it should be noted, has biographical details of all Alliance personnel.)

The Alliance failed to develop new techniques of campaigning, except perhaps for its foundation of a news agency. Illusory statistics — in 1888 it held over 4,000 meetings attended by over 1,000,000 people — show only an ability to move the same stage army of the converted from place to place. The Alliance might excel at the appearance of agitation, one supporter distributing 50,000,000 tracts at his own expense, but essentially the correct analogy was with a 'closed' religious sect. It was left to the Salvation Army to modernize agitation.

Dr Dingle treats the convoluted parliamentary aspect of prohibitionism with equal skill. Professor D.A. Hamer, in his *Liberal Politics in the Age of Gladstone and Rosebery* (1972) looked at the question from above; here we have the view from below. Individual politicians play rather a small part. Gladstone, though willing to trim, was no help; as Harcourt said, surely rightly, 'at heart he abhors temperance'. Stating the obvious, Gladstone in 1894 described local prohibitionism as no more than 'a partial and occasional remedy' and preferred municipalization as the only policy 'either promising or tenable'. Chamberlain too preferred municipalization, possibly as a shrewd way of sitting on the fence. Salisbury offered local option with compensation in 1885 as an election gambit, knowing ratepayers had little desire to compensate dispossessed publicans, and this became the Conservative line. Harcourt, the only major figure to take up the temperance cause, did so for reasons which were murkily connected with leadership struggles among Liberals.

In 1871–2 the Alliance caught the radical tide of the late 1860s just as it was going out, and was left with the weak act of 1872. Not till the 1880s did it regain momentum. By 1883 the Liberals were pledged to reform, with compensation to publicans. During the mid-1880s the Alliance captured the National Liberal Federation. In 1893 and 1895 Liberal governments went further, and brought in bills, without compensation. The triumph was technical only. The Liberal leadership had been turned round, on paper, to an extraordinary degree by lobbying and penetration between 1872 and 1893. But the 1893 bill was dropped after being introduced, while the 1895 bill only went to a first reading.

The greatest achievement of the Alliance was negative. Its rooted objection to compensation destroyed the moderate Conservative reforms of 1888 and 1890, and the 'whisky money' thus set free was used for technical education (1890). Their double success in the late 1880s, which over-impressed Liberal leaders, should not be misconstrued, the point being that it was little sacrifice to Conservative ministries to drop troublesome reforming legislation.

Nineteenth-century agitations were remarkably successful in getting people to agitate. The question cannot be left there. They were perhaps equally unsuccessful in getting governments to comply. This applies not only to the classic radical and reforming agitations, but also to some extent to the Anti-Corn Law League, the anti-slavery agitation, O'Connell's campaigns for Catholic emancipation and repeal, and the various stirrings of the agricultural right. A book might be written on the subject — entitled *Studies in Failure*? Dr Dingle's scholarly and shrewd study takes us a very useful step in the right direction.

J.R. VINCENT
University of Bristol

Joseph Chamberlain: A Political Study. By Richard Jay. Oxford: Clarendon Press. 1981. ix, 383 pp. £16.95.

Joseph Chamberlain's political career continues to fascinate historians and Richard Jay's new survey is a useful addition to an already extensive corpus of studies. The coverage is necessarily concise, but Jay provides a clear exposition of many of Chamberlain's tortuous political manoeuvres. In general, the book is easy to read; the style is polished and elegant while the comments are often thoughtful, or prudent. The short-comings of the book are usually not those of commission and omission directly so much as those of emphasis and implication. Jay eschews hagiography and attempts to give a judicious and critical assessment of Chamberlain's career. He even tardily admits — on the last page of the Appendix — that Chamberlain was 'an ambitious man and, it must be said, not a very nice one'. However in the main text he often fails to point out that Chamberlain was a past master at subverting his friends as well as his enemies. But the brisk pace of the book leaves little scope for the study of Chamberlain's personal relations. Thus his family background and connexions receive little attention, although they played an important part in moulding his career. For example, his family's Unitarian faith largely influenced Chamberlain's views on the education and land questions, which were vital elements of his radical Liberalism. But Jay pays little attention to Chamberlain's Unitarianism, just as he fails to examine the significance of his marriages into the Kenrick family. The latter provided Chamberlain with the basis of his subsequent influence in Birmingham. Jay adds nothing new to our knowledge of Chamberlain's activities in Birmingham and in general shows relatively little interest in the subject. Yet he rather exaggerates Chamberlain's municipal achievements and his influence over the city's radicals. It was neither the caucus, nor the National Liberal Federation which gave Chamberlain control over Birmingham's parliamentary representation. In reality, it was the Unionist compact of 1886 and the goodwill of Churchill, Balfour and Salisbury which delivered the keys of Birmingham to Joe. In other words, his ascendancy was created by Tory rather than by radical votes.

For most of Chamberlain's career, Ireland was the foremost problem facing British politicians. Thus an examination of Chamberlain's Irish policies is peculiarly pertinent. Jay sketches the outlines of Chamberlain's evolving views on Ireland, but he seldom illuminates them. He fails to explain why Chamberlain — who supported land reform and opposed coercion — became eventually a vindictive opponent of Parnell. By comparison, Churchill combined enlightened Unionism with a measure of respect for the Irish Nationalists. Chamberlain's curious relationship with O'Shea may well have coloured his thinking, but this association is not satisfactorily explained by Jay. The latter is however probably right in claiming that Chamberlain regarded the Irish as merely one group in the radical empire rather than as an autonomous tribe. The Home Rule crisis of 1886 was the decisive event in Chamberlain's career. His defection from Gladstone cut him off from most of his natural supporters and left him the junior partner in the minority Unionist party. Chamberlain thus forfeited any chance of the premiership, but gained instead a much more prolonged spell in office than would have been his lot if he had remained a Liberal. Chamberlain's eight years at the Colonial Office ensured that the major preoccupation of his later career was the union of the empire. Jay's account of Chamberlain's involvement in the South African imbroglio is generally judicious. He rightly criticizes Chamberlain's conduct in 1899 and leans to the view that it was Milner who provoked the war. But he neglects the important role played by Chamberlain's under-secretary, Selborne, and under-estimates the influence of the Uitlanders and the Randlords. But Jay quite justifiably claims that Chamberlain played the key role in the Unionist victory at the 1900 general election and greatly enhanced his popularity with the Tories as a result. This made it possible for him to embark on what Jay aptly describes as 'the climax and great disappointment of Chamberlain's life', the Tariff Reform campaign. Jay sees this initiative as a response to the immediate electoral problems facing the Unionists — and especially the Radical Unionists — after 1902. There is much truth in this, but Jay's account of this crucial episode is not fully comprehensive. He pays very little attention to the composition of Chamberlain's Tariff Reform group or to the latter's relations with their leader. Above all, he fails to explain why the great majority of the Tory party willingly and rapidly supported Chamberlain's initiative. In other words, Jay fails to consider how important Chamberlain's personal contribution was to the revival of the fiscal question in British politics.

   Jay's study suffers from his failure to pay much attention to Chamberlain's relations with other politicians. Indeed he did not apparently consult the papers of other leading politicians. This is unfortunate for several reasons. One of the enigmas of Chamberlain's career is why, at crucial stages in his career, did other leading politicians attach such importance to his role? Obvious examples that spring to mind are Morley and Dilke in the 1870s; Gladstone in 1880; Churchill in 1885–6 and Balfour in 1889. Since Jay acknowledges that Chamberlain's personal parliamentary following was always very small, he should have produced some convincing explanation for Chamberlain's apparently overblown prestige. But Jay generally neglects to assess the influence which other politicians had on Chamberlain's career. Thus he quite fails to emphasize, for example, what a crucial role Bright played in both Chamberlain's rise and conversion to Unionism. Although incidental allusions are made to Bright, the latter is largely dismissed by Jay as 'a declining force'. By failing to compare Chamberlain's policies with those of his contemporaries Jay has exaggerated Chamberlain's 'sheer originality and creativity as a political actor'. His combination of domestic radicalism and imperialism owed much to Dilke, whose vision of 'Greater Britain' Chamberlain spent his later years trying to implement. Likewise the concept of progressive Unionism was pioneered by Churchill and then taken over by Chamberlain. The latter generally reflected rather than created the prevailing ethos of his time. Thus he adopted French-style radicalism in the early 1870s and federal imperialism in the 1890s. Chamberlain was never as bold an innovator as Jay implies. The latter admits that at crucial times in Chamberlain's career, his aims and motives 'are very unclear'. Surely this was because Chamberlain was usually reluctant to screw his courage to the sticking place. His handling of the education, temperance, social reform, Home Rule and South African issues all betray a chronic indecisiveness which conflicts with his popular reputation. By contrast, Chamberlain's Tariff Reform initiative appears, superficially, to be a bold, unexpected and decisive move. But, in reality, the ground was already well prepared, while Chamberlain, by leaving office, avoided direct responsibility for the consequences of his policy.

Jay's thoughtfulness and powers of exposition are seen to best advantage in his concluding essay. This is an overview and assessment of Chamberlain's career: an invaluable exercise often burked by political biographers. Jay points out that Chamberlain's direct contribution to British policy was surprisingly slight, partly because he never held a senior Cabinet post. He claims that Chamberlain believed in municipalization, not nationalization, and was thus more successful in Birmingham than at Westminster. But Chamberlain's very failure and his change of party allegiance are regarded by Jay as evidence of his exceptional stature. Chamberlain thus emerges as a hero in the classic mould, though his motivation and his tragic flaw remain obscure. Jay's conclusion — respectful, but not reverential — will probably satisfy most readers. But I am rather disappointed that Jay has not presented a more original portrait of Chamberlain. I believe there is still scope for a more radical — in the historiographical sense — interpretation of his career. Nevertheless, Jay's study is a considerable achievement. Just how considerable it is can best be judged by those who have themselves attempted to master that difficult historical *genre*: political biography.

ROLAND QUINAULT
Polytechnic of North London

Colne Valley: Radicalism to Socialism. The Portrait of a Northern Constituency in the Formative Years of the Labour Party 1890–1910. By David Clark. London: Longman. 1981. xiii, 225 pp. £12.00.

Colne Valley is a fascinating place for connoisseurs of odd electoral facts. In its time it has elected the earliest left-wing rebel from the Labour Party, and replaced him by the only M.P. ever to have been deprived of his seat under the Lunacy (Vacating of Seats) Act, 1886; however, it has never elected a Conservative. It has alternated between Labour and Liberal in a cross-grained sort of way. (Labour lost it in both January 1910 and February 1974, for example). David Clark has forgiven it for ejecting him in 1974 and has written an affectionate history of the first 20 years of the Colne Valley Labour Union, from 1890 to 1910.

Much of the book is a local chronicle which will strike more chords in Slaithwaite and Marsden than in foreign parts such as Sheffield and Manchester, but it contains many themes of more than local importance which Dr Clark illuminates, though a little fitfully at times. There are two common explanations of why Labour took root in some places sooner than others — and Colne Valley is important because it fits neither of them. The first argument looks for trade union strength and class solidarity. It tends to find them at their highest in large impersonal factories, where the workers' lack of control over their own labour power is most evident. Marx thought that capitalism was digging its own grave when it herded workers into factories like that: the very economic pressure which led capitalists to set up the largest plants with the division of labour pushed to extremes would lead the workers to form trade unions which would, in due course, form the vanguard of socialism.

The first half of Marx's argument was right, and Colne Valley neatly illustrates it. The constituency was mostly located east of the Pennines, but spilt over into the fringe of the Lancashire cotton belt on the west, around Mossley and Delph. In the west, there were large factories and strong trade-unionism; in the east, small concerns where the employer still dealt with his men (or women) face to face — and weak trade-unionism. The Yorkshire woollen industry was more 'primitive' than Lancashire cotton, and probably the factories in the small towns and villages of the Colne valley were smaller even than those in Dewsbury or Huddersfield.

The second half of Marx's argument was right only in a very qualified way. Areas with strong trade unions did elect many of the first Labour M.P.s (Durham coal, Lancashire cotton) — but they were not socialists. Trade unions have never formed the vanguard of British socialism.

The first Labour candidate in Colne Valley, Tom Mann, was impatient with his constituents' failure to get organized into trade unions, and threatened to withdraw his candidature unless union membership in the constituency rose. It didn't, however, and the isolated Lancashire part where membership was high was too small to give him victory on its own. Nor could it serve as an example to the rest of the constituency. Mossley and Marsden might have been in different continents.

The rival theory, of course, derives the Labour Party from Methodism not Marxism. And here another shock awaits schematic historians. Colne Valley was not particularly Nonconformist — in fact less so than any other West Riding county constituency. Only an estimated 9.1% of the electorate were members of a Nonconformist church. Of course early socialist oratory had a revivalist air; on 26 November 1905 Councillor Pickles lectured to the Meltham I.L.P. on 'Socialism, Religion and Morality' and 'Ethics and Evolution'. But Dr Clark's meticulous collections of lists (and what lists they are, such as to outshine my previously most treasured collection of obscure facts, a reprint of the Cambrian Railways working timetable for 1904) show that there were more talks on 'Beauties of Manxland' or 'The Life of Rabbie Burns' than on anything religious.

If neither classic explanation of early Labourism fits Colne Valley, how about an alternative (not considered by Dr Clark): that it wasn't actually good Labour territory at all, and only seemed so because of Victor Grayson's freak by-election victory in 1907? The Colne Valley Labour League was too weak to put up a fight in 1900 and 1906, and the 1907 by-election, which Grayson won with only 35.2% of the votes thanks to a very even split of the rest of the vote, was only one of three Labour gains in the same month. Maybe Colne Valley was not a very Labour place, but July 1907 was a very Labour month. Incidentally, between the lines of Dr Clark's account lies an unmade point: just what a disastrous M.P. Grayson was. We already knew that he was an absentee and an exhibitionist loner: this book makes it clear that he was a dreadful scrounger as well. He attacked trade unions for not being socialist but wanted them to pay the whole of his parliamentary salary; he never repaid his debts to the Colne Valley Labour League, but actually charged them for every speech he made in the constituency! Perhaps only the vehemence with which every other Labour M.P. denounced him as a fraud has prevented modern students from realizing that he really was a fraud.

Sir Lewis Namier once showed us that it was possible to build broad generalizations, and even general theories which denied that they were theories, upon the meticulous collection of thousands of apparently disconnected facts. Dr Clark is no Namier, but he has done a thoroughly useful service to the study of national politics through local politics. May he have many imitators — and let his imitators remember that other parties too have local roots.

IAIN McLEAN
University College, Oxford

The People's Budget 1909/10: Lloyd George and Liberal Politics. By Bruce K. Murray. Oxford: Clarendon Press. 1980. ix, 352 pp. £17.50.

The strange after-life of Liberal England is still with us. In the last decade historians such as Michael Freeden, Michael Bentley, H.V. Emy and Peter Clarke have busily examined the intellectual and electoral machinery of the Liberal Party and pondered on the promise of the 'New Liberalism'. Few topics in modern British history have excited such sustained interest and discussion. Yet there is still more to say, as Dr Bruce Murray's very good monograph demonstrates. Grateful for recent scholarly studies, he summarizes their findings neatly in his introduction and does not feel called upon to take up an elaborate position of his own in relation to general theories either of decline or vitality. Clinical autopsies are eschewed and there is no role for the rogue bus in this account. Instead, the approach is painstaking and careful, if a little prosaic for such a potentially dramatic theme. Without fuss, the author reminds us that the 'People's Budget', from which so much stemmed, was a piece of legislation and by making good use of Treasury papers we can still learn a good deal from a study of its drafting and subsequent fate. Of course, biographers of leading Edwardian politicians and constitutional historians have all said a good deal *en passant* about the Budget but no one hitherto has looked at the episode in the round or produced an account so firmly based upon the ample manuscript collections now available.

Like other recent writers, the author accepts that the central issue of the age was not so much the necessity or desirability of 'social reform' but how it should be paid for. The Campbell-Bannerman government (and Asquith at the Exchequer) had already found itself committed to higher defence expenditure than it had anticipated. It was unlikely that circumstances would permit a reduction, at least not in the short term. Although this external aspect does not find as much place in Murray's account as one would expect, he is right to stress the increasing pressure to finance social expenditure in these years. Yet it was very evident that conventionally acceptable sources of taxation would prove insufficient — and this was not just a discovery made by the Liberals in 1908. It was one of the factors which propelled Joseph Chamberlain in favour of Tariff Reform. Additional revenue was needed in 1908, and needed quickly. Many New Liberals were not at all averse to using the resources of the community, as they liked to put it, for a programme of social regeneration. If the government refused to move in this direction and to contemplate further 'progressive' graduated taxation it would, allegedly, alienate working-class support and boost the nascent Labour Party. Successful implementation of such a strategy, on the other hand, would have the additional benefit of preserving Free Trade.

Such a presentation of the problem was plausibly over-simple. If, as the New Liberals alleged, a willingness to tax wealth was an indication of progressive respectability, it was also apparent that increased direct taxation could hit the pockets of middle-class Liberal voters. Somehow, a path had to be steered which would keep the party together and enhance its reforming image. That is why the sub-title of this book — 'Lloyd George and Liberal Politics' — is entirely appropriate. If the arguments about what could and could not be done were financial, the underlying issues were political. And it was Lloyd George who was the man of the hour. He grasped the need for decision when many of his colleagues vacillated and worried about the House of Lords. However, it was not self-evident that Lloyd George's appointment to the Exchequer would produce such a firm grasping of nettles. Murray notes that a major measure of social reform or new provision for labour was conspicuously lacking from Lloyd George's time at the Board of Trade. But what had emerged from this period was evidence of his flexibility and fertility of mind. In a letter to Balfour, McKenna ruefully noted that the Conservatives did at least understand the Liberal principles they rejected; Lloyd George did not! That was only partly true, but it was already apparent that the Welshman had successfully established a reputation, an unusual one, both for platform eloquence and administrative skill of an unconventional kind. This latter judgment was one which his permanent officials grudgingly confirmed — and the obstructive activities of Treasury knights form not the least interesting aspect of the story.

Lloyd George was given his head not because of a wave of social reforming enthusiasm in the Cabinet but because, by the end of 1908, his colleagues could not see any sound alternative. Murray greatly admires the preparation of the Budget, suggesting that there was hardly a question which could be taken to come under its purview which he did not tackle. Politically, it was the Chancellor who was fashioning a policy to give the government a sense of direction and purpose. Asquith seemed quite content to give him quiet support in Cabinet — Lloyd George may even have exaggerated the importance of such backing. When the Budget reached ministers, doubt and uncertainty were widespread — Murray suggests at least a third objected to its fundamental design, chiefly because the scale and nature of the direct taxes would alienate middle-class support. As the author notes, the Budget did not escape unscathed from Cabinet criticism — the straight penny tax on the capital value of land and the proposed changes in the duty for settled property were both discarded and there were other alterations in detail. Yet, in the end, the Chancellor carried the day because his colleagues had accepted that only by a finance bill could they hope to attain some of their objectives against the wishes of the Lords. This process of acceptance is carefully charted and certain details in existing accounts are corrected.

After the Cabinet came the Commons and the country. Ironically in view of some of his later oratorical performances, Lloyd George's speech on 29 April in bringing forward his proposals was not a success. Haldane was only too pleased to be able to agree that it was the speech of a man who, at least on certain points, did not understand what he was reading. Later, at Limehouse and Newcastle, the Chancellor seemed in his element. By the autumn, sensing that a rejection by the Lords was imminent (though Lloyd George had not specifically set out to provoke such a conflict), he saw his task as the mobilization of the working classes, specifically the English working classes. The rejection of the Budget would be an electoral asset for the Liberals. Why, then, did Lansdowne and Balfour force an election they knew they would lose? Murray argues that they were desperate at least to restore the Unionists to a formidable minority in the Commons and felt that, if the Budget passed, the initiative would rest entirely with the government. The chapter on the Budget Election itself does not go much beyond Blewett's comprehensive analysis and concludes with J.A. Spender's assessment that the

Liberal performance was much better than it would have been a year earlier and the credit for the recovery rested with Lloyd George and the Budget.

If, at times, the Budget somewhat disappears from sight while the general political situation is considered, the central financial problem returns to the fore in an excursus on the 1914 Budget. This time the government was forced into a retreat on the site value rating and the reorganization of local finance in part by a 'cave' of business Liberal M.P.s. Even so, Murray disputes whether the Liberal Party as a whole had rejected the financial implications of the New Liberalism. He draws attention, on the other hand, to the fact that in 1914 the large majority of income taxpayers were less heavily taxed, even after that year's Budget, than they had been when the Liberals came into office. While some claimed that it was easier for a camel to pass through the eye of a needle than for a rich man to remain in the Liberal Party, a good many rich men did remain. The final message of the book, therefore, is that the Liberal Party coalition, subjected to strain though it was, had been kept together in the hope of 'Better Times', as Lloyd George himself put it.

KEITH ROBBINS
University of Glasgow

Baldwin Thwarts the Opposition: The British General Election of 1935. By Tom Stannage. London: Croom Helm. 1980. 320 pp. £19.95.

Dr Stannage provides a good deal of useful information about electoral arrangements between 1931 and 1935, and a thorough description of the election campaign and results. His book will no doubt be of substantial interest to the dedicated psephologist, though for the political historian it is curiously disappointing. Its oddities begin with the title, which is not just awkward, but also inaccurate if it leads the reader to expect an extended analysis of Baldwin's overall strategy and electoral appeal. The first sentence unfortunately sets the tone of the book: 'there is a flatness about the 1935 general election which has as depressing an effect on the historian as it had on the voters at the time.' Dr Stannage does say that the election 'is not without interest or importance', but it is clear that the real justification for his book is given in the second paragraph — that it fills an hitherto vacant gap in the list of twentieth-century election studies. Unhappily, the 1935 election seems to be a disappointment to the student of elections: the National Government's victory was expected, there were no 'scares' or other surprises during the campaign, and so there seems little to explain.

In fact, there *are* interesting and important matters to be explained about this election; it is a pity that Dr Stannage has not discussed these more fully. This may be because the action mainly occurred before the election was announced — even though it would seem important to examine those events during a run-up to an election which determine the electoral stance of politicians and the way they are perceived by voters. Dr Stannage does indeed devote his first three chapters to a discussion of 'electoral politics' from 1931 to 1935. Here there are valuable details on such matters as the electoral bargaining between the partners in the National Government, and their difficulties in reconciling their separate identities with the maintenance of a 'national spirit'; the Labour Party's financial problems and recruitment campaigns; and the dilemmas of the fragmented Liberal Party. But neither here nor elsewhere in the book is there an adequate examination of more immediate factors shaping the election. There are only a few sentences referring to the 'New Deal' and the 'Council of Action', Lloyd George's major efforts to storm the government and dominate the election. The Cabinet's negotiations with Lloyd George in early 1935 — which must reveal something about ministerial attitudes towards the approaching election — are merely alluded to in a footnote. There is no discussion of the activities of Cecil and the League of Nations Union, and only a gesture towards analyzing the Peace Ballot (the results of which were announced in June 1935) — again, to be found in a footnote. Cripps and the Socialist League receive little more treatment, and we are simply informed that Attlee replaced Lansbury as Labour leader in October; the leadership crisis is not studied, although it occurred just weeks before Baldwin announced the election. More broadly, one might have expected a thorough attempt to assess the effects of mass unemployment: its impact in the various constituencies and consequent influence on voting patterns, the difficulties it raised in the presentation of the government's economic policies, and the reasons why the Labour Party was unable to exploit it more successfully. However, the economic problem is only referred to in general terms. There is more on foreign policy and defence issues, as is necessary given the prominence of the Abyssinian crisis throughout the election period, though the background of debate about the League of Nations and rearmament is insufficiently drawn. In short, Dr Stannage has interpreted 'electoral politics' in too narrow a sense.

The consequence of neglecting these wider aspects is that his account of the actual election is weakened. The discussion of Baldwin's calculations concentrates on his choice of election date, while the larger questions of his response to Lloyd George and to the Peace Ballot, his treatment of unemployment, rearmament and the League, and his choice of platform, receive comparatively little analysis. So the hoary question of Baldwin's reticence about defence requirements is not confronted. The success of his electioneering performances is mentioned several times; one would have liked an examination of the qualities which made him so popular and effective. There is a useful blow-by-blow account of the course of the national election campaign, and the manifestos are paraphrased and compared. But the significance of the content of speeches and manifestos in terms of policy dilemmas and electoral strategies is not brought out adequately. However, Dr Stannage's description of the contribution of the cinema, the B.B.C., and the newspapers is very full (although the relations between politicians and the press might have been better illustrated if the private archives of newspapers, proprietors and editors had been consulted). He provides much information about the candidates — their numbers, affiliations, social backgrounds, education, parliamentary service and age. And he gives a comprehensive analysis of the election turnout and results, including the degree of 'swing' according to region and type of contest. A further, exhaustive, compilation of election statistics appears in the 40 pages of appendices. Given all this material, it is rather disappointing to find just three pages of general conclusions on the reasons for the National Government's victory. It is ascribed to the government having presided over 'a general increase in the country's prosperity', to the Labour crisis, to Baldwin's success in occupying the liberal 'centre', and to the shift of public opinion towards acceptance of limited rearmament. These are convincing reasons, but they cannot be said to have been thoroughly discussed in the body of the book.

The weaknesses of the book may be due partly to the material on which it is based. Having been submitted as a thesis in Cambridge in 1973, it was prepared for publication in Australia, far from the archives. So Dr Stannage has been unable to use the MacDonald papers (which became generally available in 1976, and contain much of relevance to this subject), nor a number of other important private and party collections. On the other hand, those collections which were consulted do not appear to have been fully exploited; for example, it is surprising to find so little on Neville Chamberlain. Even books listed in the voluminous bibliography seem to have been used sparingly. Rather, the weakness seems chiefly to arise from too close an adherence to the style of the Nuffield studies of contemporary elections, which are not, perhaps, the perfect model for a historian. Being 'instant' productions, they necessarily contain more reportage than explanation. Dr Butler and his collaborators are better placed to observe the attitudes of voters, but in discussing the politicians they have to make the most of speeches, party propaganda, media reports, and tendentious information yielded in interviews. The techniques and format used to present this sort of material are not necessarily those most suitable for the historian, who has greater opportunities for explanation. Although he has no opinion polls, the historian has the advantages of access to government, party and personal records with which to make a tolerably accurate examination of policy-making and electoral calculation, and also a larger perspective to help him distinguish the significant from the less significant among the mass of other information. So — most notably — Dr Blewett in his study of the 1910 elections adapted the Nuffield model and produced an important contribution to historical explanation. The same, unfortunately, cannot be said of Dr Stannage's book. He has, however, assembled much important information, and historians will find his work a useful source.

PHILIP WILLIAMSON
University of Durham

The Commons in Perspective. By Philip Norton. Oxford: Martin Robertson. 1981. vi, 265 pp. Hardback £15.00; paperback £4.95.

Philip Norton sets out the purpose of his book quite simply in his Preface. 'It seeks to provide an overview', he writes 'of the contemporary House of Commons, in as concise a form as possible, for the undergraduate and for anyone else with a serious interest in the subject of politics.' For the undergraduate just embarking on a serious study of the British political scene and without any real background knowledge of the House of Commons, Philip Norton has succeeded admirably. He brings together virtually all an undergraduate needs to know about the working of the Commons; and he summarizes splendidly all the main controversies about the role of the Commons and the way ahead. His footnote references to what other people have written and his 'Select Bibliography' will also be most helpful to the enterprising undergraduate who wants to study the subject at a more sophisticated level.

Philip Norton's book, in one respect, at any rate, seeks to break relatively new ground. This is the chapter where he attempts to compare the impact the Commons makes on foreign and defence policy with its impact on social policies and on economic policies, for example. His analysis here is not particularly subtle; but at least it is enough to remind us that an enormous amount of work still needs to be done in this particular comparative field — and, perhaps inadvertently, it reminds us, too, what an extraordinarily difficult problem this is to tackle.

As Philip Norton goes over the familiar ground he frequently whets the appetite of the more sophisticated reader with the promise of the 'Norton view' to be revealed later. It is all the more disappointing, therefore, that when that view is revealed it is rather superficially presented. The 'Norton view' is about the various proposals for parliamentary reform which have been advocated in recent years. These he presents succinctly, covering the reformed select committee system, reducing the size of the Commons, ending the Prime Minister's power of dissolution, proportional representation, a Bill of Rights and so on. Then we come to the 'Norton view', which he says (pp. 219–20),

> takes issue with the other approaches so far identified. It emphasises instead the importance of attitudes within Parliament, and the potential and actual power available already to members, as the basis on which the Commons might achieve an effective role of security and influence.

So Philip Norton argues that since the House of Commons retains the basic power that 'if a majority of members disagree with a proposal or motion advanced by the Government, they [the M.P.s] can vote against it in the division lobbies' (p. 225) — then by being more ready to use this power M.P.s 'can exercise a greater degree of scrutiny and influence' (p. 226). To support his case he points out that in the 1970s 'Government back-benchers, first under a Conservative Government and then under a Labour one proved willing to enter whipped Opposition lobbies to impose defeats on the Treasury bench' (pp. 226–7). Philip Norton sees this as a useful beginning and believes that this more independent attitude can and will go further. But he does not stop to consider whether there were special features about the party political balance and party attitudes in the Commons in the 1970s that make such little independence by M.P.s as he manages to identify the exception rather than the rule. More important, though, he does not consider at all in this context the importance to back-bench M.P.s of getting on their respective ministerial ladders. Unless we are to have a breed of M.P.s who prefer independence to ministerial promotion — or unless something of a career structure (e.g. succession to chairmanships of committees with appropriate additional salaries) can be created for M.P.s in the House as some alternative to the ministerial greasy pole, the development of back-bench independence does not seem likely to get very far. But Dr Norton has no discussion of points like these. More serious though, in this context, is his total failure to consider whether the Commons is so overloaded with business that M.P.s simply do not have the time or opportunity to score more than a few glancing blows against minute parts of the vast flow of executive decision-making and executive-produced paper (much increased by Common Market membership) which now almost completely overwhelms it. Nor does he consider whether the staff of the Commons has to be significantly increased before they can exercise the greater degree of scrutiny and influence the Norton thesis expects and demands. Certainly a respectable case can be made for the view that until our centralized Whitehall decision-making machine is made to shed a lot of its work to regional governments the House of Commons will never be able to cope — and even if that happens the Commons will need a greatly enlarged and professional staff to have the sort of influence Dr Norton wants. But none of this gets any airing.

It is a pity, therefore, that the 'Norton view' is so superficially presented. It merits a much fuller exposition.

LORD CROWTHER-HUNT
Exeter College, Oxford

Works of Art in the House of Lords. Edited by Maurice Bond. London: H.M.S.O. 1980. 108 pp. xxxi + 94 illustrations, 10 in colour. £3.95.

'Good God! I am just returned from the terrific burning of the Houses of Parliament ... The comfort is there is now a better prospect of painting a House of Lords', wrote B.R. Haydon, the history painter. Mr Bond, in his introduction to this amply illustrated guide, remarks not only on the opportunity that the destructive fire of 16 October 1834 afforded of erecting a purpose-built legislature, but also on the long-standing tradition of wall-decoration at Westminster, particularly works of an historical or narrative character. Haydon, who as early as 1812 had proposed adorning the Lords' Chamber with a 'grand series' of historical paintings, failed in the subsequent open competitions, but his successful rivals created that 'Victorian vision of the British past' that lines the visitor's route through the extensive premises of the House of Lords: a reflection of early nineteenth-century enthusiasm for national history.

Charles Barry, architect of the new palace at Westminster, who grew up in the shadow of the old palace at a time when access to the Parliament buildings was far easier than it is today, himself had a clear concept of his building as setting forth England's history — but in the more permanent form (as he hoped) of sculpture and carving. A programme of history painting was imposed on him by the rival authority of a royal commission. Melbourne as Prime Minister had insisted that there was no prospect of the House of Lords being ornamented by painting (Haydon's diary, 13 October 1835), and Barry clearly envisaged an interior largely panelled. Mr John Charlton, in his lucid account of the artistic endeavours, failures and partial successes in the decoration of the House of Lords, points out that the 'prime mover' in the appointment of the Royal Fine Arts Commission was that notable connoisseur, Sir Robert Peel. In 1841 a Commons select committee had considered 'the promotion of the fine arts in this Country in connexion with the rebuilding of the Houses of Parliament'. Of that body, Peel was chairman. When, as Prime Minister, he sent its report to the Queen (24 September 1841), he proposed setting up a royal commission to conduct further inquiries, 'without reference to party distinctions': it might, he thought, include members from each House whose attention had been directed to the cultivation of the fine arts, as well as two or three distinguished artists. When Peel proposed that the Queen's young husband should be chairman, Prince Albert at once showed that he would be no mere figurehead, telling Peel that 'there had better be no artist by profession in the Commission'. Artists' opinions could be better obtained by their giving evidence, as more views could be obtained, and lay members would not be inhibited in expressing their opinions by the presence of 'distinguished professors'. Peel, convinced by his arguments, appointed the commission of connoisseurs that Haydon in 1846 blamed for the failure to achieve a national triumph.

The idea of fresco painting, already explored by the select committee, was taken up enthusiastically by the commission under the prince's guidance, but in result proved a fiasco. Mr Charlton blames 'the damp English climate accentuated by fogs and sewer gas from the Thames', so that the walls may never have been dry enough when the fresco was applied, even in those few months of the year in which conditions were propitious. Dyce's progress was so slow that he gave his address in the Royal Academy Yearbook as 'Royal Robing Room, House of Lords' — though, Mr Charlton remarks, he was simultaneously working on more congenial subjects at All Saints', Margaret Street. 'I feel how much of life has been wasted in ... writing in the sand. Time's effacing fingers began to obliterate at one end, while we were painfully working at the other', was the sad comment of C.W.

Cope, who depicted Stuart history in the Peers' Corridor. Mr Charlton concludes his essay with a useful summary of the restorations of the frescoes during the four subsequent periods of conservation, based on Mr R.J.B. Walker's invaluable unpublished catalogue of works of art in the Palace of Westminster.

The third and final section of the guide is a descriptive narrative by Jeremy Maule to accompany the visitor on the line of route from the Royal Robing Room to the Lords' Chamber, with a concluding note on the sculpture in the Norman Porch, at the head of the Royal Staircase. Text and illustrations call attention to the unjustly neglected series of oak bas-reliefs, the story of Arthur, by H.H. Armstead in the Robing Room, and of Tudor portraits by pupils of the Royal School of Art, South Kensington, in the Prince's Chamber. We may hope that this attractively designed and splendidly illustrated booklet will contribute to making this morsel of the national heritage better known and more appreciated.

M.H. PORT
Queen Mary College, London

Vol. LV No. 132   *November 1982*   *Price: £4.00*

BULLETIN OF THE
INSTITUTE OF HISTORICAL RESEARCH

Edited by F. M. L. Thompson

Contents:

Historical News
UNIVERSITY OF LONDON: INSTITUTE OF HISTORICAL RESEARCH
SENATE HOUSE, LONDON WC1E 7HU

UNIVERSITY OF LONDON: INSTITUTE OF HISTORICAL RESEARCH

SENATE HOUSE, LONDON, WC1E 7HU

UNIVERSITY OF LEICESTER
HISTORY DEPARTMENT

Occasional Publications. General Editor: Aubrey Newman

No. 1. *A Register of Parliamentary Lists, 1660–1761.*
Edited by David Hayton and Clyve Jones. (Reprinting.)
'Invaluable guide . . . extraordinarily useful'
    J.R. Jones, *English Historical Review*

No. 3. *A Register of Parliamentary Lists, 1660–1761: A Supplement* (1982). £1.00.
Available from Dr A.N. Newman, Dept. of History, University of Leicester, Leicester, LE1 7RH; Prof. R.W. Davis, Dept. of History, Washington University, St. Louis, Mo. 63130.